Israel

EVERGREEN is an imprint of TASCHEN GmbH

Under the direction of Michel Buntz
Text: Hugues Demeude
Photographs: Philippe Roy
Layout: Roger Donadini
Map and illustrations: Jean-Michel Kirsch
Editor: Corinne Fossey
Cover design: Angelika Taschen, Cologne

Translated by Rae Walter
In association with First Edition Translations Ltd, Cambridge
Realisation of the English edition by First Edition Translations Ltd, Cambridge

Printed in Italy
ISBN 3-8228-5871-4

Israel

Text

HUGUES DEMEUDE

Photographs

PHILIPPE ROY

evergreen

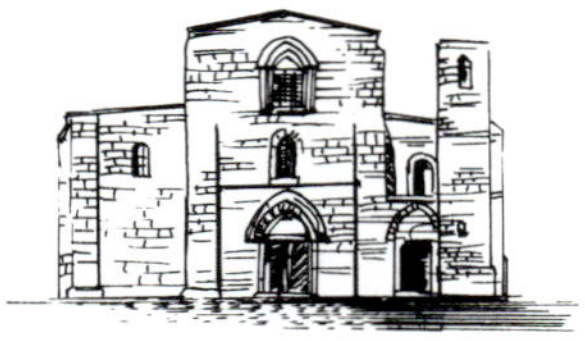

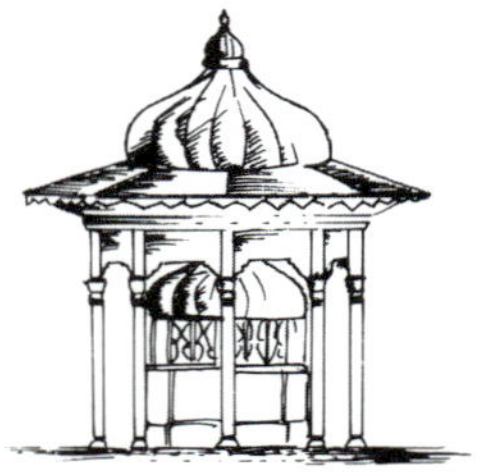

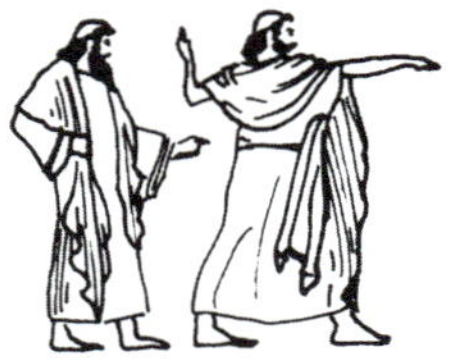

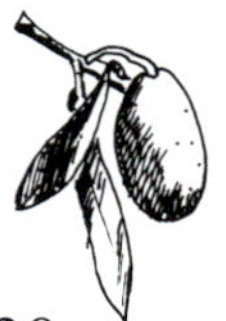

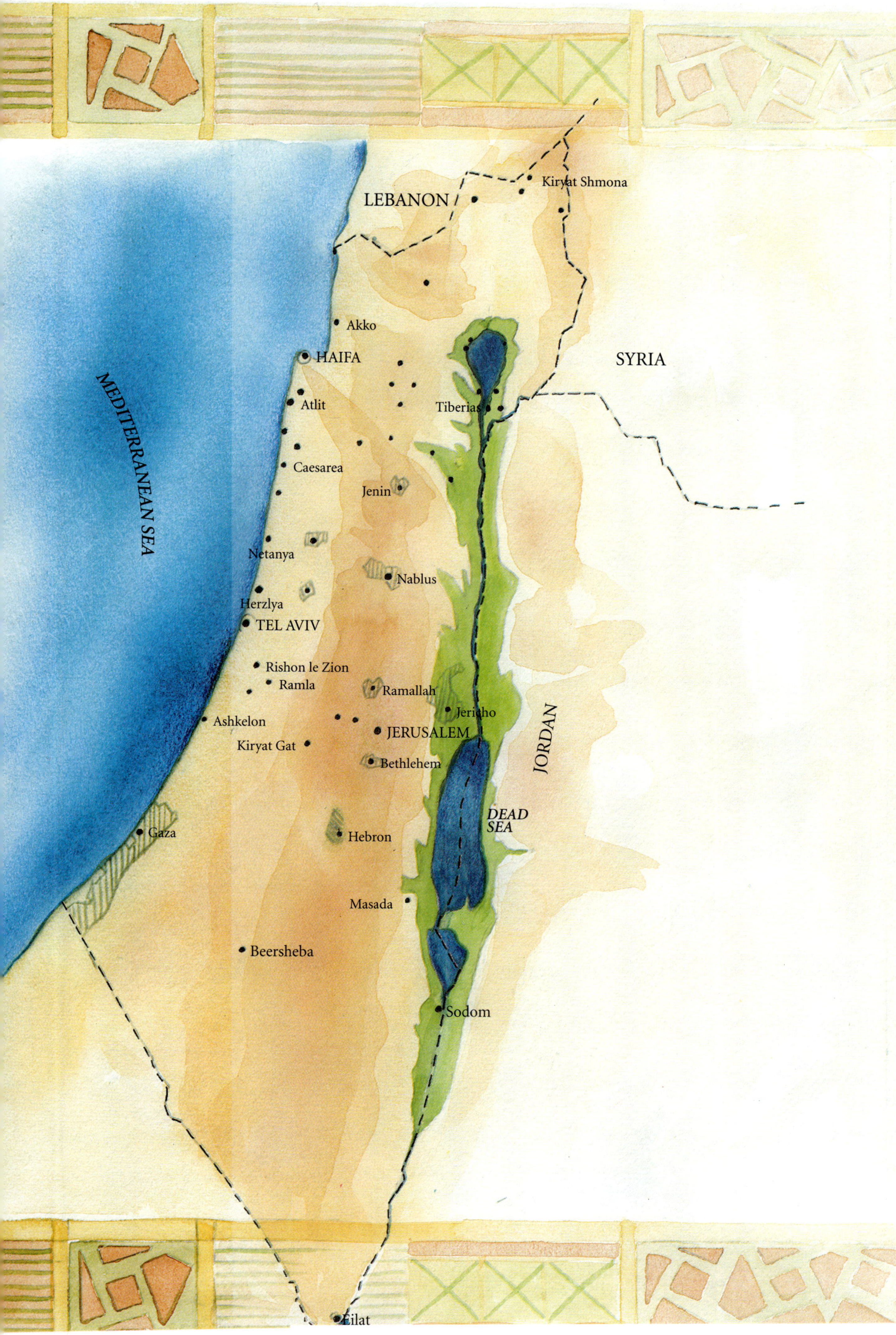

LEBANON
Kiryat Shmona
SYRIA
MEDITERRANEAN SEA
Akko
HAIFA
Atlit
Tiberias
Caesarea
Jenin
Netanya
Nablus
Herzlya
TEL AVIV
Rishon le Zion
Ramla
Ramallah
Jericho
Ashkelon
JERUSALEM
Kiryat Gat
Bethlehem
JORDAN
DEAD SEA
Gaza
Hebron
Masada
Beersheba
Sodom
Eilat

Since its creation in 1948, the state of Israel has constantly occupied the front of the international stage, leaving no-one truly indifferent, and even seeming to carry on a passionate relationship with observers all over the world as they strive to follow its destiny.

It is a young country, with geographical dimensions that are inversely proportional to its historical importance, and it has always, for better or for worse, been under the current affairs spotlight. But if this country attracts attention when the spotlight is turned on, it is because there is something out of the ordinary about it, something approaching excess, on the edge of reason. Everything about it is intensified, accentuated, exploited. So, in this land which has been defended by many people, armed and ready to make the ultimate sacrifice, they have carried out remarkable projects. They have built a vast city on sand, made the desert fertile, diverted the waters of the Jordan, and drained the marshes to create verdant valleys. They have adapted the landscape to meet the needs of a population which has grown from 650,000 to 6 million inhabitants in 50 years, founded a nation, and organised profoundly different individuals arriving from all over the world into a stable society.

The ruins of the heritage of a country situated at the crossroads of several civilisations are equally disconcerting; there are traces of its illustrious biblical past, and the ancestral rites of Judaism, which have turned memory into the object of a living cult. Moreover, travelling in Israel inevitably creates a feeling of returning to one's roots, a sense of pilgrimage. Lying at the meeting point of the Mediterranean and the Arabian desert, between Africa and Asia, present-day Israel is indeed a focal point where fifty centuries of history have seen the greatest Mediterranean and oriental civilisations succeed one another. For example, in the city of Jericho, thought to be one of the oldest in the world, and probably founded some 9,000 years ago. Here there are many sites and relics bearing the marks, both moving and informative, of the passing of the Canaanites, the Philistines, the Assyrians, the Romans, the Byzantines, the Crusaders, the Mamelukes, the Turks, and even the

British. There are so many different aspects to this cultural heritage that this in itself could be enough to justify a stay in Israel. But when it comes to searching for one's origins, visitors still prefer working on their past in a way which allows them to delve down towards other roots. They favour a more spiritual approach, in this case one which highlights the landscapes where monotheism was born.

For it was indeed here, in the Holy Land, that it all began. Reflecting 3,000 years of the history of Judaism, 2,000 years of Christianity, and 13 centuries of the spread of Islam, this land of revelations and prophets – which a great part of humankind can look on as a cradle, and whose sacred character continues to this day to be cultivated by the Jewish state of Israel – still, of course, contains a wealth of places which are the embodiment of faith. Jerusalem, Safed, Tiberias and Hebron (ceded back to Palestinian authority), the four symbolic cities of Judaism, occupied in one way or another by the Israeli community all through the course of history; Bethlehem (also ceded back), Nazareth, the Sea of Galilee and Jerusalem again, where many pilgrims come to affirm their piety out of love for Christ – these places are bastions of such great religious significance that they make the soul of the believer tremble. They are also so steeped in stories and legends that they delight the non-believer.

But even if Israel is a country whose religious, historical, and political dimensions continue to leave their mark on people's minds, its actual physical surroundings and human geography remain largely unrecognised. This is regrettable, because it is not only a land of many and varied landscapes, which has been greatly altered and has much to teach us through the diversity of its population, but also and perhaps – as its religious inhabitants believe, most importantly – because it is the earthly kingdom of a holy nation, whose constitution can be traced in the divine law of the Torah (imparted by God to Moses on Mount Sinai). The four main regions of this land, spread out between the four seas which frame the country (the Mediterranean Sea, the Sea of Galilee – also known as Lake Tiberias – the Dead Sea and the Red Sea), comprise to the west the coast and the coastal plain, and to the

*Following pages:
The ancient city of Jerusalem seen from the Mount of Olives.
In the foreground, the Dome of the Rock; to the left, the cupolas of the Holy Sepulchre; in the background, some of the tower blocks in the modern city which is still growing.*

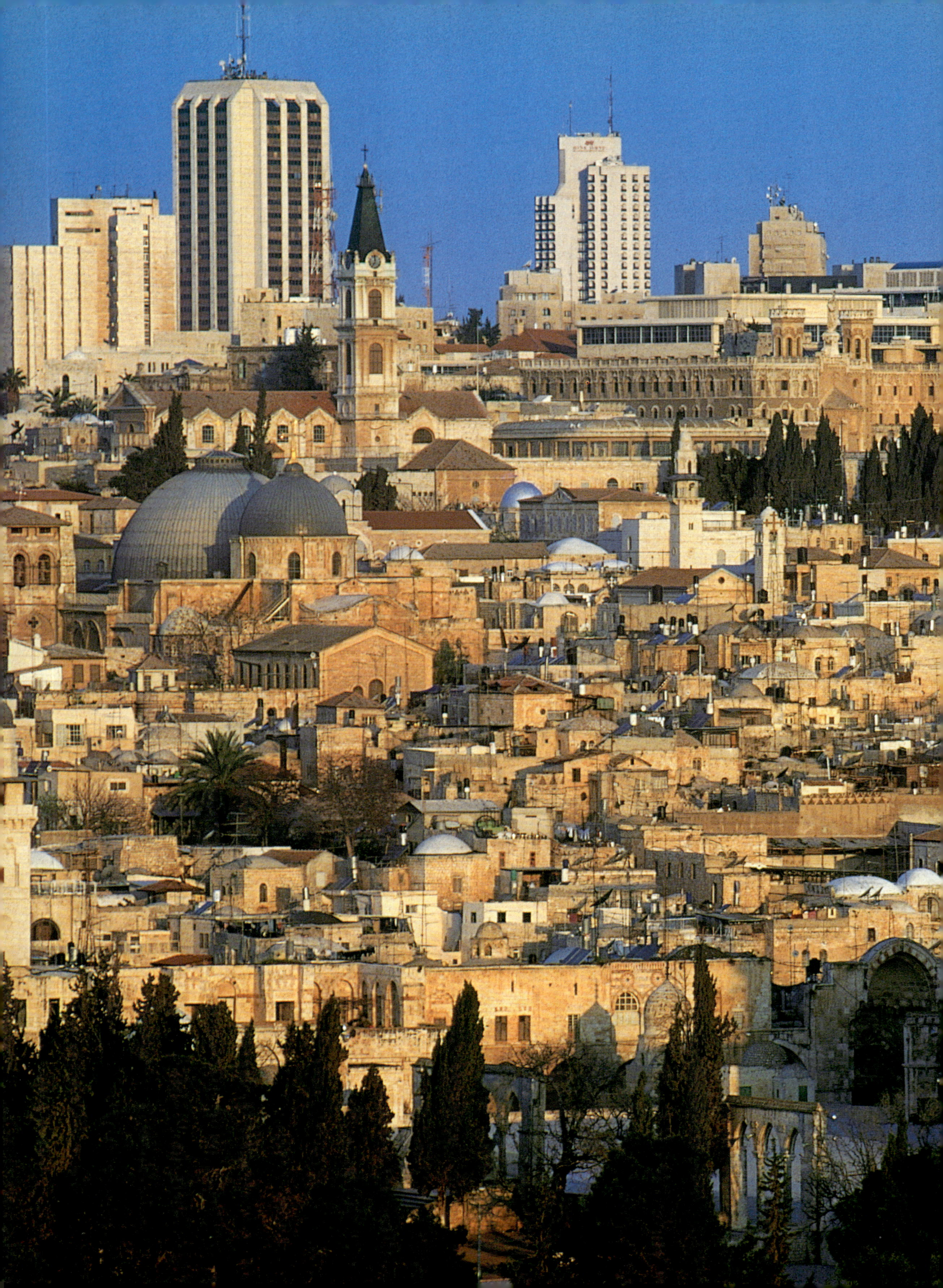

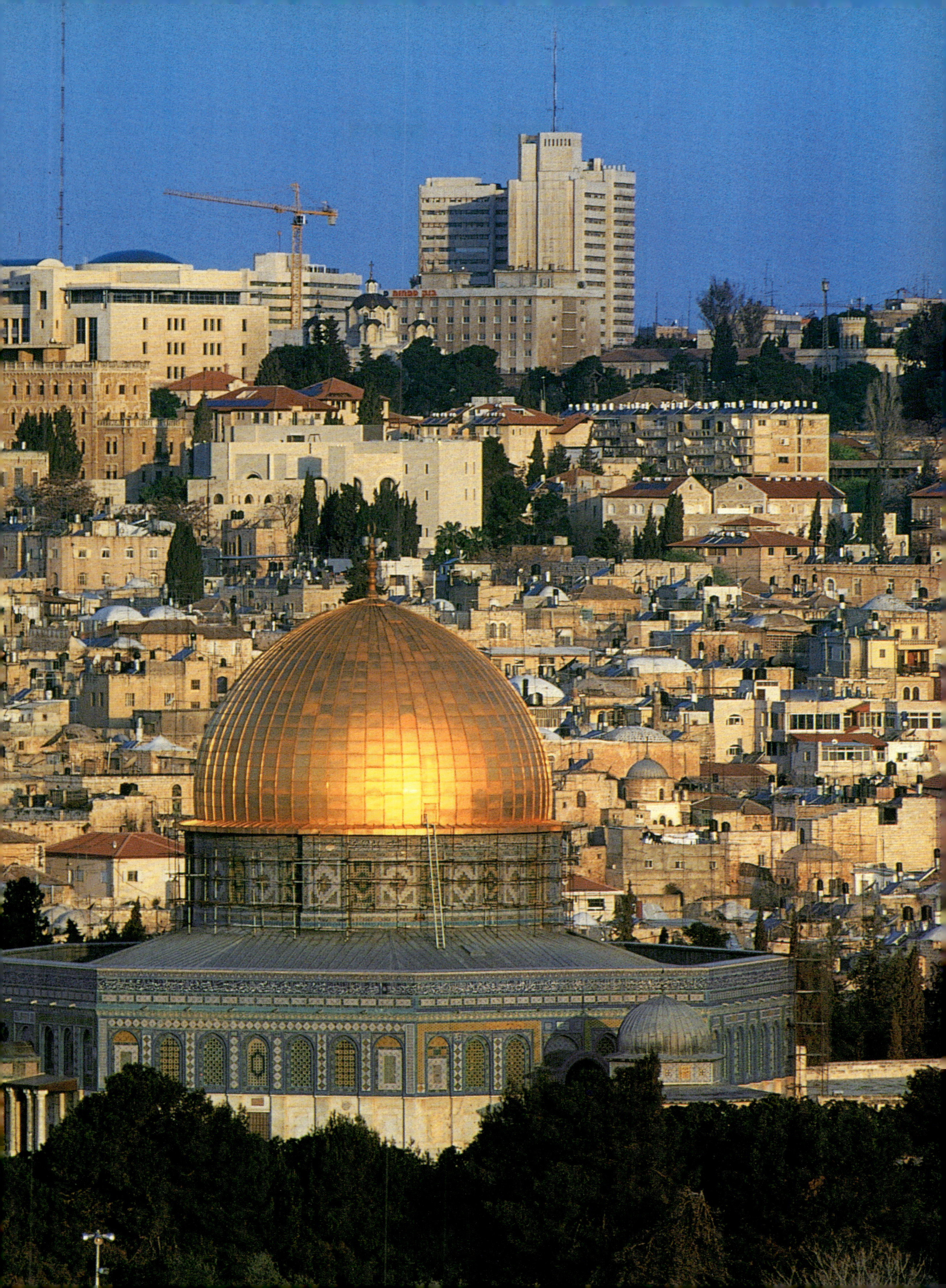

east the verdant Jordan Valley, part of the huge fault in the earth's crust known as the Great Rift Valley. In the centre are the mountains of Galilee, Samaria, and the mountains of Judaea, with the mythical Jerusalem growing at their heart; and finally, to the south, the Negev Desert which stretches from its chief city of Beersheba to Eilat, the highly esteemed coastal resort on the Red Sea.

Washed by the Mediterranean and looking towards the setting sun, the Israeli coast is edged by a sandy coastal strip. Despite the fact that its access to this sea, by which so many warriors and pioneers arrived, has been reduced to barely 200 km (125 miles), the major part of the country's vital forces is concentrated here, and the area contributes greatly to the nation's wealth. There are sharp contrasts to these models eulogising the success, individualism, enjoyment, and pleasures which characterise the western lifestyle of the half of the Israeli population living in the coastal cities – with Tel Aviv, of course, at the forefront. The unfailing vigilance of the inhabitants of Safed, who make sure that Hebrew roots maintain their pre-eminence; the obedience to the divine breath which caressed the religious city of Jerusalem; the uneasy attempt to spread the pioneering spirit of the members of the *kibbutzim* throughout the countryside; and the determination of the colonists who wish to continue development within the Palestinian territories of the West Bank – all these give the impression of belonging to another world. For the rest, the heterogeneous nature of this country's human geography is confirmed by the deep divisions which fragment Israeli society. But these divisions also reflect a splendid variety. This richness is not only that of a nation with many faces, a society in a permanent state of change, whose principal characteristics remain the same despite the feverish attempts to maintain a balance between tradition and modernity and the enormous capacity to integrate and yet to mobilise in individual units when faced with adversity; it is also that of a community for whom belonging is joyful and fraternal, fervent and respectful. It is a nation for whom this exhortation inscribed on one of the walls of the Diaspora Museum in Tel Aviv was written: "Remember the past, live the present, trust in the future."

A series of flights of steps in the Jewish quarter of the old city.

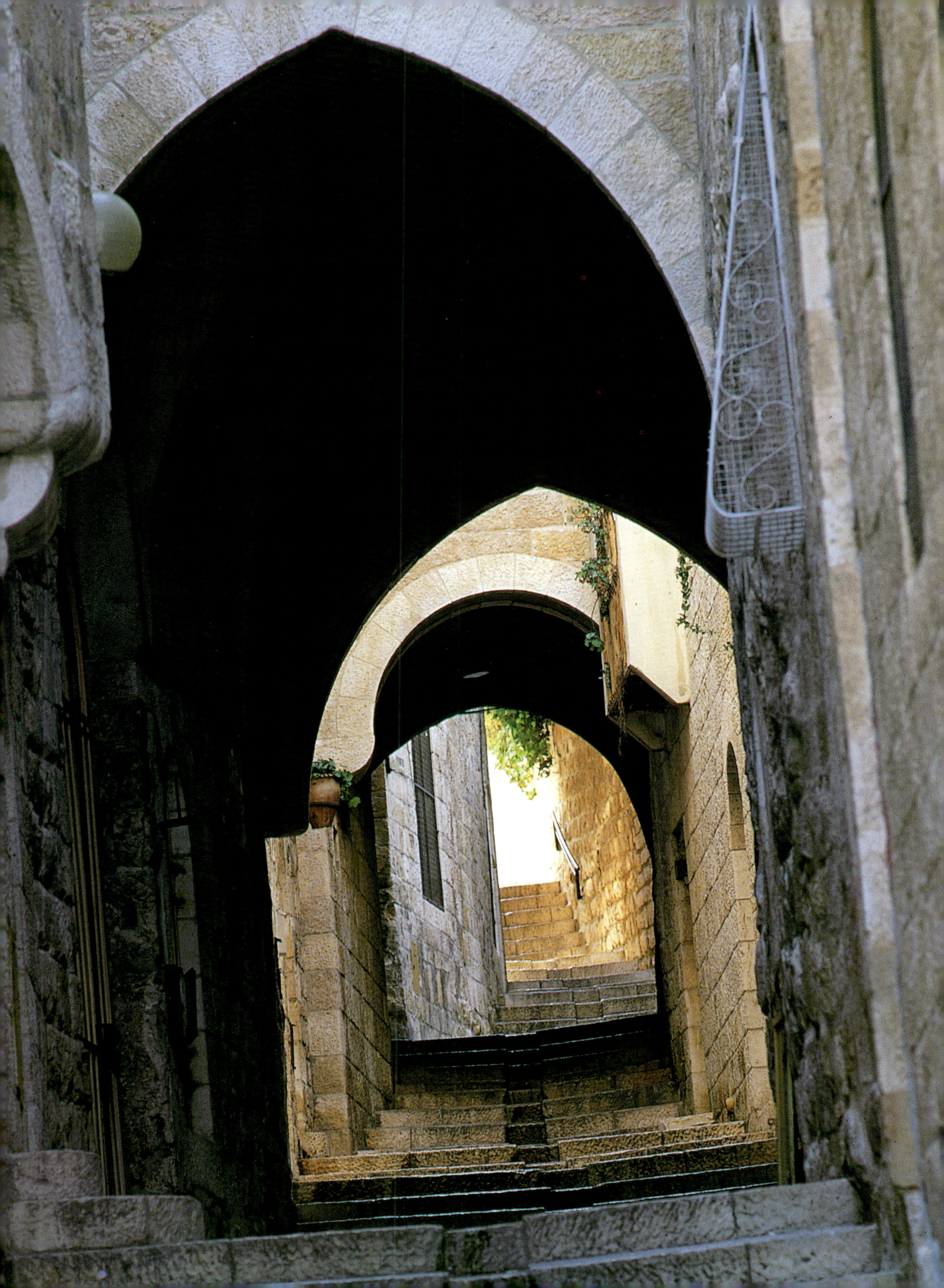

If Jerusalem and its suburbs appear to be a mosaic of zones, with lay and religious Jews, Muslim Palestinians and Christians co-existing on their borders, today the old city is a true meeting-point, where the districts inhabited by the three great monotheistic religions come together.

Jerusalem, *thrice holy but lacking in wisdom*

The eternal capital of Israel for the Jews, a holy city for Muslims – especially the Palestinians, who think of it as the legitimate capital of their future state – and the heart of the ancient Latin kingdom, which has become the holy centre of the Christian world, Jerusalem is held sacred by the three great monotheistic religions. Its status and prestige are unparalleled, and in the course of a long and tumultuous past, this has manifested itself in frequent attempts at domination, followed by rebellions. Jerusalem is a city of myths and martyrdom, which over the years has had to suffer the thirst for conquest of besieging powers wishing to reign over its past. Since its creation as the city of David, king of the Hebrew nation, 3,000 years or about 120 generations ago, Jerusalem, as Jean-Claude Guillebaud reminds us in his book *La traversée du monde* (Crossing the World), "has been Jewish for five and a half centuries, Persian and Greek for four centuries, Frankish for a short eighty-eight years, Mameluke and Ottoman for almost eight centuries. Finally Israel has been demanding its reunification under the authority of the Hebrew State since 1967, and is methodically encircling the city with Jewish colonies resembling military bunkers." Of course, its reconquest by Israel in the twentieth century is still at odds with the Palestinian people's demand for partition.

Going up and down the great flight of steps which opens out into the Via Dolorosa can be not just an effort but a real exercise of skill.

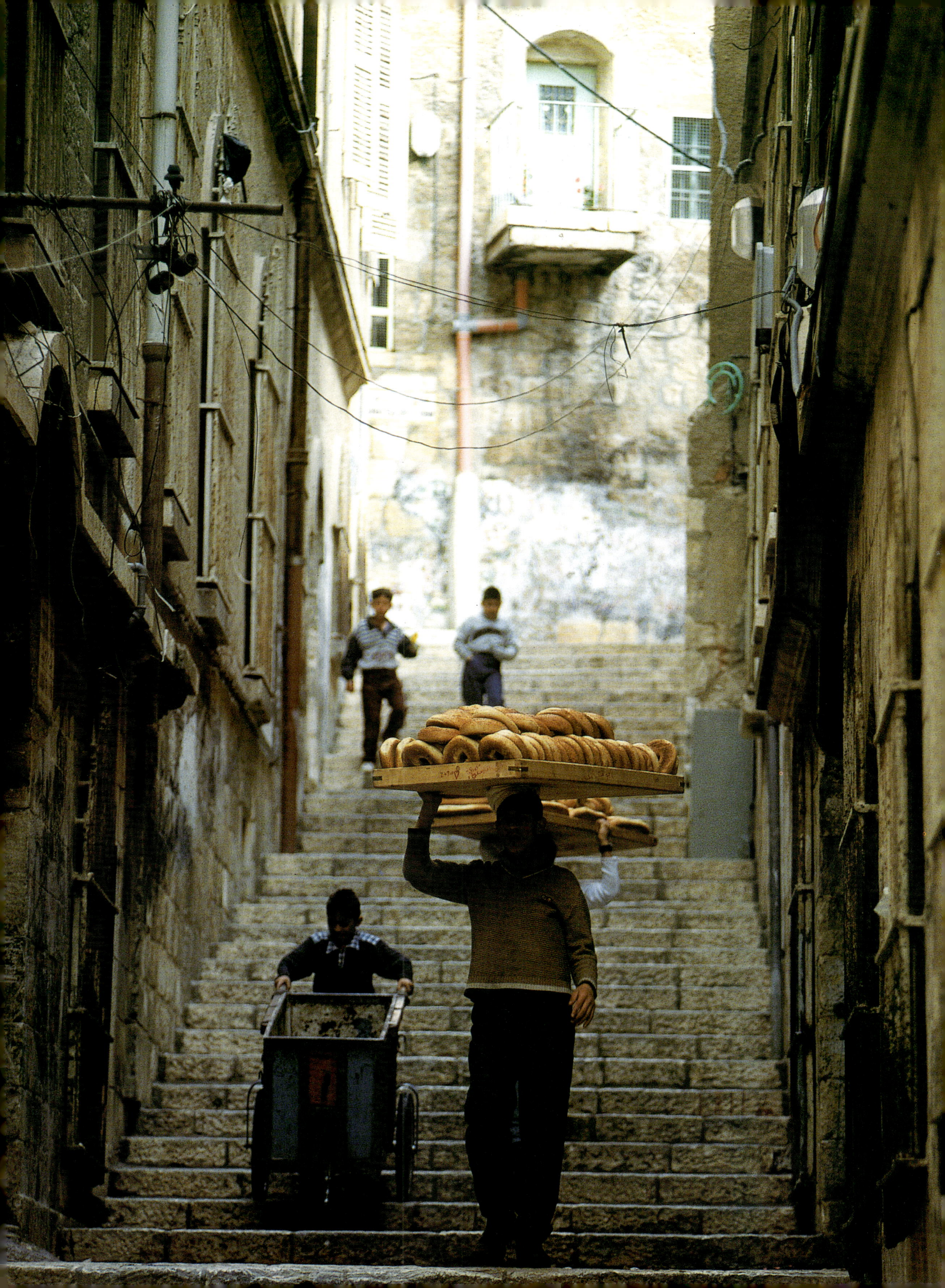

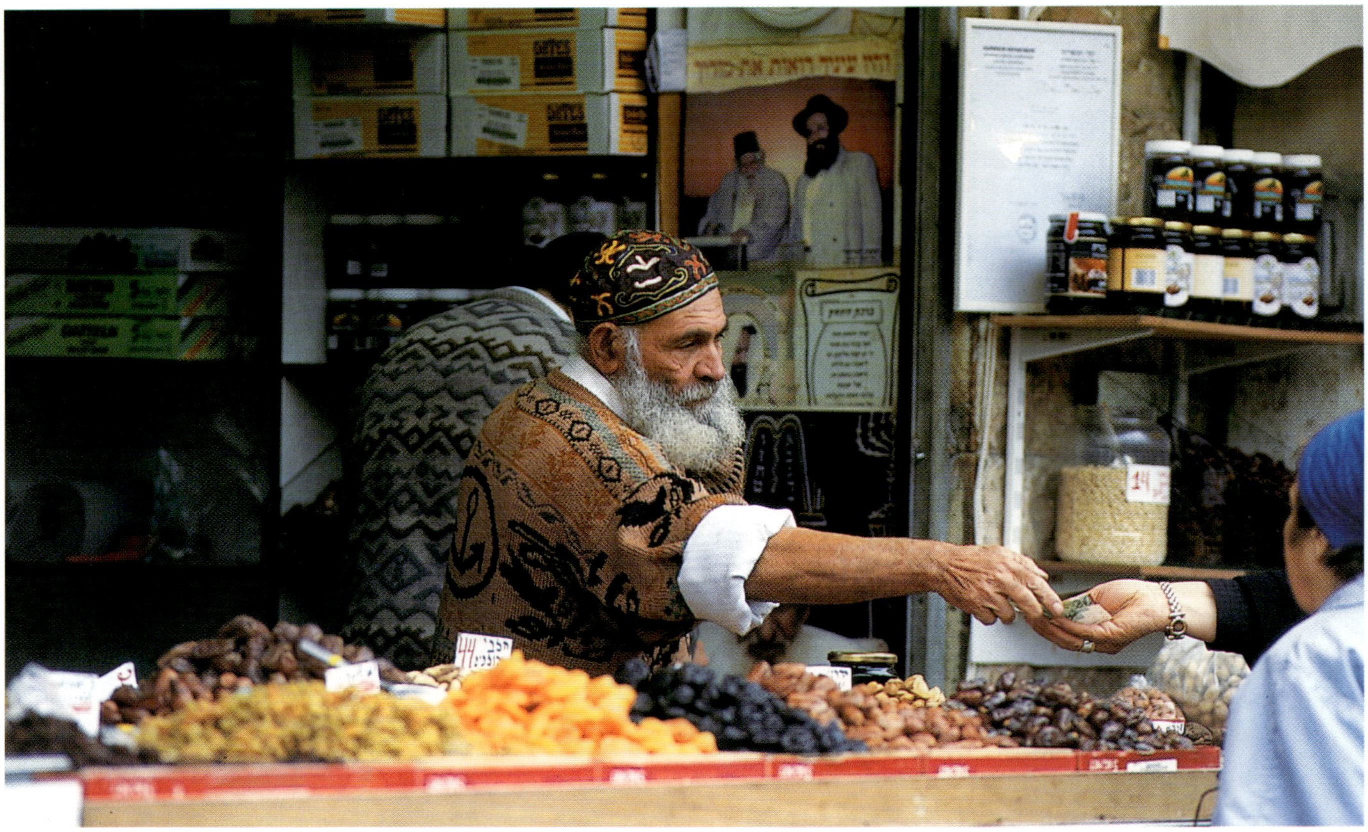

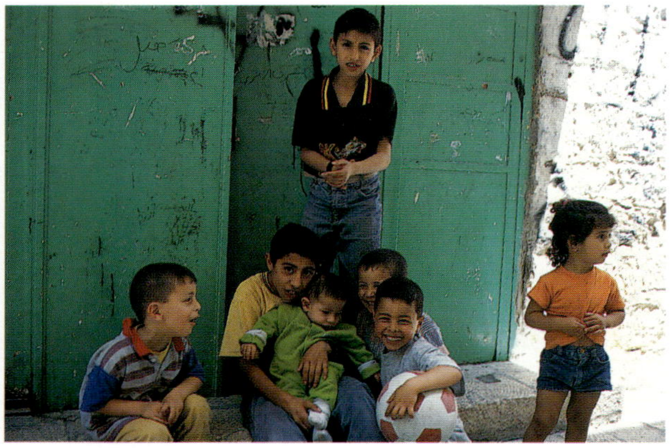

Jewish shopkeeper in the ultra-religious district of Mea Shearim. Children playing in the Muslim quarter of the old city.

That is the nature of Jerusalem; the new replacing the old, ever newer strata covering up a past which must be obliterated so that it can be completely subsumed. Moreover, one of the main attractions here is the feeling of how much history may be engraved on the stones of the city. As long ago as the end of the eighth century before Christ, some hundred years before the destruction of the First Temple, which David wished to have built and which was erected a generation later by his son Solomon in order to house the Ark of the Covenant, the prophet Isaiah, witnessing the Assyrian army's attempts to seize the city, observed that "you counted the buildings in Jerusalem, and tore down the houses to strengthen the wall". This sacrifice proved to be in vain, however, as in the end, after the Assyrian attacks had been repulsed, it was the Babylonians under their king Nebuchadnezzar who finally – in 587 to be precise – demolished the defences of the capital of the kingdom of Judaea. As a result, part of the city was devastated, the First Temple destroyed, and the élite of the population deported to Babylon.

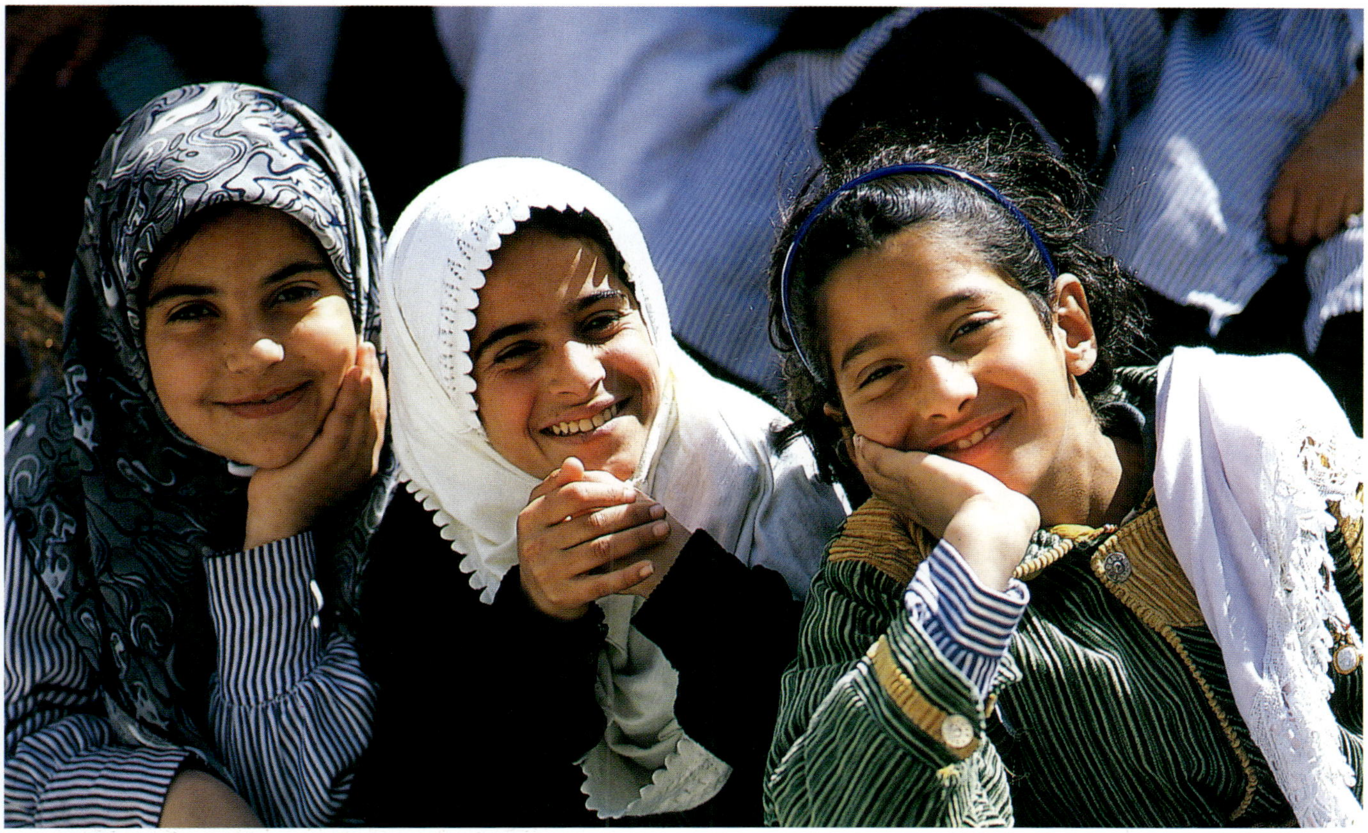

Later, when the Temple had been rebuilt by the Hebrews on their return from fifty years of exile, and subsequently enlarged by King Herod at the end of the last century before the new Christian era, it was the turn of the Roman legions of the emperor Titus brutally to seize Jerusalem, which was at that time under the control of the Jews after a four-year rebellion against the authority of Rome. In fact in 70 AD, after Jesus was crucified on Golgotha, at the place where the church of the Holy Sepulchre would later be built, the Romans again destroyed the city and the holy Temple, built of characteristic white limestone blocks. From this time, which can be considered the end of the period of the Second Temple and marks the beginning of the Jewish Diaspora, there still remains the last solemn, mysterious vestige of this Temple dedicated to the eternal God: the Western Wall, also known as the Wailing Wall.

But travellers entering the thrice holy city for the first time – whether they are pilgrims, lovers of history, or simply visitors returning to their Judeo-Christian roots – are surprised at first glance by the absence of

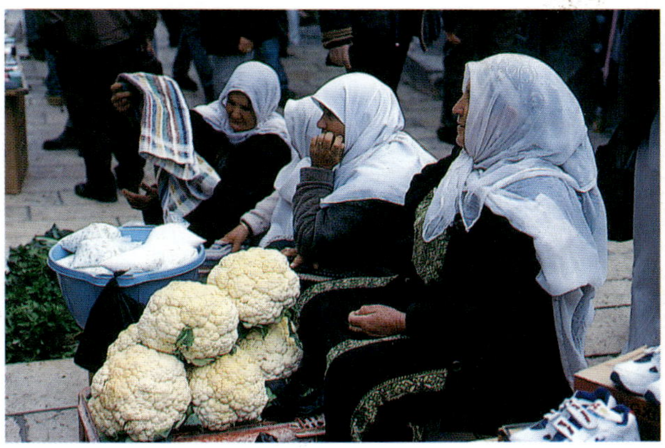

The bright eyes and persevering spirit of Muslim girls and women in East Jerusalem.

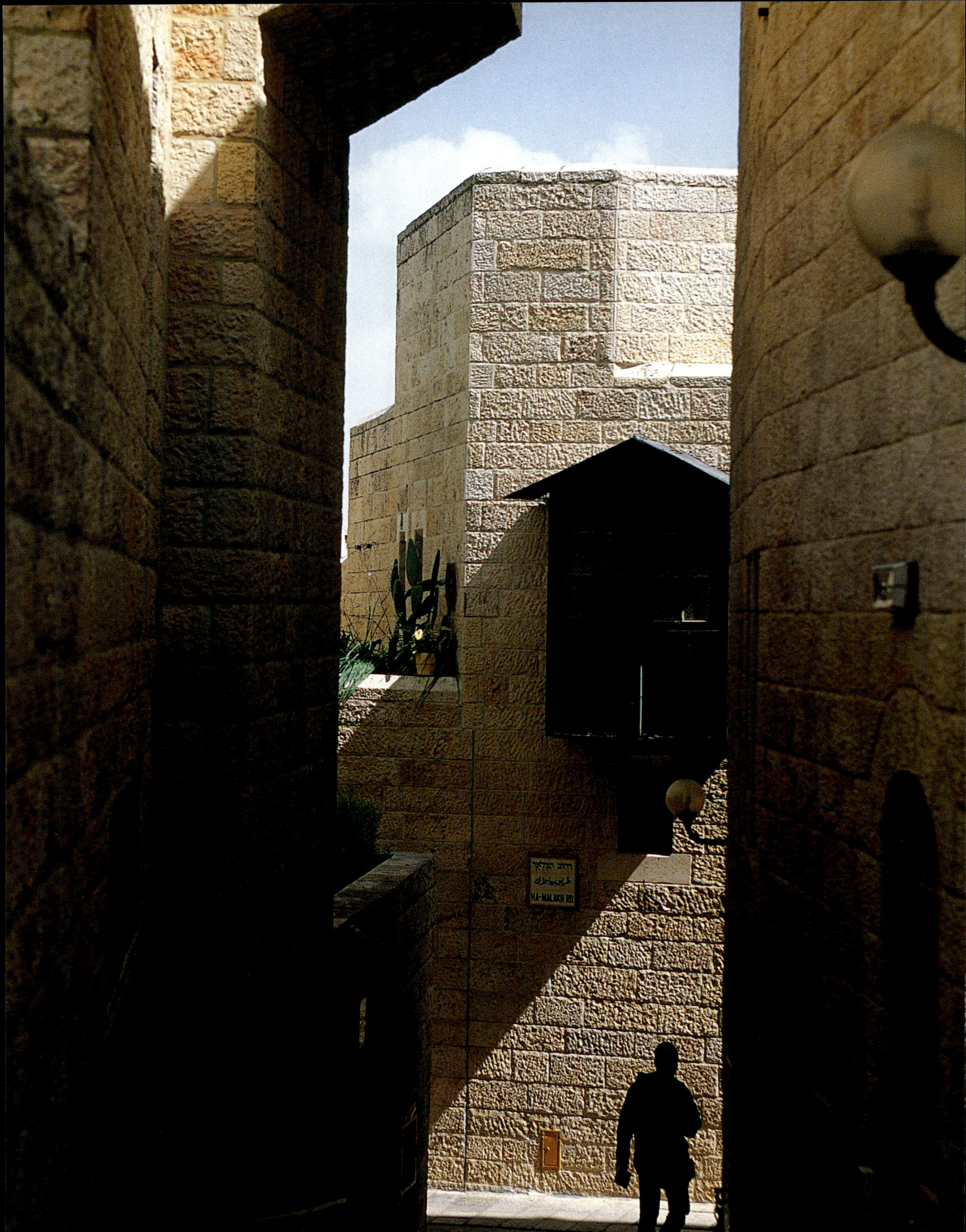
רחוב המלאך
HA-MALAKH RD.

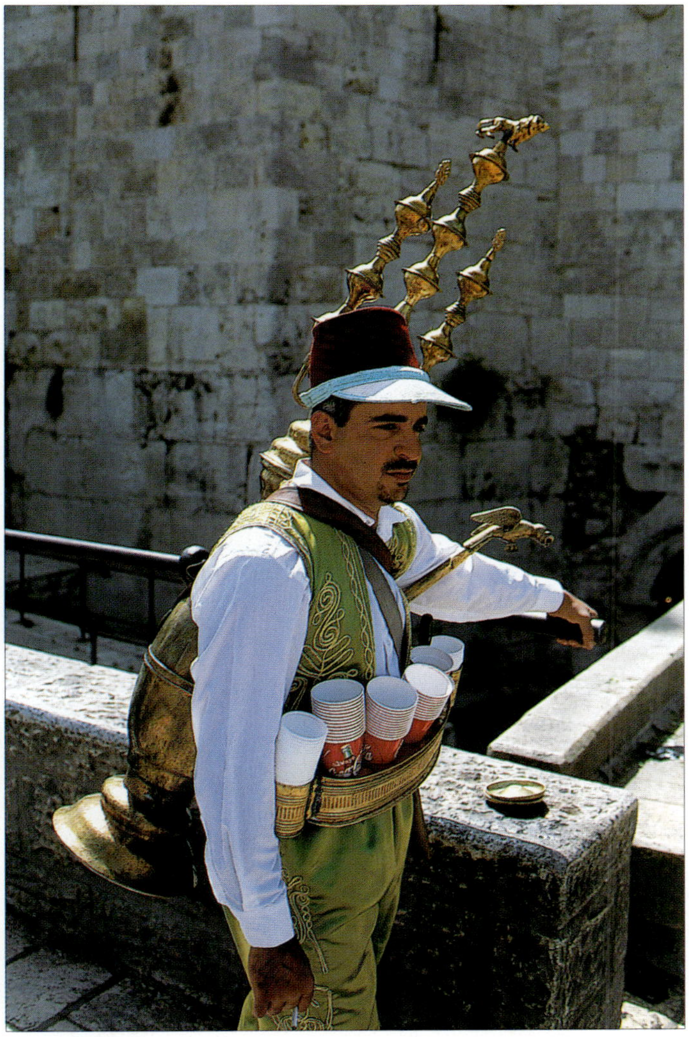

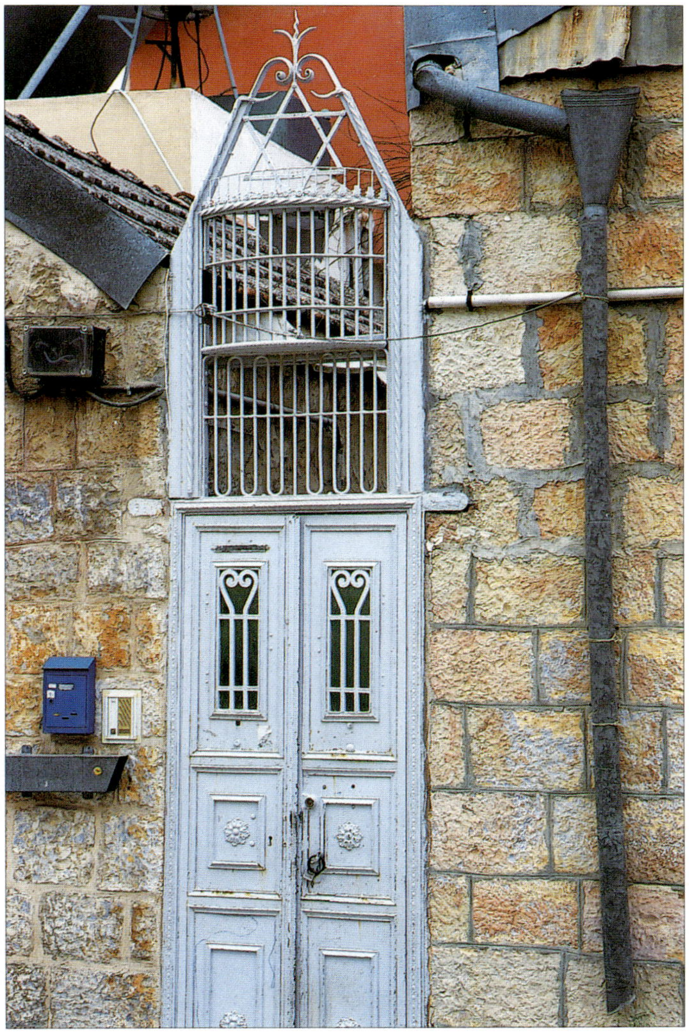

anything which might illustrate the imagined motives for their journey or the images of their dreams. What they discover on arrival is not the tangle of stones, the labyrinth of narrow streets, or the criss-crossing of church towers and minarets in an eastern sky such as are seen in the familiar pictures of Jerusalem, but merely a modern city. At its heart, the old city now appears reduced in size because of the profusion of residential areas around its ramparts. On one side is West Jerusalem, which has developed on several hills as the population has increased (there are around 450,000 Jewish inhabitants), and has many centres of activity and interest; on the other side lies East Jerusalem, the Arab city, much less extensive than its rival, less populous (the Muslim population is estimated at about 150,000), and markedly less well endowed from the

A water-seller by the Damascus Gate.
Front door of a house in Mea Shearim.
Facing page:
Restored area in the Jewish quarter of the old city.
Following pages:
Pictured here beside the Jaffa Gate, the citadel of Jerusalem is an imposing defensive wall, presided over by the Tower of David.

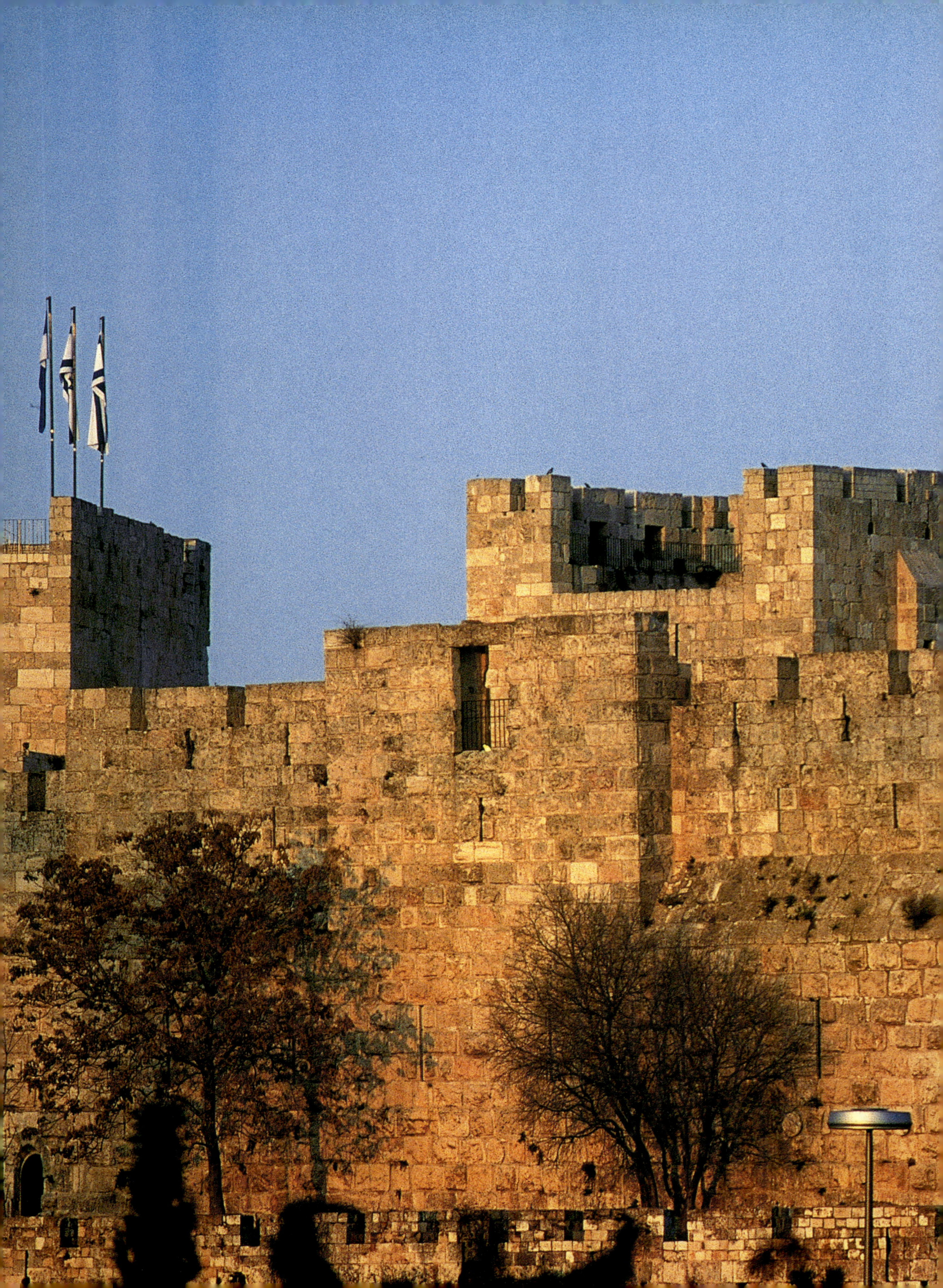

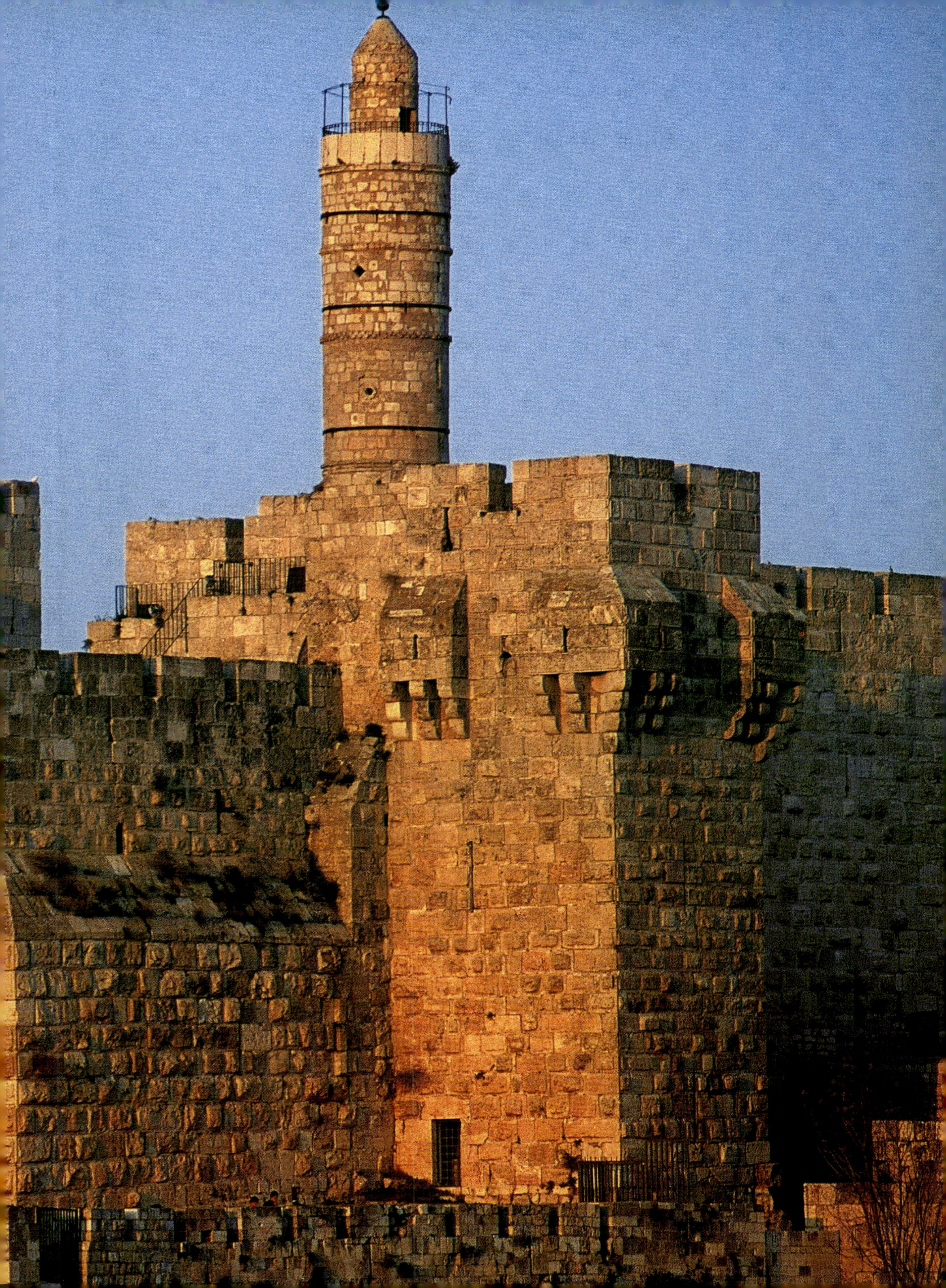

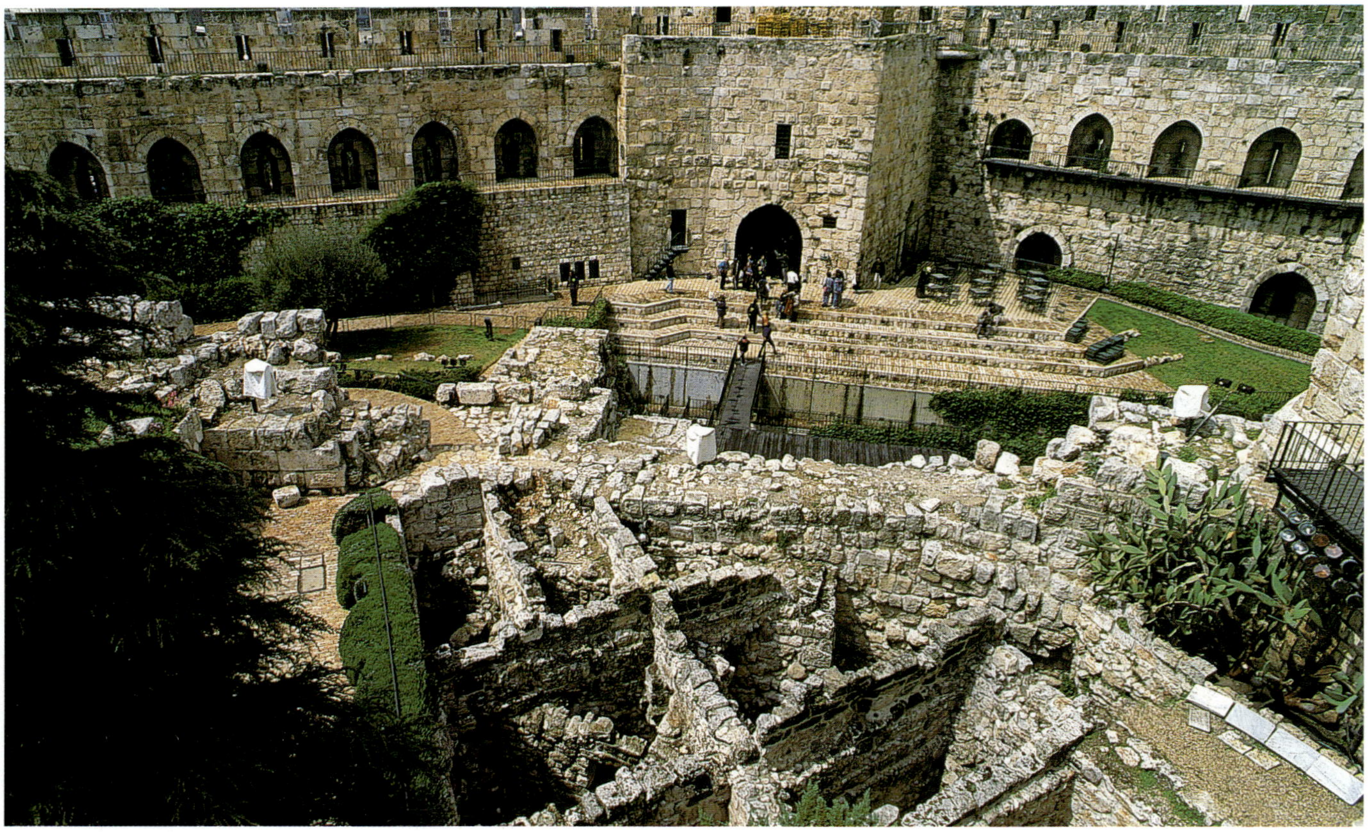

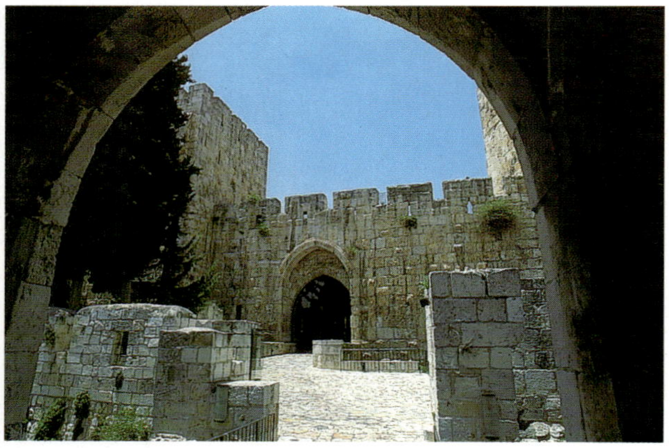

The inside of the citadel, showing some archaeological remains.

point of view of urban infrastructure. But although the separation is absolutely real on the ground and in the mind, the Jews have so completely taken over the city that this division has almost become obsolete. Reinforced by the transfer of the entire Israeli administration as soon as independence was declared in 1948, the Jewish presence literally became a takeover when it was decreed that a large number of houses should be built. The intention was on the one hand to accommodate the flood of immigrants, and on the other hand to gain a foothold in the east by entirely surrounding the old city, so that Jerusalem gradually but inevitably became a single, indivisible entity.

In the new city, the liveliest districts are those which, at the beginning of the twentieth century, already extended outside the walls along the Jaffa Road. Shops, small hotels, bars, and restaurants are clustered in a triangle formed by the recently refurbished pedestrian precinct of Ben Yehuda Street (a part of King George V Street) and the Jaffa Road (at the end of which is the bus station, where you can catch buses to various

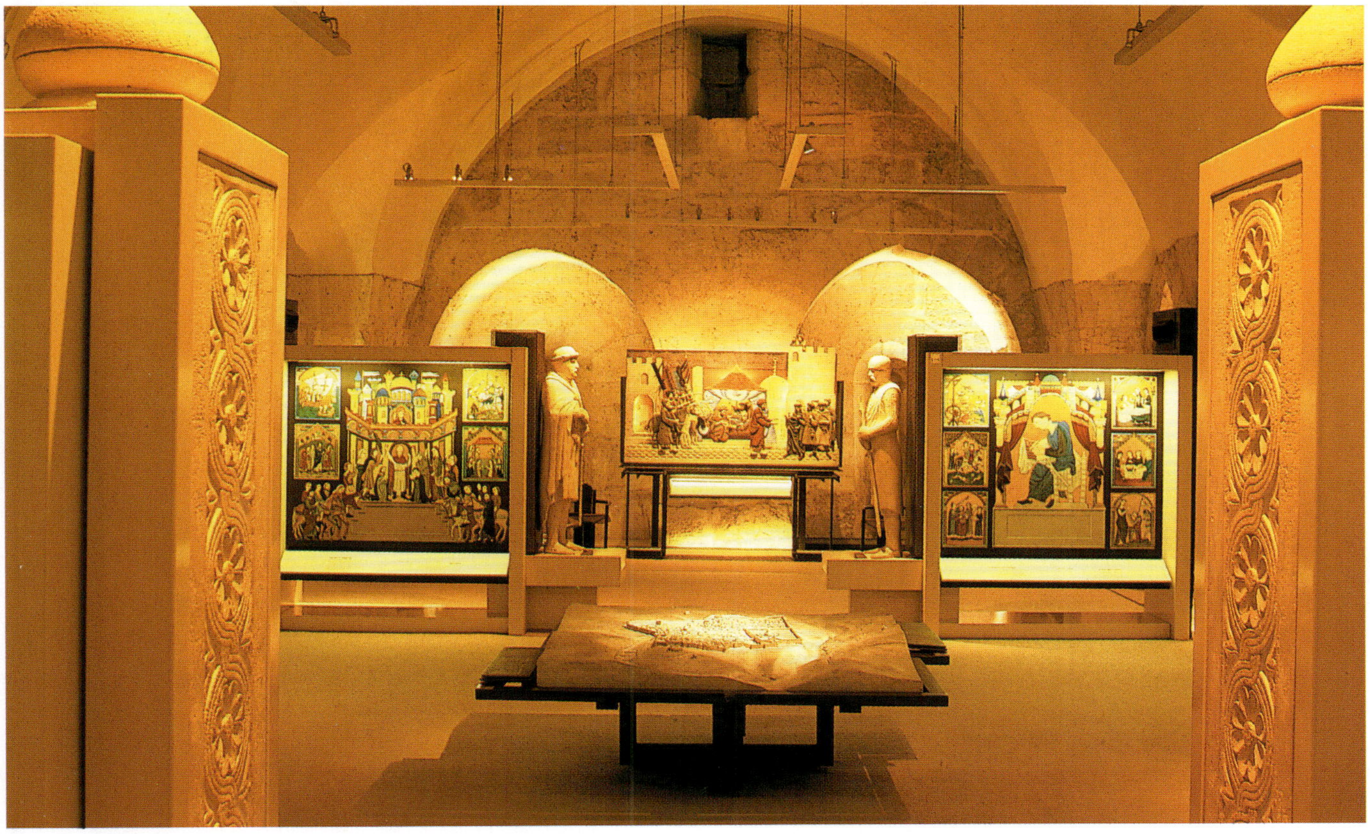

destinations in the country). Around this triangle, crowds of people gather almost every evening, even on the Sabbath – the seventh day of the week, which begins at sundown on Friday, and demands strict observance of the rule that no work should be done for 24 hours to commemorate the creation of the world by God. Salomon Street and Nahalat Shiva, which have one bar or restaurant after another, and the Russian quarter where you find the most fashionable bars, make Jerusalem look like any western city. Or almost, because for one thing there is the constant but always slightly surprising presence in the Israeli countryside of young soldiers carrying sub-machine guns. And then there are the ultra-religious who come and go, dressed in black, with their hats and beards, and their hair in curl-papers on their temples, making it clear – with the utmost conviction and perhaps a hint of proselytism – that their values and their way of life are the absolute opposite of those of wealthy societies. Mea Shearim, the ultra-orthodox district of Jerusalem, inhabited solely by followers of the mystical Hassidic movement, who group together to

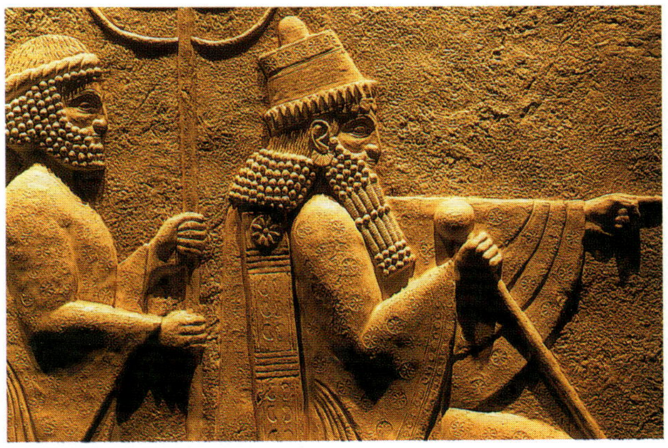

The Citadel Museum comprehensively traces the history of Jerusalem. The Crusades Room, for example, is very instructive. There are many images on view, like this one showing the exile in Babylon.

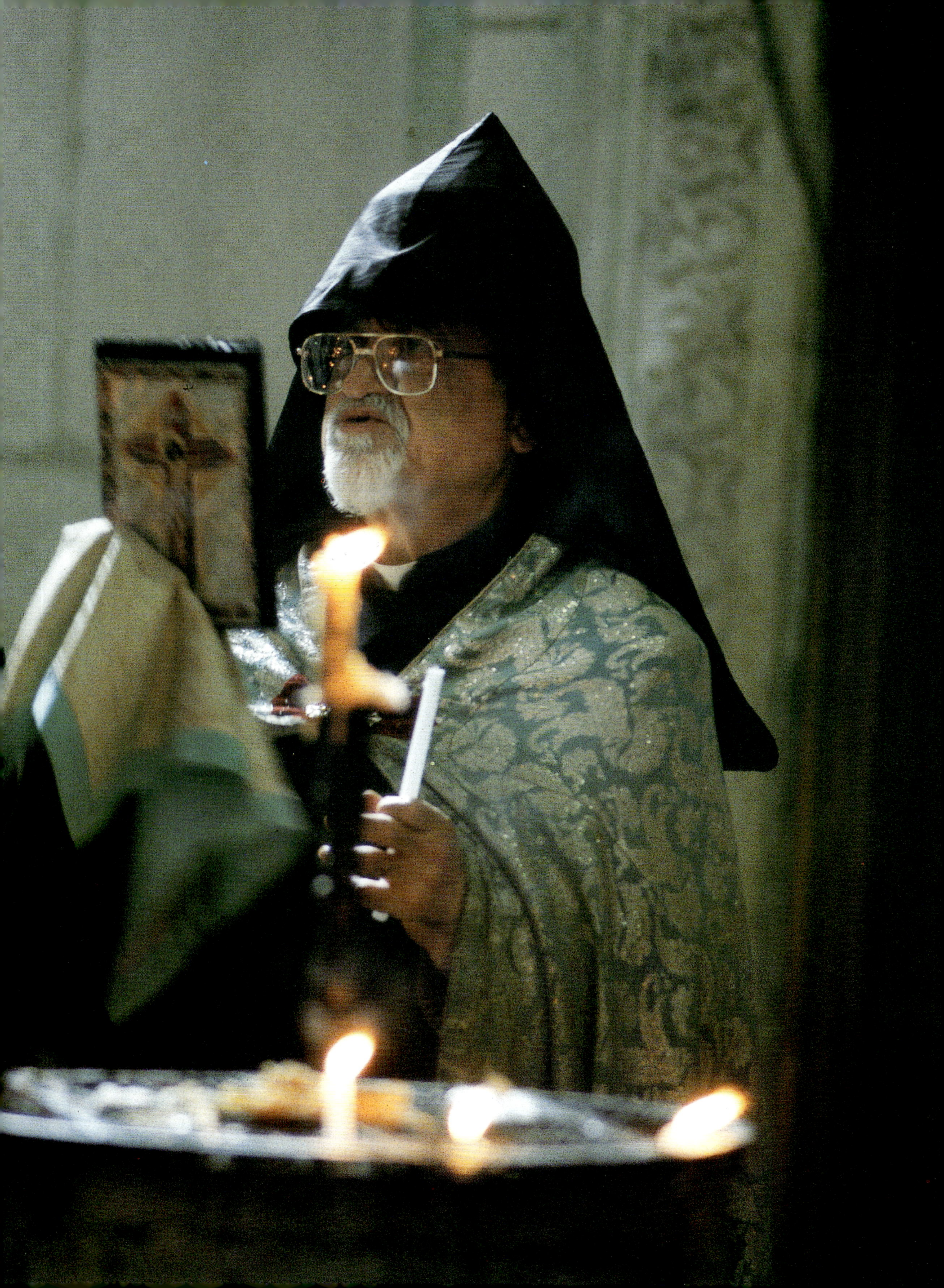

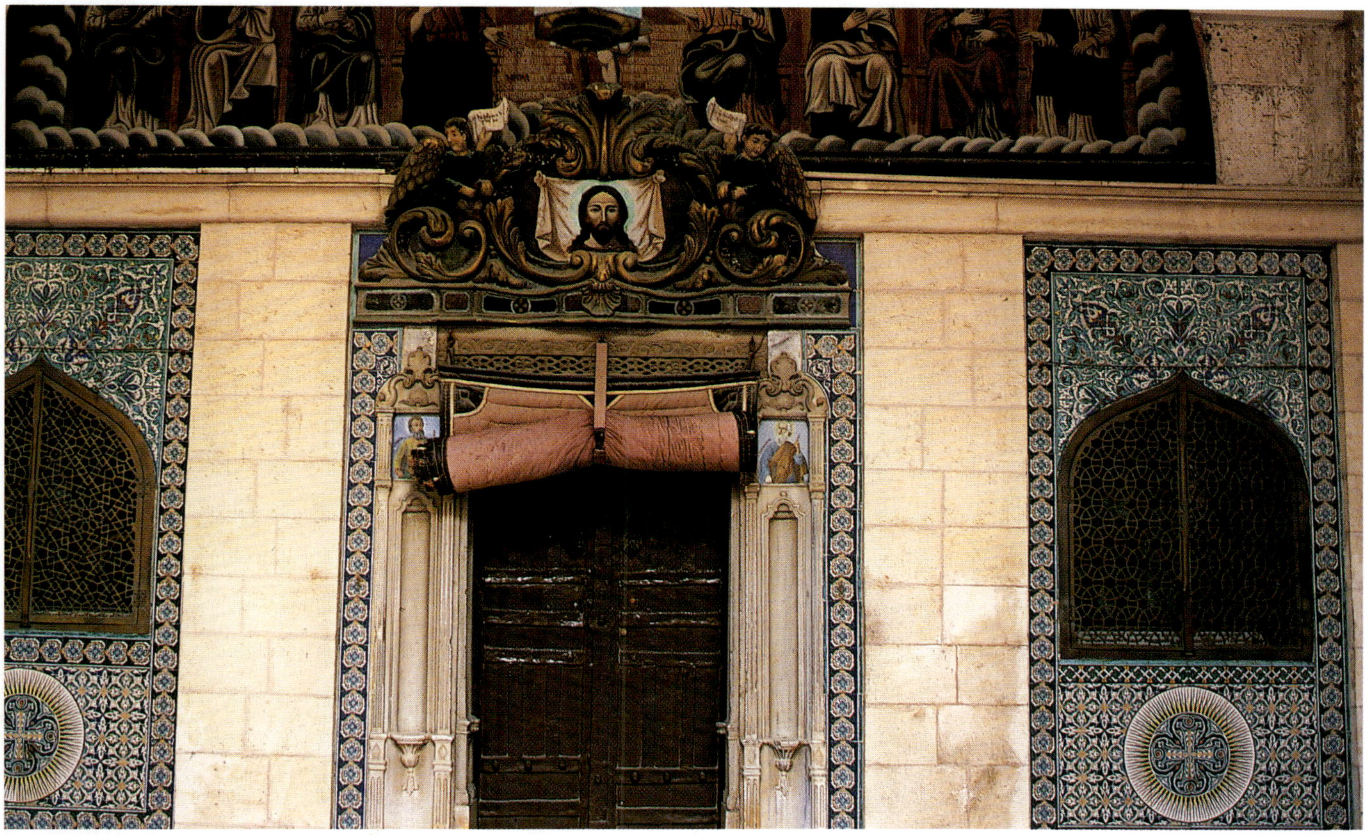

avoid being disturbed by those who do not share their passionate love of God, is an amazing contrast to the central districts of the new city of which it is a part. When you walk through this district along Mea Shearim Street or Ha Nevim Street – which actually means the street of prophets and marks the true boundary between the world of those Israelis who are integrated into the nation's life and the world of the ultra-religious anti-Zionists who, for example, object to the state of Israel as an absurdity which conflicts with the prophecies – what strikes you most is the impressive number of children being raised and taken for walks by every couple. It is not uncommon to see families of eight or ten walking briskly through the streets of this picturesque district, especially on the Sabbath, when no cars are allowed there. Another striking characteristic is their extreme closeness to one another.

It might be a group of teenagers walking briskly, marching in step as if they were part of the same body, or men coming out of a synagogue in the midst of a passionate discussion, waving their arms to emphasise

The Armenian cathedral of St James is one of the most beautiful jewels of Christianity in the eastern world. Prettily carved, decorative, and pleasing to the eye, the gates and the abundance of ironwork at the windows also allow evil spirits to flee away, according to ancient superstition.

Facing page:

The high priest, a dignitary of the Armenian Church, celebrates the liturgy in the church of the Holy Sepulchre.

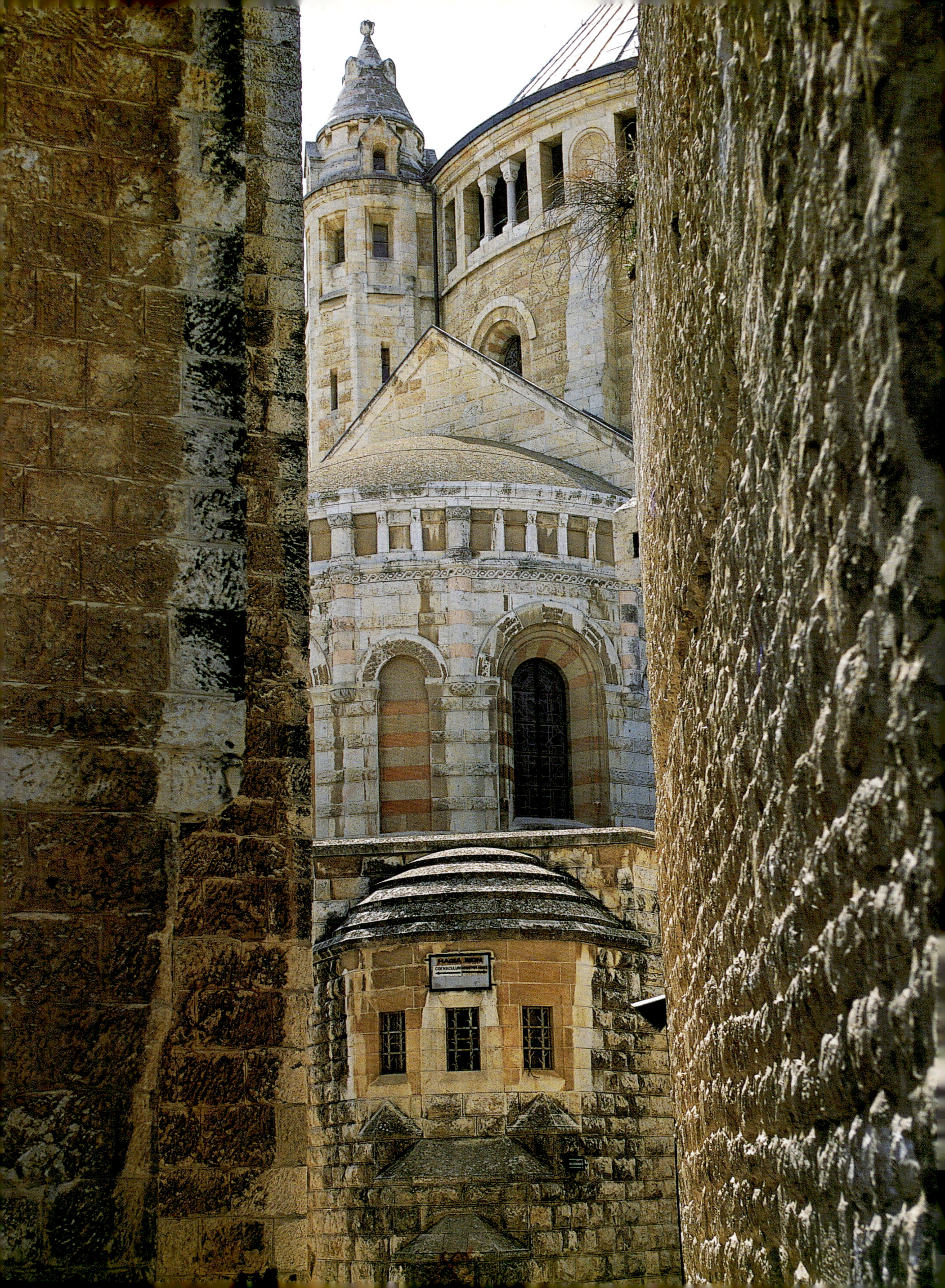
HAGIA SION
COENACULUM

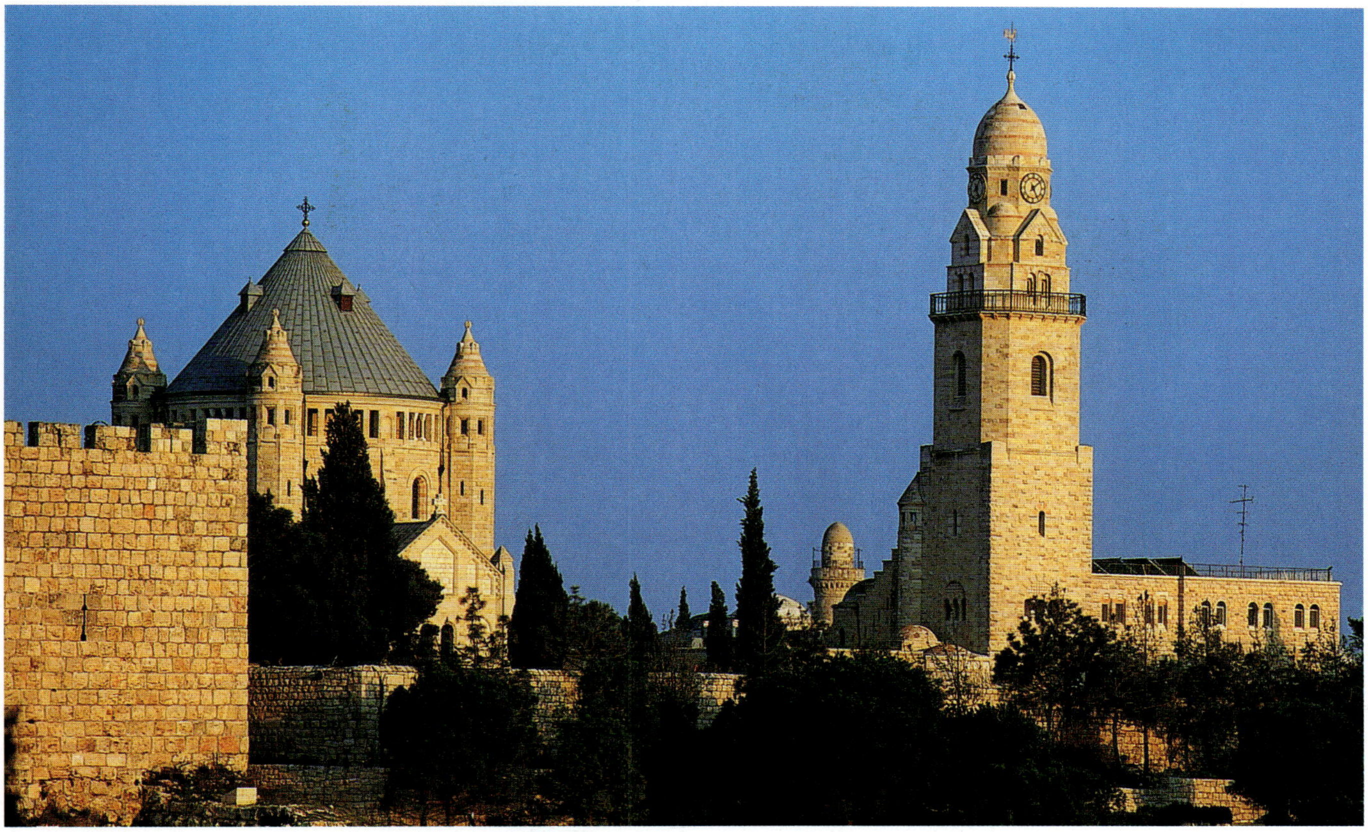

their points and clearly enjoying the argument. These religious people, who are so scrupulous about the rites of *kashrut* laid down by their rabbi, and far more attuned to the quest for divine ecstasy through singing and dancing than to the painstaking study of the texts of the Torah, show as much solidarity towards their own closed society as distrust of strangers. If Jerusalem and its suburbs appear to be a mosaic of zones, with lay and religious Jews, Muslim Palestinians, and Christians co-existing on their borders, today the old city is a true meeting point, where the districts inhabited by the three great monotheistic religions come together. Jewish, Armenian, Christian, and Arab quarters are joined to one another inside the fantastic ramparts which encircle them.

The present-day appearance of these fortifications dates back to the Ottoman Sultan Suleiman the Magnificent, who decided to adorn Jerusalem with mighty walls, pierced by impressive gates, along a line already established by the Romans. The eight gates, spaced at regular intervals along the ramparts, which encircle the city over a distance of

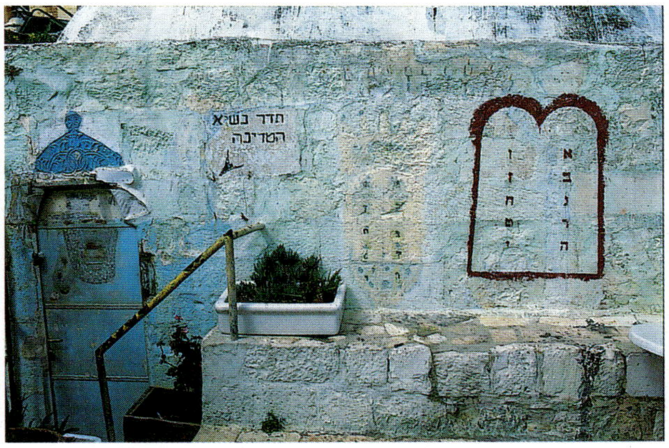

Mount Zion, which stands apart from the wall surrounding the old city, houses the tomb of King David and is also the site of the two important churches, St Saviour's in the foreground, and Dormition abbey a little further back.
Close to the tomb of David, the cell of a Muslim monk.
Facing page:
Dormition abbey stands on Mount Zion, at the place where the Virgin Mary is said to have fallen into eternal sleep.

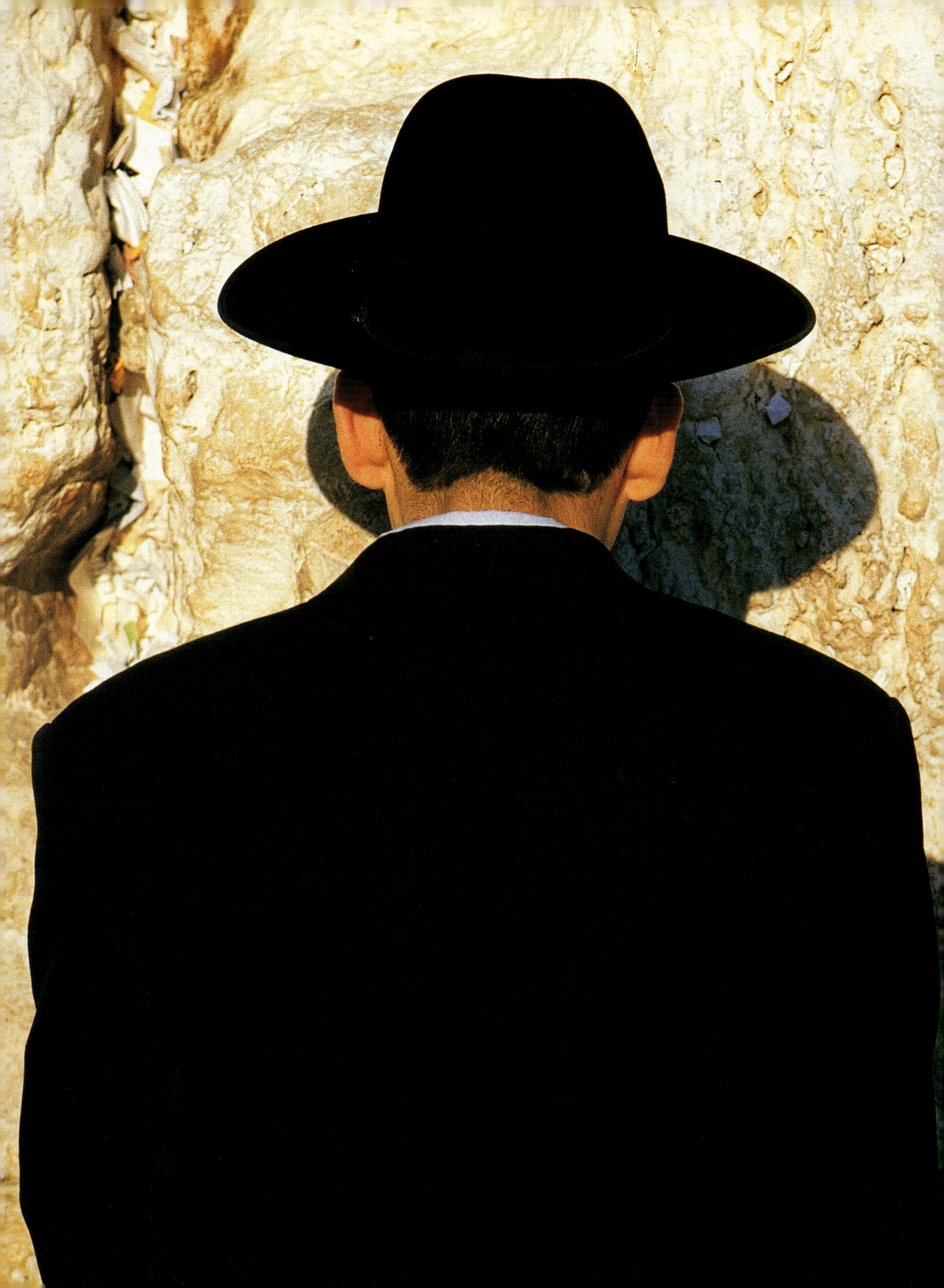

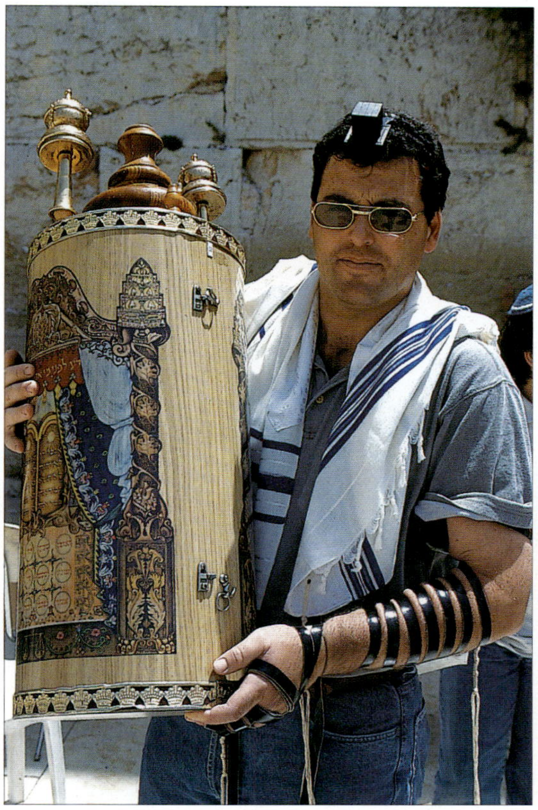

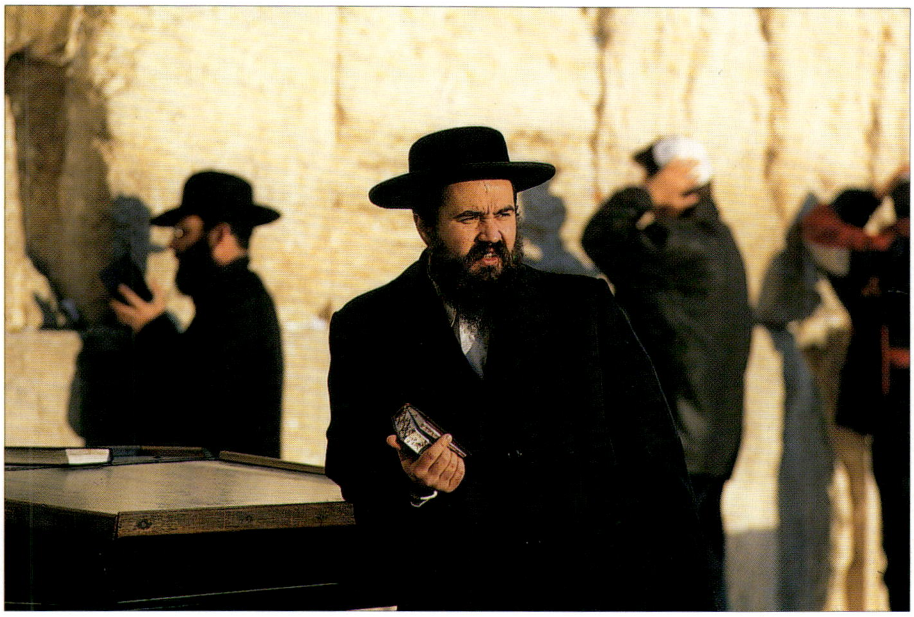

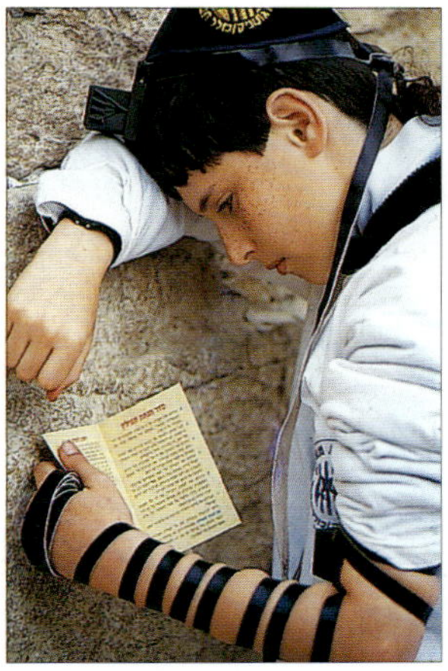

A young member of the Jewish community prays assiduously at the wall, wearing tefillin on his left arm and his forehead.
These tefillin, or phylacteries, contain passages from the Pentateuch; those on the arm symbolise action, those on the forehead, thought.
Near him, men of the ultra-religious Hassidic movement, dressed all in black, commit themselves every day to almost ecstatic prayers.
Facing page:
A religious man meditates and prays by the Western Wall, commonly known as the Wailing Wall.

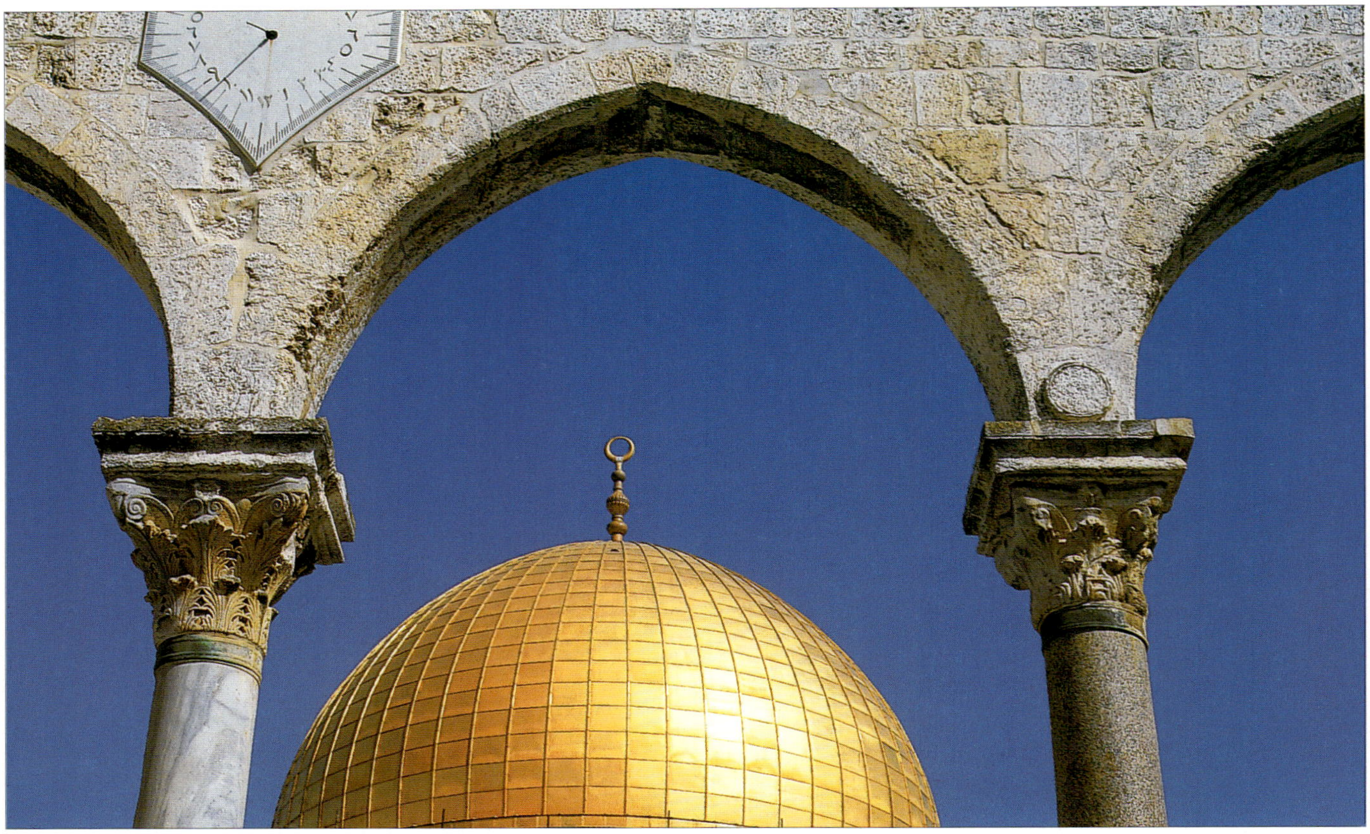

The Dome of the Rock, near the Al Aksa mosque, towers over the esplanade of Mount Moriah.

• The Dome of the Rock •

It shines in the Jerusalem sky, a symbol of the holy city, and is the highlight of any photograph, regardless of where it is taken from. It was built in 691 by the great Muslim Arab builders of the Omeyyad dynasty. The octagonal sanctuary is covered by a dome, re-gilded in 1963, which previously shone only with the gleam of copper, and contains a rock revered by both Muslims and Jews. According to tradition, this rock on Mount Moriah is the place where Abraham prepared to sacrifice Isaac, and also the rock from which Mohammed ascended into heaven to hear the angel Gabriel confirm his destiny. The exterior of the building has an abundance of geometrical motifs, while the interior ornamentation draws inspiration from every conceivable kind of vegetation. People may circulate around the rock. Beneath it is a cave, where visitors may go to meditate.

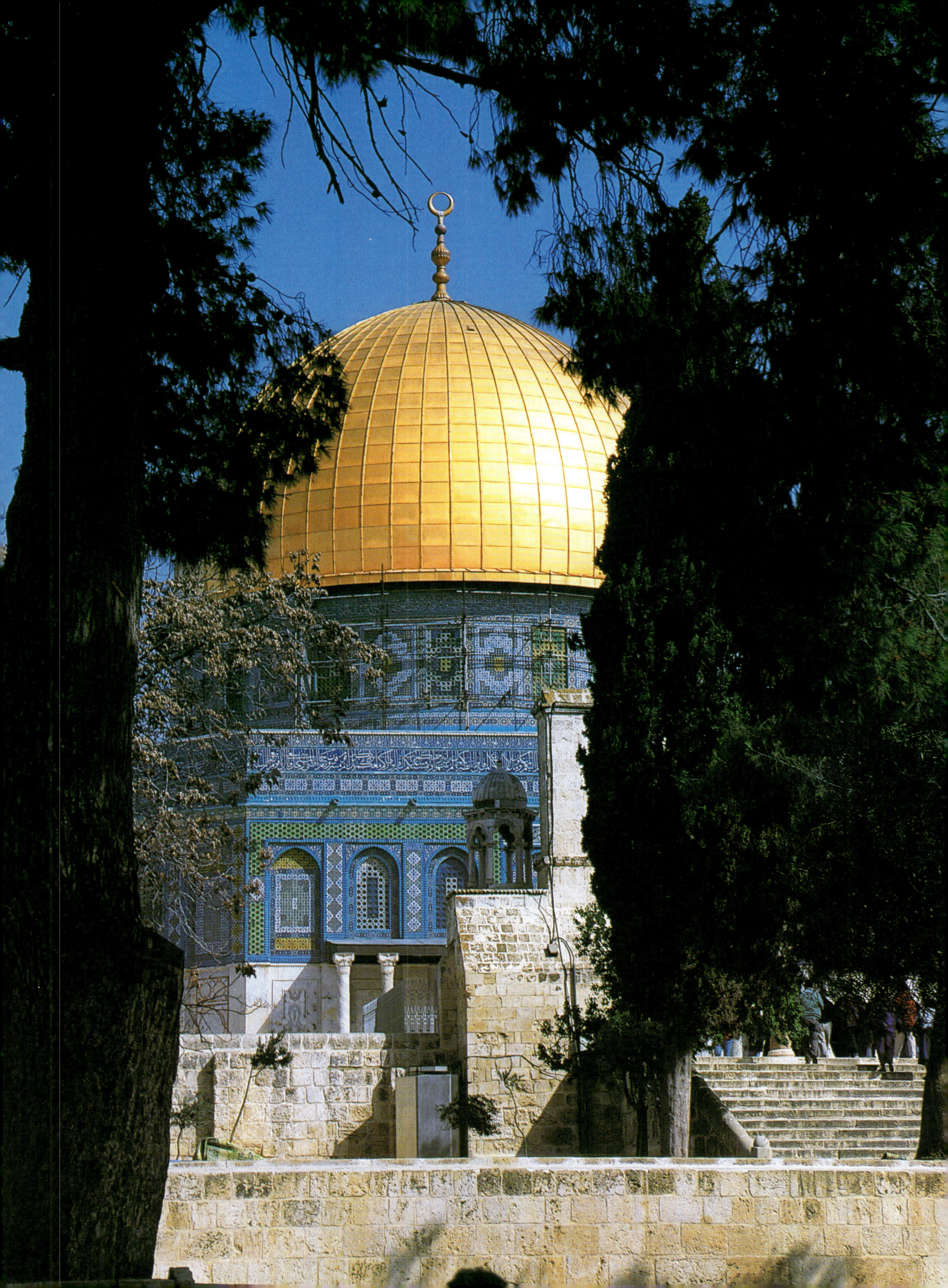

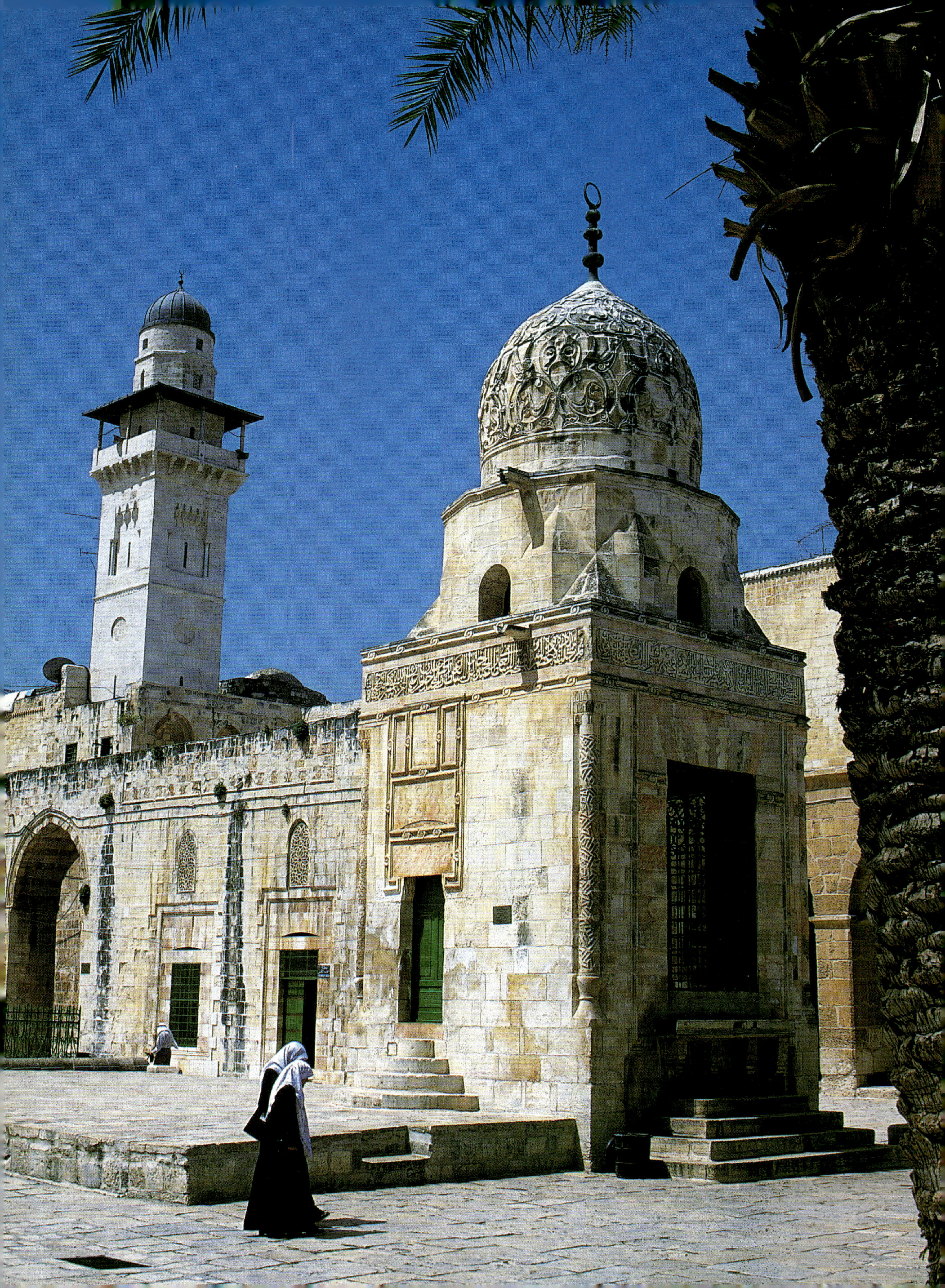

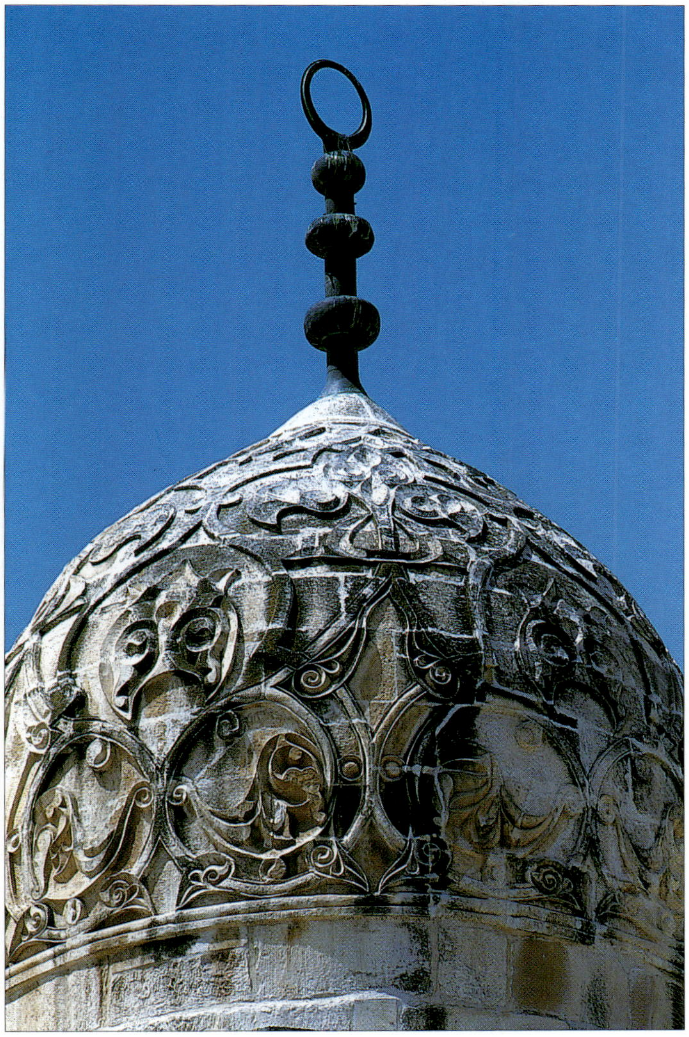

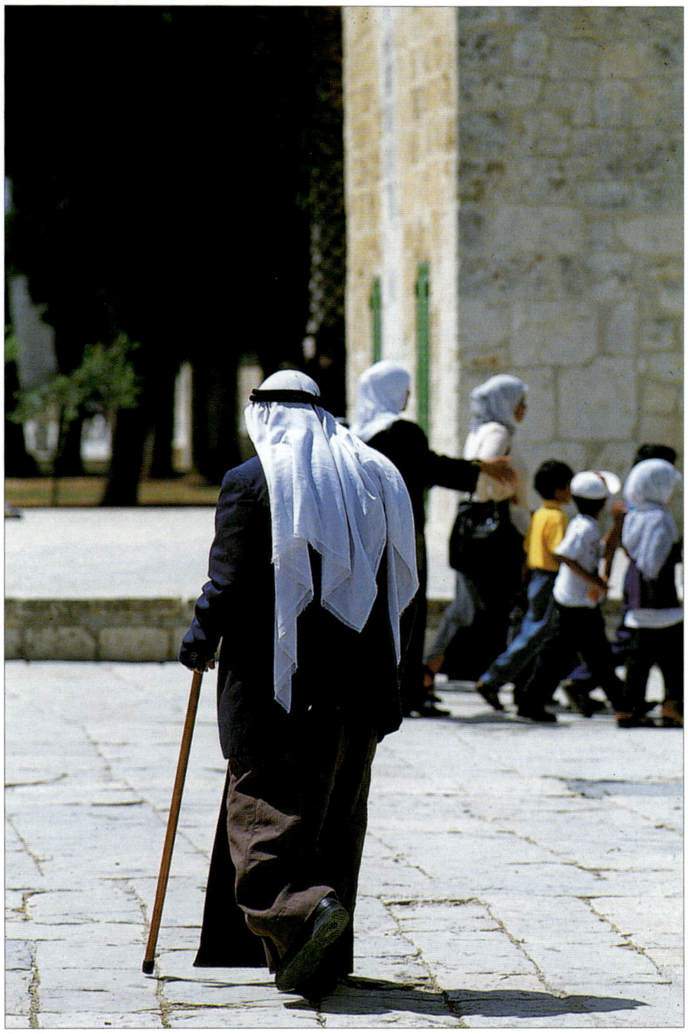

more than 4 km (2½ miles) and whose height varies from 5 to 15 m (16 to 50 ft), have names which fill the mind with dreams of the past, even before one enters this legendary city. Probably the most frequently visited is the Jaffa Gate, which lies to the west and takes its name from the Philistine city on the coast, to which it gave access. To the north-west is the most recent, the New Gate, built by the Ottoman rulers in the nineteenth century to allow the Christians easier access to their quarter. The Damascus Gate to the north takes its name from the Syrian capital towards which it faces, and is the main entrance to the Arab part of the city.

To the north-east, Herod's Gate, smaller and less often used, owes its name to the palace of Herod Antipas, the son of the king who beautified

The esplanade is a holy place, where thousands of Muslims go every day to meditate, and also to meet each other and rest in the shade of the green foliage.

Facing page:
The spring of Sebil Qait Bey is one of the many buildings to be found on the esplanade of Haram esh-Sharif.

Following pages:
The square in front of the church of the Holy Sepulchre gives you the opportunity to appreciate the building before you enter.

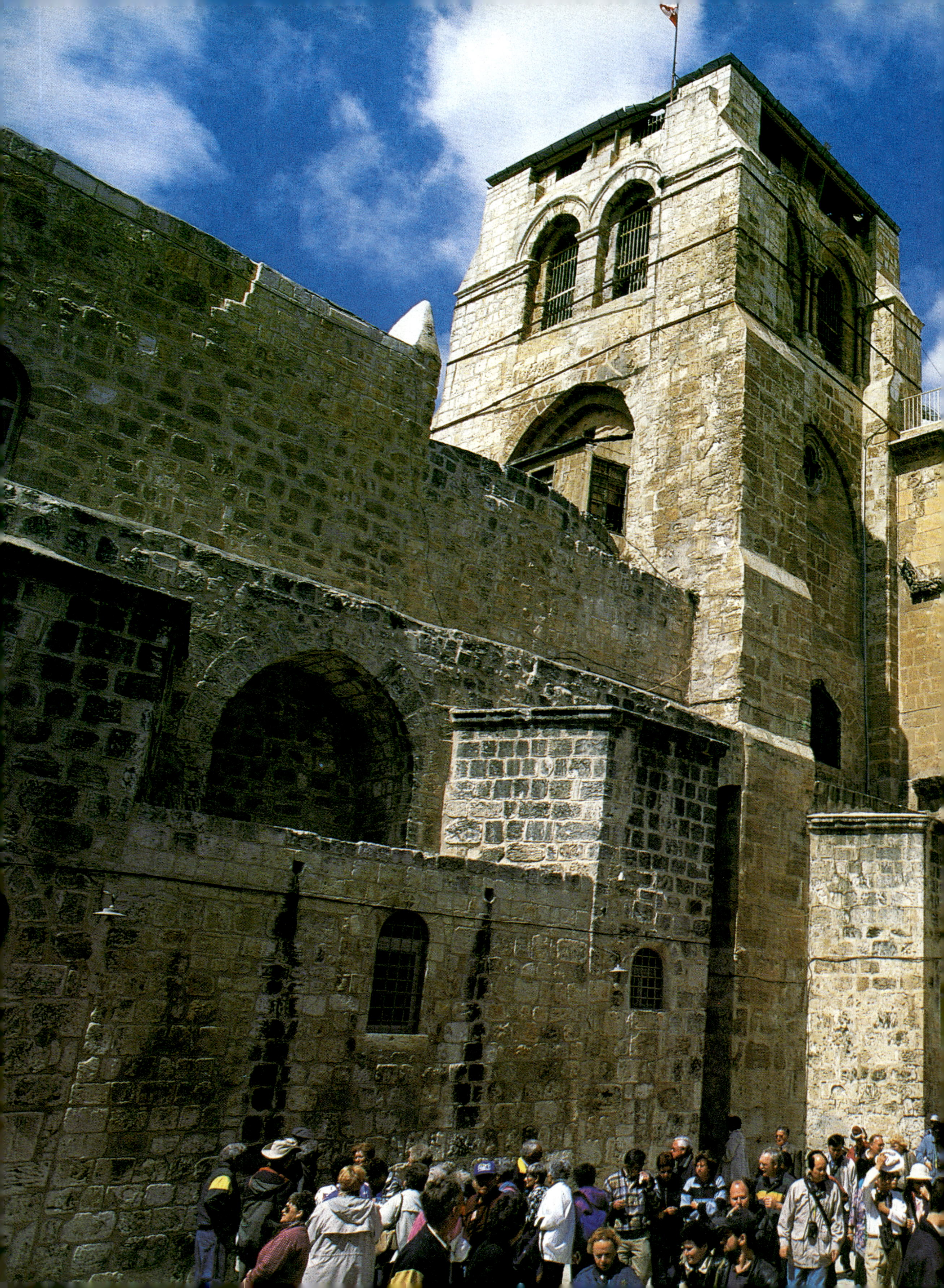

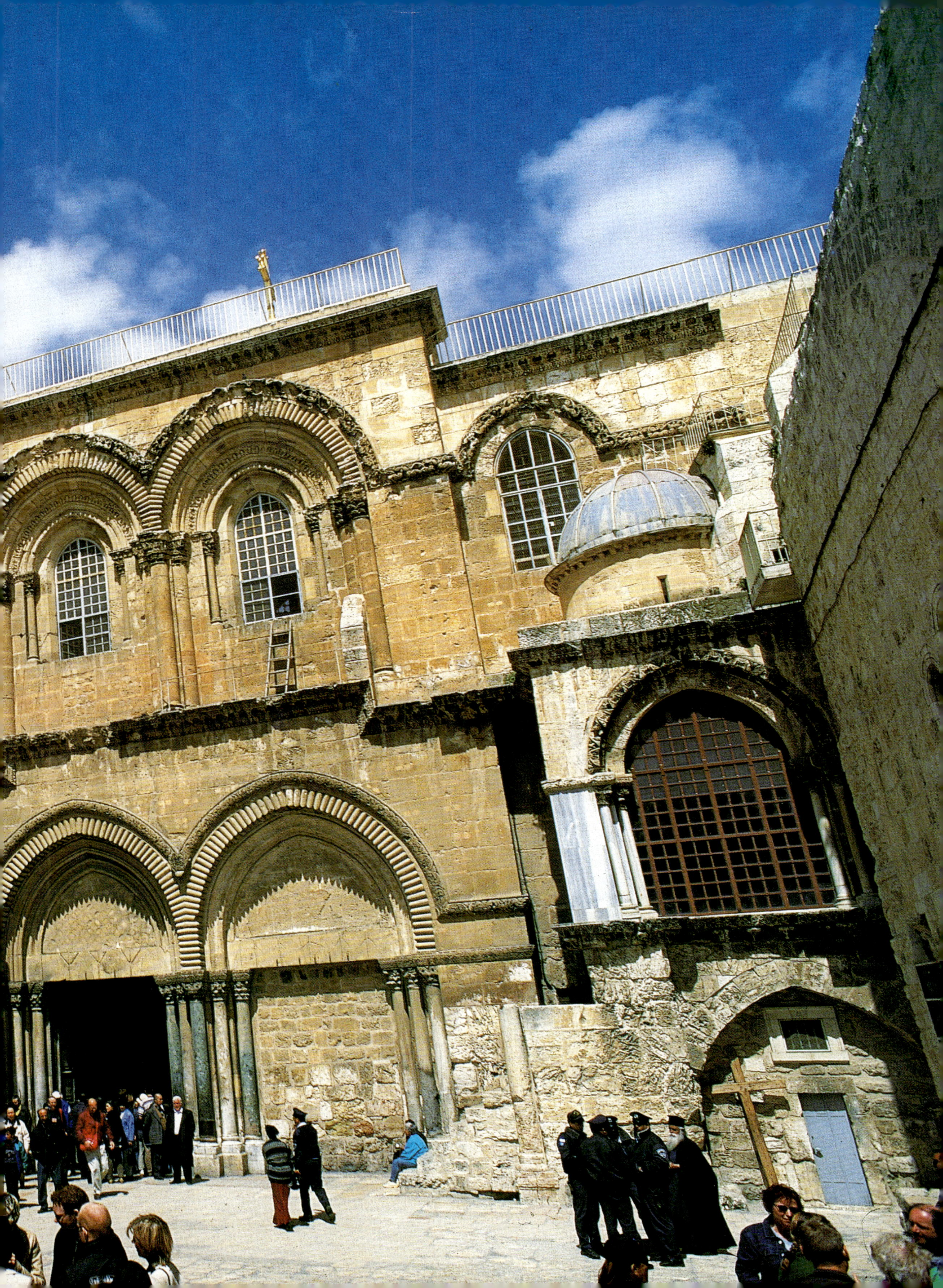

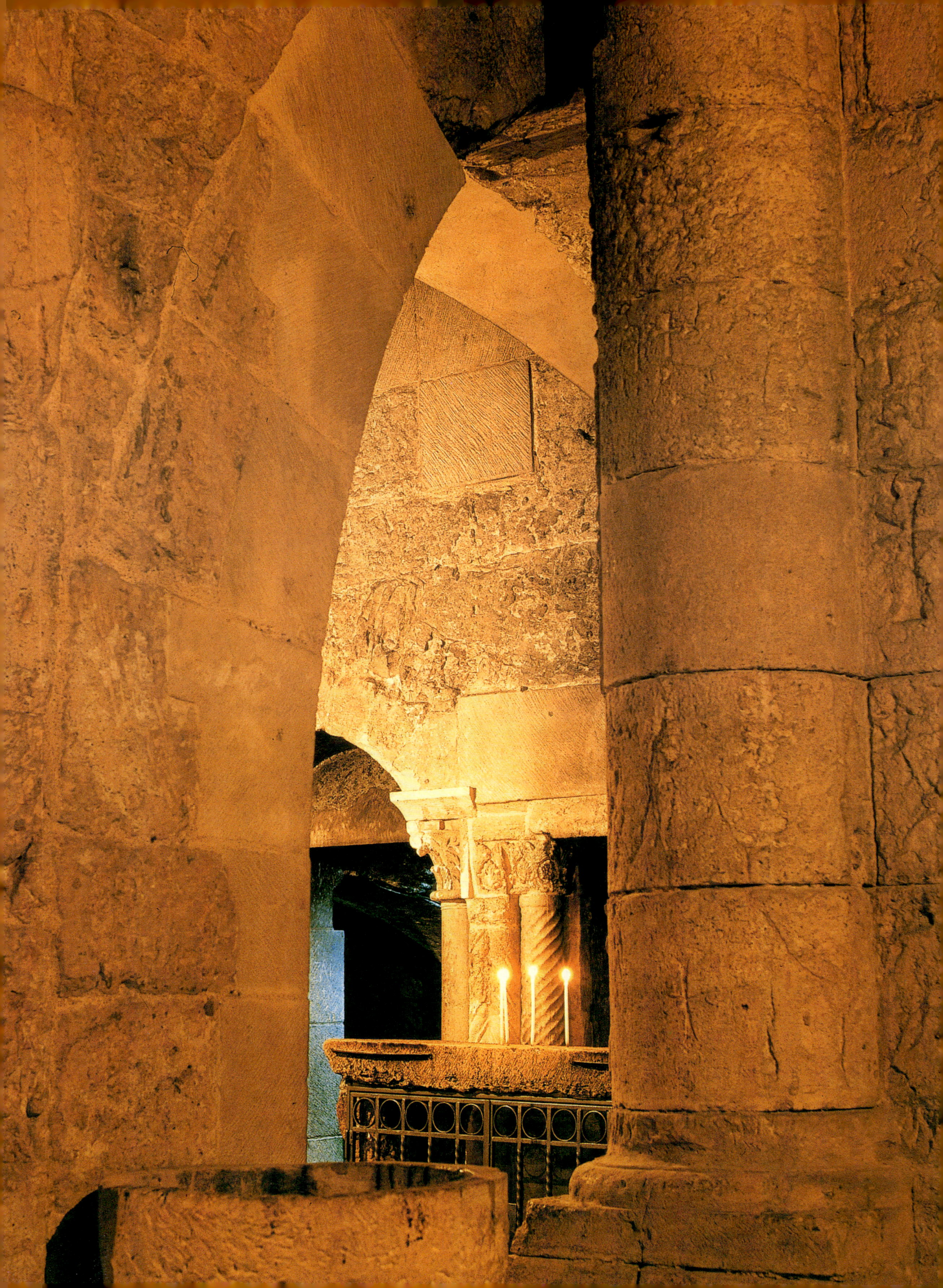

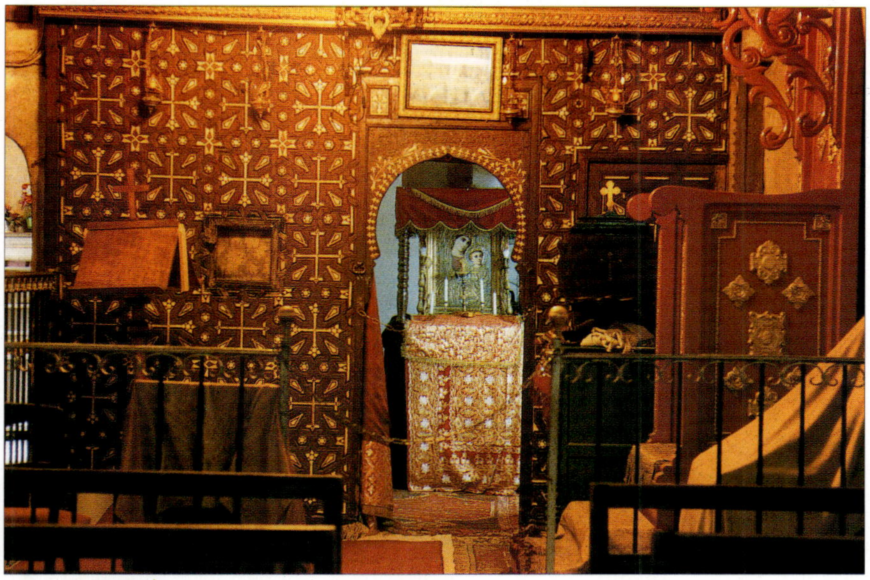

The Catholic, Latin, Greek Orthodox, Armenian, Coptic, Syriac, and Ethiopian communities each have their own chapel in the church of the Holy Sepulchre. The rituals and sacred images vary from one to another.
Here a mosaic in the Greek Orthodox choir represents Christ with an emaciated face.

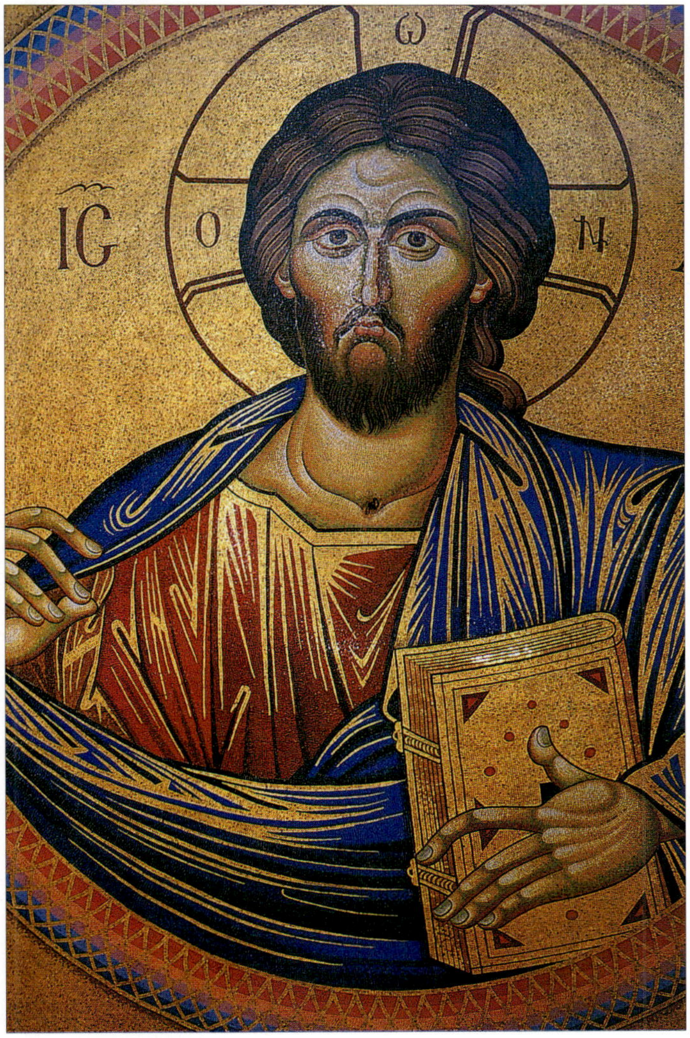

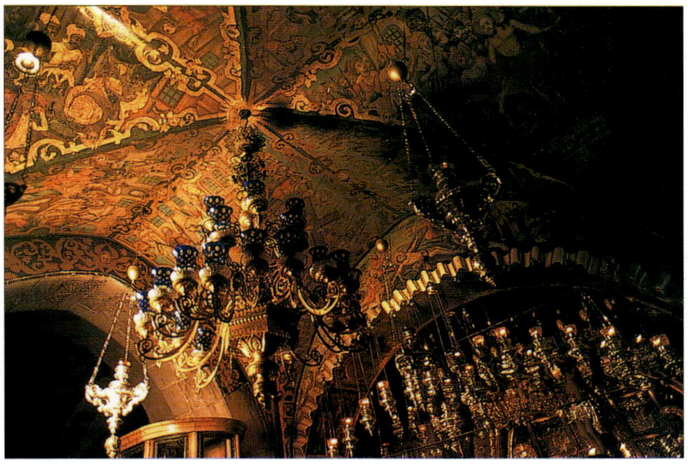

Facing page:
The church of the Holy Sepulchre is a complex building, with many rooms, hidden recesses, underground chambers, and other nooks and crannies. In the semi-darkness, there is always a candle ready to bring light and warmth to the darkness of hearts which have gone astray.

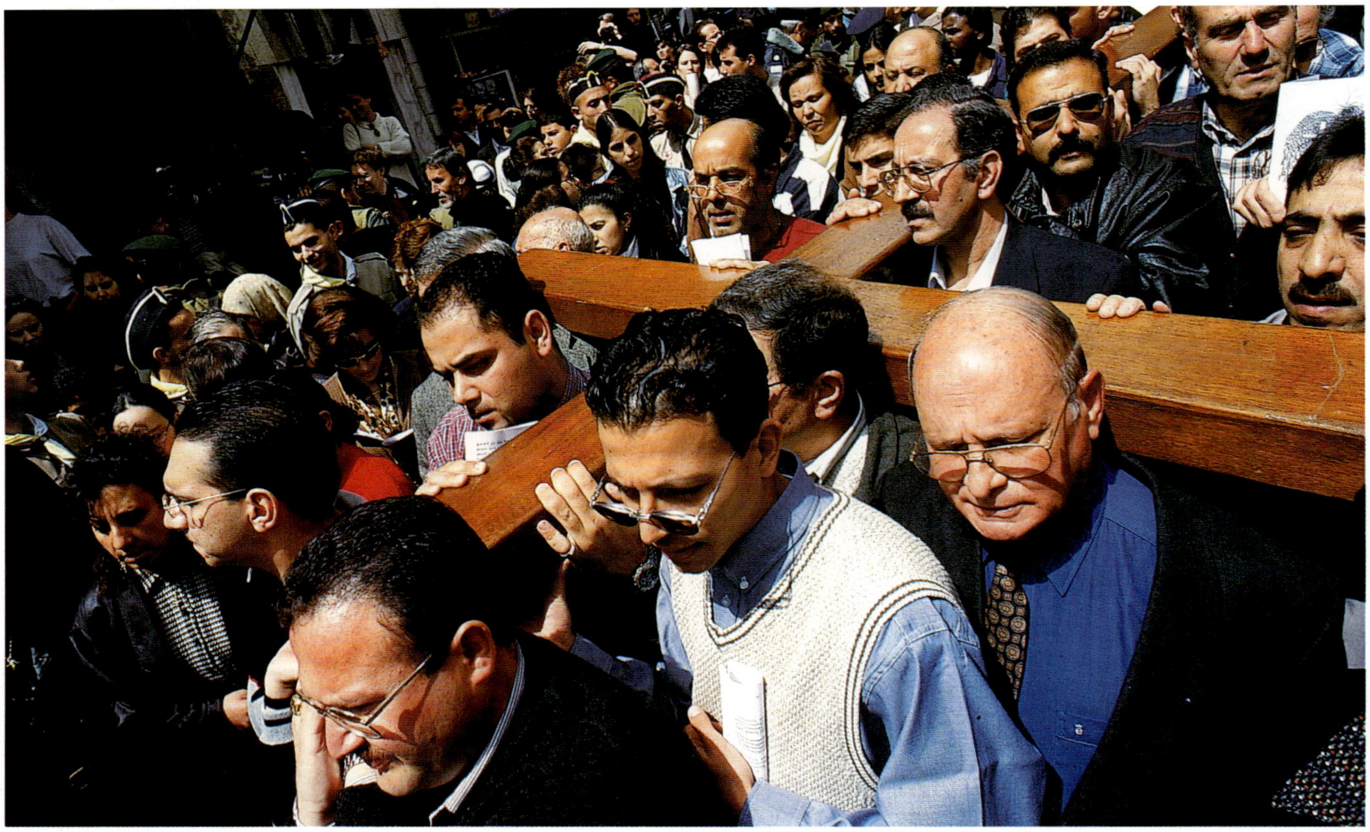

The Good Friday processions along the Via Dolorosa always attract a dense crowd.

the Second Temple. To the east, the Lions' Gate, also called St Stephen's Gate, opens directly on to the Via Dolorosa, Christ's road to Calvary. The Golden Gate, also in the east wall, was blocked up by the Arabs several centuries ago, so that the Messiah awaited by the Jews should not enter through it. Finally, in the south, there is the Dung Gate, so called because of the refuse which was taken out of the city by this route to the Valley of the Cedron below. And, still in the south, the Zion Gate, built in the seventeenth century, not far from the tomb of David on Mount Zion, bears the distinguishing marks where it was riddled with bullets during the violent struggles of the War of Independence in 1948. The Mount of Olives, situated just beyond the Lions' Gate, makes an ideal observatory from which to see the various views of the old city. From its western slopes, at the very spot where sacrifices were made in the time of David – now the site of a very impressive ancient Jewish cemetery – a spectacular panorama is revealed to the visitor. This is also the place to which Jesus went before the Passion and where, looking out over the holy

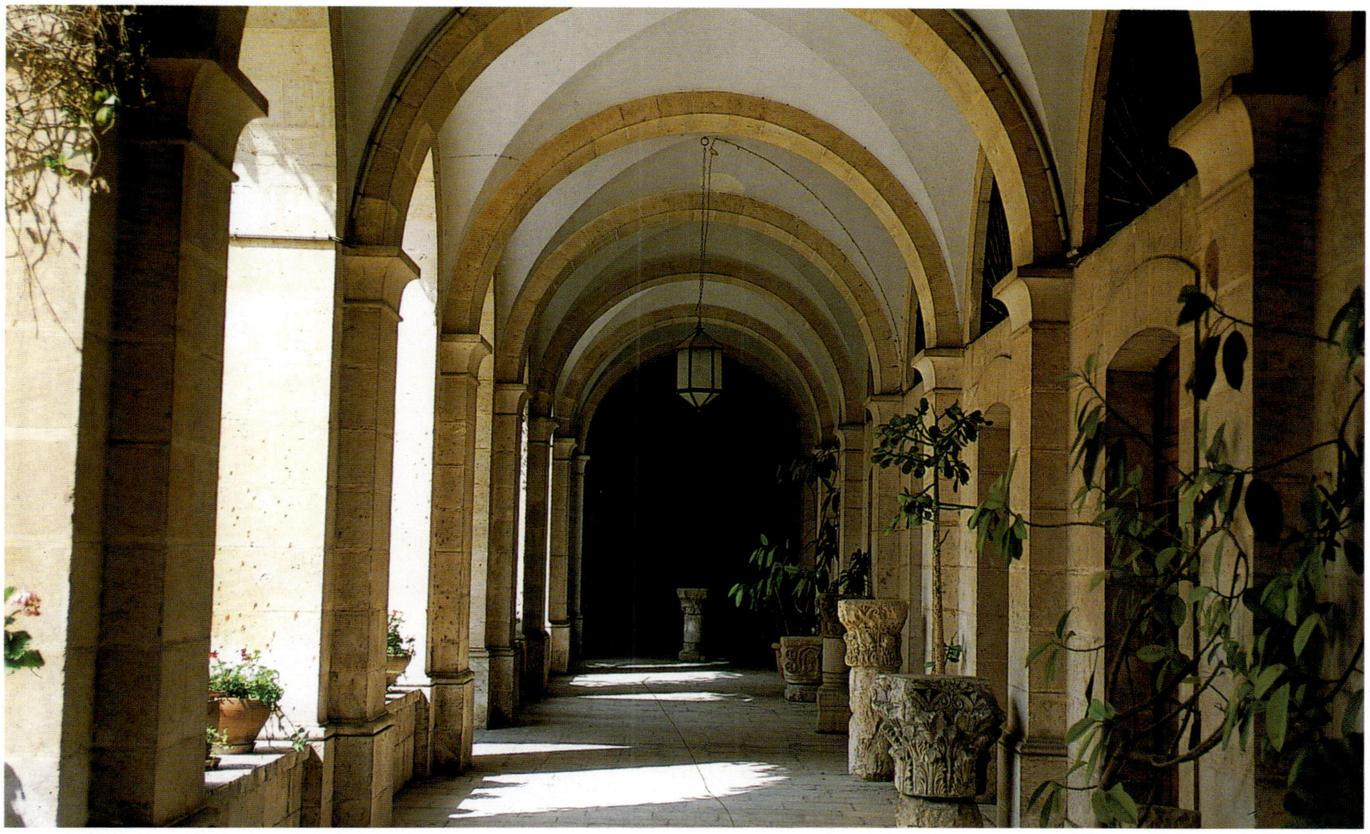

city, he wept for "Jerusalem, you who kill the prophets and stone those sent to you." (Matthew 23:37).

The crenellated walls of time-worn limestone blocks; the famous Dome of the Rock, built in the seventh century and covered with gold on the initiative of King Hussain of Jordan; the minarets and church towers calling the faithful to prayer; and, of course, the cupolas of the church of the Holy Sepulchre, each topped by a shining cross; all these ensure that the traveller fully experiences the spiritual dimension of this city surrounded by barren hills. This spiritual dimension is further intensified when the sun bathes the city in a bronze light, warming the stones and giving them new life.

Newcomers most often enter the city – which can seem small when you have surveyed it many times in all directions, but nevertheless deserves a stay of at least several days on your first visit – by the Jaffa Gate. All you need to do is follow the Jaffa Road, then take the Carob Walk along the Western Wall, which has many palm trees planted at its foot and is tinged by the last caressing rays of the sun. As soon as you have entered, and

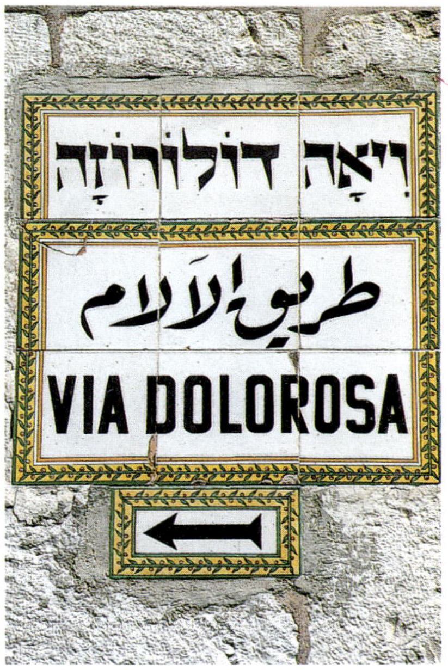

The tranquillity and coolness of a convent cloister offers the requisite atmosphere for lengthy meditation.

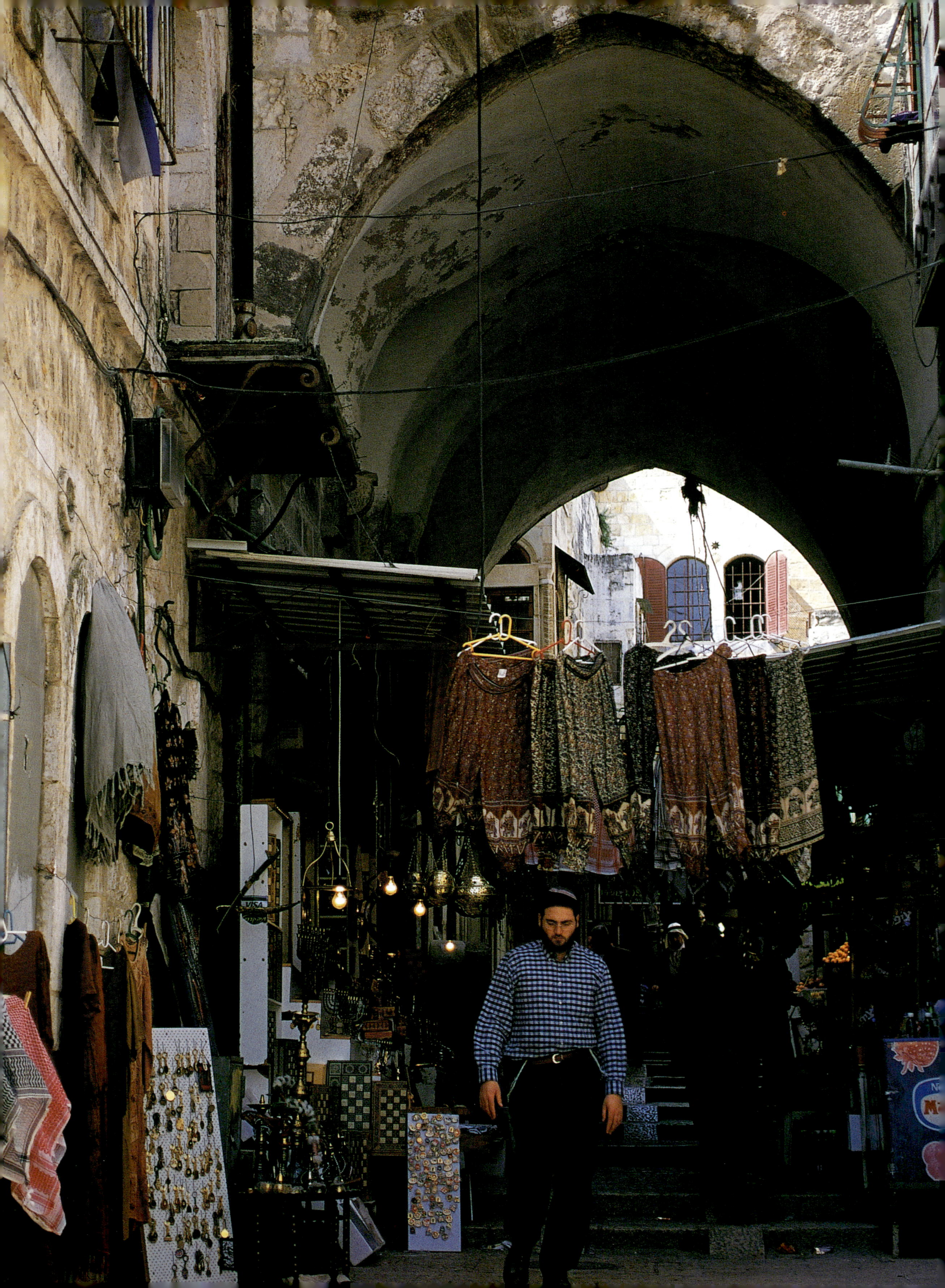

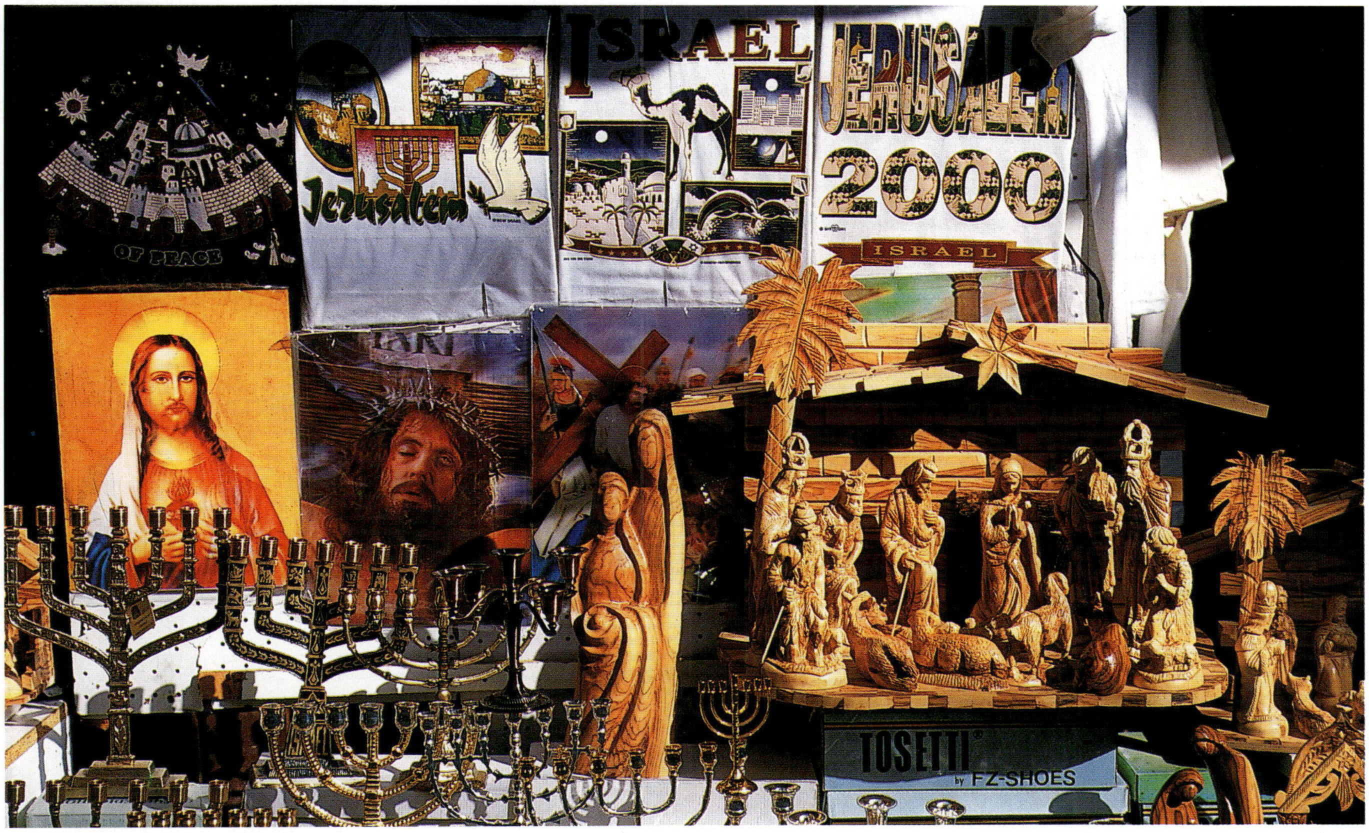

some have touched the mezuzah on the gatepost of the great gate, you begin to sense an oriental atmosphere, already quite distinct from the prevailing ambience of the new city. Then you can start to wander about, discover the city, let its atmosphere pervade you. And there is always a choice of possible routes. For instance, if you come in from Jaffa, you can visit the Tower of David and its historical museum, go up on to the ramparts and walk along as far as the Dung Gate, head south towards the very peaceful Armenian quarter and St James' cathedral and on towards Mount Zion to pay your respects to the tomb of David, or you could go directly into the narrow alleyways of the souks, which are the living heart of the old city.

At the end of the little square by the Jaffa Gate, the entrance used by cars wanting to enter the Jewish quarter, stands the Hotel Petra, a small establishment that caters for travellers on a low budget. The terrace of the Hotel Petra is open to everyone and offers a breathtaking view of Jerusalem. When the city is seen from this vantage-point high above the

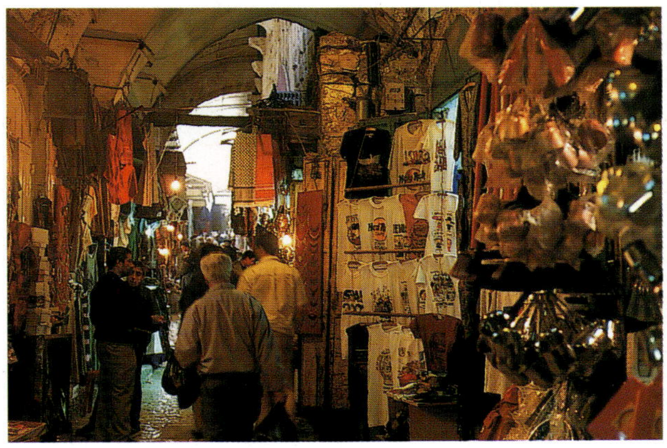

A typical small religious souvenir shop, and a view of life in the souk.
Facing page:
An entrance to the souk in the Muslim quarter, not far from the Damascus Gate.

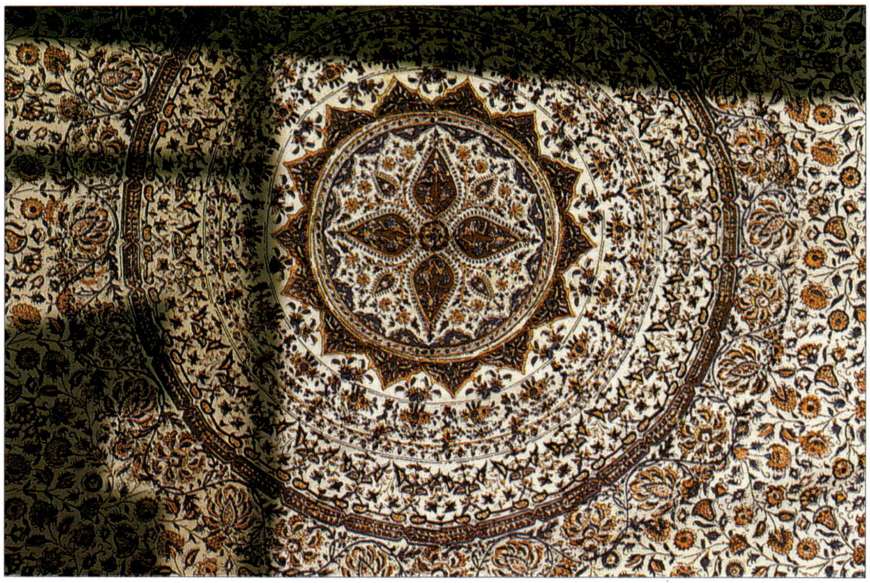

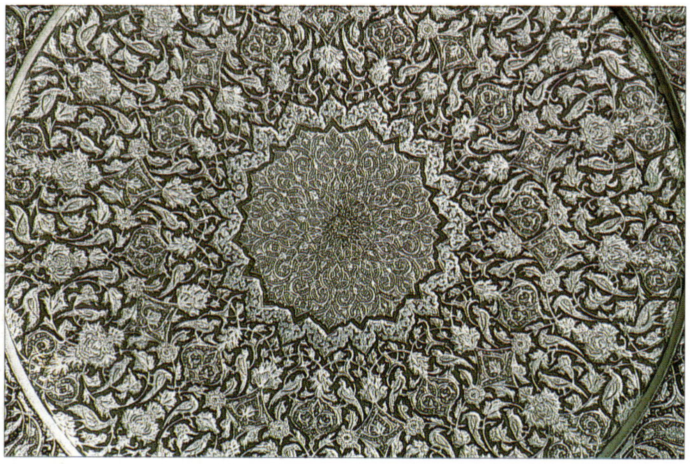

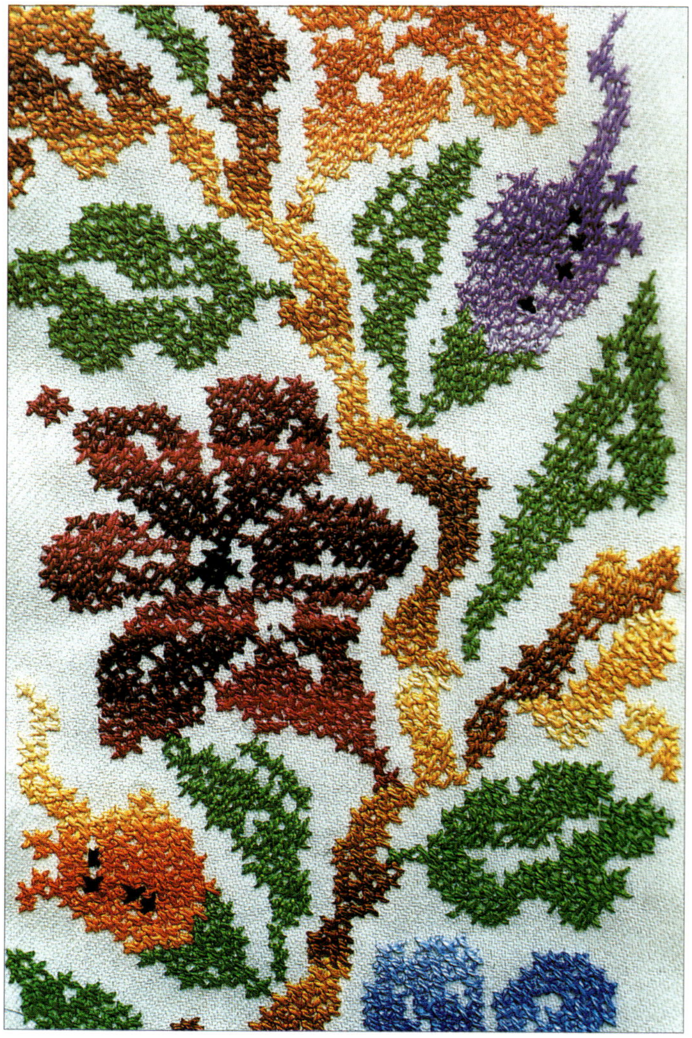

Among the many treasures to be unearthed in the souks are wares such as this finely worked tablecloth, intricately wrought tray, and embroidery from a Palestinian dress, whose subtle delicacy is shown in the detail.
Facing page:
The magnificent door of a house in the Jewish quarter.

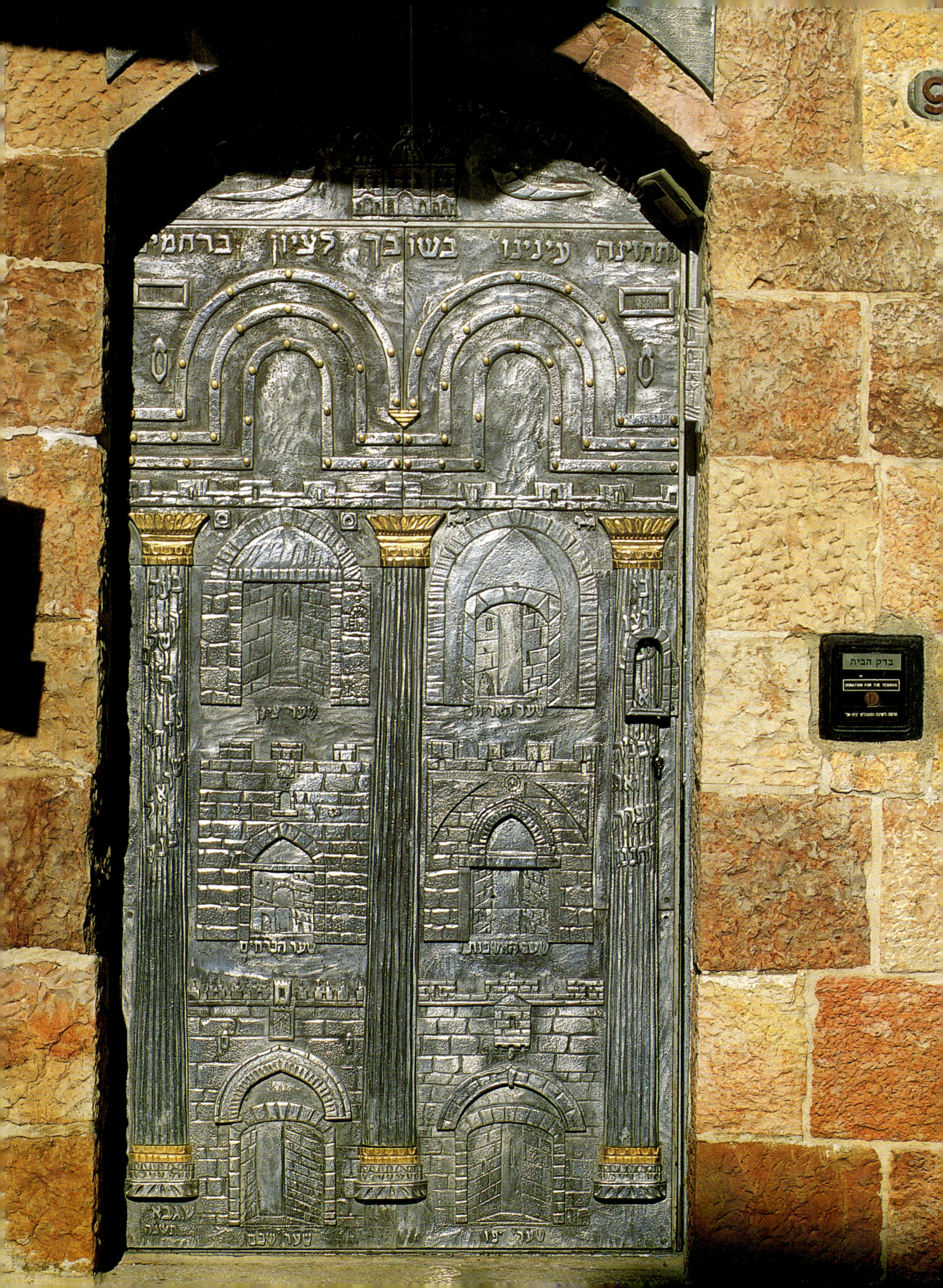
ותחזינה עינינו בשובך לציון ברחמים
שער ציון
שער האריות
שער הפרחים
שער האשפות
שער שכם
שער יפו
בדק הבית
DONATION FOR THE YESHIVA

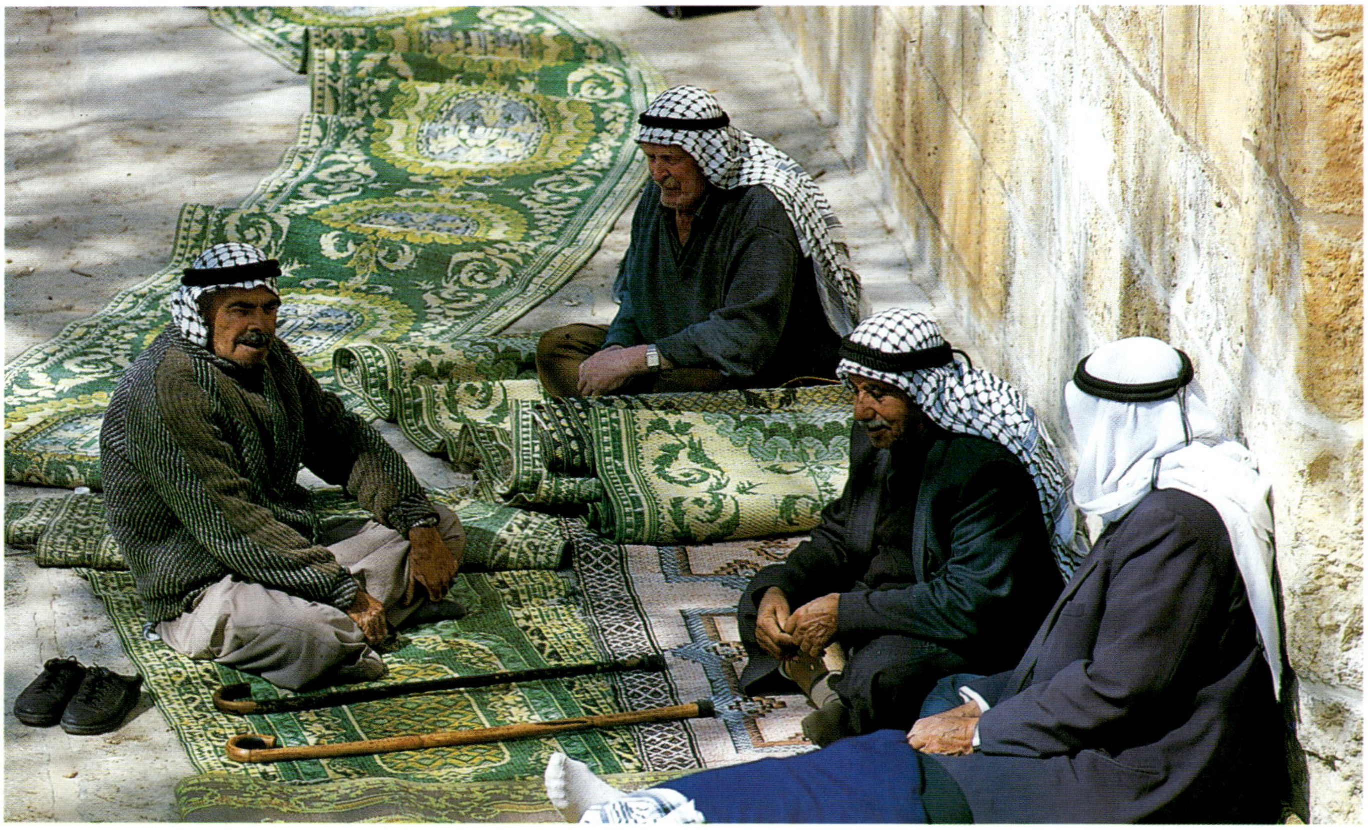

Palestinians wearing the traditional keffiyeh, resting after prayer, letting time go by.
Following pages:
Detail of the crenellated wall framing the Lions' Gate or St Stephen's Gate to the east of the old city.

terraced rows of cube-shaped houses with their aerials and satellite dishes sticking up on top, it seems at first glance like a jumble of ageing stones, with no continuity of architectural style or construction. But in reality it has a unique and amazing physical presence, largely because of its unusual building material, the white, so-called Judaean limestone, which has acquired a golden patina and now verges on the beige. This overall picture, which is even more spectacular when seen from the top of the 41 m (135 ft) high Lutheran church of the Redeemer, also brings home the fact that the three holy places – the Holy Sepulchre, the Western Wall, and the Dome of the Rock – are all situated within a very small area of each other, in barely 1 km^2 (less than half a square mile).
In order to reach the Holy Sepulchre – the vibrant core of the Christian quarter which has linked Calvary to the tomb of Christ since Byzantine days – the customary route for pilgrims is to follow the Way of the Cross, along which the fourteen stations represent the events of Jesus' walk to his crucifixion.

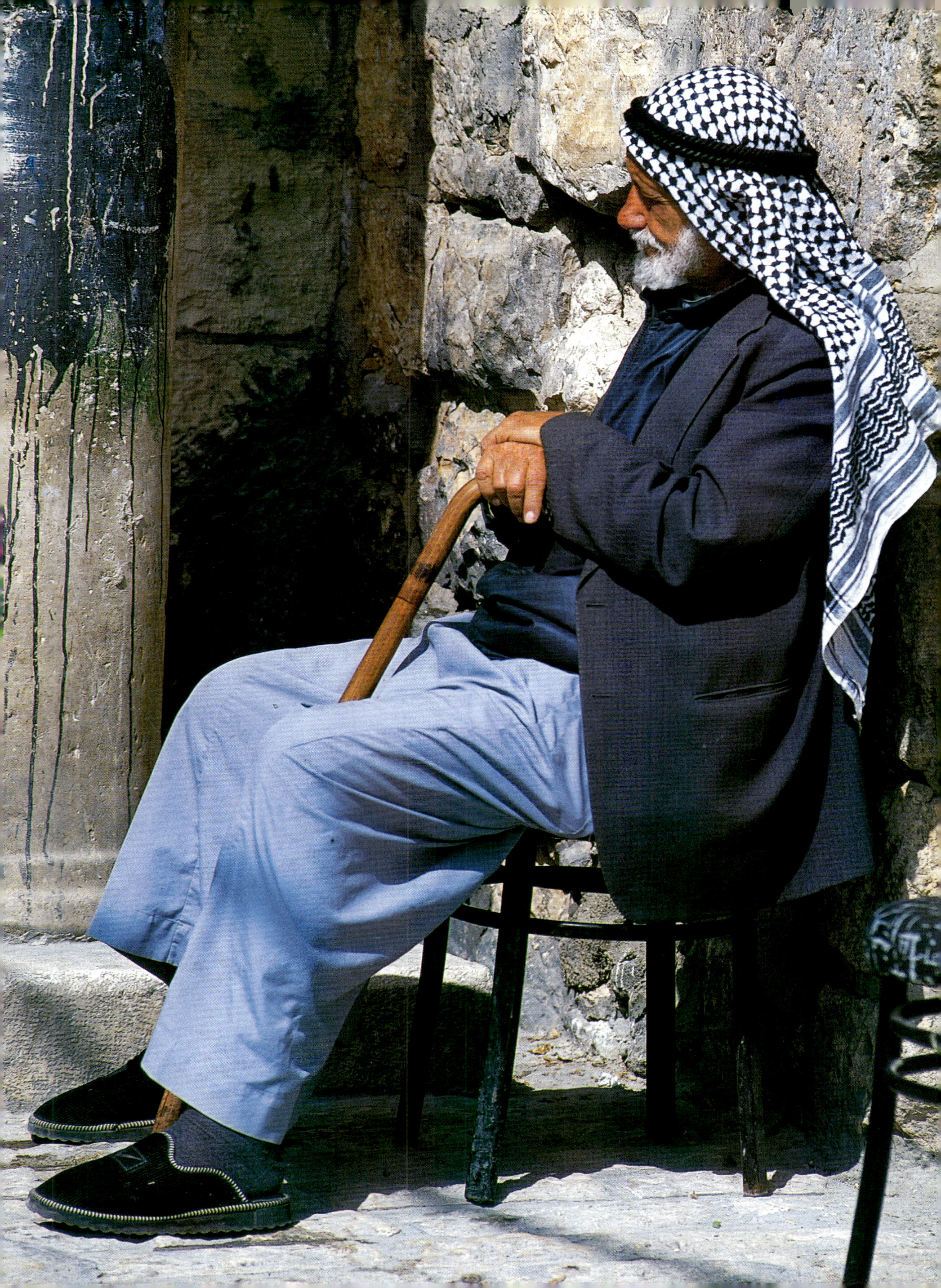

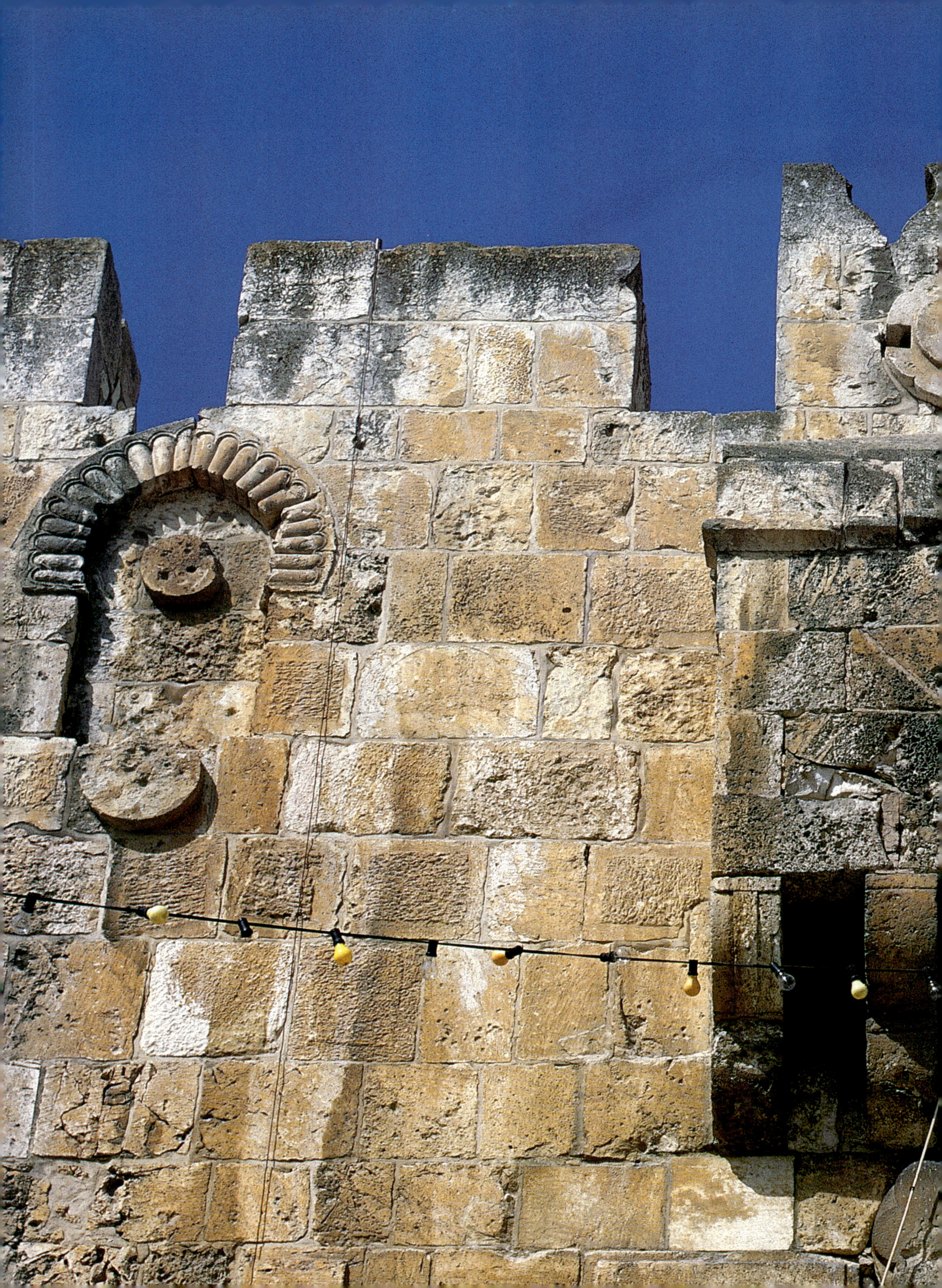

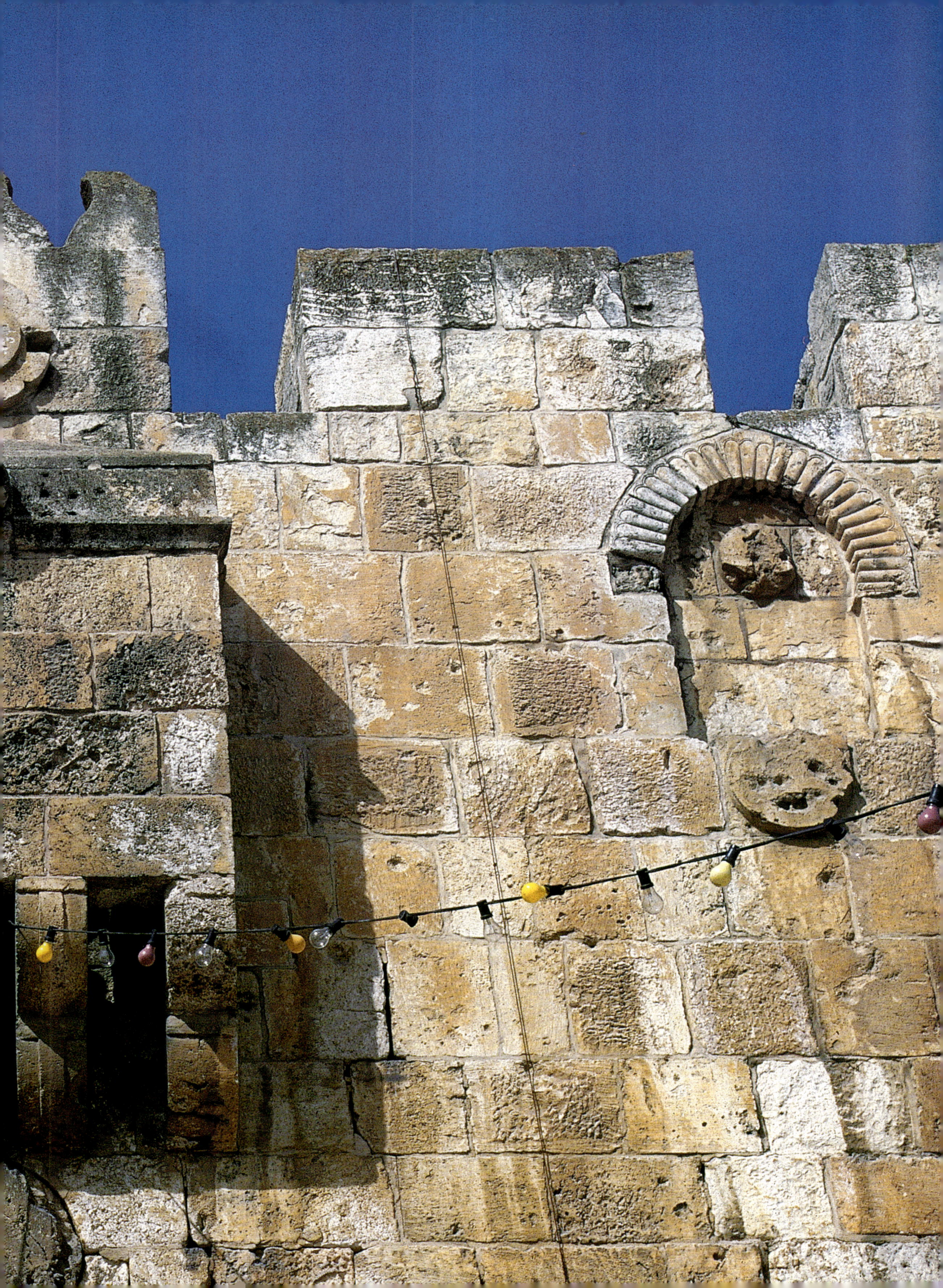

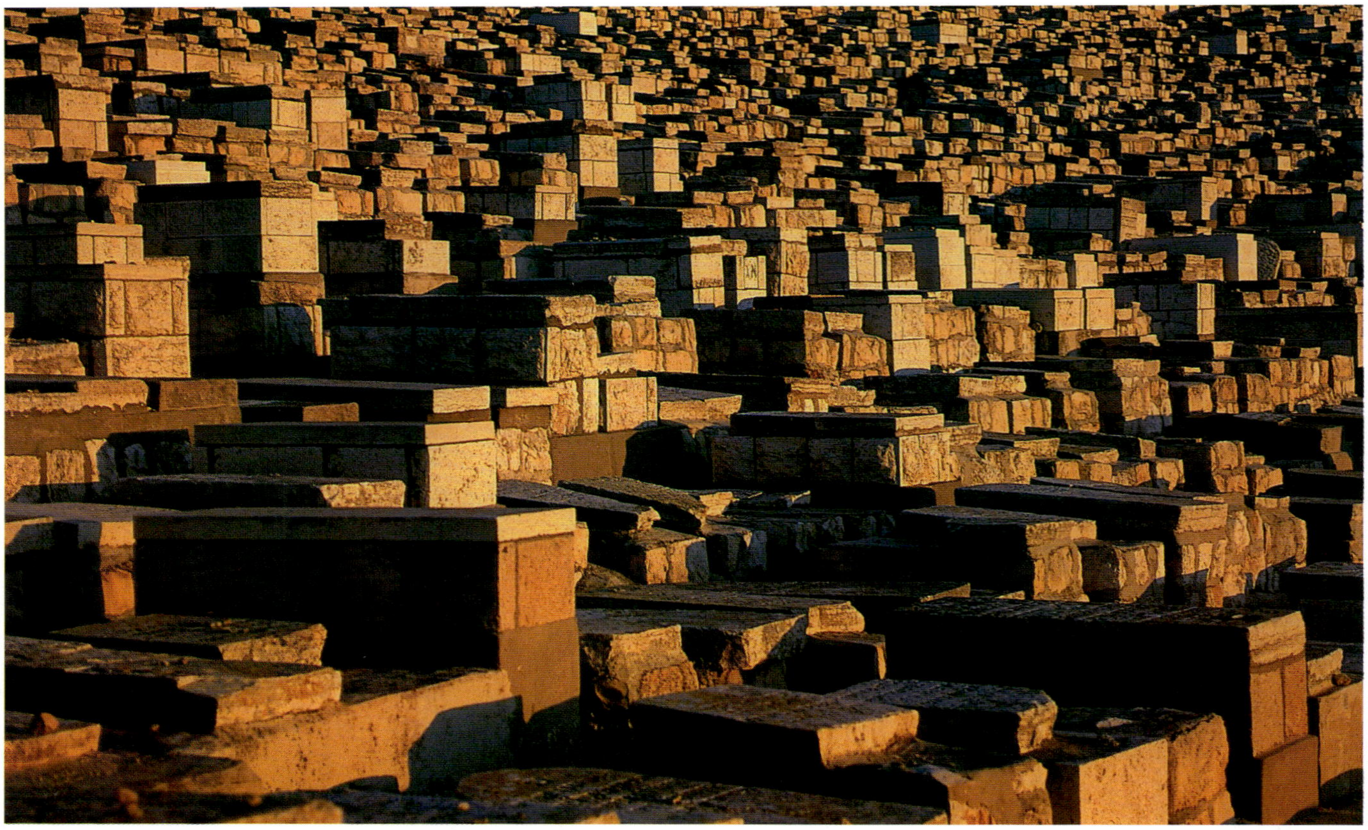

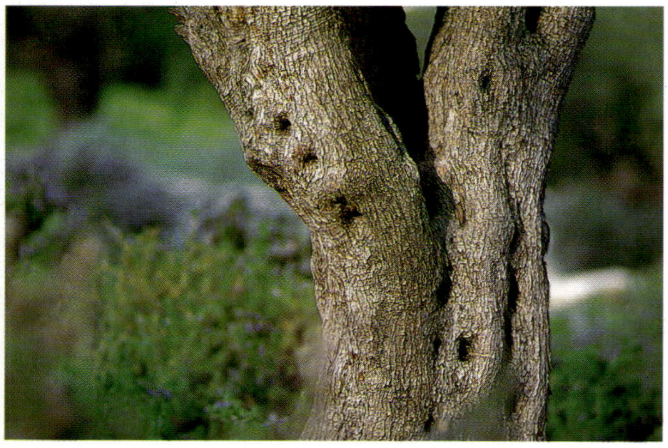

The vast, ancient, Jewish cemetery on the Mount of Olives is the most sacred necropolis in Israel.

On the first part of the Via Dolorosa, which comprises the stations recalling the places where Jesus was sentenced, where he received the cross and where he fell for the first time, there are many buildings and ruins of great significance for Christians. Among them are the remarkable Frankish church of St Anne, the church of the Flagellation, and the triple arch built by the Roman emperor Hadrian, known since the sixteenth century as the Ecce Homo Arch in memory of Pontius Pilate's cry of "Behold the man!" The fourth station, commemorating the place where Jesus encountered Mary on the road to Calvary, is situated at a crossroads. To the north of this is the Damascus Gate, mainly used by Muslims, and to the south is the place where security controls have been set up at the entrance to the esplanade of the Western Wall, behind which stands the Dome of the Rock. This wall, known to Christians as the Wailing Wall, is the Jews' most sacred place because it is the last remaining part of the Second Temple on Mount Moriah and has received the prayers of a persecuted people over nearly 2,000 years.

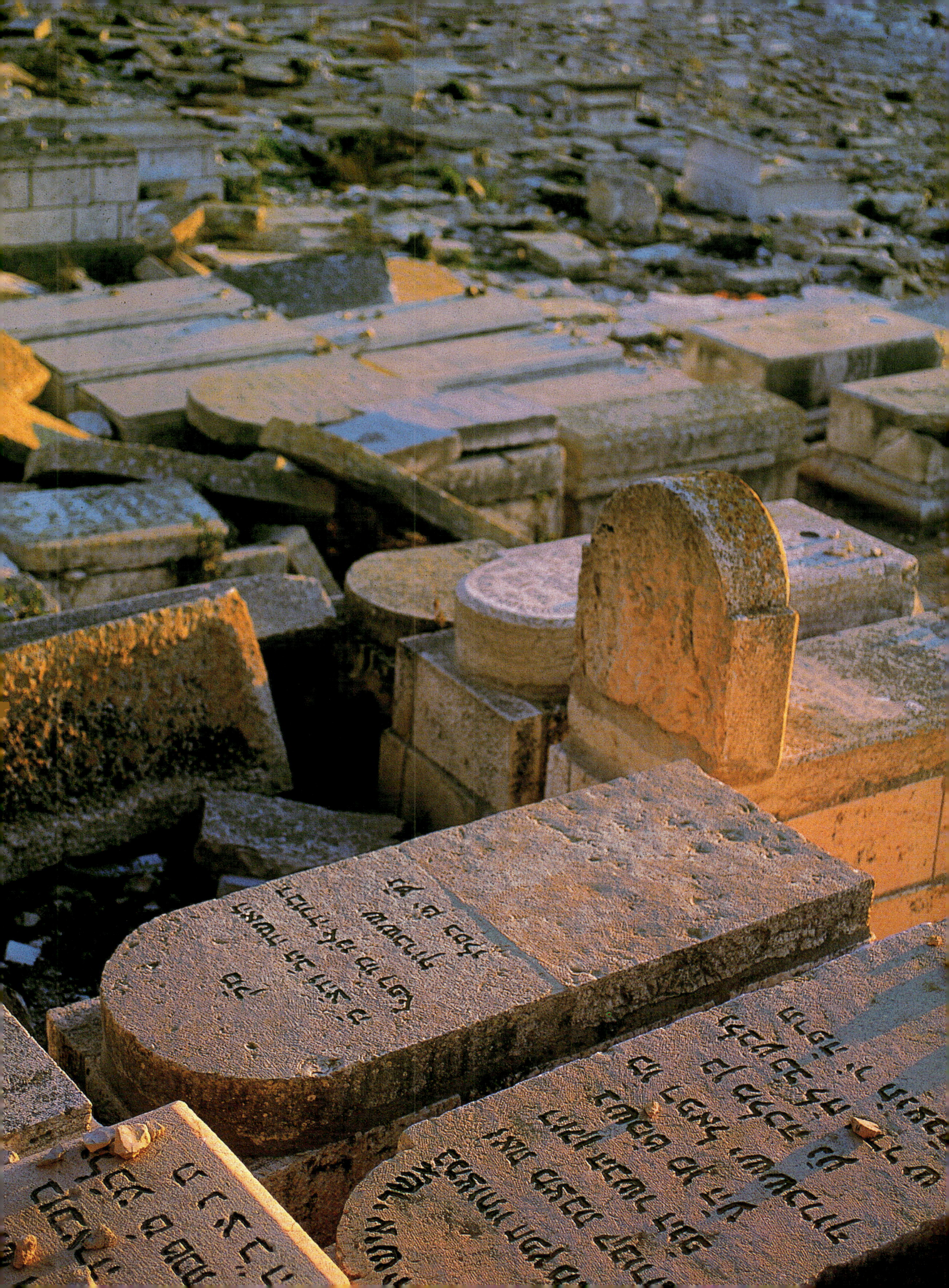

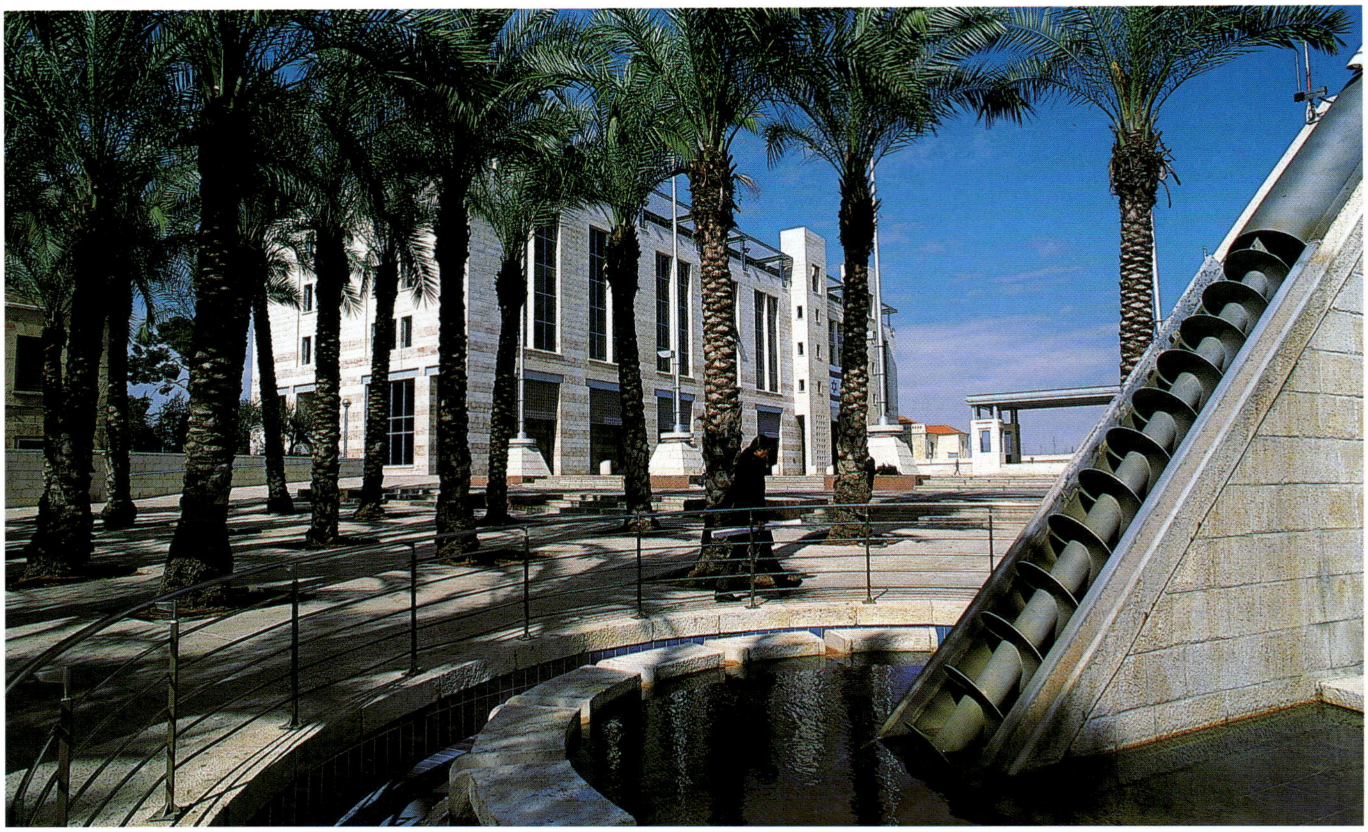

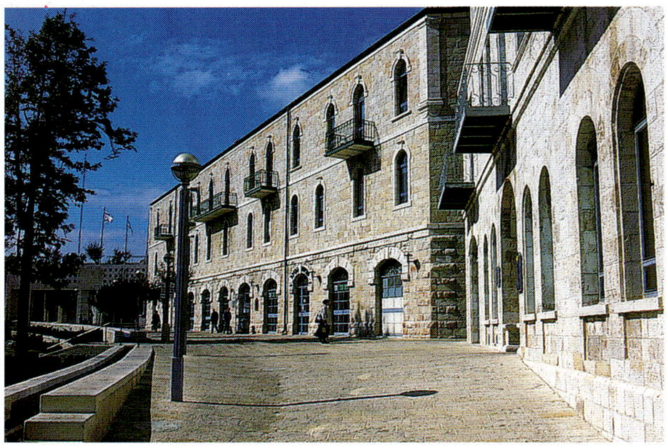

The esplanade in front of the City Hall, which opens out on to the Jaffa Road close to the old walls, is one of the recently refurbished parts of the new city.
Even the nineteenth-century houses, relics of the first moves to extend the old city beyond its walls, appear rejuvenated.

Today, of course, it is still the object of the most fervent attention and the most ardent prayers of those for whom belief in one God and the sanctity of human life continue to be the supreme values of Judaism, and for whom the Torah and its commandments encompass all possible experiences of human life. Moreover, many Bar-Mitzvahs – religious ceremonies during which 13-year-old boys become adult members of the community – are organised beside the wall. These take on a special significance when the young initiate begins to read a passage from the Torah, which makes him an active member of the people of the Book. To continue the road to the last four stations of the cross – the nailing of Jesus to the cross, his death, the handing over of his body to his holy mother, and the placing of the body in the tomb – you must go up to the west through the souks with their well-stocked handicraft stalls. The Holy Sepulchre marks the end of this pilgrimage. Entering it is a strange, very intimate experience, which invokes and fosters religious feelings in any visitor with a penchant for meditative reflection.

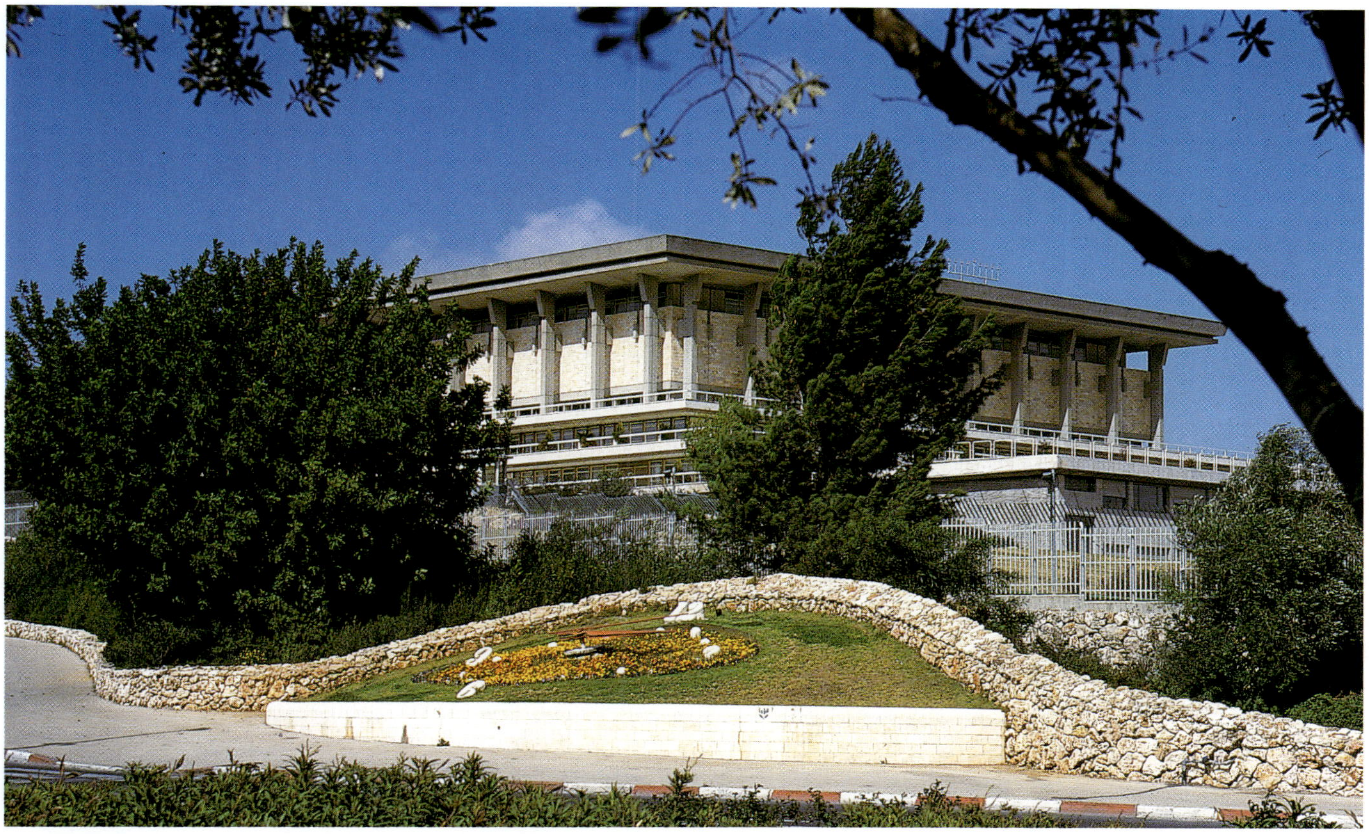

Six Christian communities are represented within the very heart of this complex and imposing building, erected in the fourth century on the initiative of the Roman emperor Constantine, destroyed by the Muslims, then rebuilt by the Crusaders in the twelfth century on this site, which is the highest point in the old city. There are Catholic, Greek Orthodox, Armenian, Coptic, Syriac, and Ethiopian communities. Each community has its own chapel and celebrates its faith according to its own rituals and timetable. The Franciscans, for example, gather regularly for a ceremony composed of a chorus of prayers repeated at every symbolic place in this sacred building and ending, of course, at the tomb of the man who, 2,000 years ago, preached love, mercy, and respect. We are now at the start of the new millennium, and respect for one another remains the chief goal and challenge for the inhabitants of this city of contrasts. A solution can only get underway through a mutual understanding, which is the first step to creating a lasting recognition between different communities, and victory for peace.

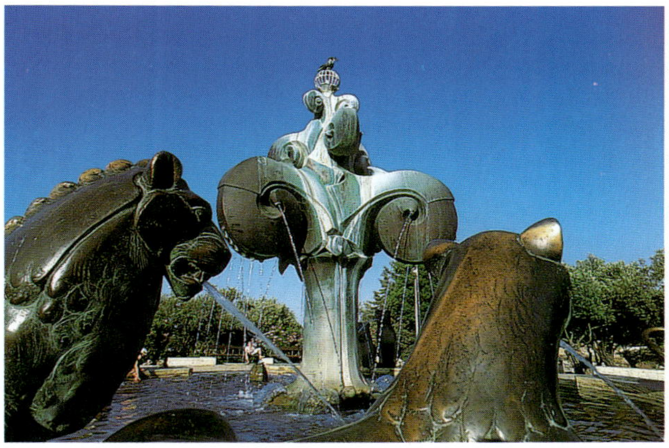

The Knesset, the Israeli parliament, presides over the heights of Ramat Gan. Beyond it is the fountain in the Liberty Bell Gardens at Montefiore.
Following pages:
The monastery of the Cross, tucked away in the heart of the wide, undulating, tree-lined area of Ramat Gan, lying to the west of Jerusalem, was built in the eleventh century on the spot where the tree which provided the wood for the cross to which Christ was nailed is said to have grown.

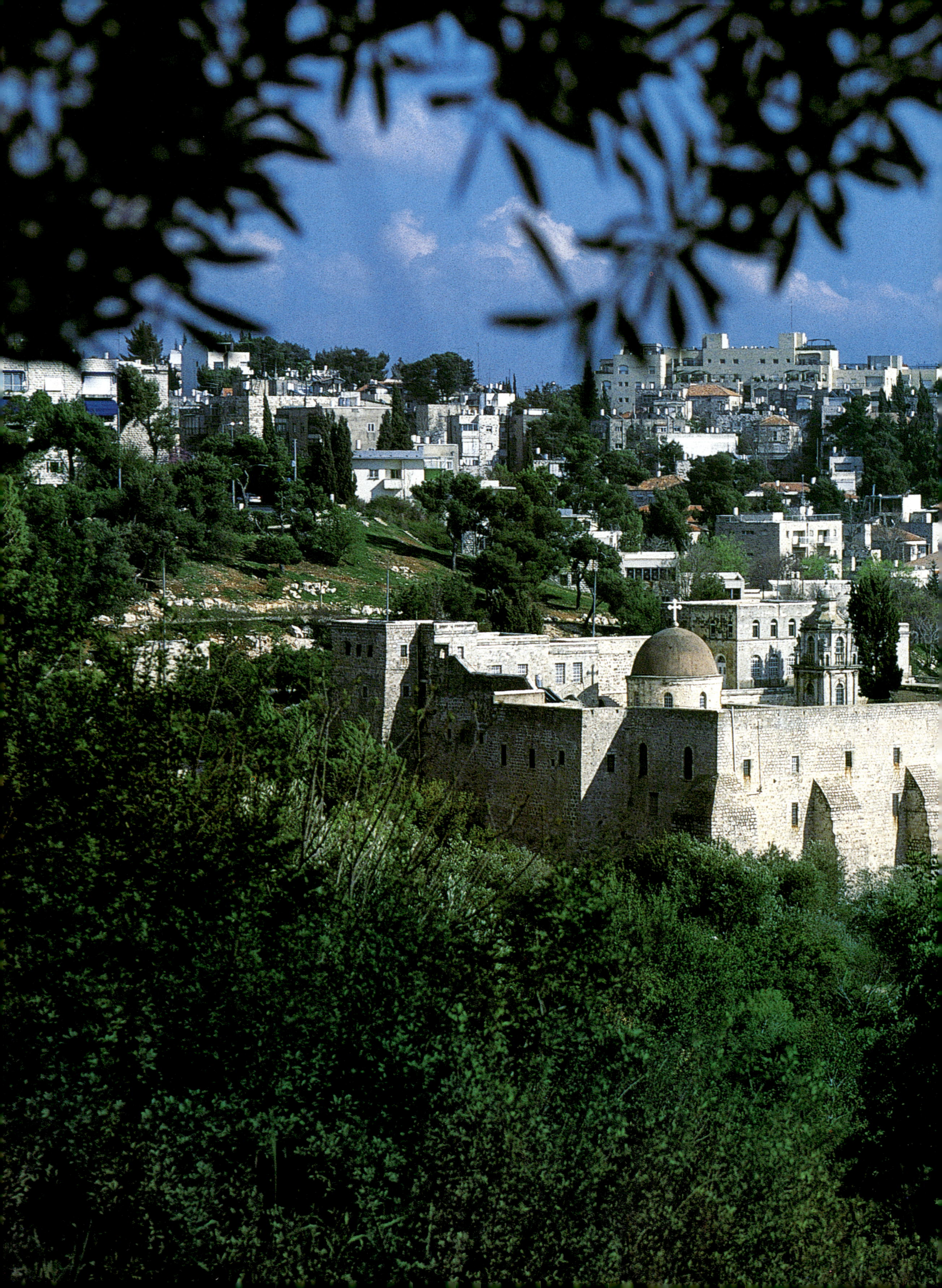

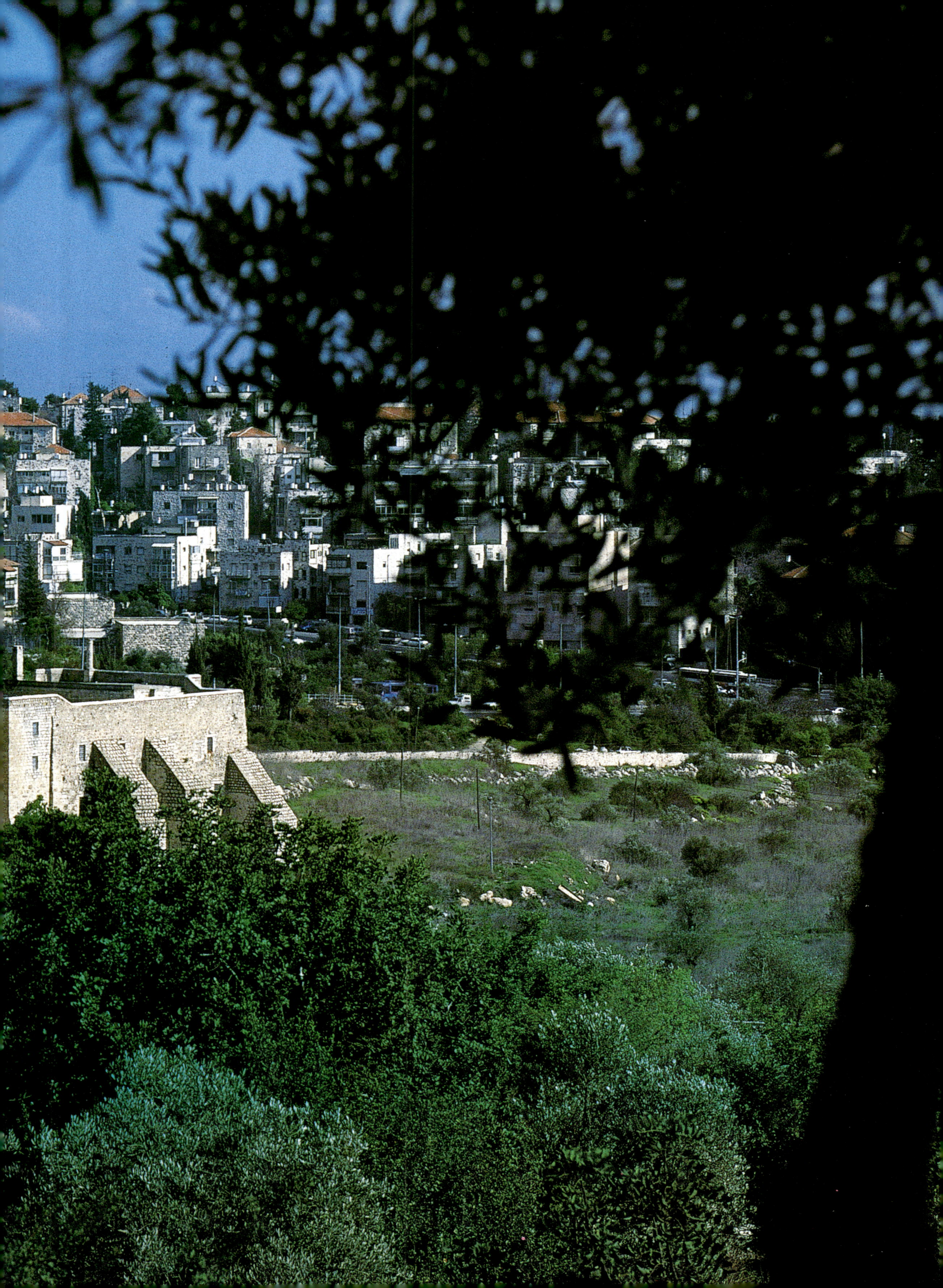

The geographical features of this area, known to some as the west bank of the Jordan and to others as Judaea-Samaria, are varied, to say the least, with fertile hills, verdant valleys, bare mountains, and a limestone desert with a few abundant, cooling springs gushing from it.

The West Bank, *the yearning to return to Palestine*

In August 1999, when a journalist interviewed Yasser Arafat, the president of the Palestinian government on his seventieth birthday and asked him what his dearest wish might be, he immediately replied: "To pray in Jerusalem, the capital of the Palestinian State." Regaining a share of sovereignty over Jerusalem, which is the third holy city of Islam after Mecca and Medina – but the first historically, since the prophet Mohammed turned to Jerusalem for the same reason as the Jews and Christians – is indeed the demand which is closest to the Palestinians' hearts. It is clearly the most sensitive bone of contention between the two communities, since the Israelis consider Jerusalem to be their eternal, unified capital. This question of sovereignty is so important and so complex that until the summit at Camp David in July 2000, it had not been addressed, either in the interim Israeli–Palestinian agreements begun in Oslo in September 1993, or in the Hebron or Wye River agreements of January 1997 and October 1998. Unfortunately, the peace talks in Camp David failed to resolve the question of Jerusalem. After the signing in Cairo, on 4 May 1994, of the agreements marking the beginning of Palestinian self-government, one can come to the conclusion that the peace process in general has not made any convincing advances. During

General view of Bethlehem from the church of the Nativity. In the foreground, the mosque of Omar.

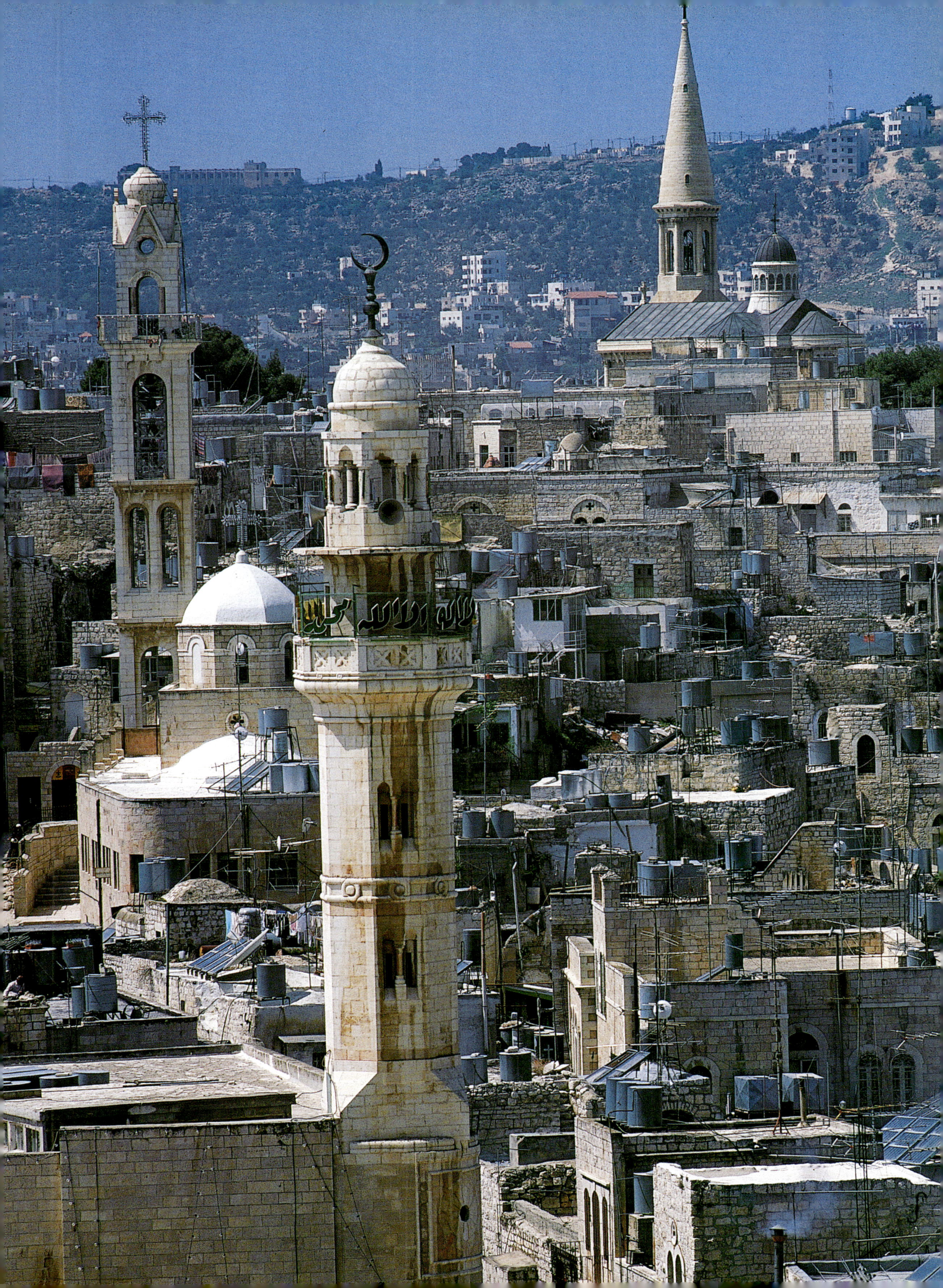

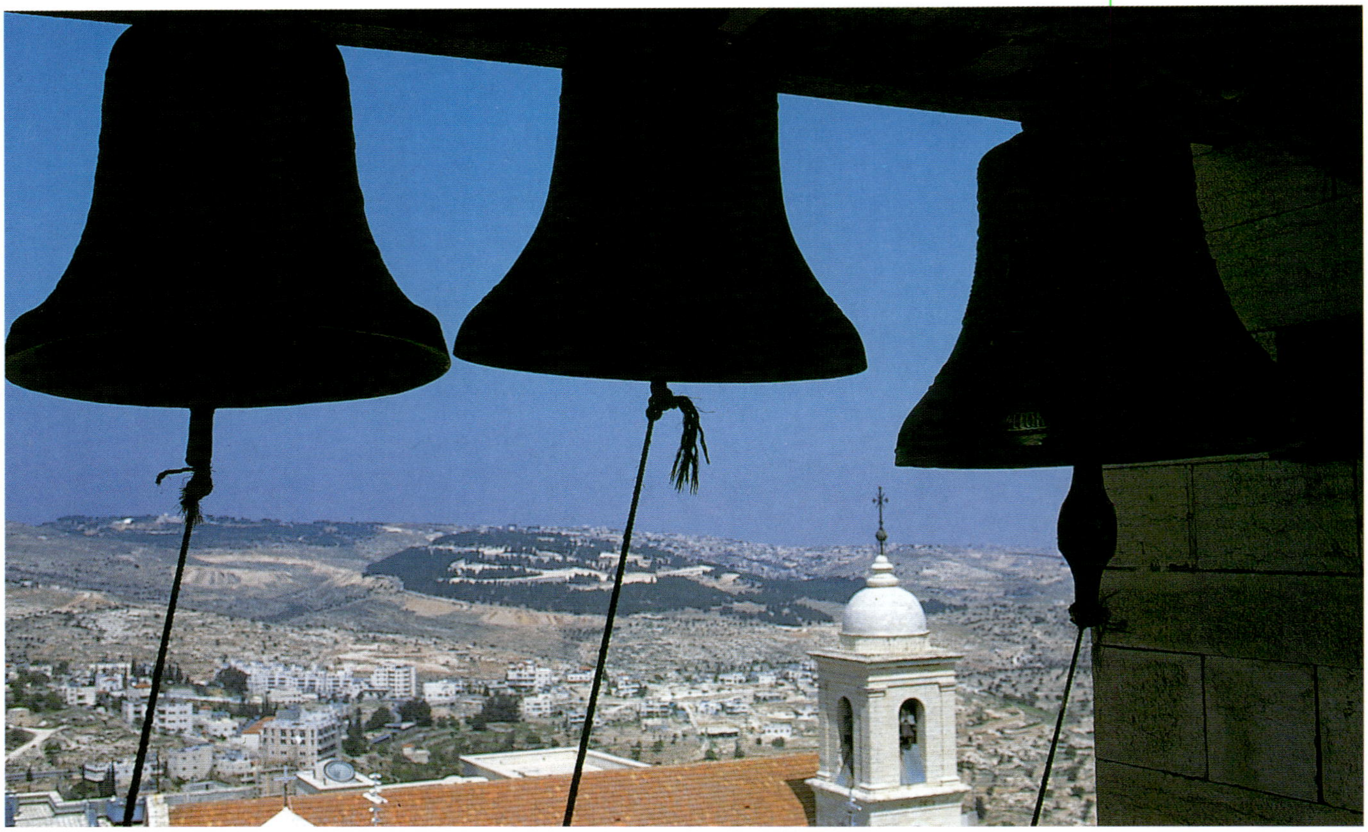

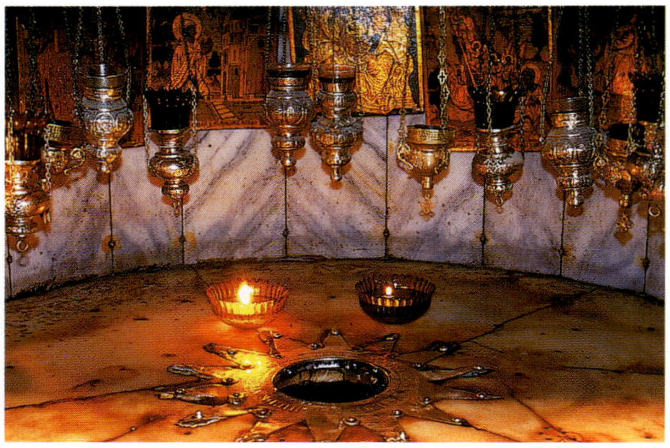

The bell-tower of the church of the Nativity offers a splendid view of the Bethlehem area.
The site of the star by the altar of the manger, which is reached by descending into a grotto, is said to indicate the precise place where Christ was born.

this interim period, Israel has so far restored only 4 per cent of the West Bank and not more than 60 per cent of the narrow Gaza Strip along the Mediterranean coast to Palestinian control.

A region of barely 6,000 km^2 (2,320 square miles), occupied and later annexed by the Israelis after the Six Day War in 1967 – which resulted in victory over their Arab neighbours – the West Bank of the Jordan had been part of the Kingdom of Jordan since 1951. At that time, the east bank was known as Trans-Jordan. In contrast to the mass exodus of the Palestinian population following the first Arab-Israeli war of 1948, the military occupation of the West Bank after the 1967 conflict did not immediately result in a huge flood of refugees, even though many people crossed the river to seek protection in Jordan. A posteriori, the most spectacular effect was rather to intensify the deep-seated link which all Palestinians have with their homeland.

There are those who consider that the territory of a possible future Palestinian state is already established in Jordan with its 75 per cent

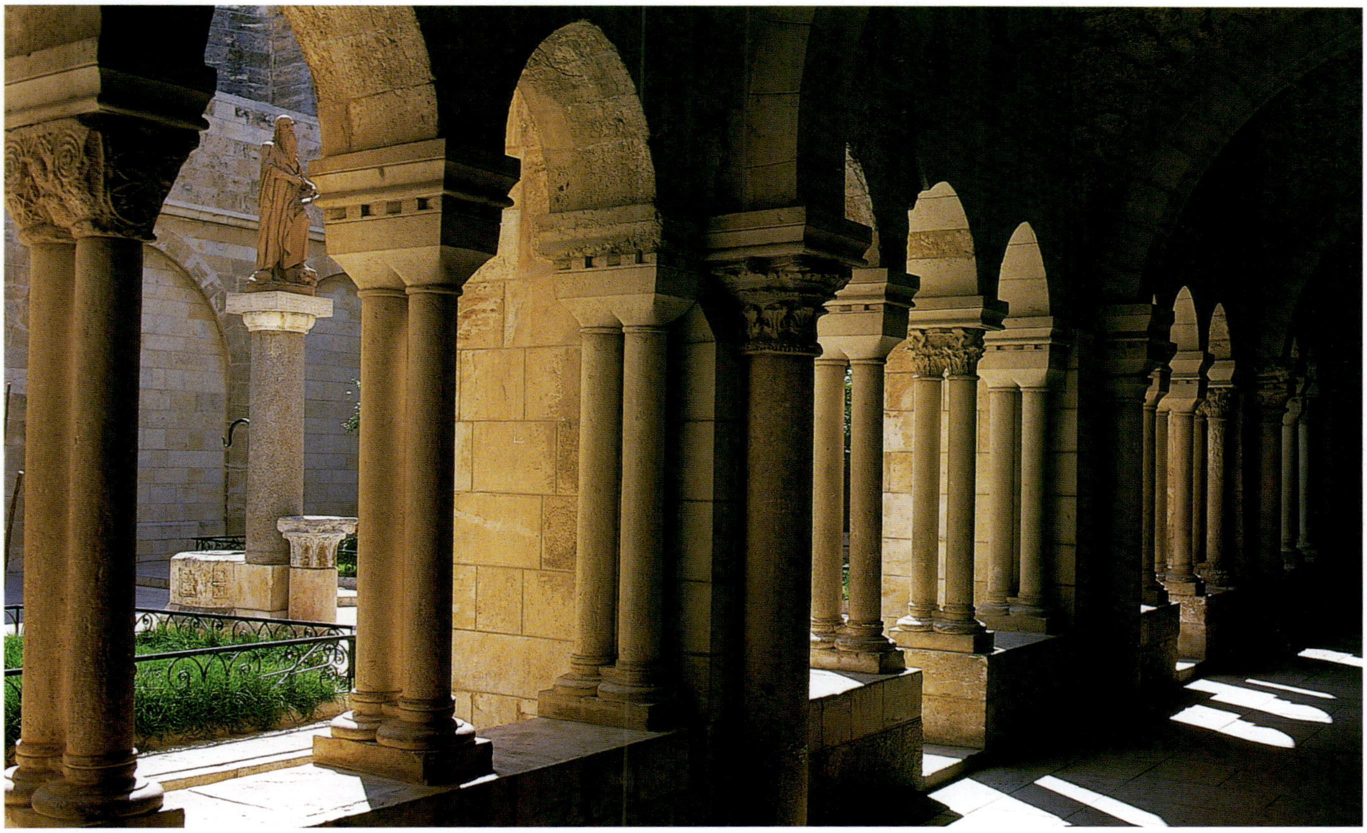

Palestinian population. But on the contrary, it seems clear that the thirty years of Israeli presence – ending in the confiscation of lands, the introduction and establishment of numerous settlements, and the confrontation during the Intifada between the *Chabab* (young adolescents) and the armed soldiers – has only reinforced the desire of Palestinian people throughout the West Bank, and to a lesser extent in Gaza, to claim the territories on the map of their heritage which all the seven million citizens in the community carry within them.

The West Bank, known to Palestinians simply as "the west bank of the Jordan" and to the Israelis as "Judaea-Samaria" – referring to the two biblical provinces in which the history of the Hebrew nation was written – brings together a wide variety of geographical features. To the north are the fertile hills of Samaria; to the east, the verdant Jordan Valley; in the centre, the drier mountains of eastern Judaea, extending on one side into the limestone Judaean Desert with the Jericho oasis, and on the other into the mountains around Hebron. This physical framework was divided by

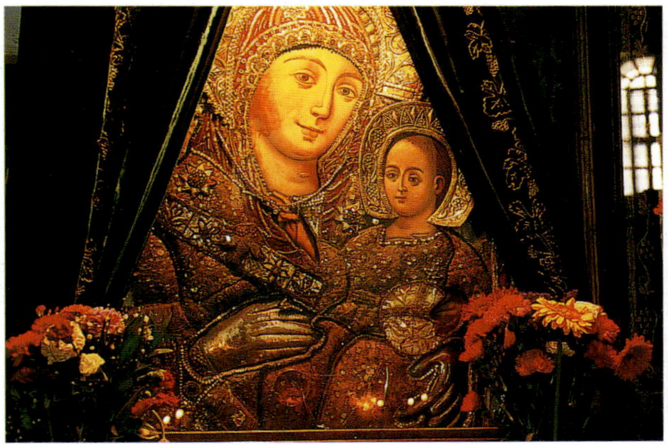

The cloister of the convent of the Nativity, and an icon in praise of the Virgin Mary and her holy child.

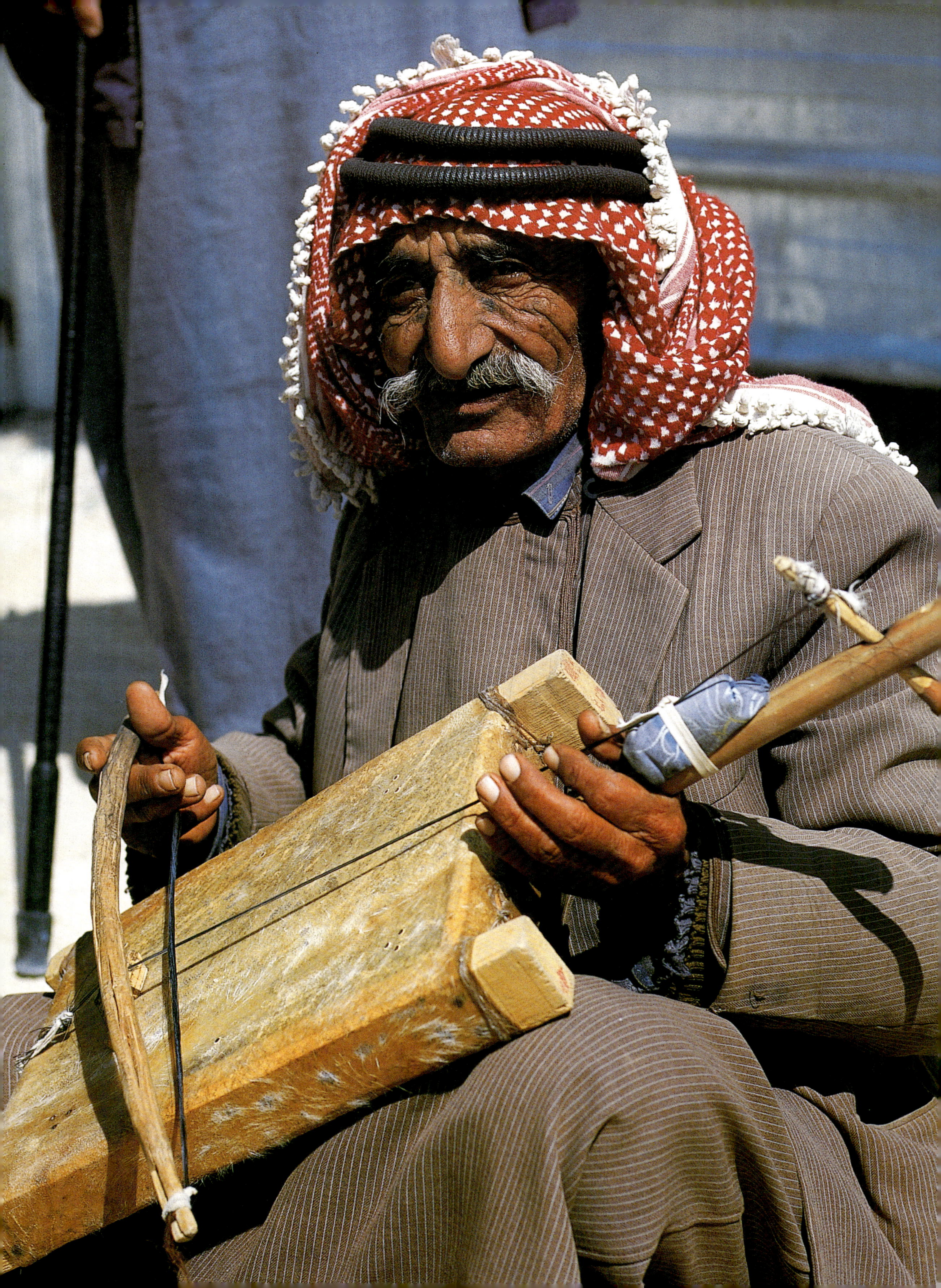

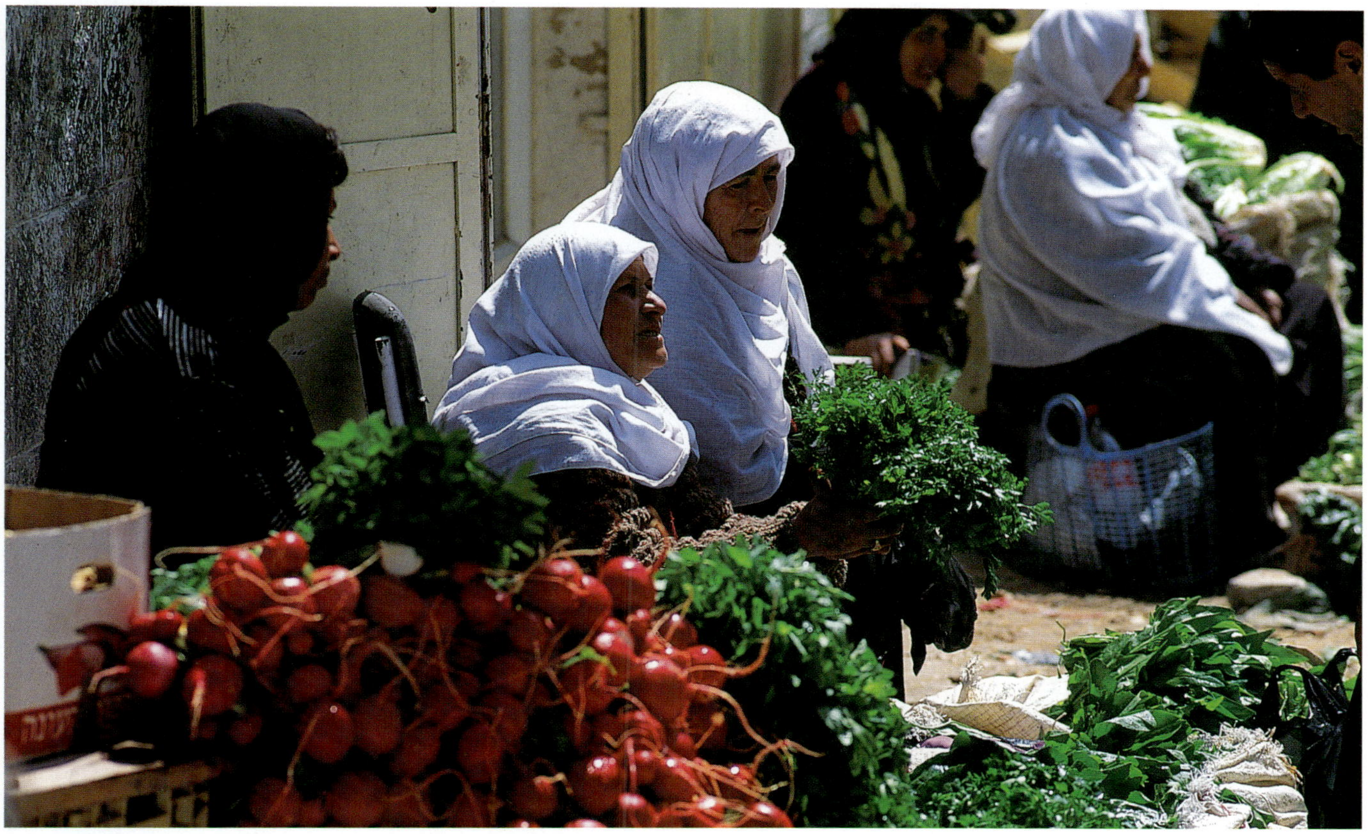

the Palestinians into eight administrative and regional districts, corresponding to the major urban areas which developed between 1948 and 1967.

Many simple families living in Haifa, Jaffa, Akko, and other coastal towns, did in fact emigrate to Jordan in 1948, swelling the population of these urban areas. At the same time, the local Palestinian élite mostly preferred to leave for capital cities in the region, such as Beirut, Cairo, and Damascus. The eight districts, in order of decreasing size of population, are: East Jerusalem, Hebron, Nablus, Ramallah, Tulkarm, Jenin, Bethlehem, and Jericho. By virtue of the Oslo agreements on the resettlement of the Israelis in the autonomous territories, the West Bank today has three faces. The first corresponds to those zones entirely under Palestinian control (in other words, the urban areas which were used to define the districts, with the exception of Jerusalem). Then there is the very fragmented area, where Palestine has control of everything except security matters, which remain the responsibility of the Israelis. Lastly

Scene of everyday life in the Bethlehem vegetable market.

Facing page:

An old man, who must already have been playing this instrument at the time of the British mandate in Palestine.

Following pages:

Terraced olive groves in the Bethlehem region. The olive tree is still a fundamental part of Palestinian life. The fruit has a variety of uses, and the wood is used to make many different objects.

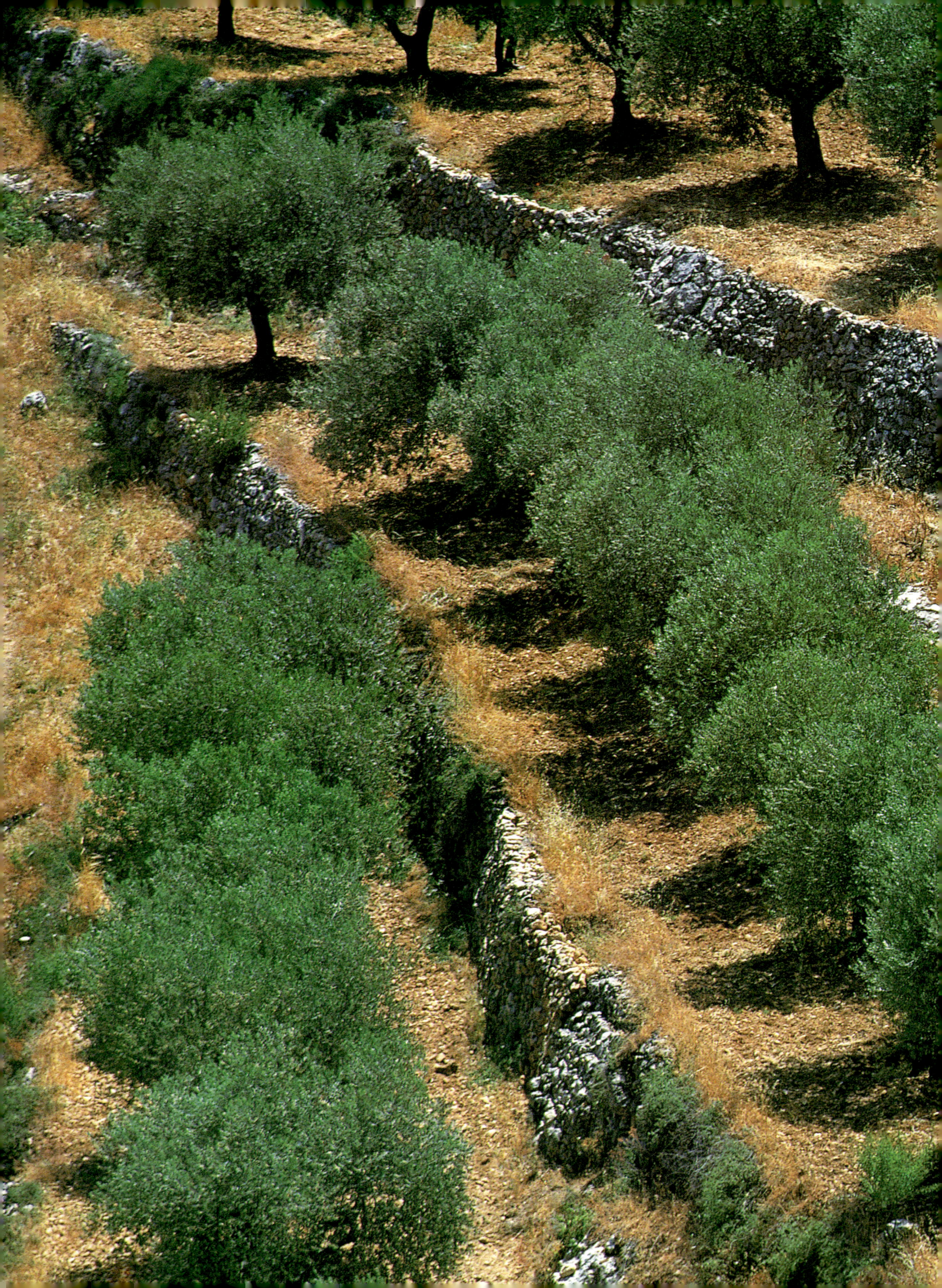

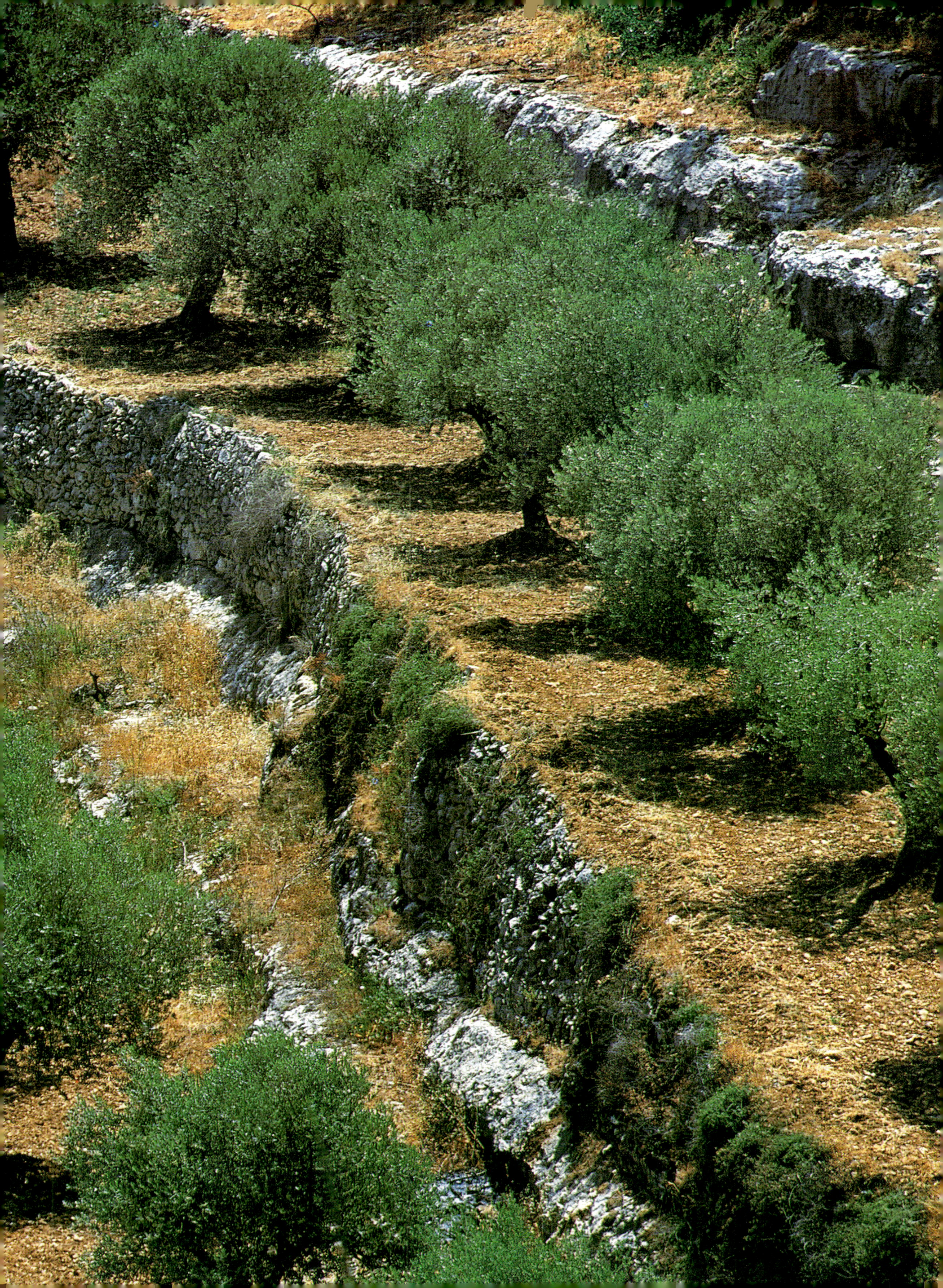

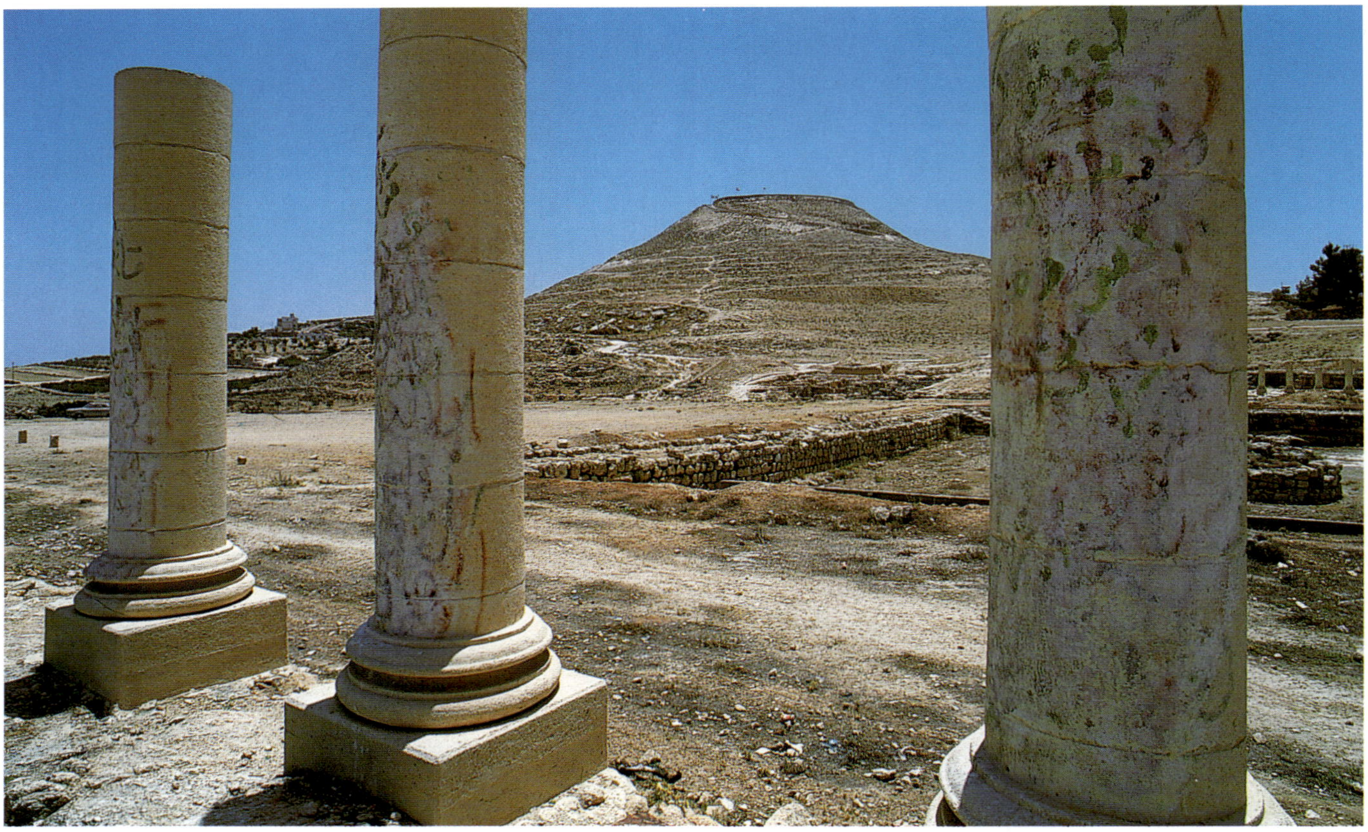

The Roman citadel of Herodion, on the top of a mountain 10 km (6¼ miles) from Bethlehem, dominates a striking landscape extending from Jerusalem to the Dead Sea.

there is the area marking the border with the State of Israel, which has fifty settlements within its confines and remains entirely the responsibility of the Israelis.

So the West Bank, is still largely under Israeli control. It is inhabited by more than one and a half million Palestinians, living in defined sectors and about 300,000 settlers – half of whom are living in new settlements surrounding these enclaves, the other half in the eastern part of the holy city, annexed in 1967. In the event of the Palestinian government proclaiming the creation of a Palestinian state – as provided for in 1947 in UN resolution 181, which dealt with the plan for the division of Palestine, then under British mandate – the land over which this new Arab State will be able to exercise its authority will be somewhat fragmented, difficult to improve, and in no position to satisfy the principle of free movement of goods and people.

Nevertheless, despite the harsh existence endured by the inhabitants, whose standard of living is much lower than that of their Israeli neighbours, and who are sometimes morally exhausted as a result of their

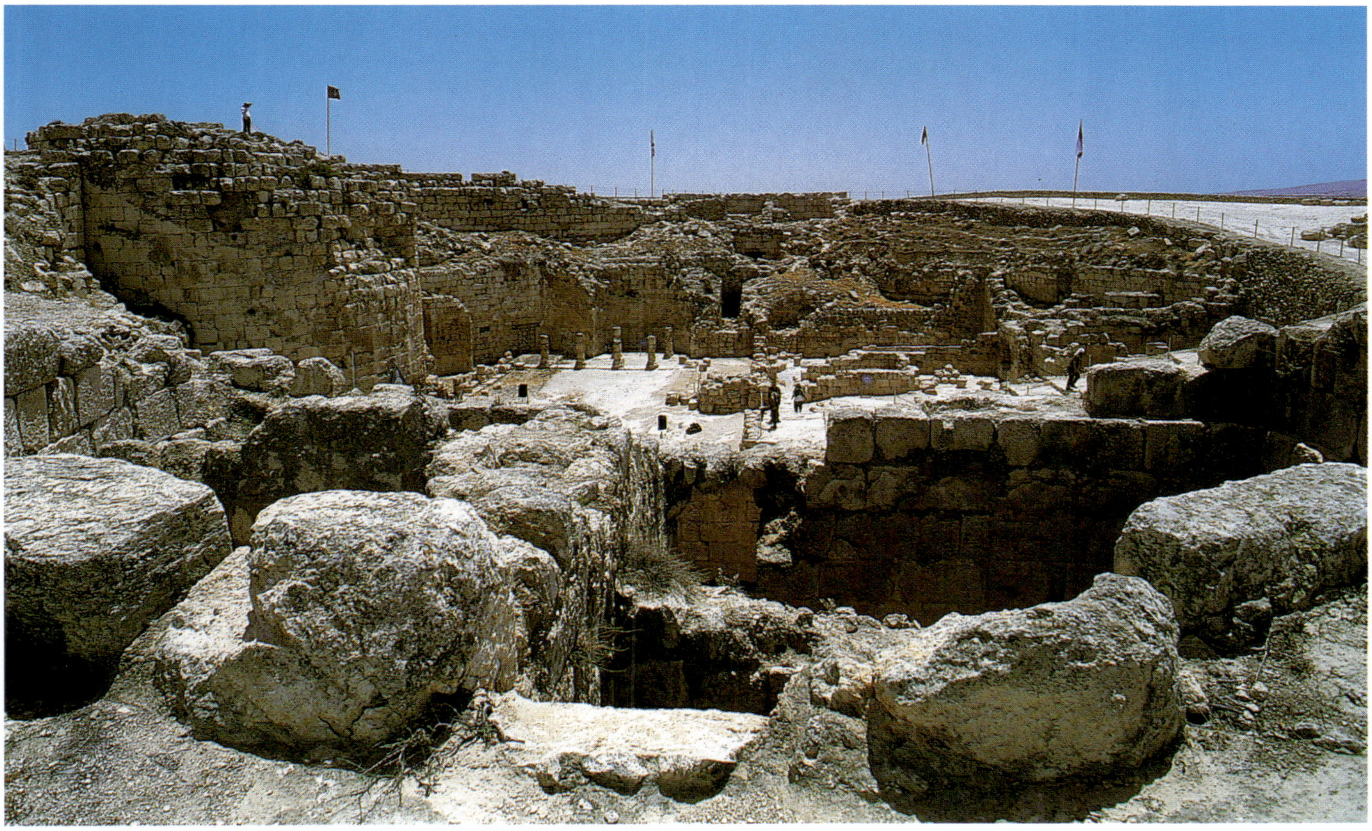

The centre of Herodion, showing interesting archaeological remains.

quest for freedom and often inclined to anger, visitors receive the best possible welcome when they choose to visit this region, which is so rich in sites to be discovered. All the same, one of the precautions you must take, which unfortunately shows how far the differences separating the two communities still are from being resolved, is to be careful about the vehicle that you are using.

Cars with yellow number plates showing they are Israeli registered are regularly attacked by young people throwing stones at them. It is therefore a sensible precaution to check the insurance policy of the Israeli hirer, or take public taxis (*sherut*), go on some of the organised tours of this region, or even arrange to hire a vehicle with a number plate from the autonomous territories.

Not far from Jerusalem lies one of the sites that is dearest to the hearts of Christians, the town where Mary gave birth to Jesus in a stable. The church of the Nativity, backing on to the recently renovated Manger Square, is a stage not to be missed on the pilgrim's journey.

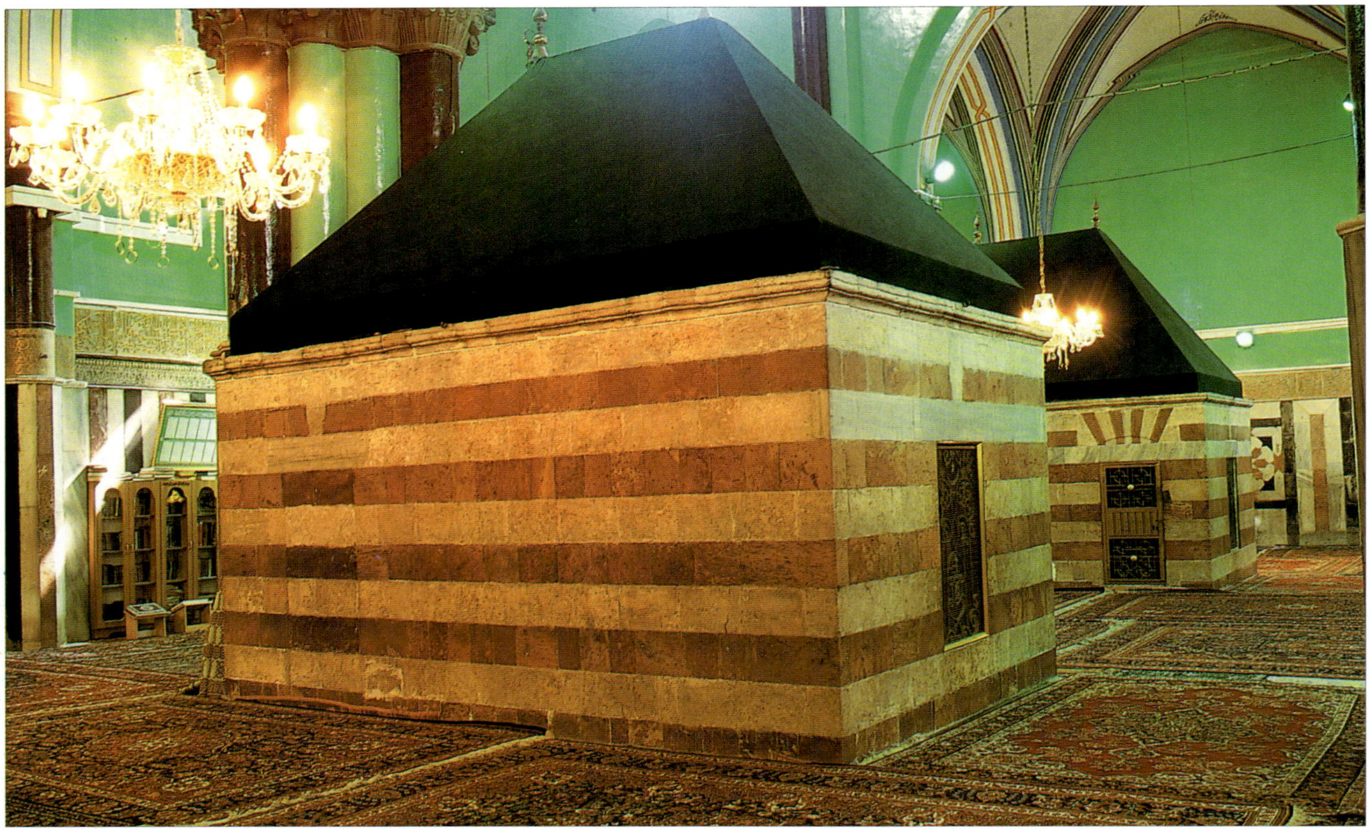

The tombs of Isaac and Rebecca in the Tomb of the Patriarchs at Hebron. Right: The minaret of the Ali Baka mosque at the Tomb of the Patriarchs.

• The Tomb of the Patriarchs •

Built at the time of Herod the Great, the Tomb of the Patriarchs – the *Machpelah* (double cavern) to the Jews, the *Haram el Khalil* (the sanctuary of the friend) to the Muslims – looks from the outside like an impressive fortress. According to tradition, the field and more particularly the cave of Hebron, which Abraham had just acquired after crossing a part of the Promised Land, became the burial place of his wife Sarah, and later the place where the Patriarchs and Matriarchs, whose lives marked the origins of Jewish history, were interred. At the centre of the monument are the tombs of Abraham and Sarah; opposite them, in a room used as a synagogue, are the monuments to Jacob and Leah. The tombs of Isaac and Rebecca are situated beside the former church, which has been turned into a mosque. Venerated by the Jews, the Tomb of the Patriarchs is also honoured by the Muslims, who recognise Abraham as the father of the Arab nations, the descendants of his son Ishmael by his maidservant Hagar.

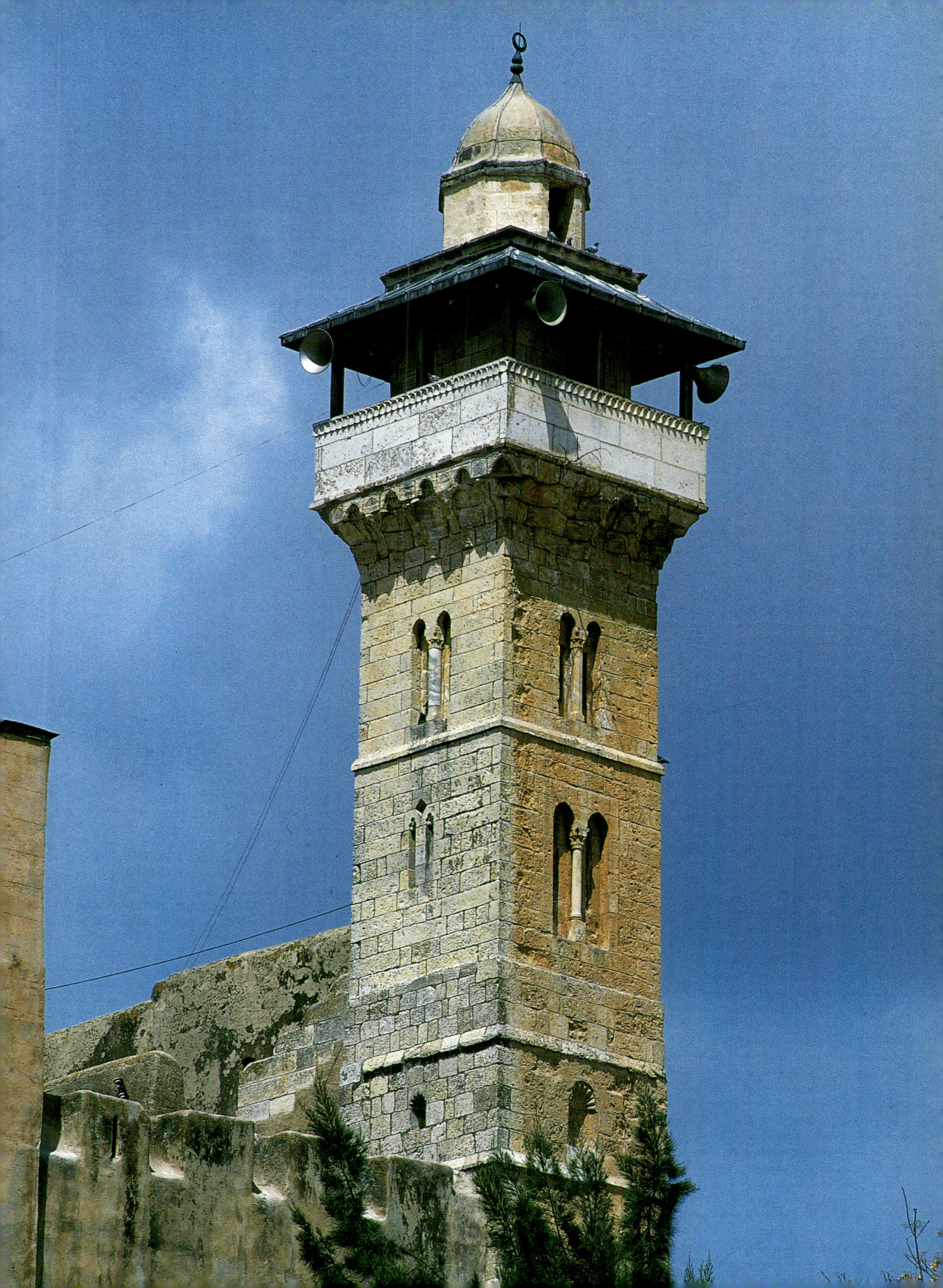

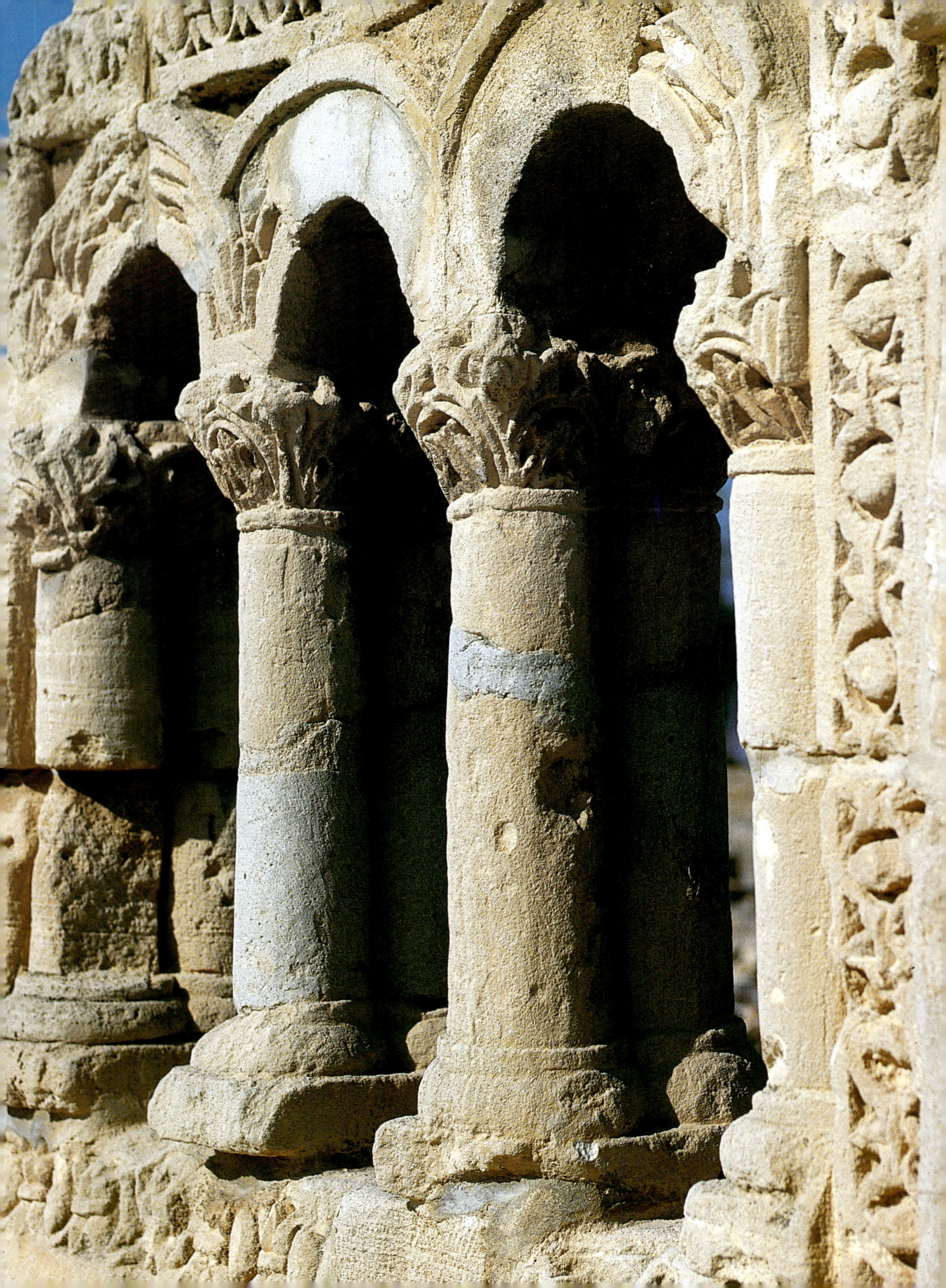

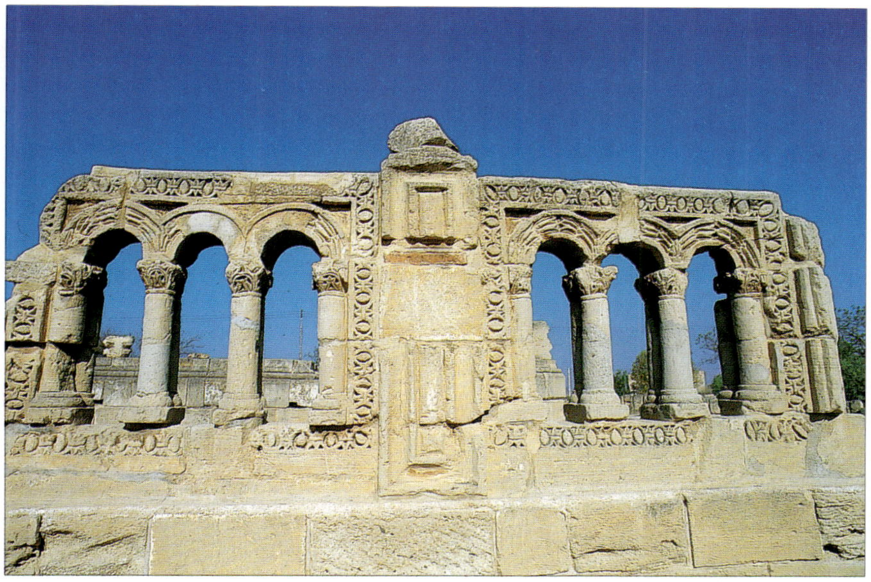

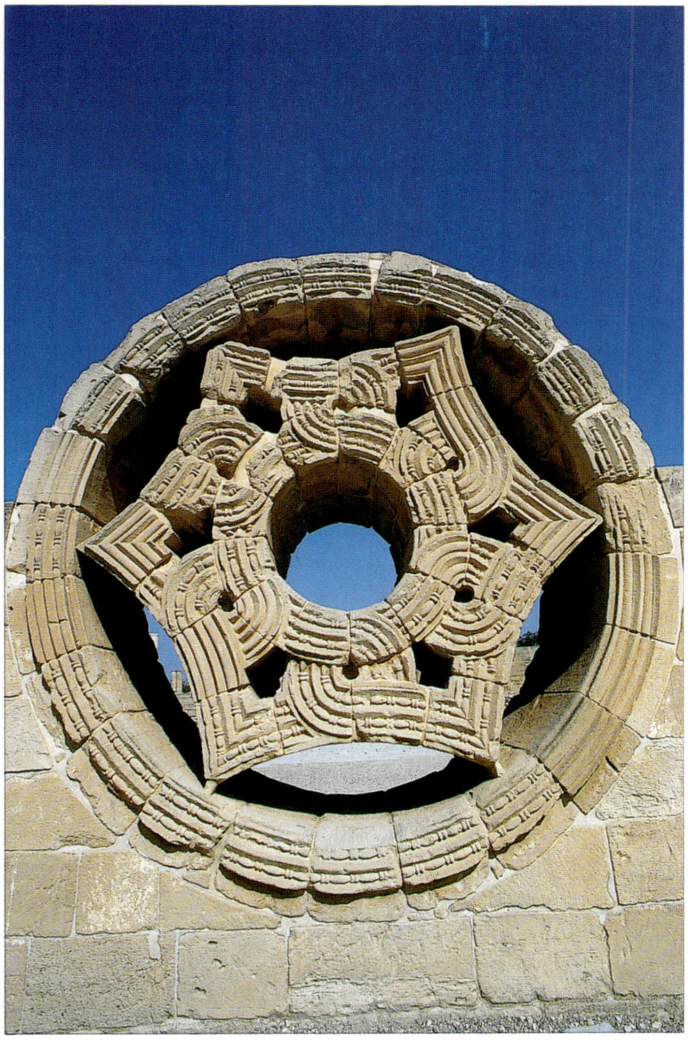

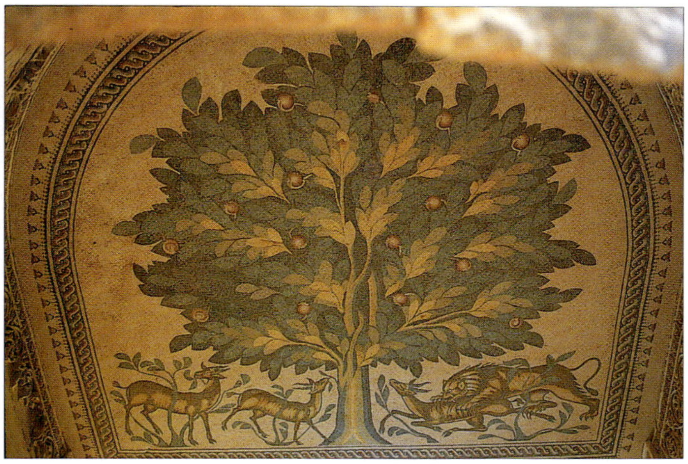

Hisham's Palace, which dates from the seventeenth century but whose foundations are said to be 9,000 years old, is one of the major archaeological sites of Jericho. The arcades of the central courtyard, the rose window which is used as the emblem of the city, and the restored mosaic of the tree of life are reminders of this city's illustrious past.

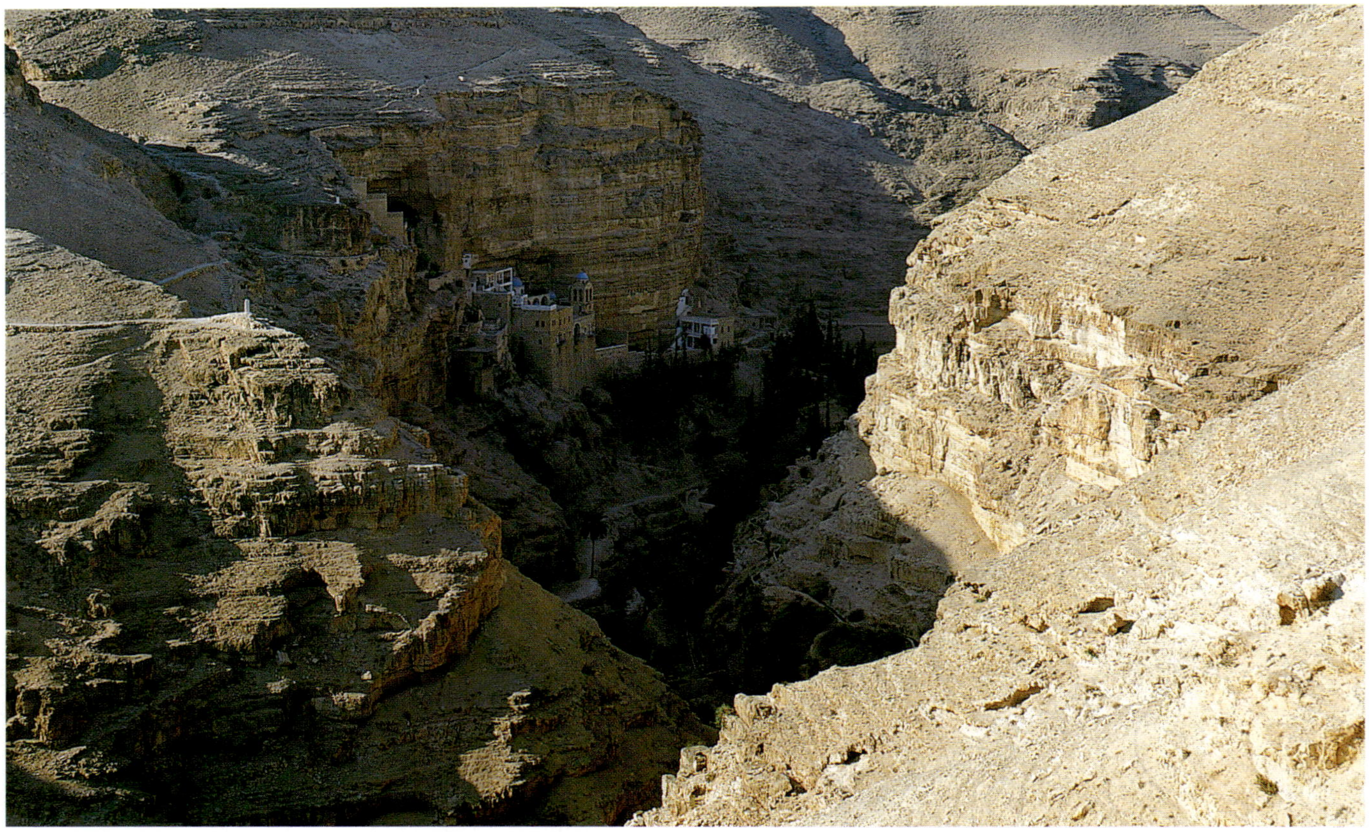

In the gorges of the Wadi Kelt in the heart of the Judaean Desert, the monastery of St George clings to the mountainside. Founded in 480 AD, it was deserted for many years after its destruction in 614 by the Persians. The existing monastery was built between 1878 and 1901.
Following pages:
View from the outskirts of Jericho over the Judaean Desert, which has always attracted prophets, hermits, and other monks.

The church, which according to tradition was built around the cave where the holy child was born, is looked after by the Orthodox Church, the Franciscans, and the Armenians. A holy place and centre of devotion, the basilica gives the impression of being several churches together, built at different times by the Byzantines under the influence of the Emperor Constantine, then by the Crusaders and the Greek Orthodox.

St Catherine's church, where midnight mass is celebrated every year on 24 December and broadcast throughout the world, forms part of this archaeological complex, and is steeped in history. Bethlehem, with its 30,000 inhabitants, is under Palestinian administration, but is also one of the important holy places of Judaism, since it contains the tomb of Rachel, wife of the Patriarch Jacob. In the book of Genesis, she is counted among the holy women (with Leah, Sarah, and Rebecca) who contributed to the building of the house of Israel. About 15 km (10 miles) further south is the city of Hebron, which is so legendary and sacred to both Jews and Muslims that it is in an almost permanent state of high tension. It is here in this city, built like

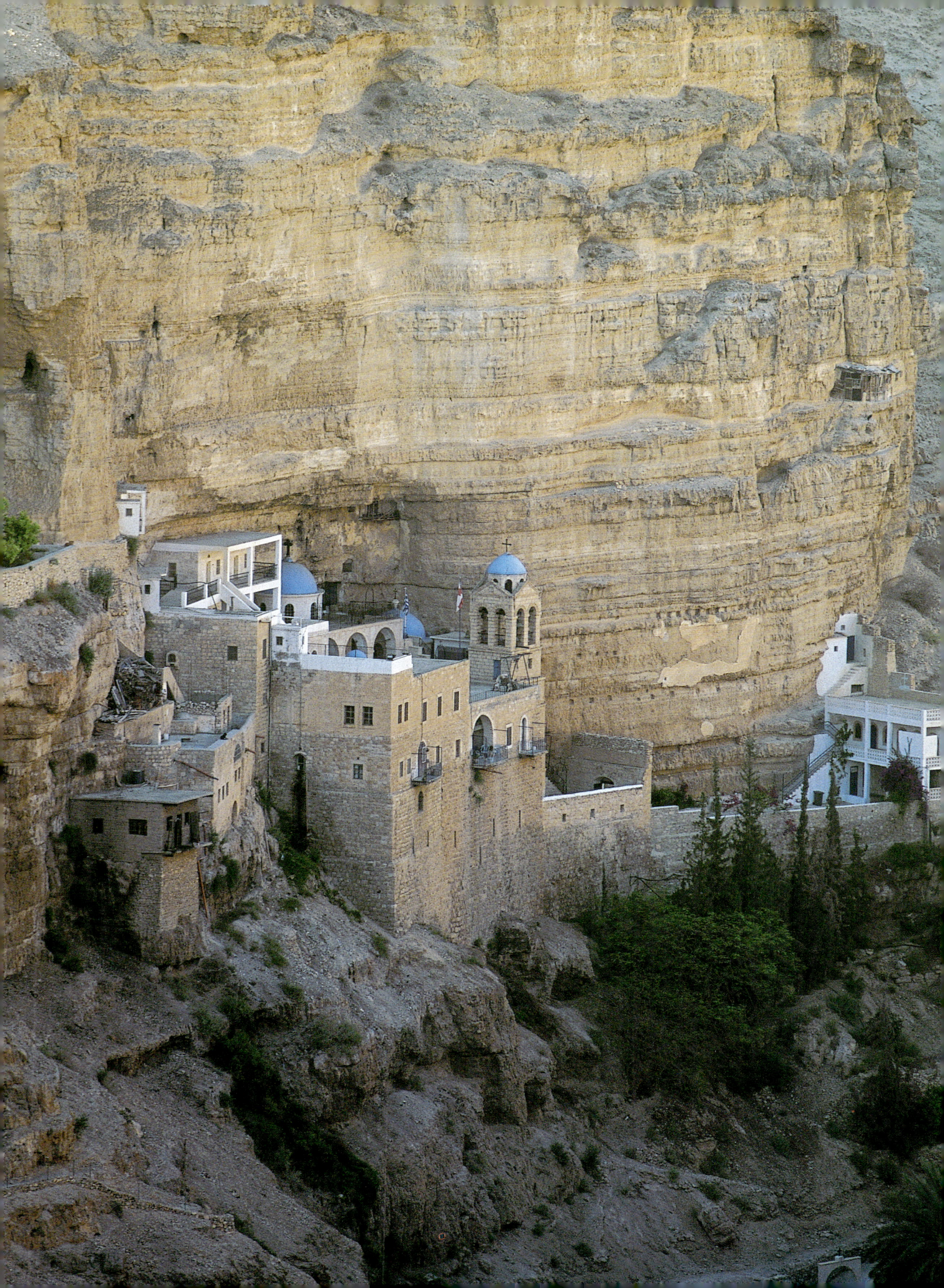

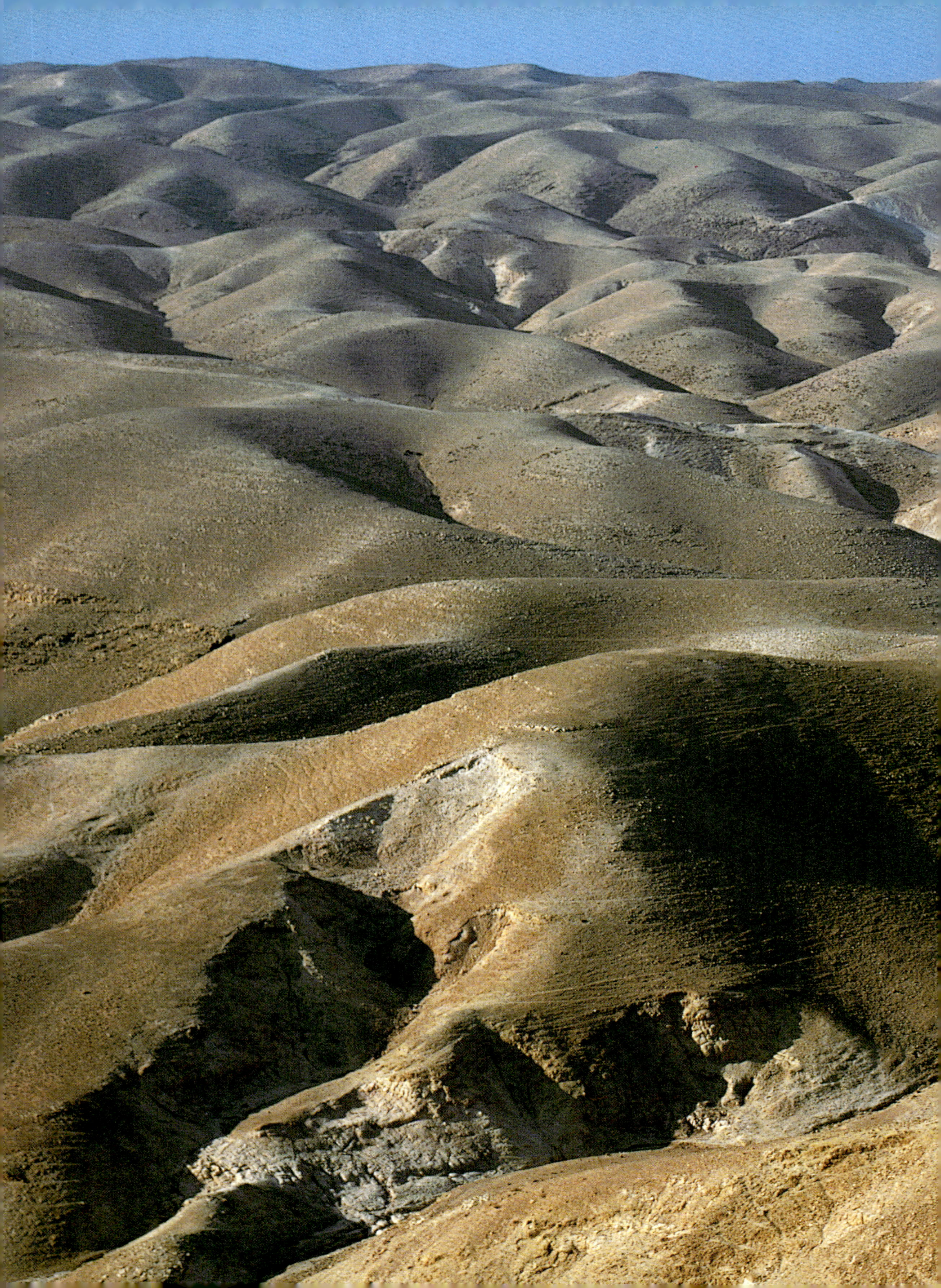

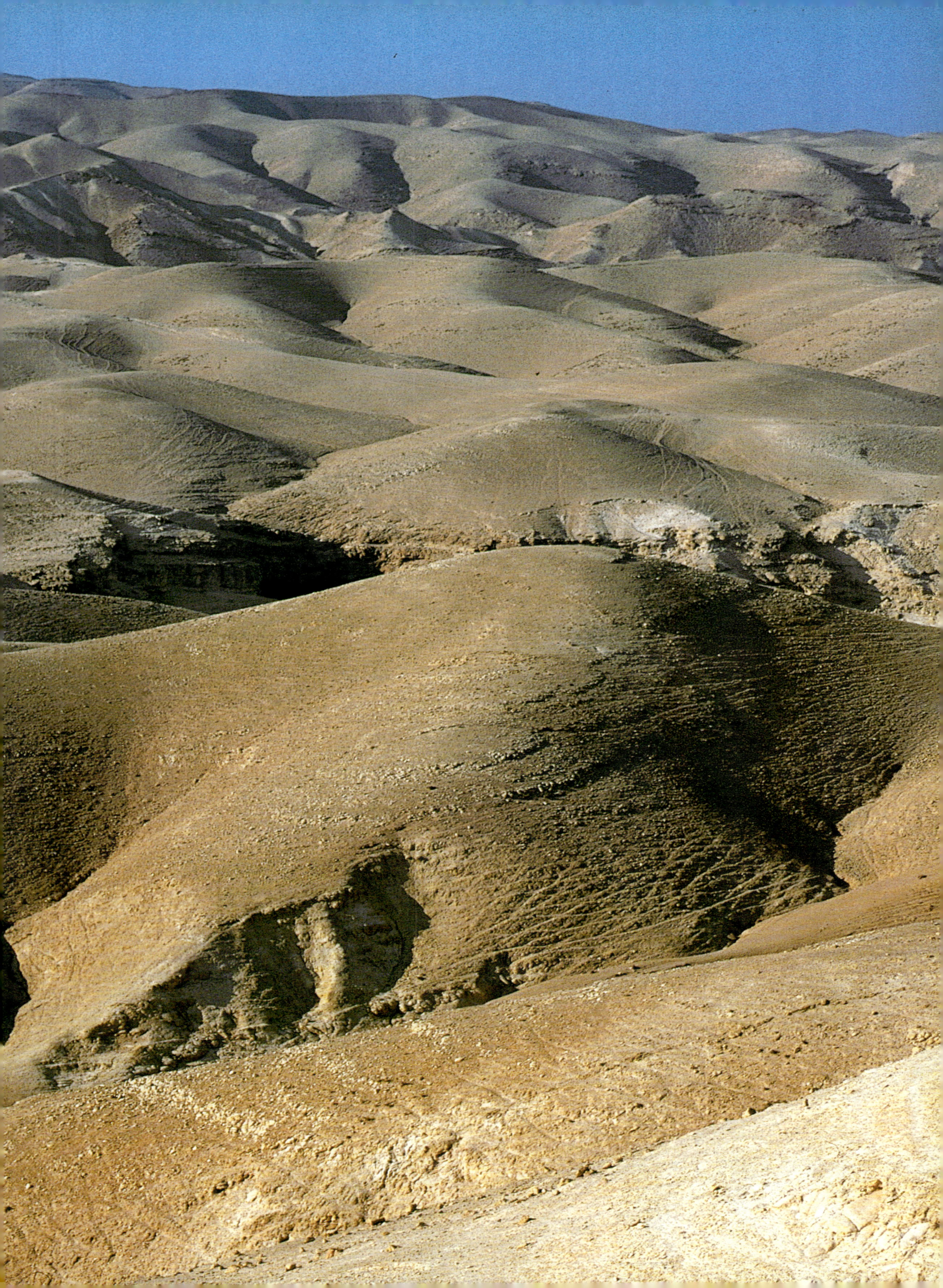

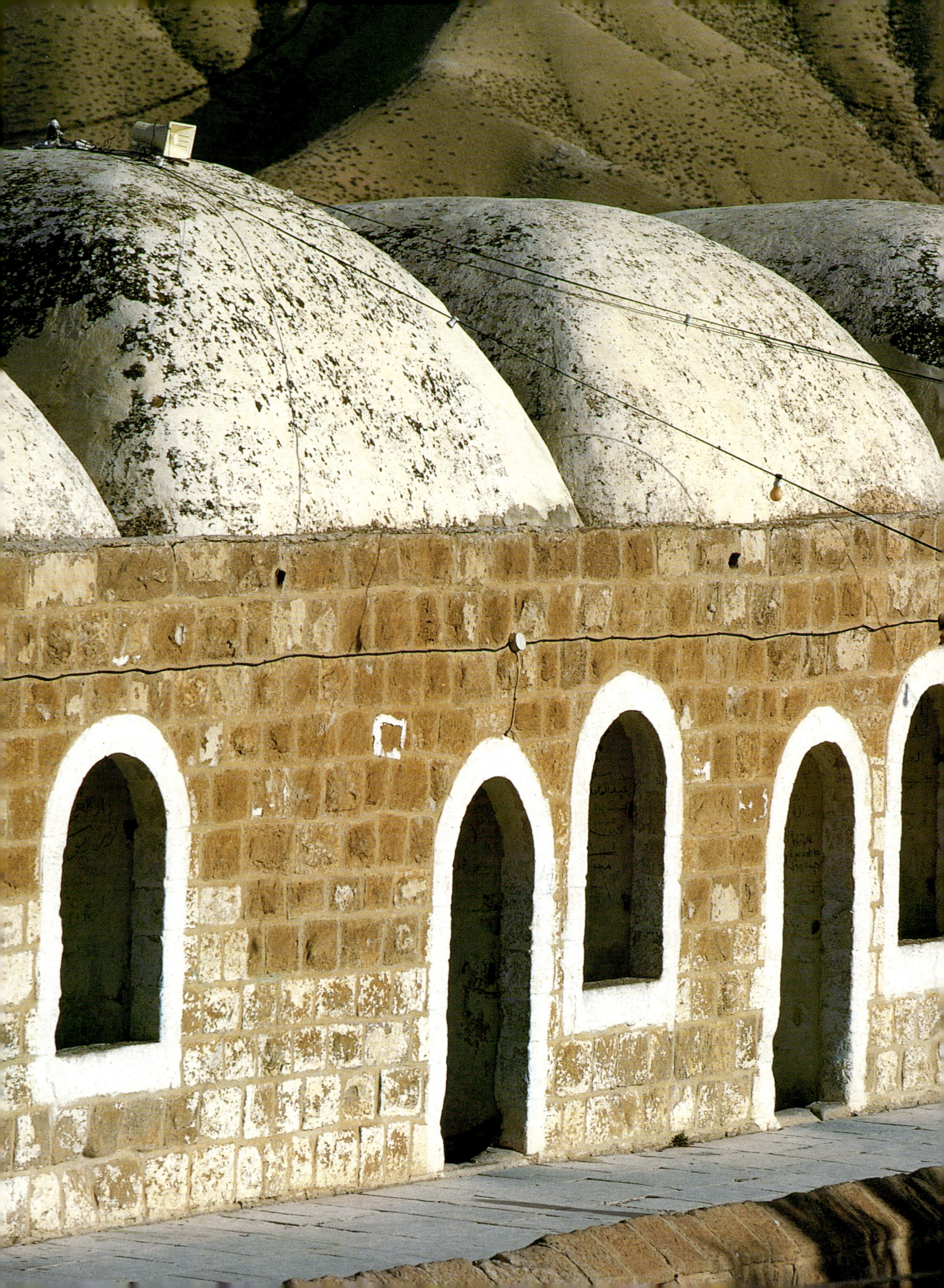

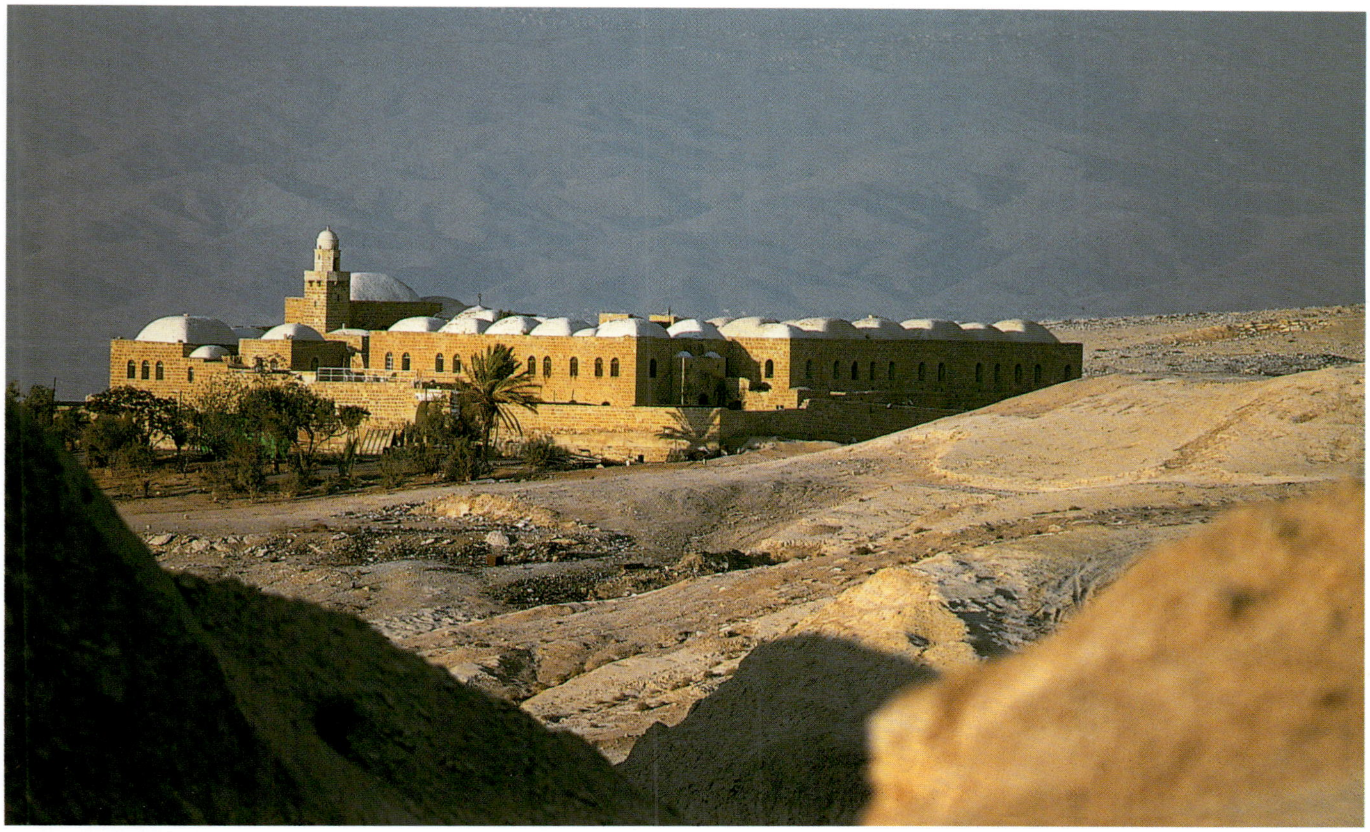

Nehri Musa is an old caravanserai in the middle of the Judaean Desert.

an amphitheatre on the Judaean hillsides, that Abraham, the common ancestor of these two communities, lies buried in the Tomb of the Patriarchs. History also tells us that it was in Hebron that David was crowned king of Israel, and that this was the city he chose as the capital of his kingdom, before he captured Jerusalem and made it his new capital.

Establishing a Jewish presence in this holy city of Judaism, 450 ultra-religious Jews live in the very heart of the old Arab city, which has forced the negotiators of the peace process and the Israeli resettlement in the territories to draft a special law for Hebron. A sizeable number of armed troops have been deployed especially to protect these devout occupants, with another 2,000 installed on the hill of Kiryat Arba overlooking the city. Before going to Hebron, it is important to get information about the current state of tension, as it may happen that – as a result of skirmishes between Arabs and settlers in the marketplace for example – the city is sealed off by the military.

Going northwards, to the east of Jerusalem, not far from the Jordan border, the ancient city of Jericho lies huddled in its oasis of greenery,

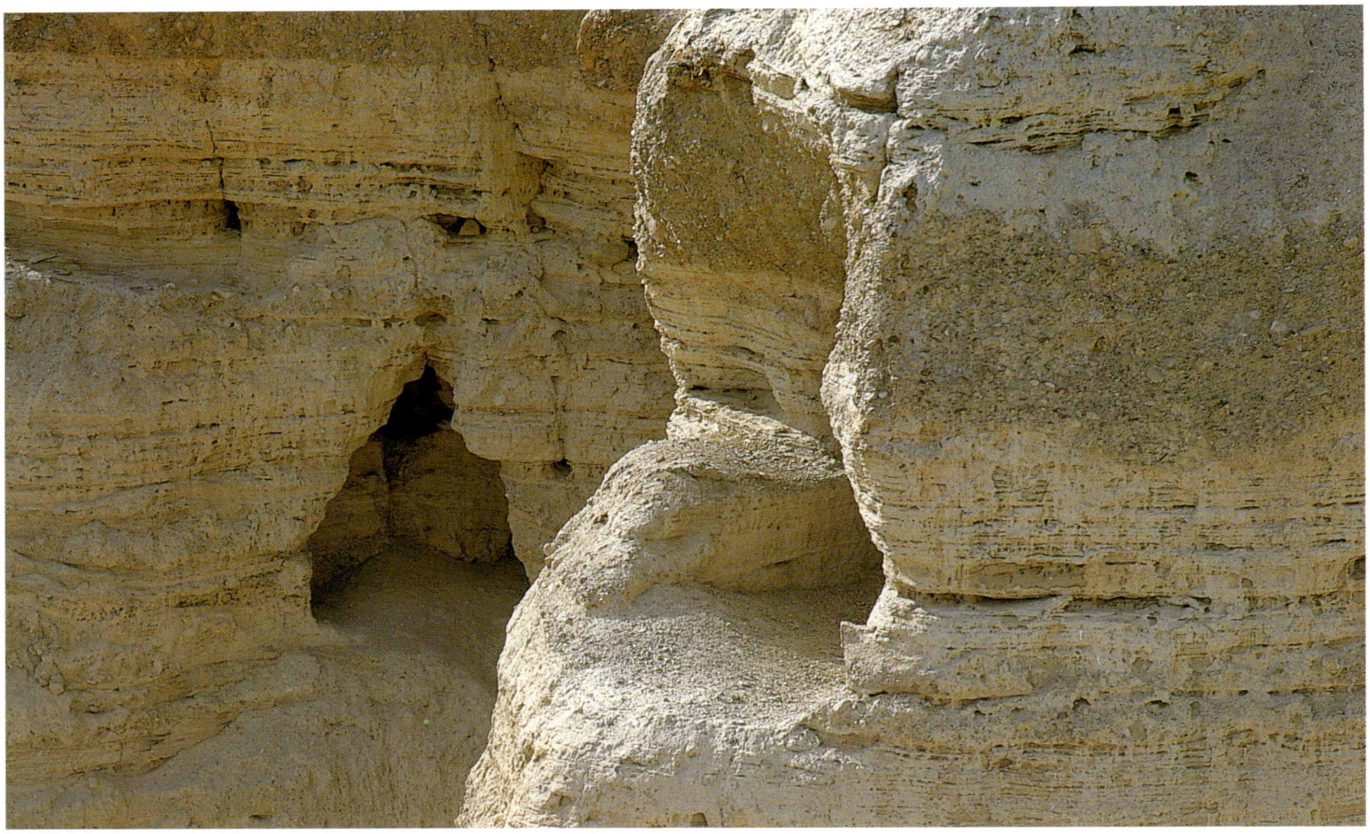

During the second century BC, the Jewish sect of the Essenes established itself at Qumran. Complete scrolls and fragments of texts collectively known as the Dead Sea Scrolls were discovered in 1947 in caves in the cliff, which the members of this sect had used as their headquarters.

258 m (846 ft) below sea level. Thought to be the oldest city in the world by archaeologists, who date the first human settlements back some 9,000 years, Jericho was also the first city on the West Bank to be handed over to Palestinian control, in 1994. The remains of its illustrious past are rare, and hard for the uninitiated to interpret.

The city has been devastated and left in ruins several times, notably by the Hebrews themselves who captured it and razed it to the ground, after Moses had seen it from Mount Nebo and Joshua had led the tribes of Israel up to its walls. Today, Jericho continues to enjoy its enviable situation in the midst of a stretch of greenery, where date-palms, orange-trees and bougainvilleas grow. Unusually for the Middle East, where gambling is generally banned, the Palestinian government has authorised the building of a casino and allowed profit to be made from it. This initiative resulted in money coming in, which could be used in part to finance projects of public interest. About 50 km (30 miles) north of Jerusalem stands Nablus, the most populous city in the West Bank region with 80,000 inhabitants.

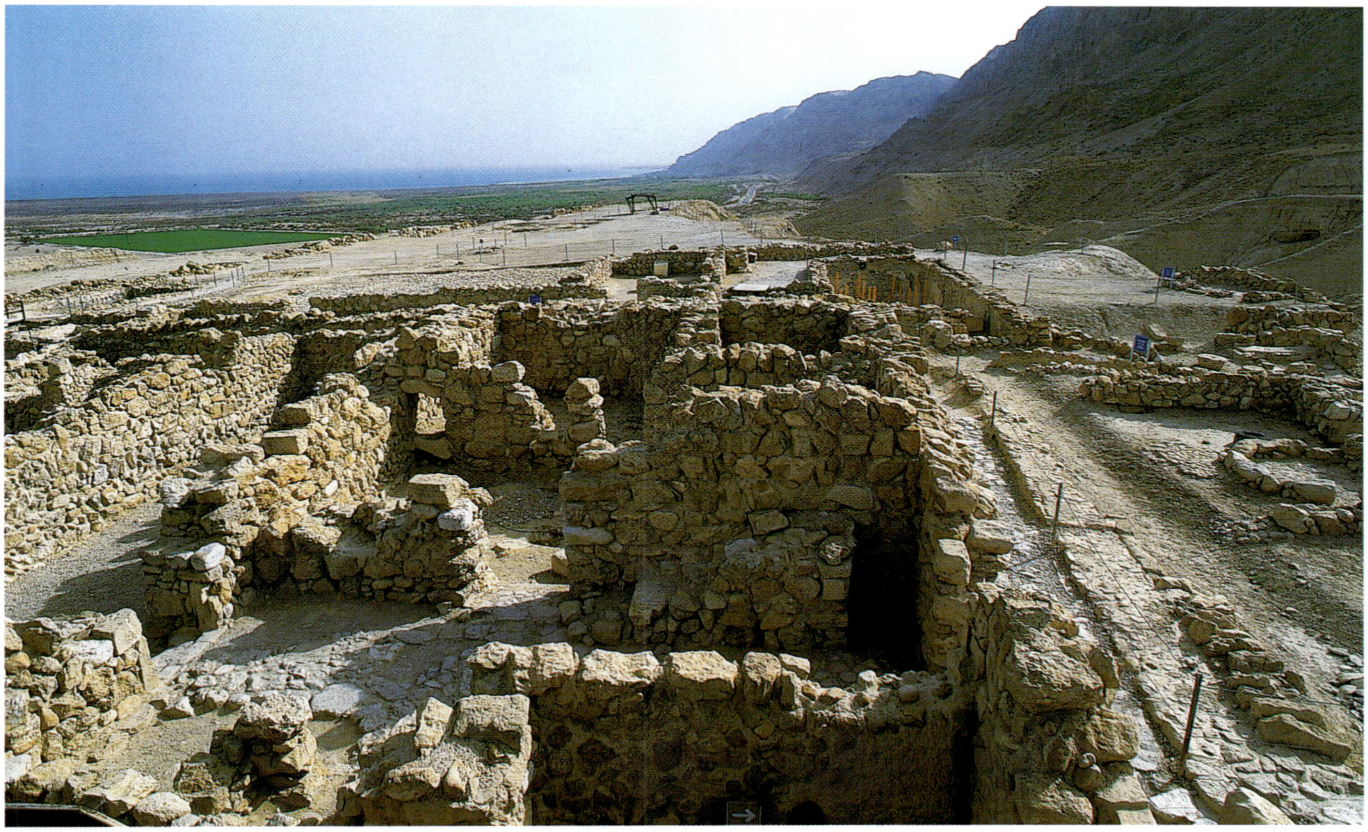

Nablus is situated at what was once the very important crossroads for the routes to Jerusalem (the road opposite the Damascus Gate, for example, is called the Nablus Road), the Mediterranean, Galilee, and Jordan. It is a very lively city, which nevertheless retains an air of considerable prestige, with its rows of small, blue-doored houses lining the hillside. But the former Samaritan capital still remains a city in which Palestinian nationalism is firmly anchored, and visitors venturing alone into the narrow, winding alleys may encounter some problems, if the tension suddenly mounts. Even though the Good Samaritan is still a symbol of brotherhood among men, it seems that it will take more than one of them to make it possible for the two communities to get closer to one another. Certainly, in the short term the involvement of the international community will play a crucial role for the establishment of a peace accord. However, in the longer term, the presence of several new generations of good Samaritans in the area could hopefully contribute to the deepening of positive steps achieved by talks between the two communities.

Because of its size and height above sea level, the Golan plateau enjoys climatic conditions which ensure abundant rainfall, so it has always been the region's "water tower", the reservoir feeding the sources of the Jordan. It is therefore not surprising that control is bitterly disputed.

The Golan, *a source of territorial conflict*

The Golan plateau is a strategic area, the cause of bitter confrontations between the Israelis and the Syrians in 1967 and 1973, and the focus of talks aimed at achieving a global peace agreement in the region. But it is also, and perhaps more importantly, one of the wonders of nature. Covering 1,150 km^2 (450 square miles) in the north-east of Israel and framed by Galilee, Lebanon, Syria, and Jordan, the Golan overlooks Lake Tiberias and the northern part of the Jordan Valley. It is an enormous basalt massif, topped by the craters of extinct volcanoes. The plateau slopes downwards from north to south, reaching over 1,000 m (3,280 ft) at the highest points, with the 2,814 m (9,230 ft) high Mount Hermon at its northern extremity, inside the Syrian border. Because of its size and height above sea level, the Golan plateau enjoys climatic conditions which ensure abundant rainfall, so it has always been the region's "water tower", the reservoir feeding the sources of the Jordan. Like the source of the River Dan in Galilee, which is surrounded by vegetation, the source of the Banyas in the Golan, 15 km (10 miles) from Kiryat Shmona, gives life to beautiful landscapes, protected within the nature reserve of Nahal Hermon. Before the Banyas, which rises in the Golan Heights, joins the Dan to form the Jordan, the river must first lose altitude, cascading down one step at a time. Its banks are lined with dense and varied vegetation. Planes, willows, and poplars grow readily on

The River Banyas rises in the Golan Heights, before joining the Jordan.

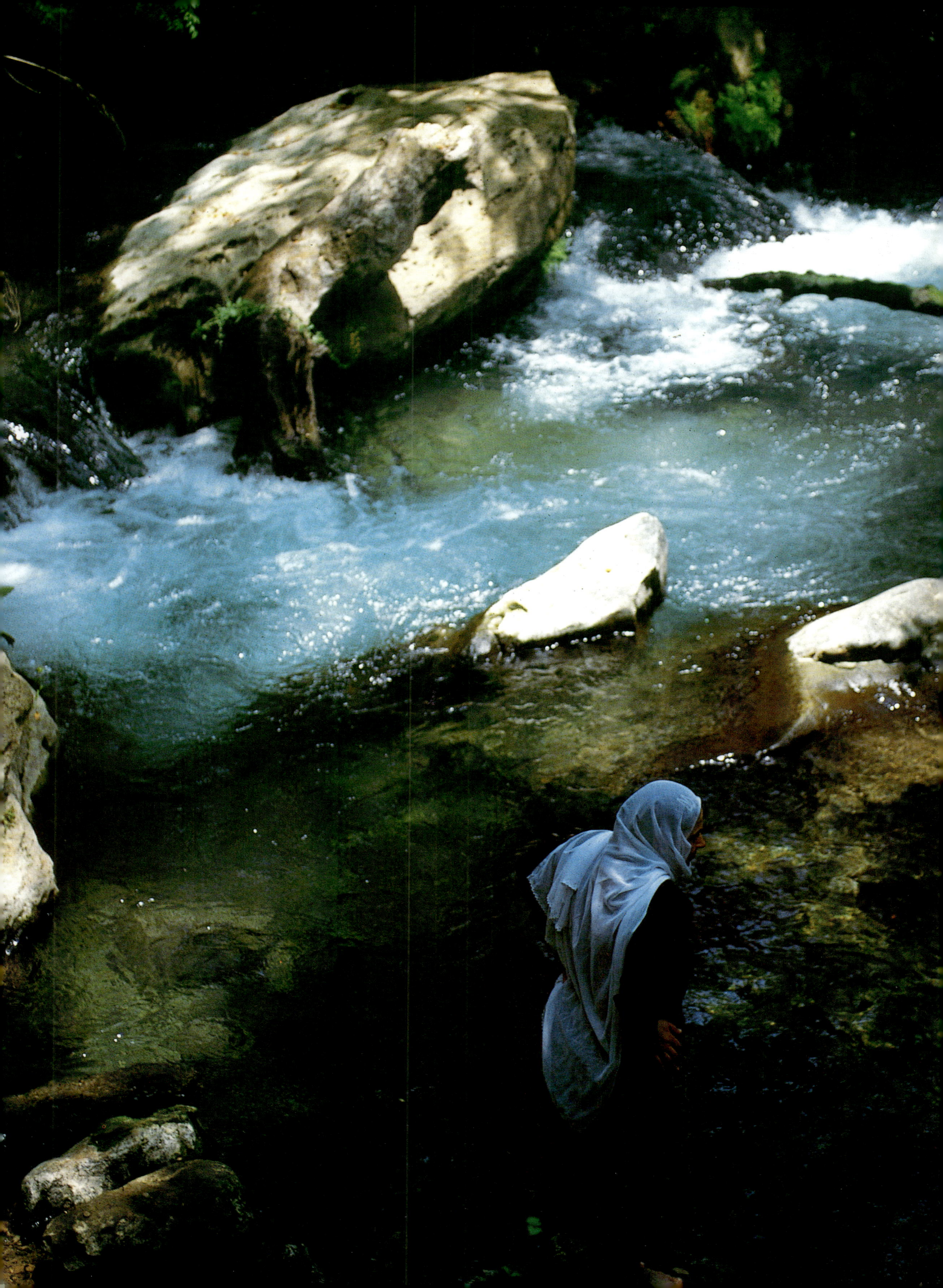

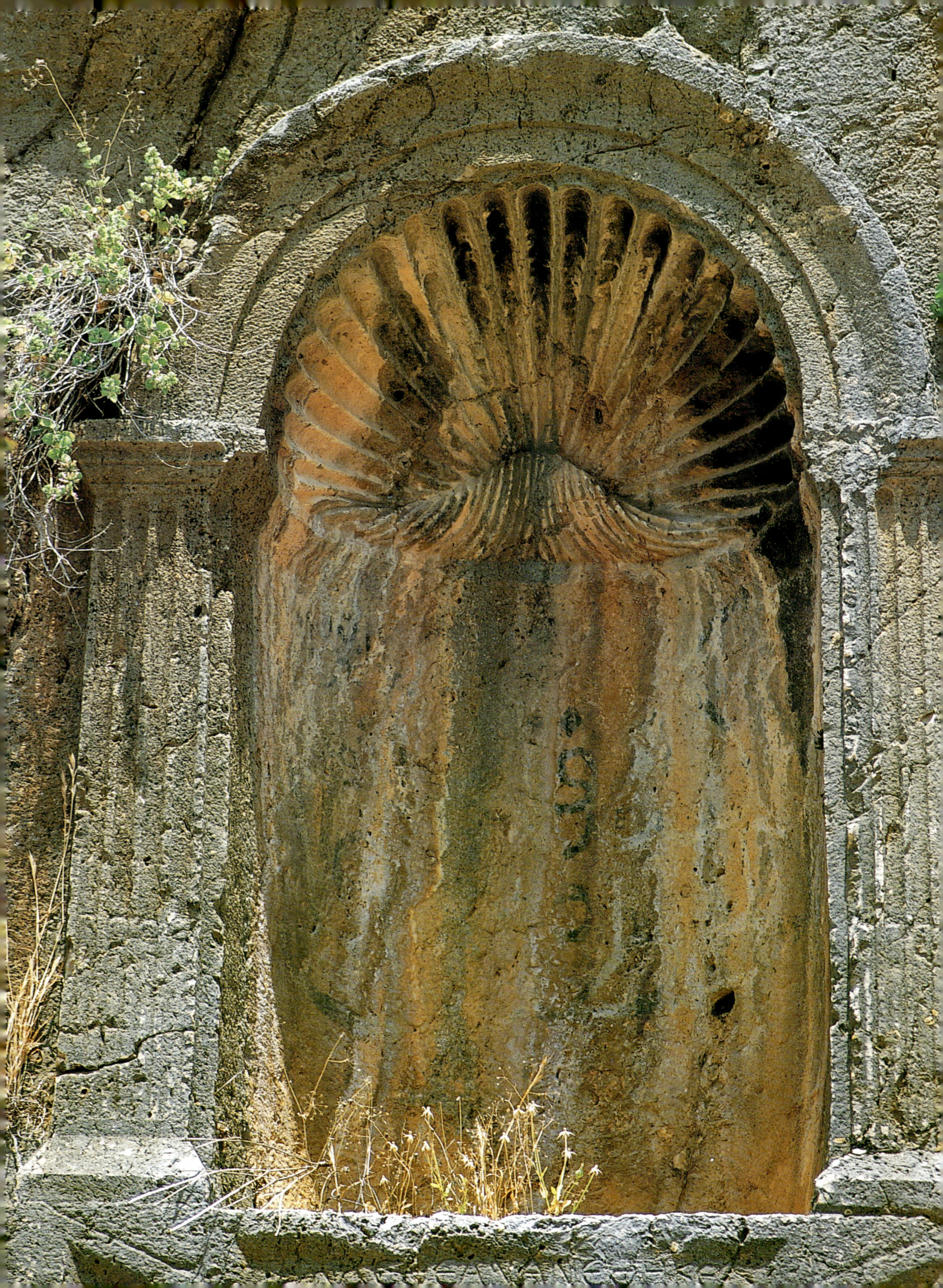

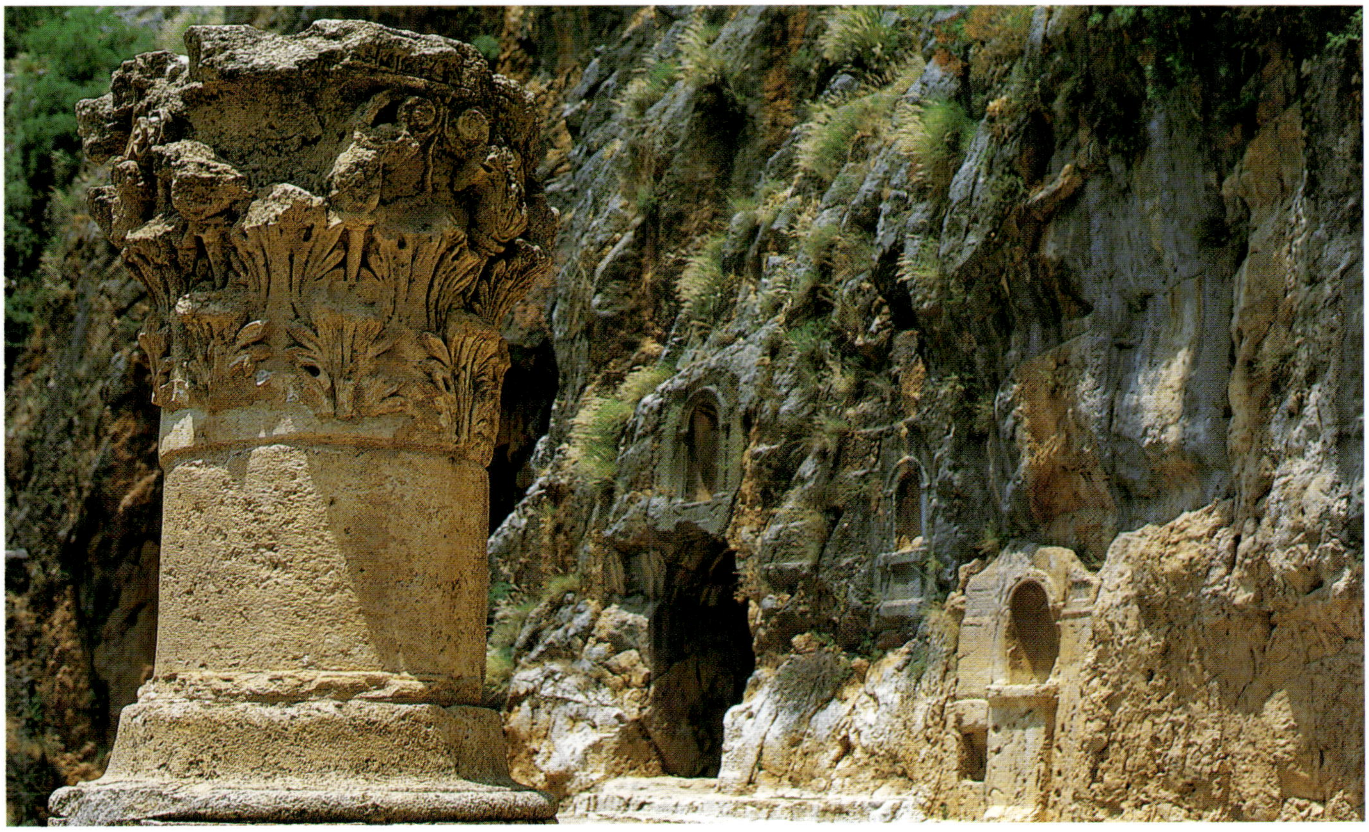

both banks, once the main bed has levelled out. Other trees have been planted, such as fig, lemon, eucalyptus, date-palm and mulberry. You can take a very pleasant walk from the entrance to the reserve, close to the source, and enjoy contact with nature at the same time as discovering an ancient heritage. The very name of Banyas is an Arabic corruption of the Greek name Paneas, or Pan, the god of nature. There is an altar dedicated to him in one of the recesses overlooking the entrance. Or, to take another example, the few remains of the temple of Augustus are what is left of the Roman city of Caesarea Philippi, which was built around the spring. And the pilgrims are not to be outdone as, according to certain interpretations of the scriptures, it was the rock of Banyas which Jesus took to be the foundation of his new building, the new message.

It is indeed here that you move from the Old to the New Testament. According to Matthew (16:18), when he came to the region of Caesarea Philippi, Jesus said to Simon Peter: "And I tell you that you are Peter, and on this rock I will build my church."

At the time of the Greeks an altar was dedicated in the Banyas rock niches to Pan, the god of nature. Pan became corrupted to Paneas, then Banyas.

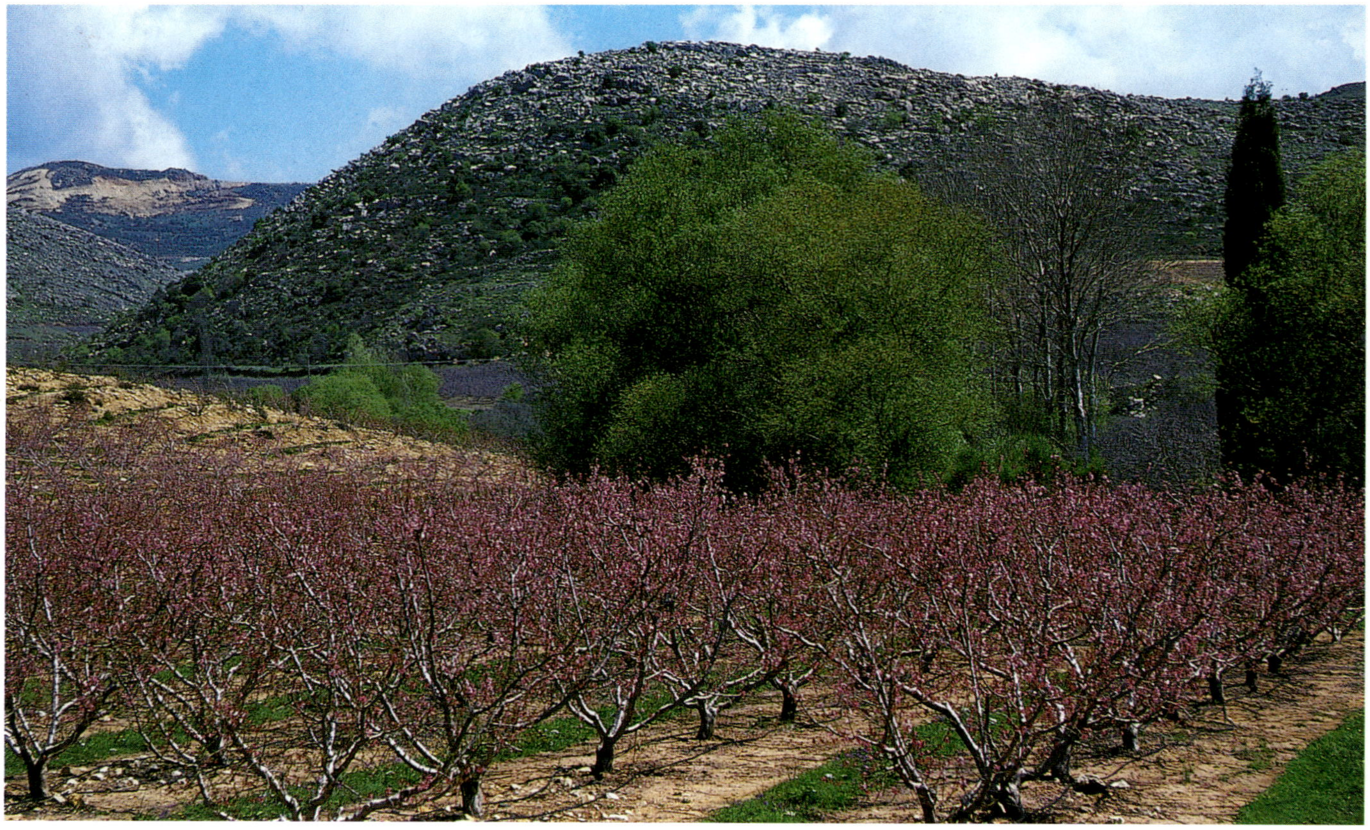

The orchards of Majdal Shams are part of the cultivated area, which brings colour to the landscape and draws profit from the land of Golan.

Leaving Banyas on route 99, visitors follow a road which takes them straight to the top of a mountain from which there is an absolutely splendid view, typical of the beauty of the Golan.

Stretching away as far as the eye can see, mountains rise at a distance from one another, leaving space in between for bowl-shaped valleys. In the background Mount Hermon, with its bleached cone, proclaims itself lord and master of this mineral kingdom. It is a vegetable kingdom too, because the sides of the valleys which can be seen in the foreground, in front of the distant barrier of mountains, are verdant and appear in sharp contrast. Carefully tended hillsides, plots of cultivated land, and fruit trees in family groups stand side by side with wilder vegetation. The farmers trying to earn a living from this beautiful and bountiful nature come from the Druze village at the top of one of the mountains. The Druzes form an initiatory religious community, which had its origins in eleventh-century Egypt, as a result of the Ishmaelian schism of the Fatimids. They have a strong presence in the Lebanon, Syria, and Israel, especially in the Golan,

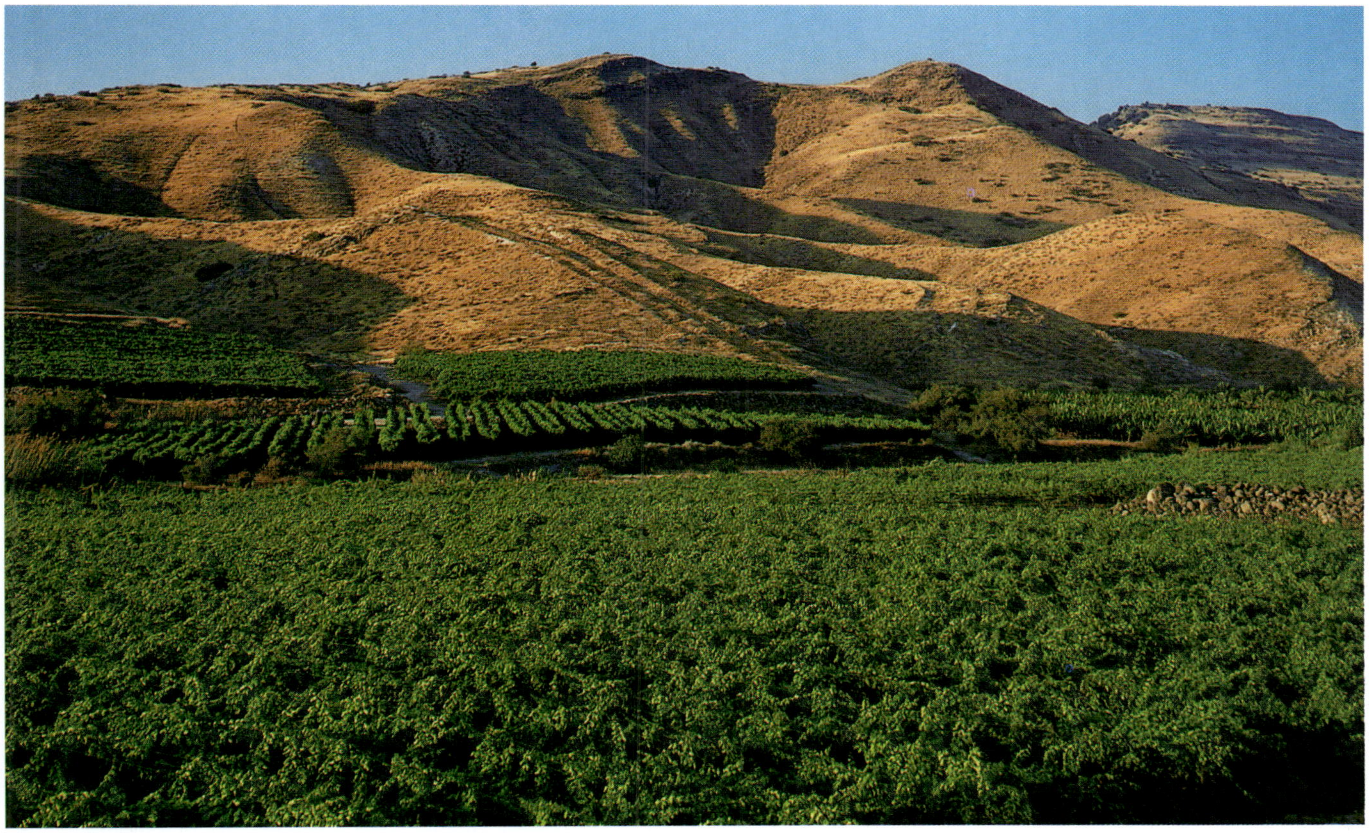

Vineyards and banana groves near Ramot, on the edge of Lake Tiberias.

where 15,000 of them remained under occupation after 1967, though there were ten times that number before this date.

Thirty thousand Israelis now live in the Golan, mainly labourers who have made their contribution to making the soil bear fruit. The fate of these settlers has been the subject of negotiations between the Hebrew State and its Syrian neighbour, which is demanding that the plateau borders be restored to where they were in 1967, before any agreement can be reached on maintaining peace throughout the region. But for the Israelis, any such restitution of land comes up against three major problems. The first is the problem of the security and protection of Israel, which could once again come within range of the Syrian artillery. Then there is the question of land, and the work the Israelis have put into its cultivation. Finally, there is the matter of water, which in this, one of the world's drier areas, is the most crucial cause for dispute and where the stakes are highest. Seen from this perspective, the Golan takes on the appearance of a fortress, and control is bound to be bitterly disputed.

Around the plantations which are beautifully maintained by the kibbutzim and the moshavim, the wild plants covering the soil of the softly rounded hills, windswept and scorched by the sun, form a carpet of ever changing reflections, which has the power to compress time and evoke the atmosphere of the pastoral poetry of biblical times.

Galilee, *the poetry of a landscape where memories meet*

The Canaanite archaeological site of Tel Hazor was once a prosperous urban centre, which flourished over several centuries, starting in the eighteenth century BC.

Galilee, with its landscape of lovingly cultivated, fertile valleys, and hills that are sometimes dry and sometimes decked with trees, whose green foliage is caressed by what some might call a divine breeze, is without doubt the most poetic and captivating region of Israel. It occupies the whole of the northern part of the country, from the mountains of Samaria to the Lebanese border, and from the coastal fringe to the eastern border, formed by the Golan plateau and Jordan. In this land, lying between the Mediterranean and the Sea of Galilee – better known by the name of Lake Tiberias – a wide variety of cultures and ways of life co-exist. Depending on whether you live in the centre of busy Haifa, in Nazareth in the Arab area, on a kibbutz in the Jezreel Valley, in the mystical city of Safed, in a Druze village, or even in Kiryat Shmona, under the constant threat of attack from southern Lebanon – the course of your life could follow a number of amazingly different paths for such a small area. There is a similar diversity in the centres of interest for tourists, and this is its chief attraction for visitors. They can choose to go on a pilgrimage tracing the places where Jesus preached; soak up the atmosphere of towns with an important heritage, such as Safed, Acco (Acre), and Beit Shean; relax in a hotel on a kibbutz; swim and unwind

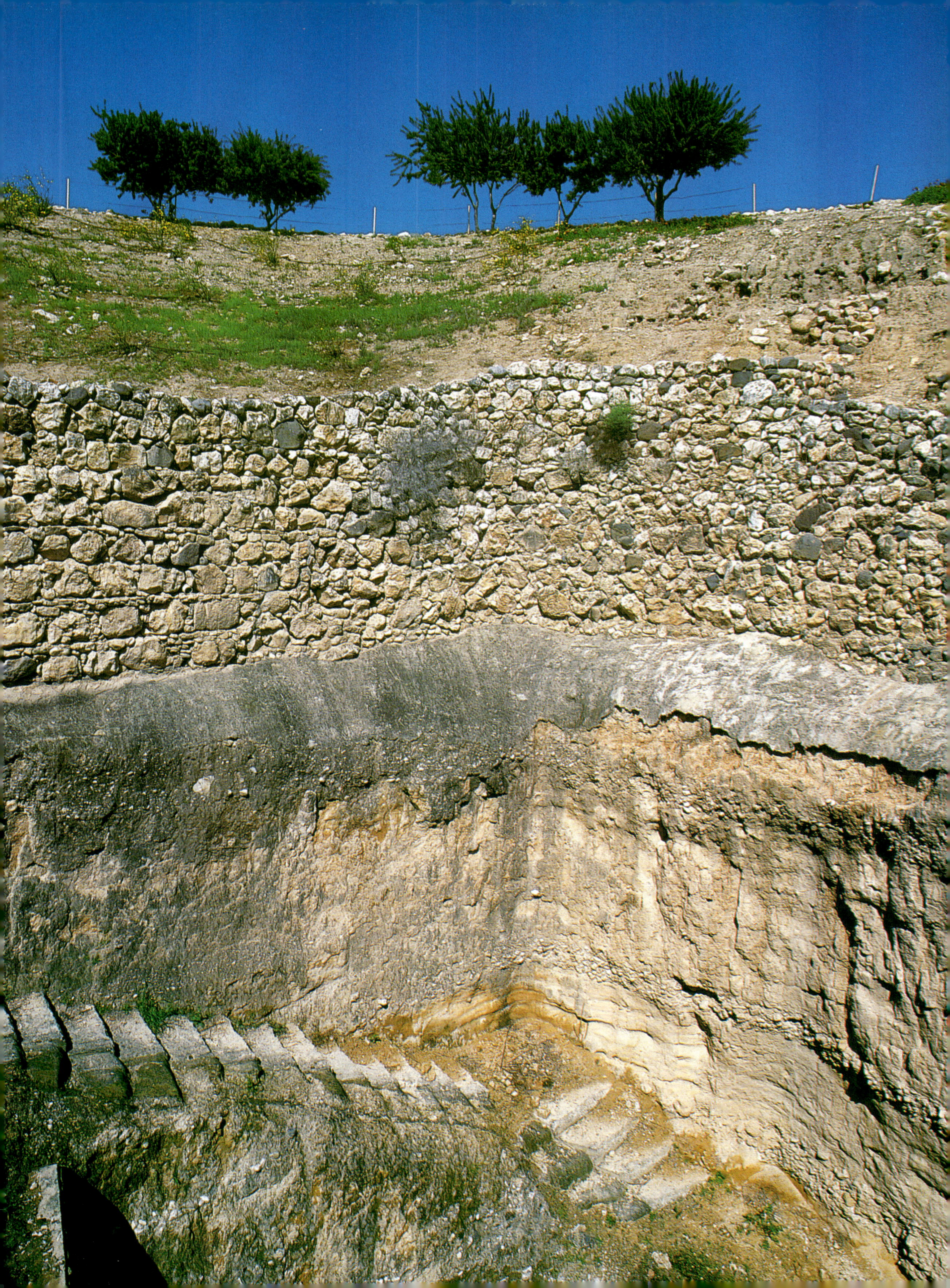

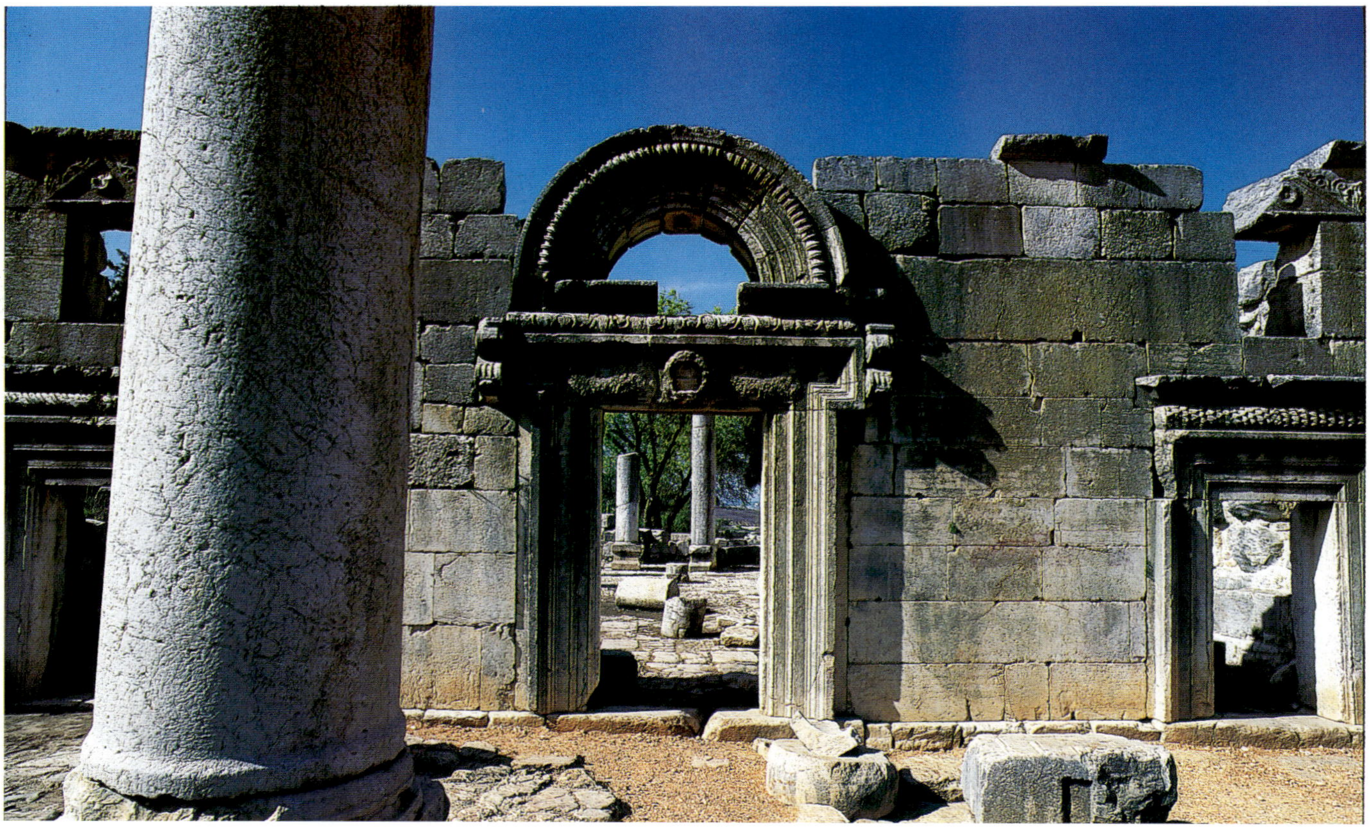

The ruins of the Bar'am synagogue near the Lebanese border, with walls, lintels, floors, and columns dating from the second century.

in the warm waters of a spring; or quite simply contemplate and feel themselves in harmony with these biblical landscapes, in which love and memory meet.

Haifa, Israel's third-largest city and most important industrial centre, is a good port of entry for exploring the centre of Galilee. It is a remarkable city, having grown up on the slopes of Mount Carmel, overlooking the bay, which extends right up to the Lebanese border, marked by the cliffs of Rosh Hanikra. It is underrated by tourists, who often remember nothing more of their visit than the splendid view of the gardens of the Baha'i temple, yet it is well worth going out of your way for. Haifa is a city of character and a pleasure to explore, not only owing to its tumultuous past, which was largely the result of its strategic position on the Mediterranean and the protection offered by its hills, but also thanks to its green and tranquil surroundings, which are the delight of the people who live in the rows of houses arranged like an amphitheatre on the slopes of Mount Carmel. From there, the perfect choice of itinerary

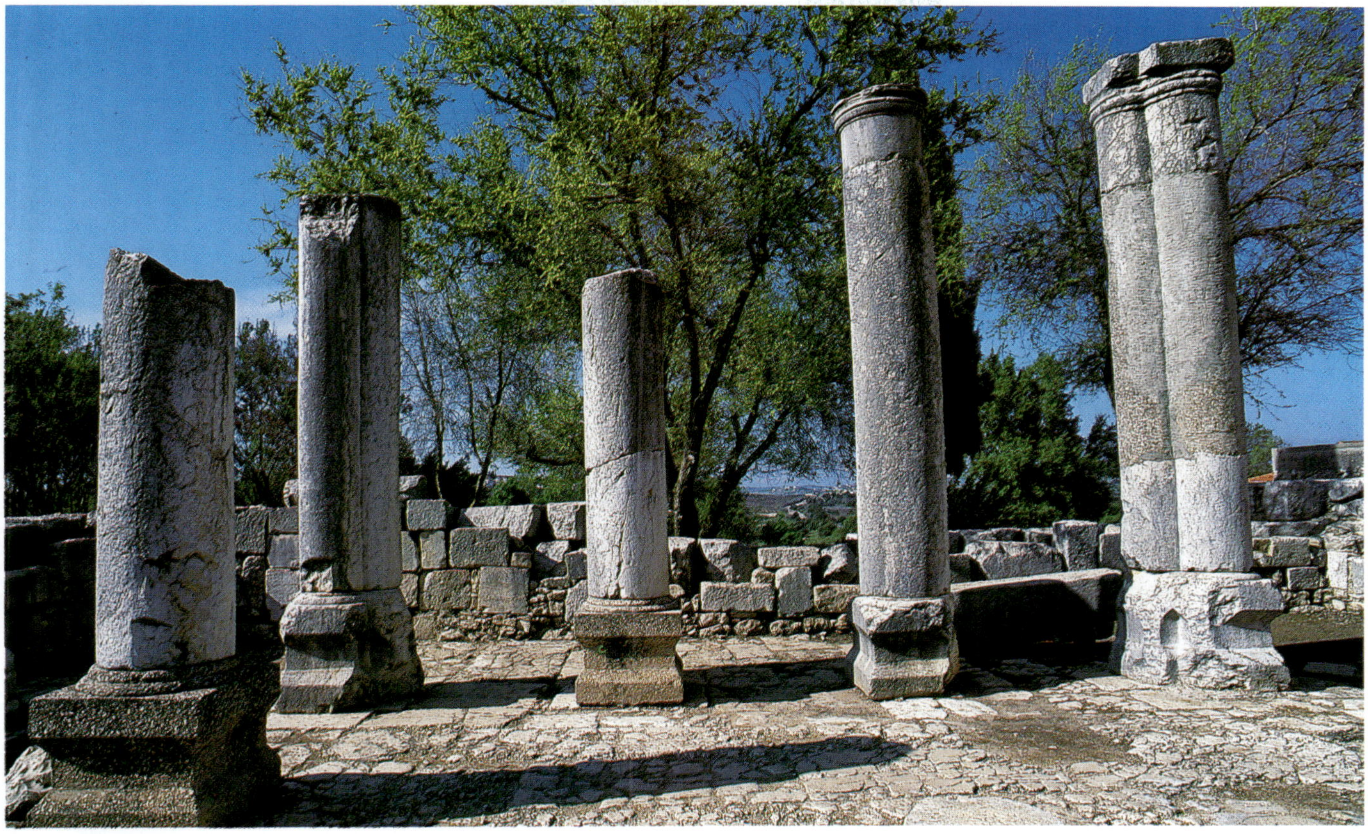

might be to take route 75, which goes all the way to the town of Nazareth, and brings you into contact with scenery characteristic of a particular part of Galilee.

Barely 20 km (12 miles) out of Haifa, the little town of Kiryat Tivon is a good example of what the good life means in this part of the world. It means living in delightful houses perched on the crest of one of the mountains of the Carmel range, protected by the majestic forest cover all around them, and with the azure sea on the distant horizon. As you leave this little oasis, you come to the beginning of the great, rich, fertile Jezreel Valley, which has been a prosperous centre of agricultural production since the first pioneers settled there. Israeli citizens continue to take pride in this production, the legacy of the first *kibbutzim*, whose members had to struggle against the harsh conditions all around them. In *Le septième jour d'Israël* (The Seventh Day of Israel), Serge Moati remembers the *kibbutzim* of Galilee: "That summer, my uncle took me to Degania, the first kibbutz in Israel (1909), not far from Lake Tiberias.

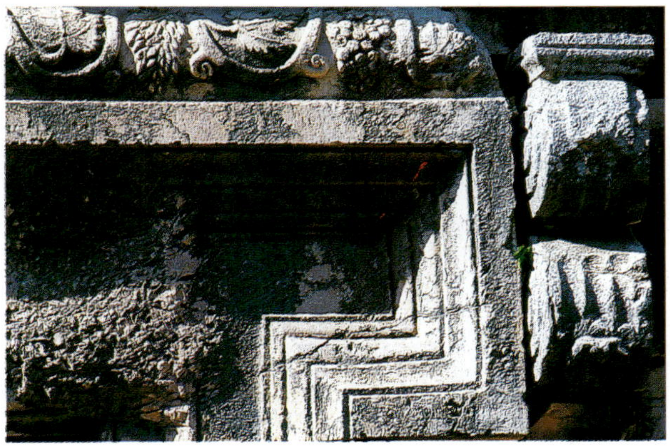

Following pages:
General view of the site of Tel Meggido, situated on the ridge extending from Mount Carmel about 30 km (20 miles) from Haifa. There are so many layers of human occupation at this place where the trade routes crossed, that houses have constantly been built one on top of another over thousands of years.

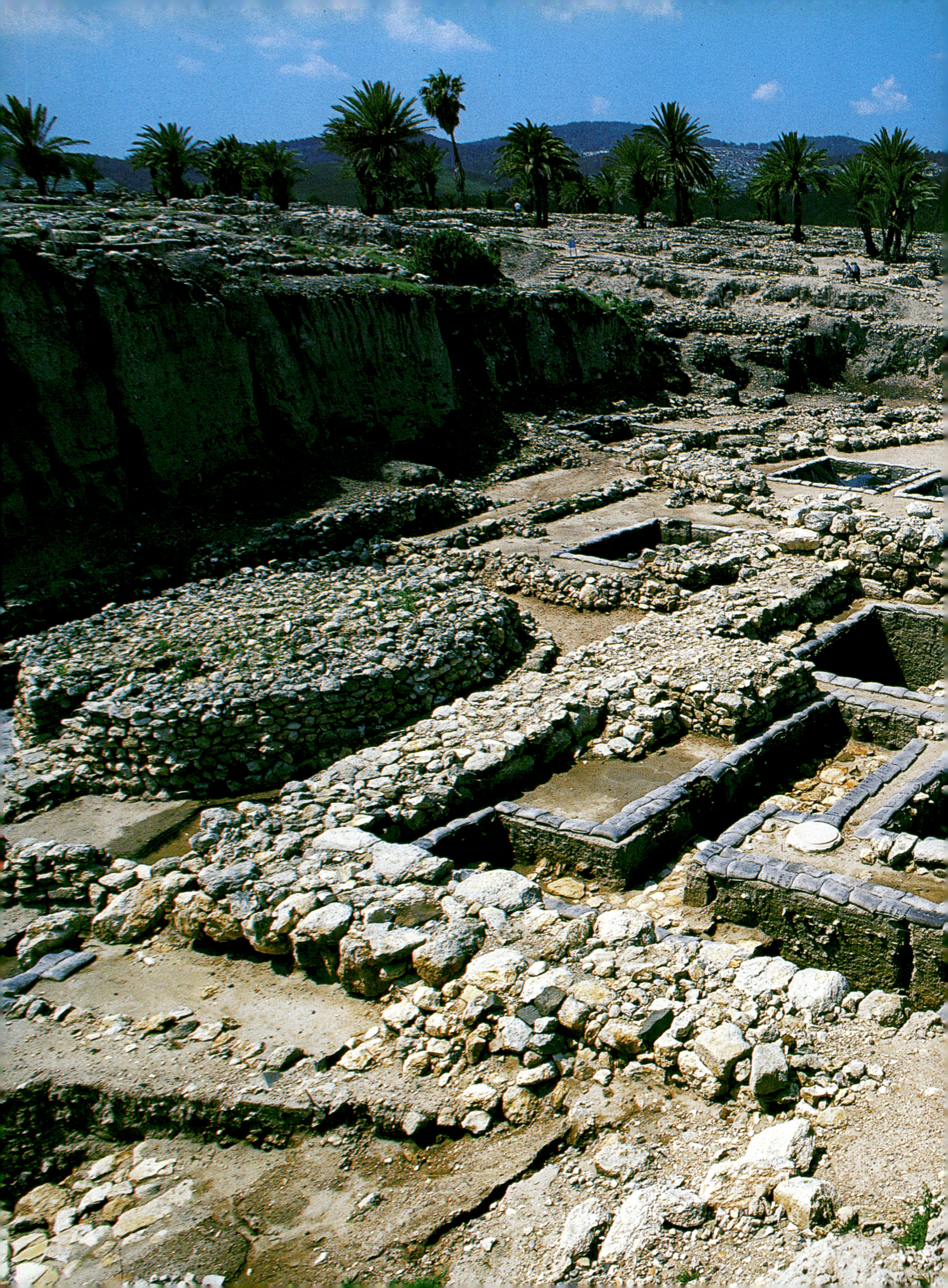

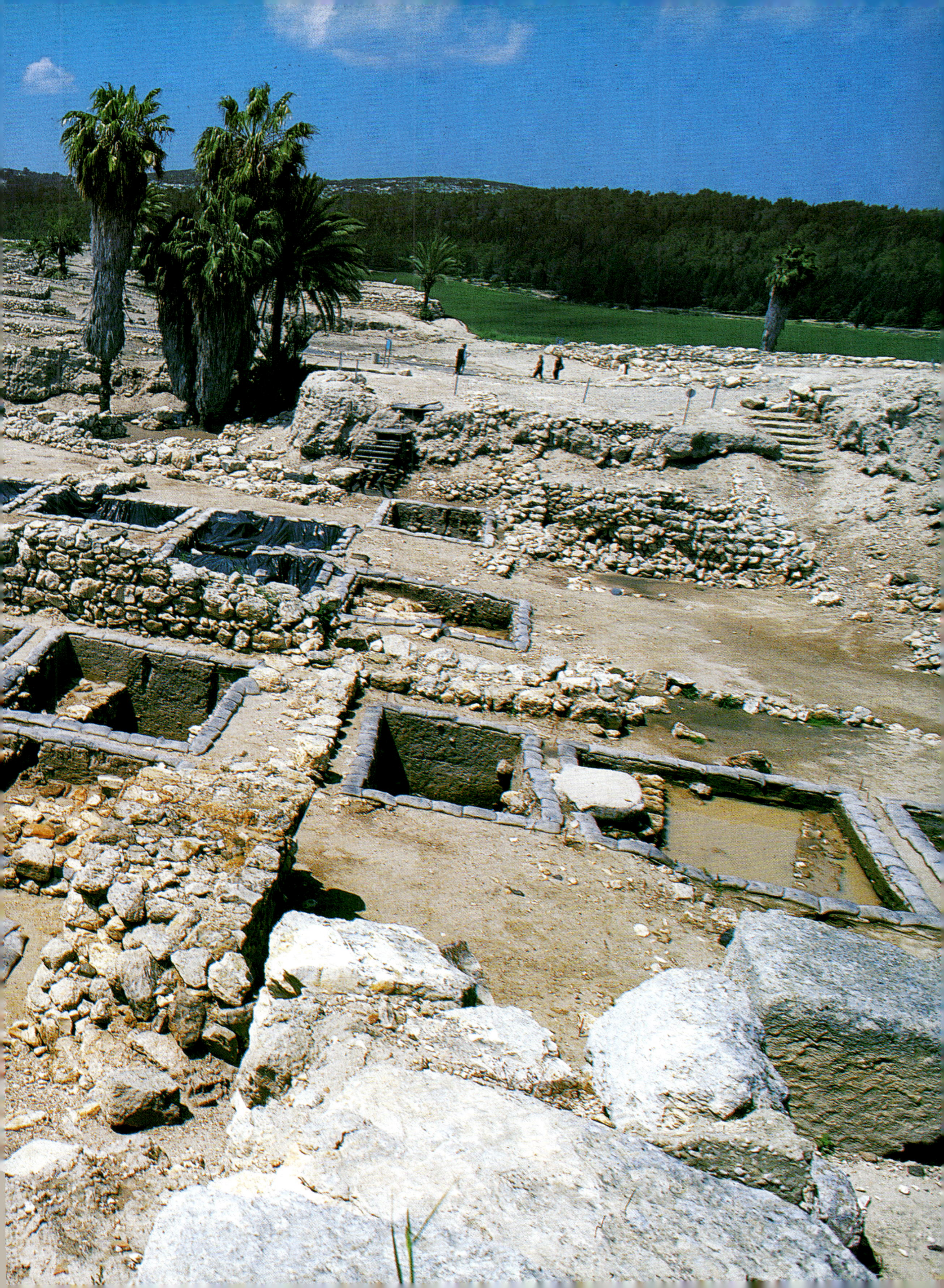

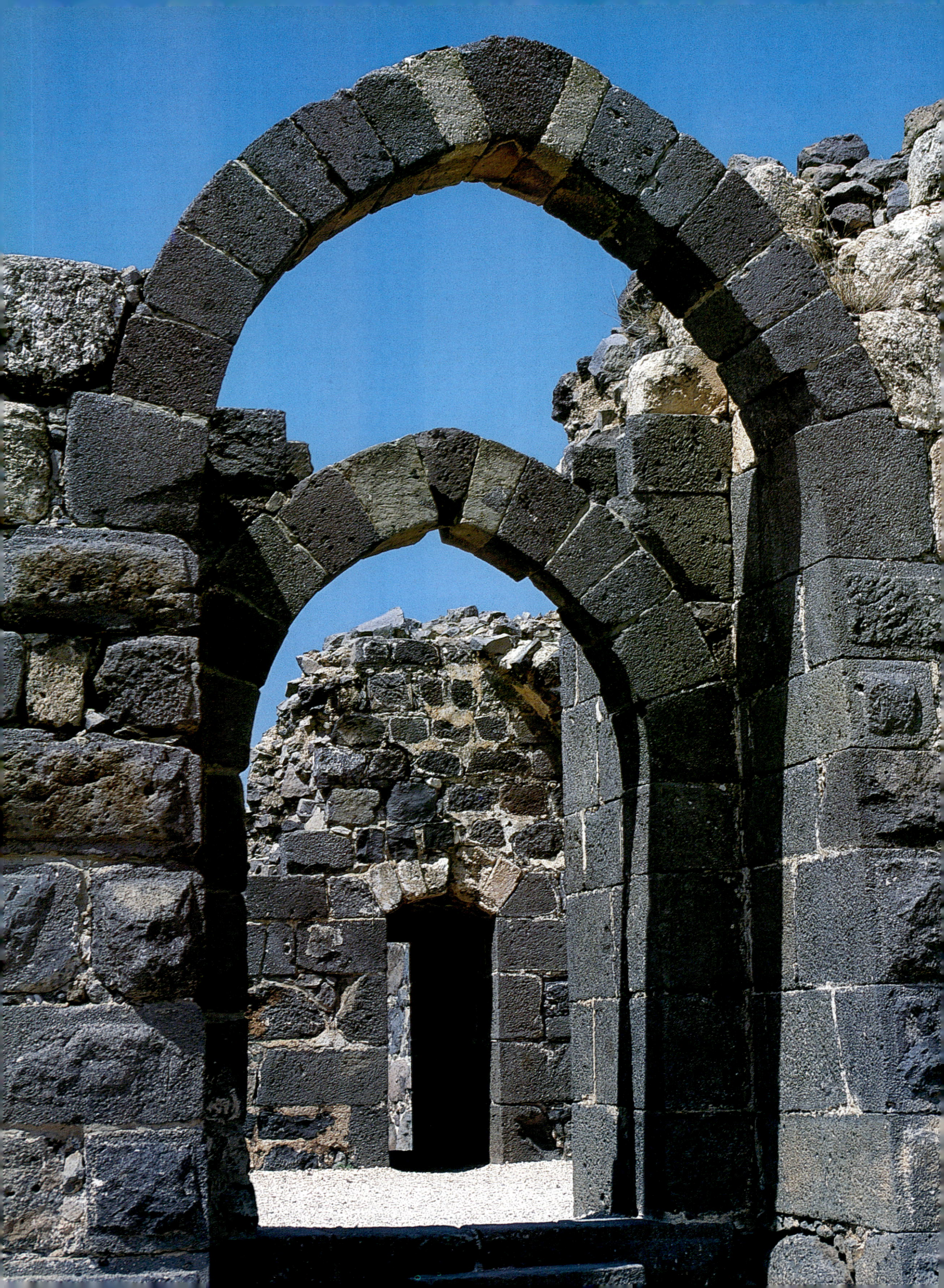

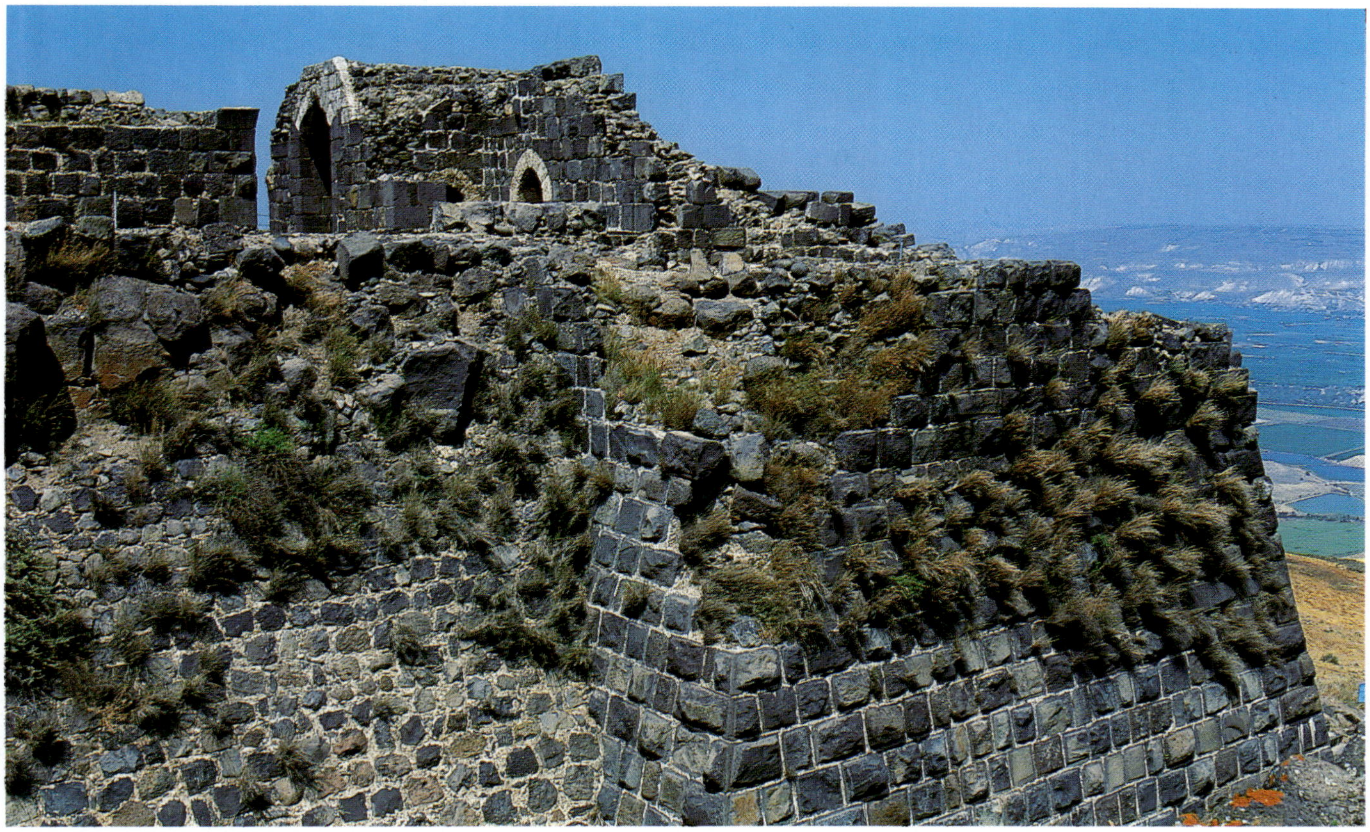

The Crusader fortress of Belvoir, dating from the twelfth century.

At that time, the *kibbutzim* were the showcase of Israel. People came to show their respect for these new kinds of Jews, who had managed to make their lives a daily miracle, building neat villages on the marshes, which they had successfully drained. They embodied the hopes of a generation, by restoring the pride of a nation bruised and decimated after the Shoah." The Jezreel Valley was not a particularly difficult area to cultivate, unlike the Jordan Valley, which had to be drained, or the part of the Negev Desert, which has been made fertile by a combination of hard work and advanced technology. Nevertheless, it has always been a model of productivity, at the cutting edge of agricultural research, especially with regard to irrigation methods, the selection of seeds and fertilisers, and crop-rotation techniques. Among the 260 working *kibbutzim* in the country, which employ around 180,000 people, some of the larger communities such as those of Israel or Harod are still farming land in the valley, often specialising in a particular fruit or vegetable crop or in raising animals.

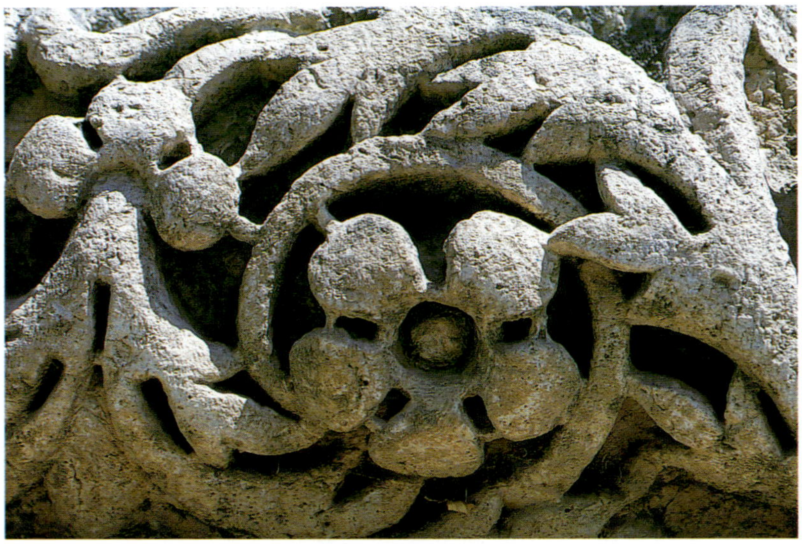

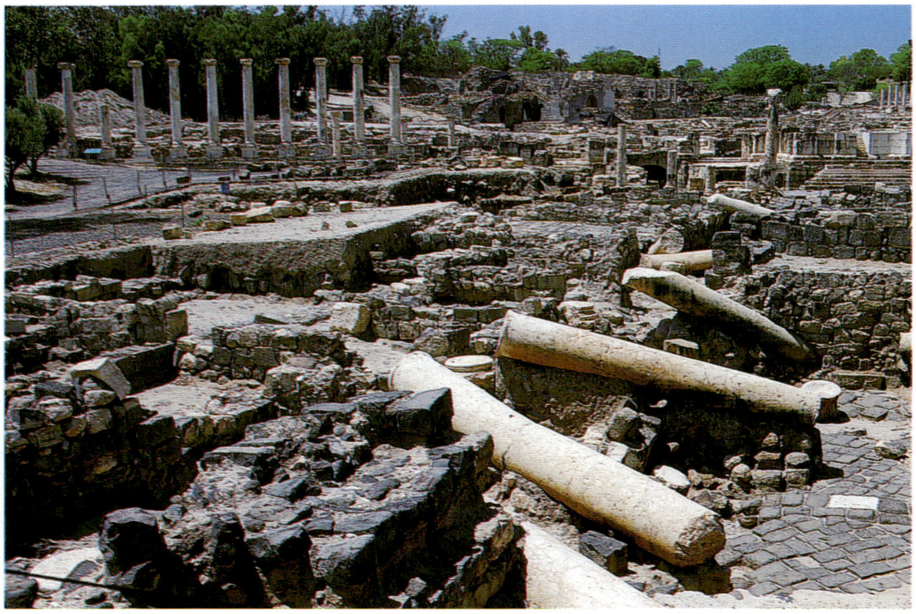

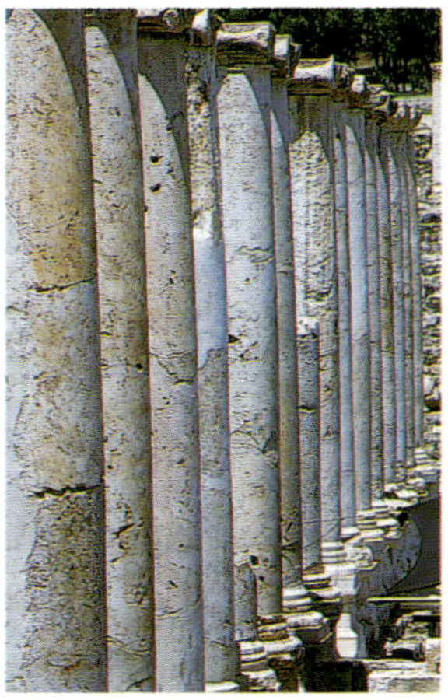

The archaeological remains on the site of Beit Shean bear witness to the town-planning skills of the Romans and Byzantines.

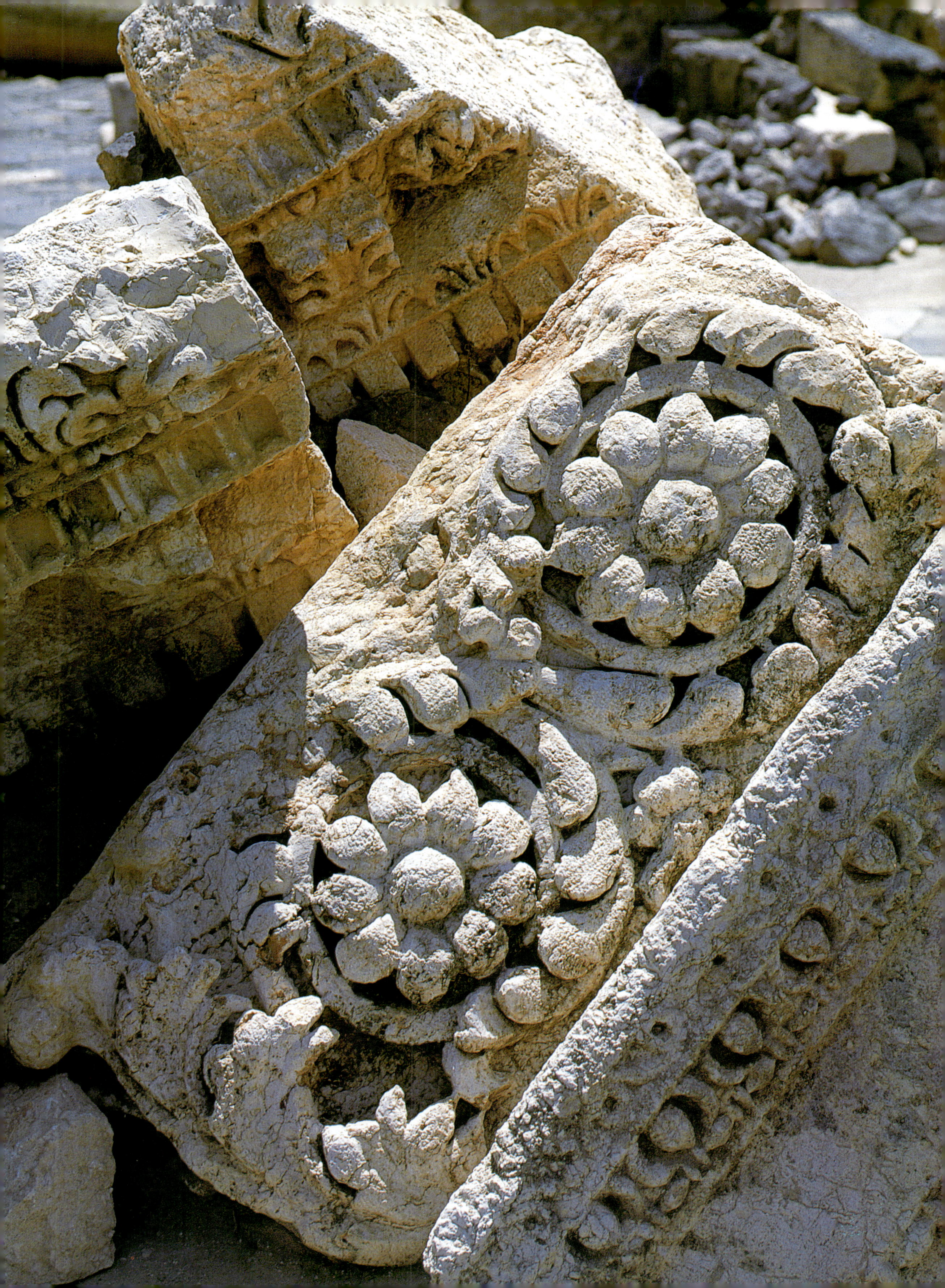

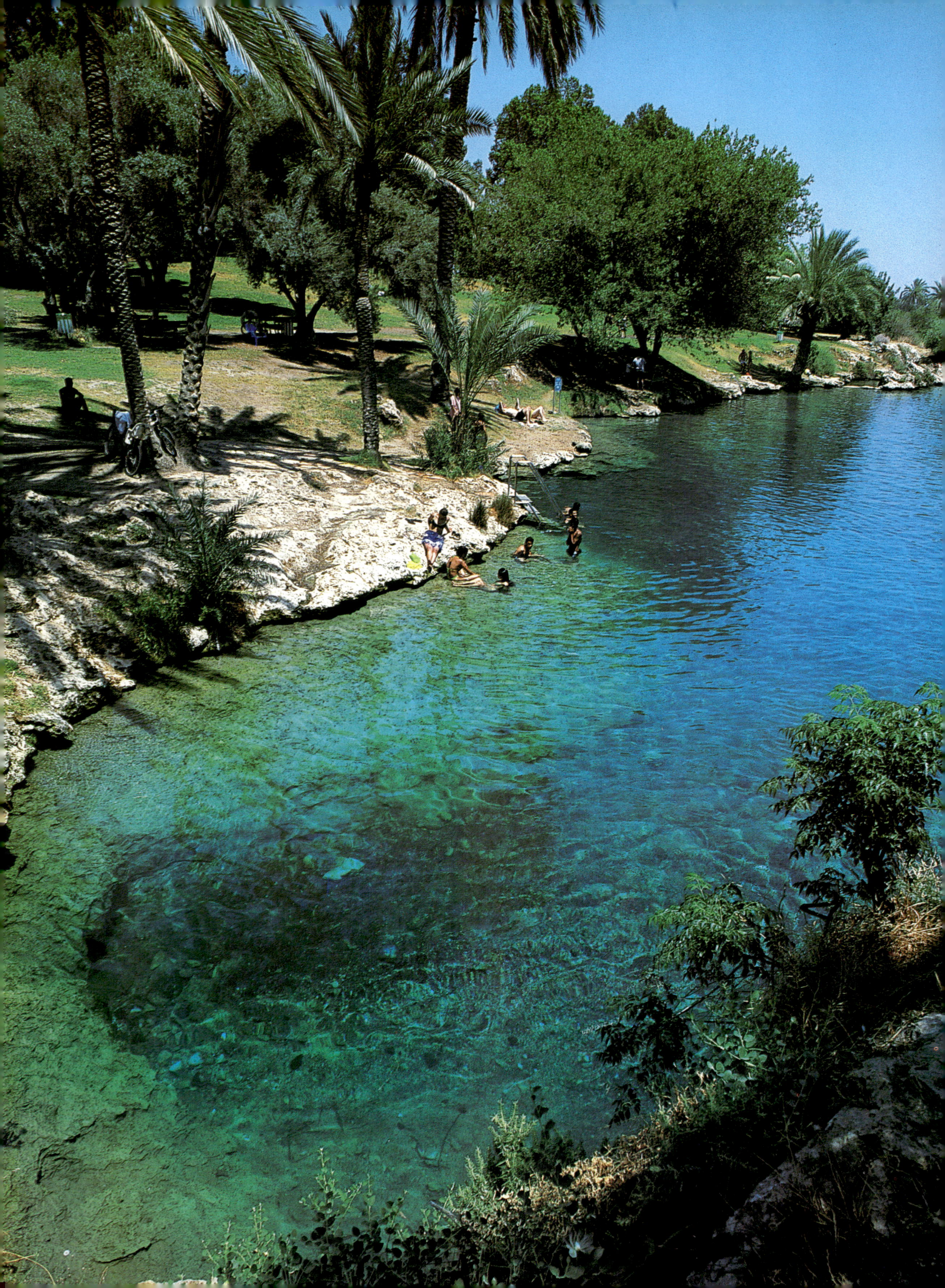

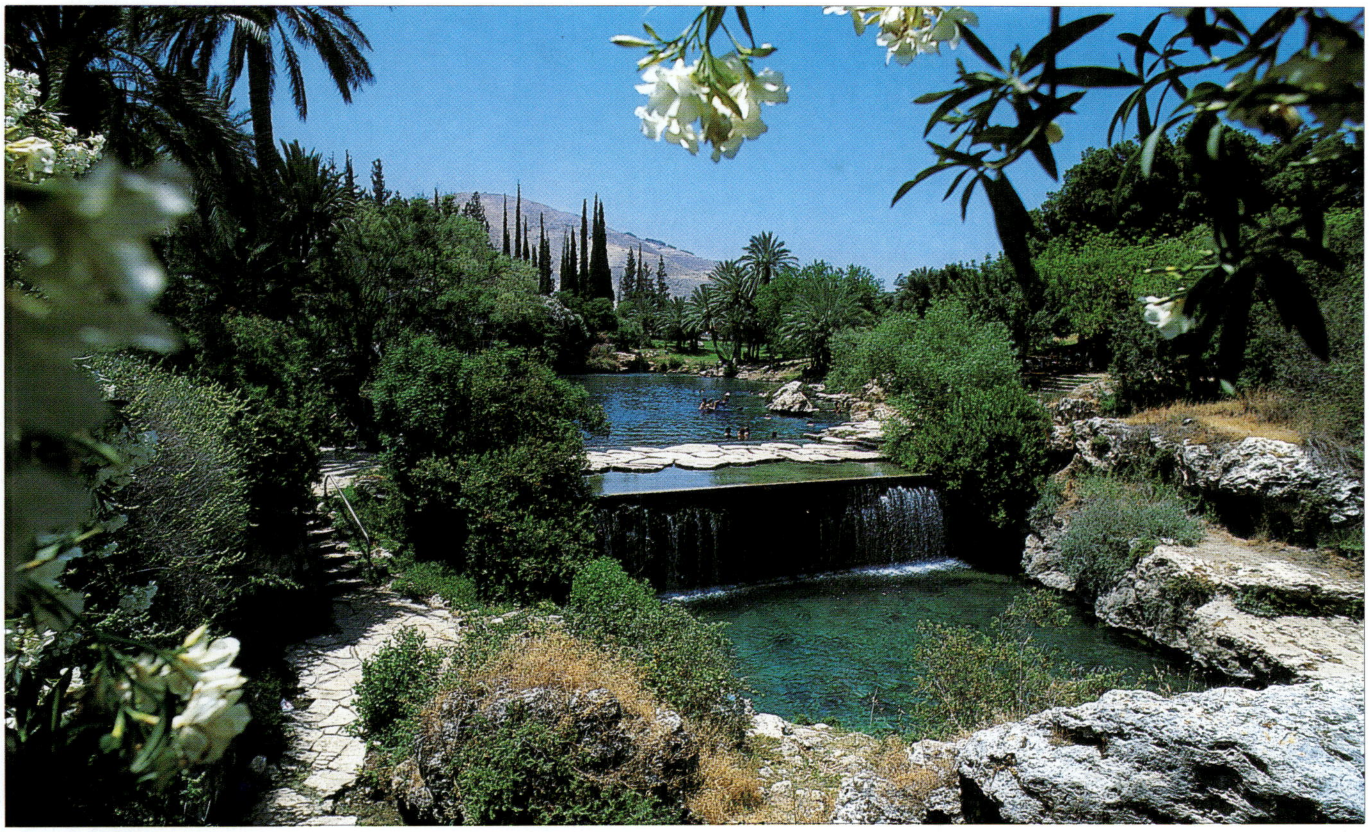

The hot springs and natural swimming-pools of Gan Ha Shelosha.

• Hammat Gader •

Bathing in the hot springs is one of the Israelis' favourite water-sports, even though they are already used to all kinds of aquatic pleasures. The five springs of Hammat Gader were already known to the Romans. The remarkable remains of the complex infrastructure of the bath-house they built around them survive to this day, and the springs continue to gush with waters adorned with healing properties, warmed by volcanic activity deep in the earth. Many families come to spend a day of leisure in the park, which has been laid out around the springs, and to enjoy the mineral-rich water, whose temperature varies between 30° and 50 °C (86° and 122 °F). Close to these natural wonders, overlooking the Yarmuk Valley to the south-west of Lake Tiberias, you can also find a Roman theatre, the ruins of a Roman bath-house, an old mosque, a former synagogue, and even a crocodile farm.

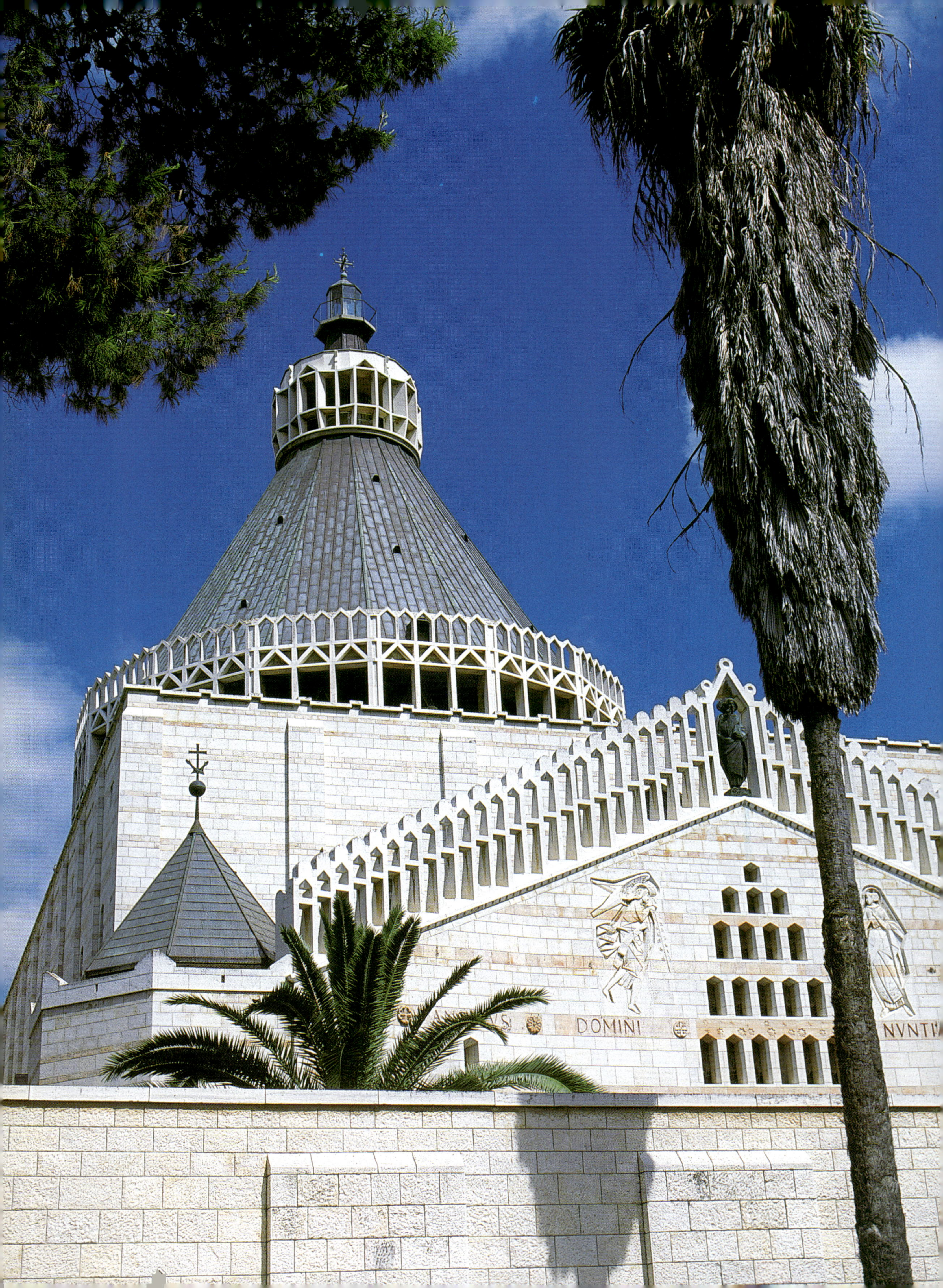
DOMINI

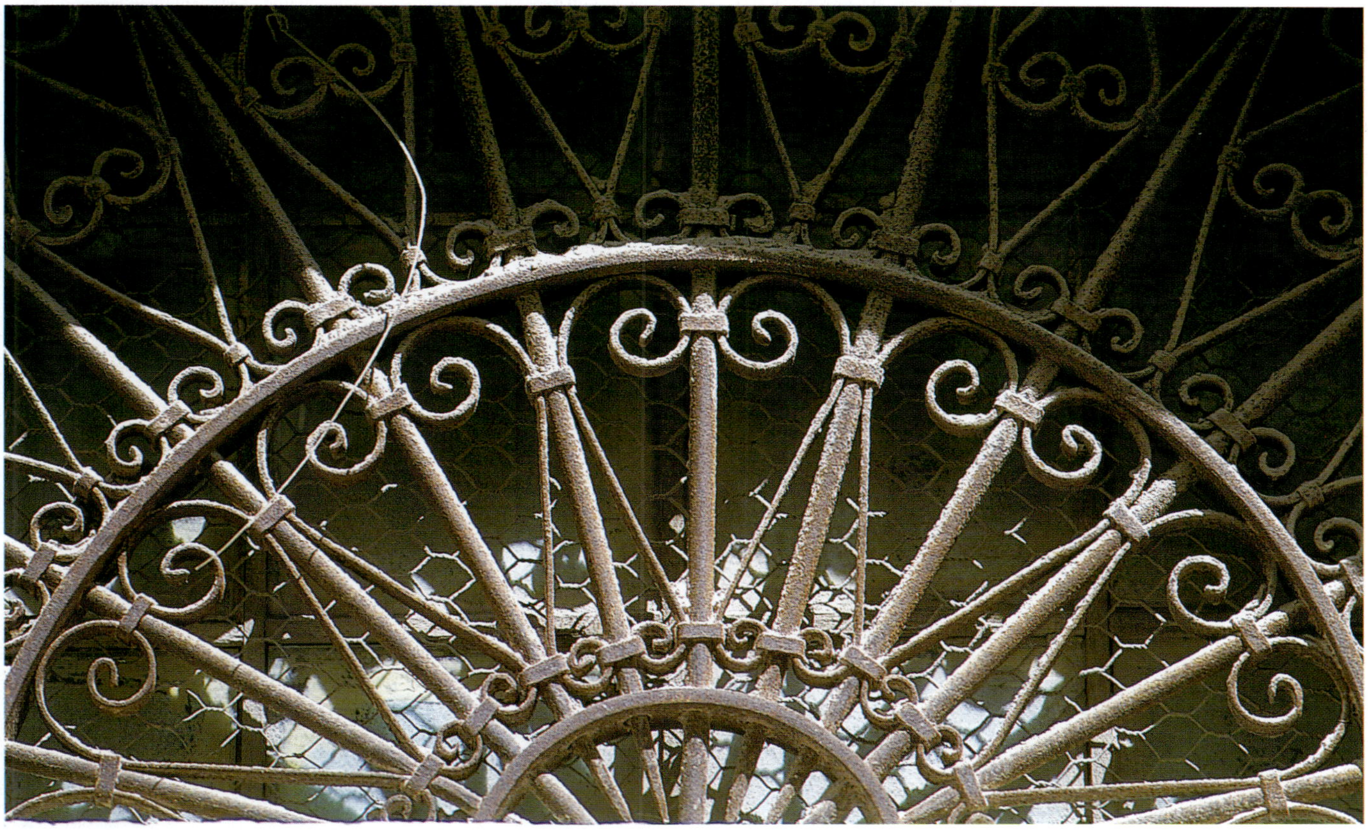

Detail of the gate of a house in Nazareth.
Facing page:
The church of the Annunciation in Nazareth, built in 1969, is the largest church in the Middle East.

The landscapes they fashion are immensely beautiful; each plot of cultivated land sends forth a riot of colour. But without going so far as to talk of a decline, it seems that the *kibbutzim* are experiencing a certain disaffection in favour of the *moshavim.* These are no longer communities whose members work humbly for the common good, but farmers' co-operatives, where people help one another and share some of the means of production in order to improve their productivity and incomes.

As you penetrate further into this region, which for Christians represents the land of their spiritual roots, Nazareth soon comes into view. The four gospels tell us that this town clinging to the hillsides was the place where Christ – Jesus of Nazareth – spent his childhood and youth. Even before his birth, it was the place where the angel Gabriel announced to Mary that she would bear the holy child. Contrasting starkly with the biblical image which people may have nurtured deep inside themselves, Nazareth today is a town of 60,000 inhabitants, who suffer from all the ills of modern civilisation – such as the unending traffic jams which have

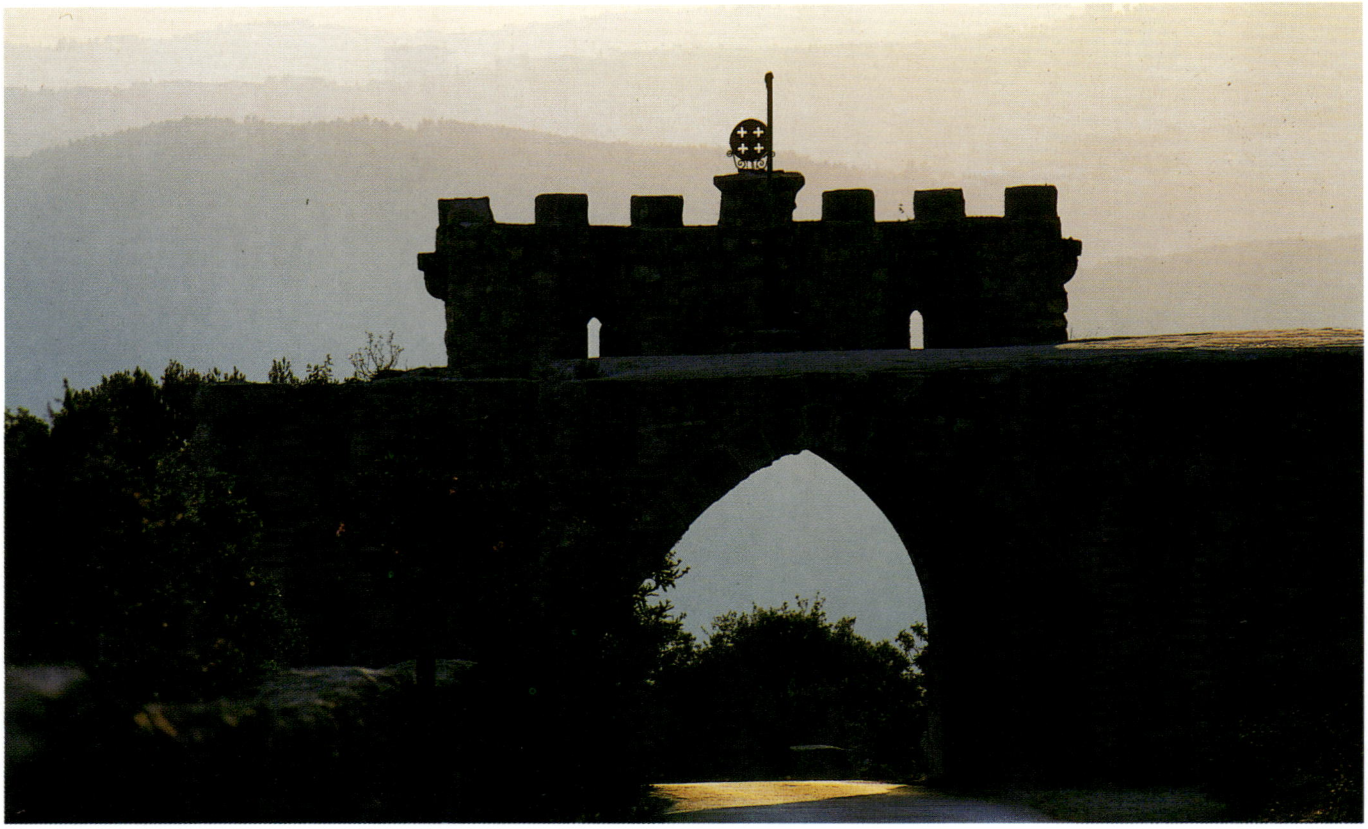

Mount Tabor, which rises in isolation to a height of almost 600 m (900 ft) above the plain of Jezreel, gives you the opportunity to enjoy a magnificent view of upper Galilee and especially of Lake Tiberias, notably from the pleasant Franciscan church built on the site of Jesus' transfiguration.
Following pages:
An old Orthodox monastery on Lake Tiberias.

become one of the features of this town with a single main street running through it.

Though Nazareth is considered to be the most important Arab town in Israel, every day a continuous flow of pilgrims and sightseers streams towards the many churches, the most important being the church of the Annunciation. This church, the largest in the Middle East, was built thirty years ago around the grotto marking the site of the annunciation, described by Luke (1:28–33) as follows: "The angel [Gabriel] went to her and said, 'Greetings, you who are highly favoured! The Lord is with you.' Mary was greatly troubled at his words, and wondered what kind of greeting this might be. But the angel said to her, 'Do not be afraid, Mary, you have found favour with God. You will be with child and give birth to a son, and you are to give him the name Jesus. He will be great and will be called the Son of the Most High. The Lord God will give him the throne of his father David, and he will reign over the house of Jacob for ever; his kingdom will never end.'"

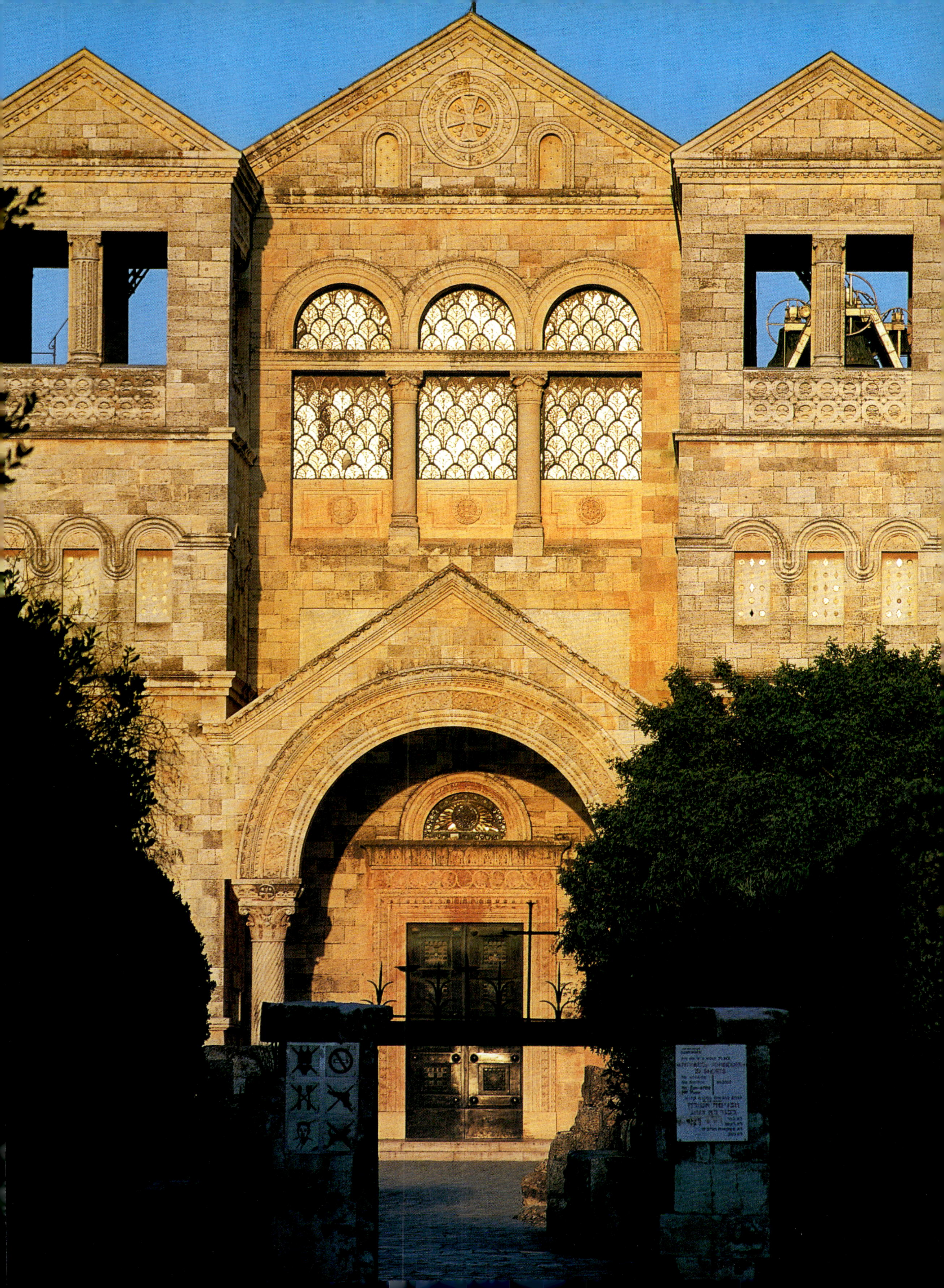

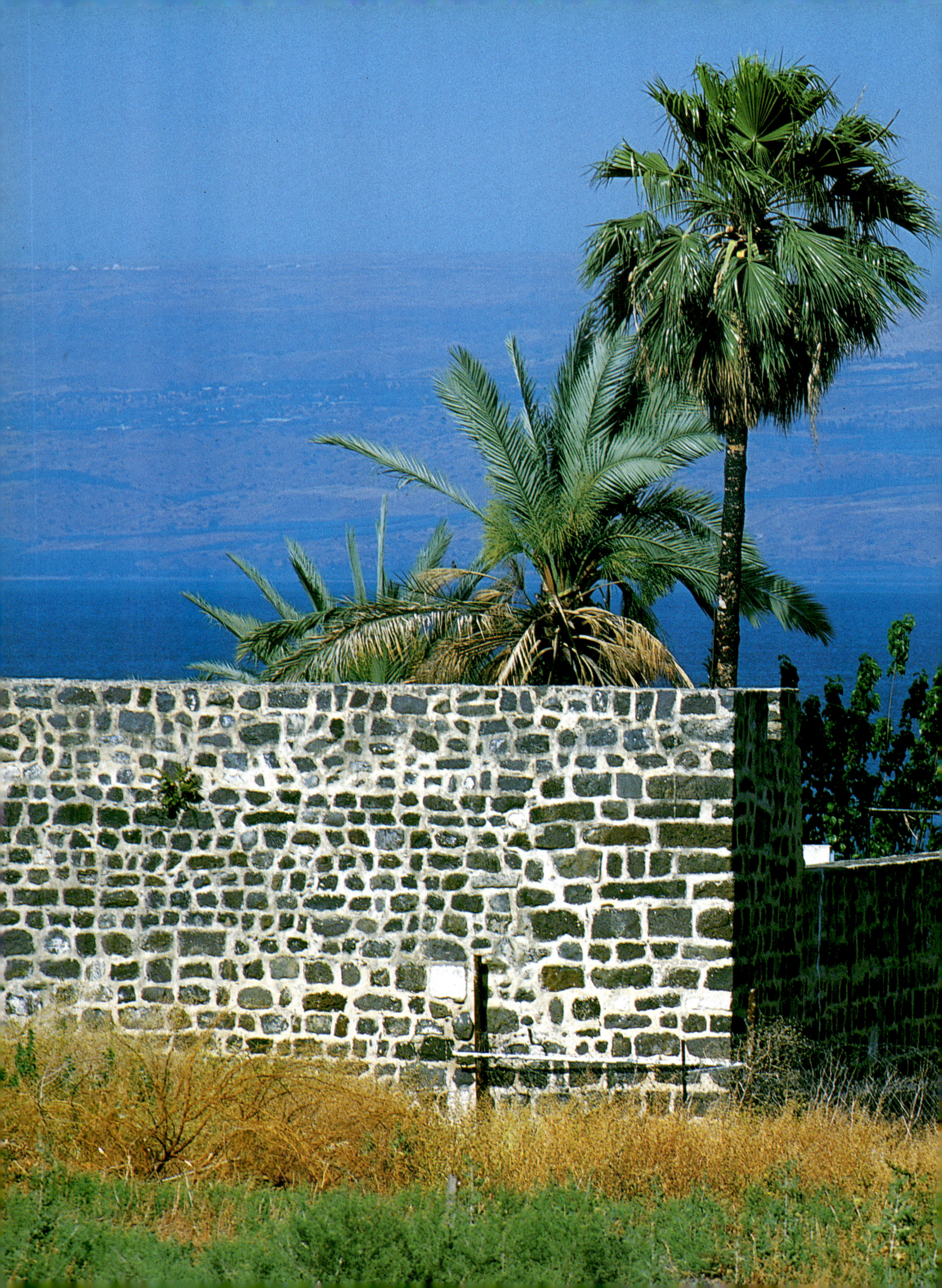

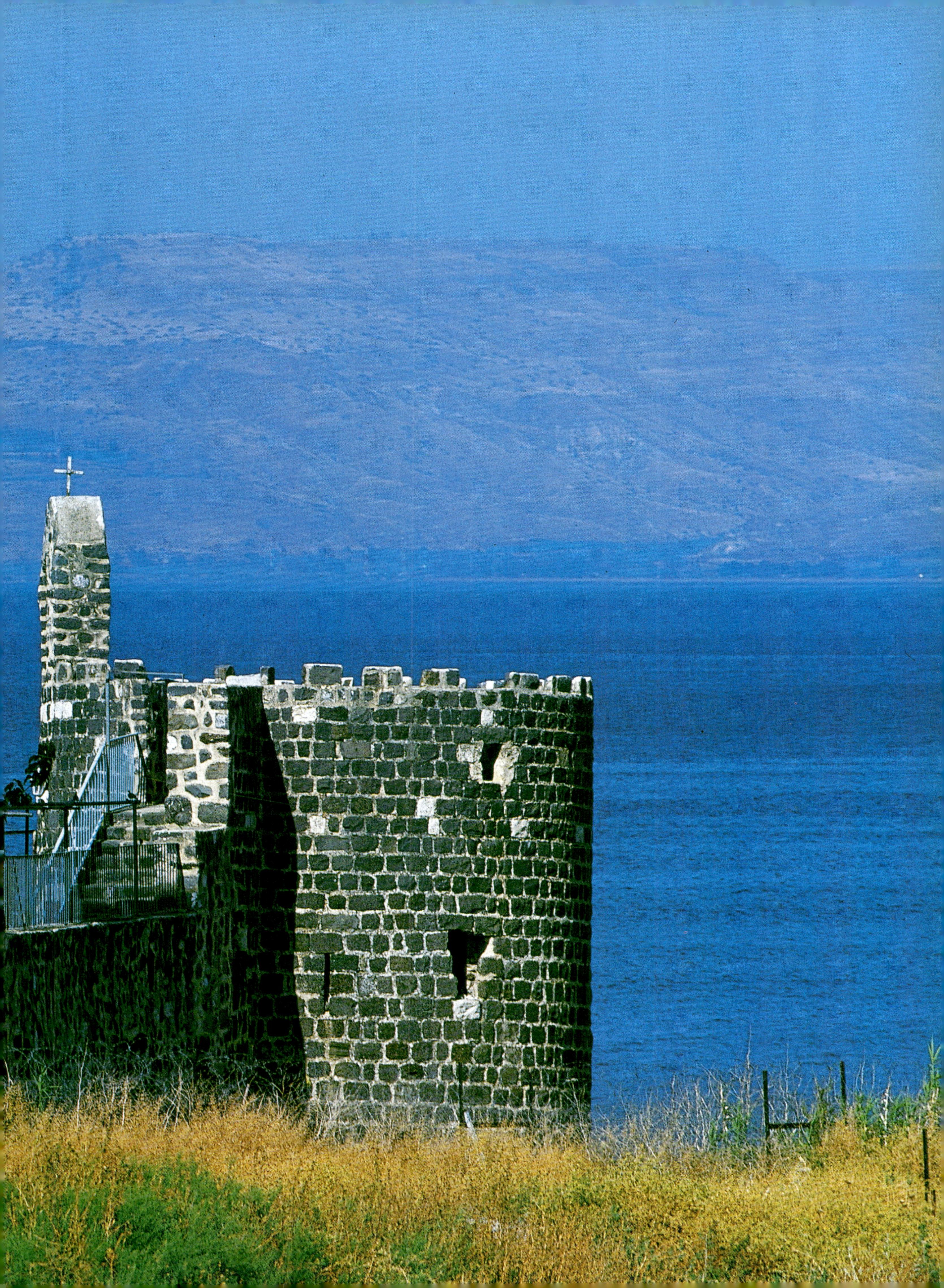

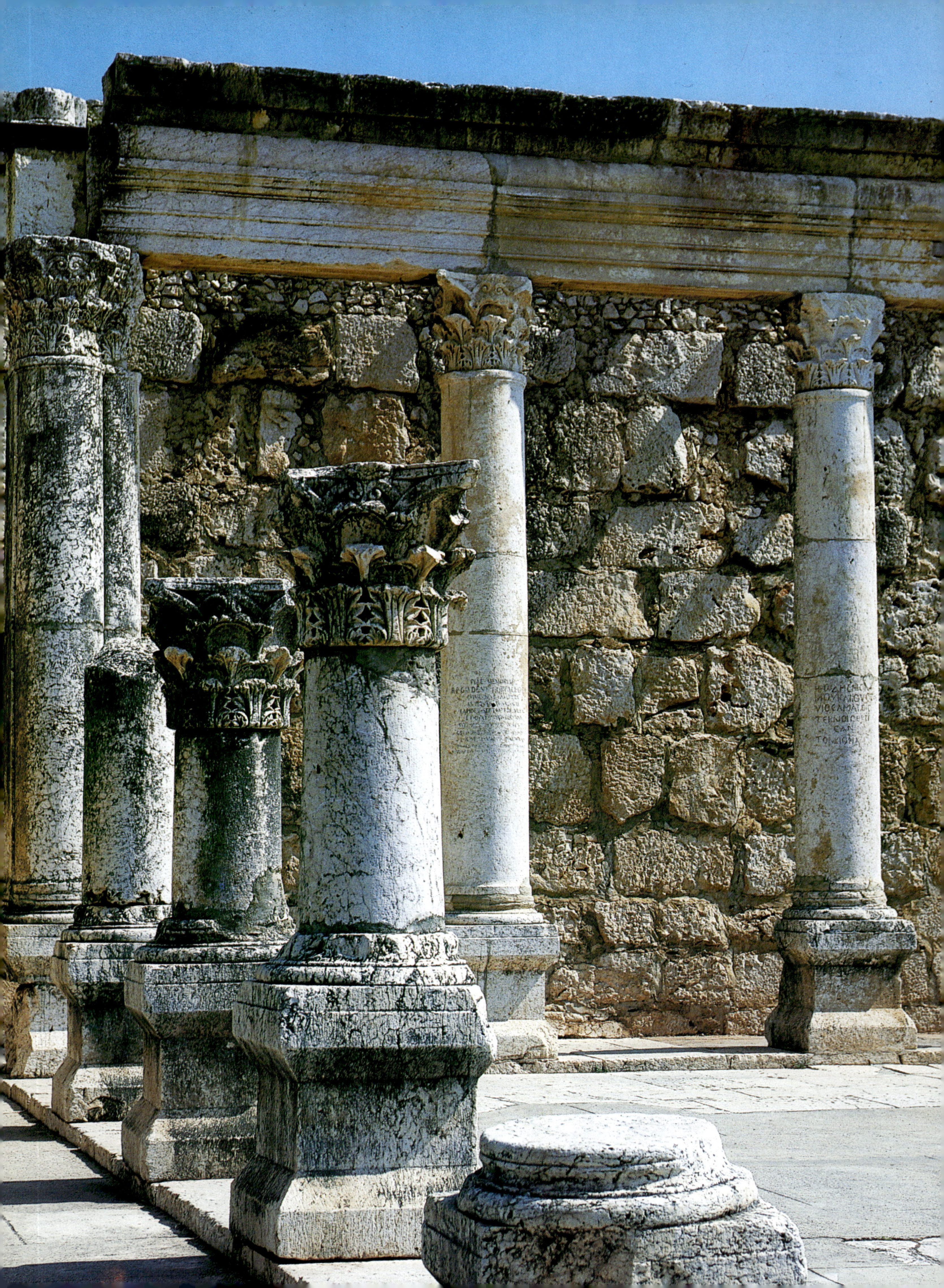

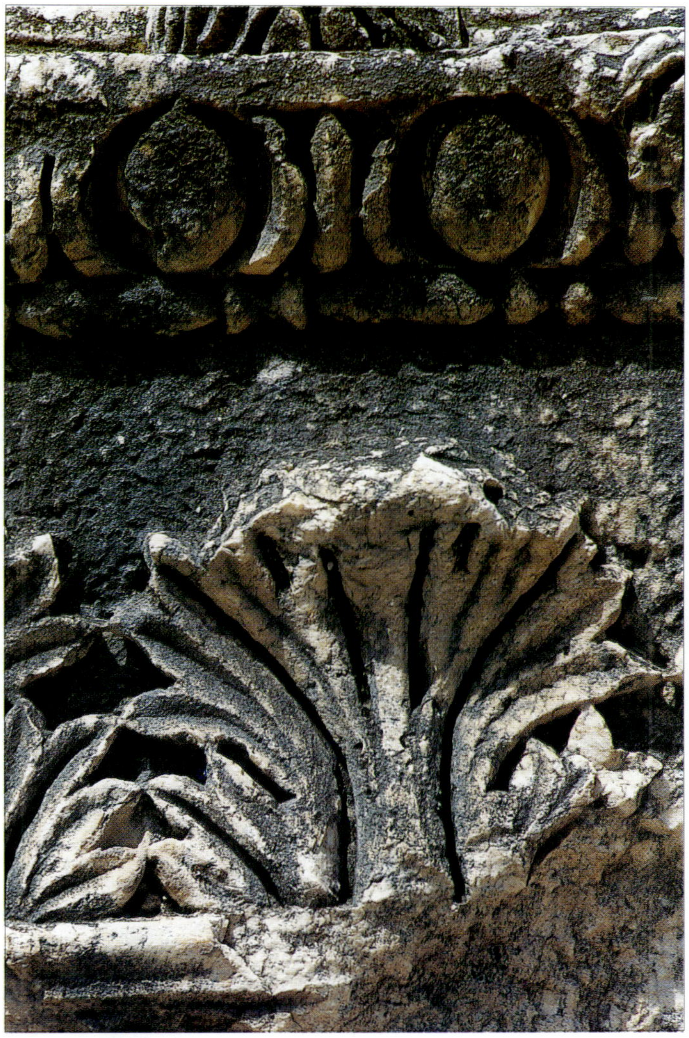

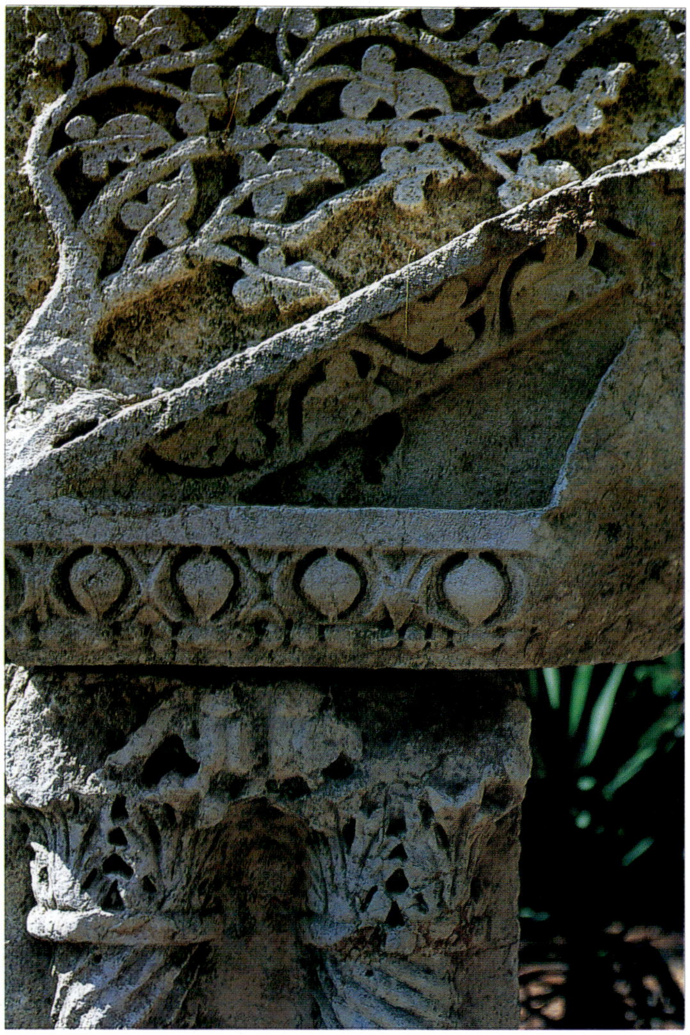

To celebrate the bimillennium of the annunciation, an urban improvement plan was drawn up, to provide the town with the infrastructure that would enable it to receive the many pilgrims wishing to spend some time in the place where it all began, in order to meditate and pray in the quiet little churches there. The pilgrims continue on their quest in the direction of the inland Sea of Galilee. After passing Cana – the site of Jesus' first miracle, when he turned the water into wine at a wedding – which now boasts three churches (a Franciscan church, a Greek Orthodox church and a chapel), visitors can trace the other important events of Christ's ministry around the lake on which the Messiah walked. ("During the fourth watch of the night Jesus went out to them, walking on the lake." Matthew 14:25).

Capernaum is considered to be Jesus' town, where he came to preach with Peter the fisherman, after leaving Nazareth. The synagogue, built in 400 BC, whose columns are still standing, is the house of God where he went to pray.

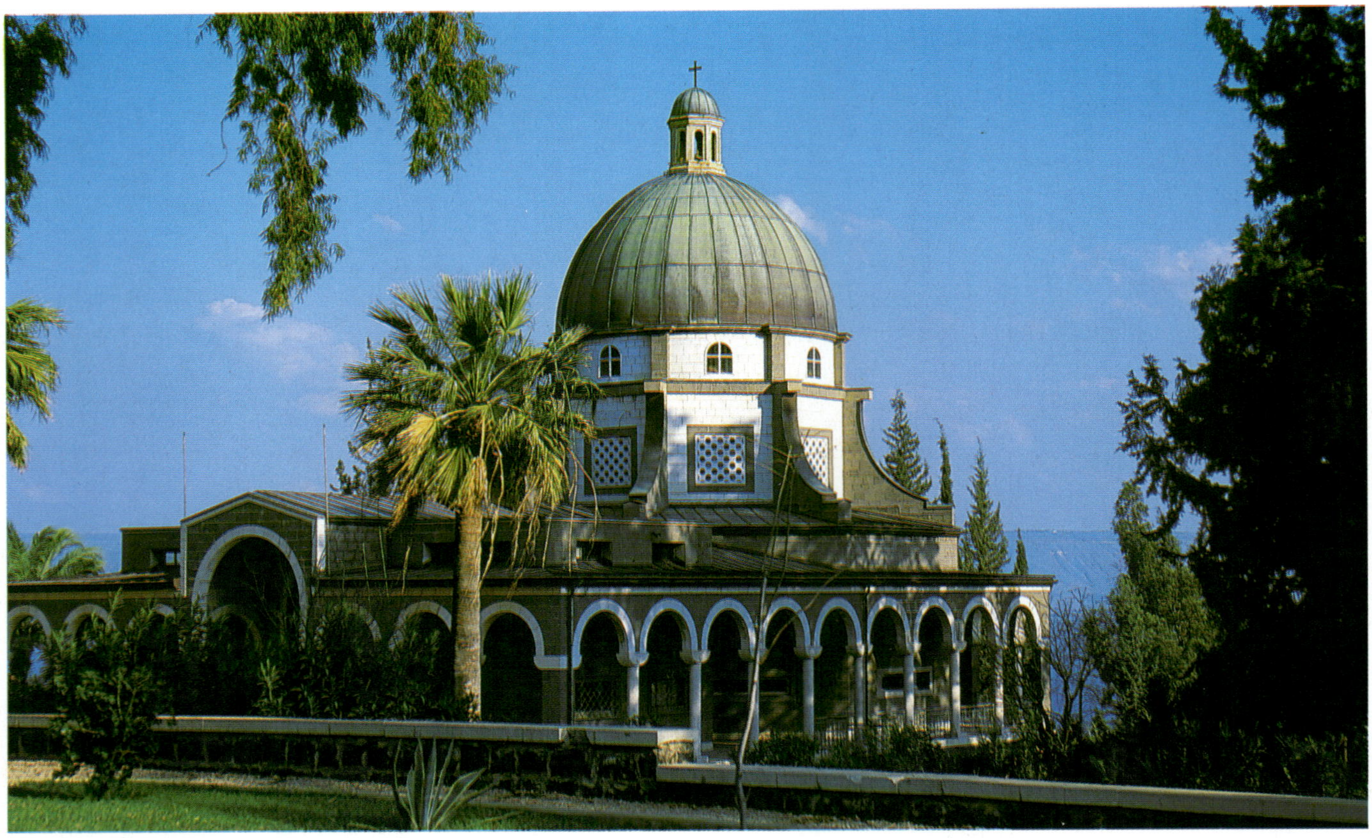

The monastery of the Beatitudes.
Facing page:
The Orthodox church in Capernaum.

But before they get there, visitors must cross undulating countryside, which has suddenly become dry and rocky, as though the trees and flowers which flecked the earlier hillsides had been mysteriously blown away. There are still a few olive trees clinging on here and there, and a few obstinately cultivated fields, but now the typical landscape is mainly stony desert. And just as an oasis appears after you have crossed the desert, so do the plantations surrounding the western shores of Lake Tiberias. They make a striking picture, because the cultivated land really stands out. Banana, avocado, olive, palm, and pine trees are clustered together, forming a veritable paradise of greenery. Around these plantations, the wild plants covering the soil of the softly rounded hills, windswept and scorched by the sun, form a carpet of ever changing reflections, which has the power to compress time and evoke the atmosphere of the pastoral poetry of biblical times.

Tabga which, according to tradition, is the site of the feeding of the five thousand (Matthew 14:19), and more especially Capernaum, the town

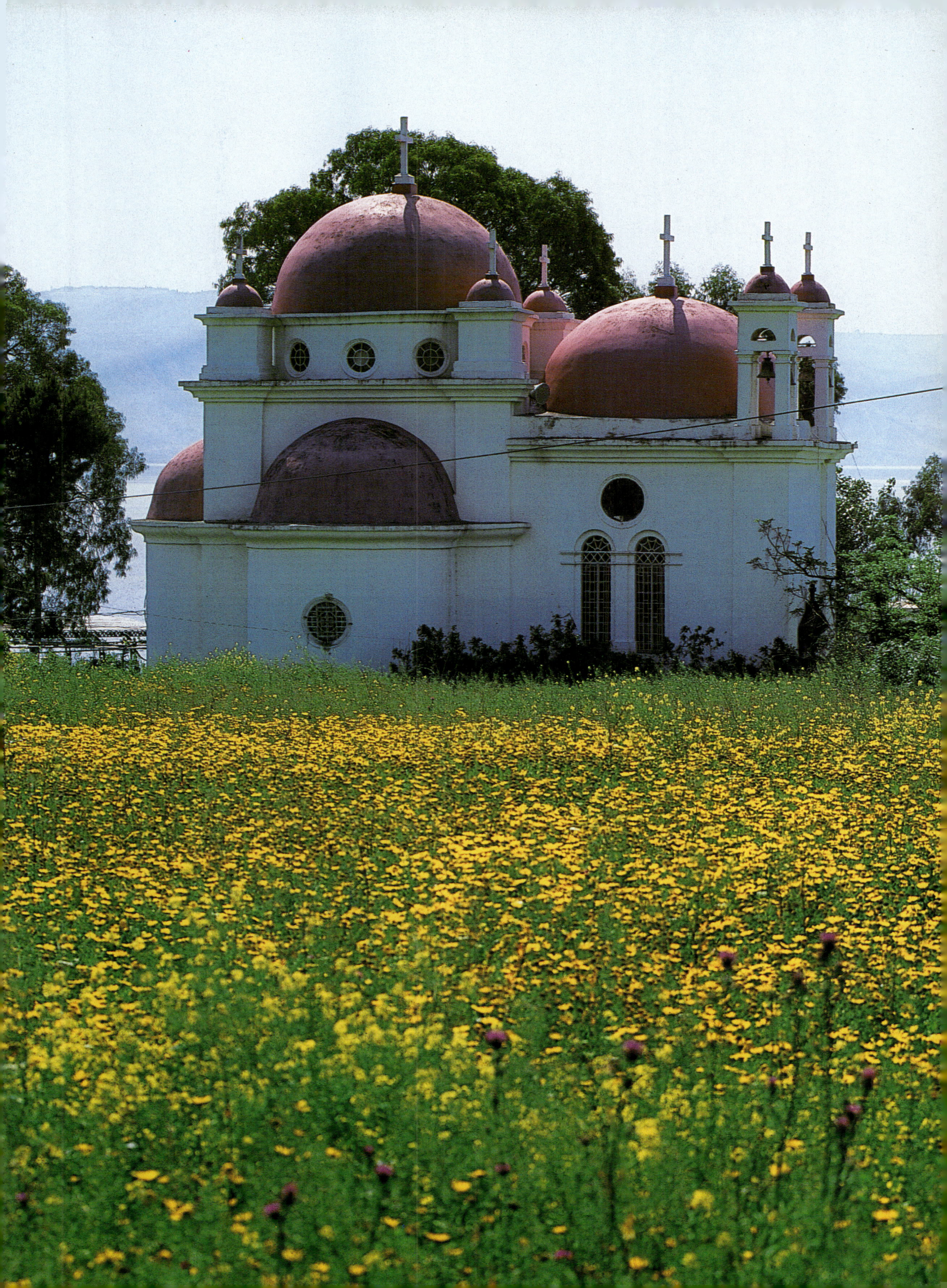

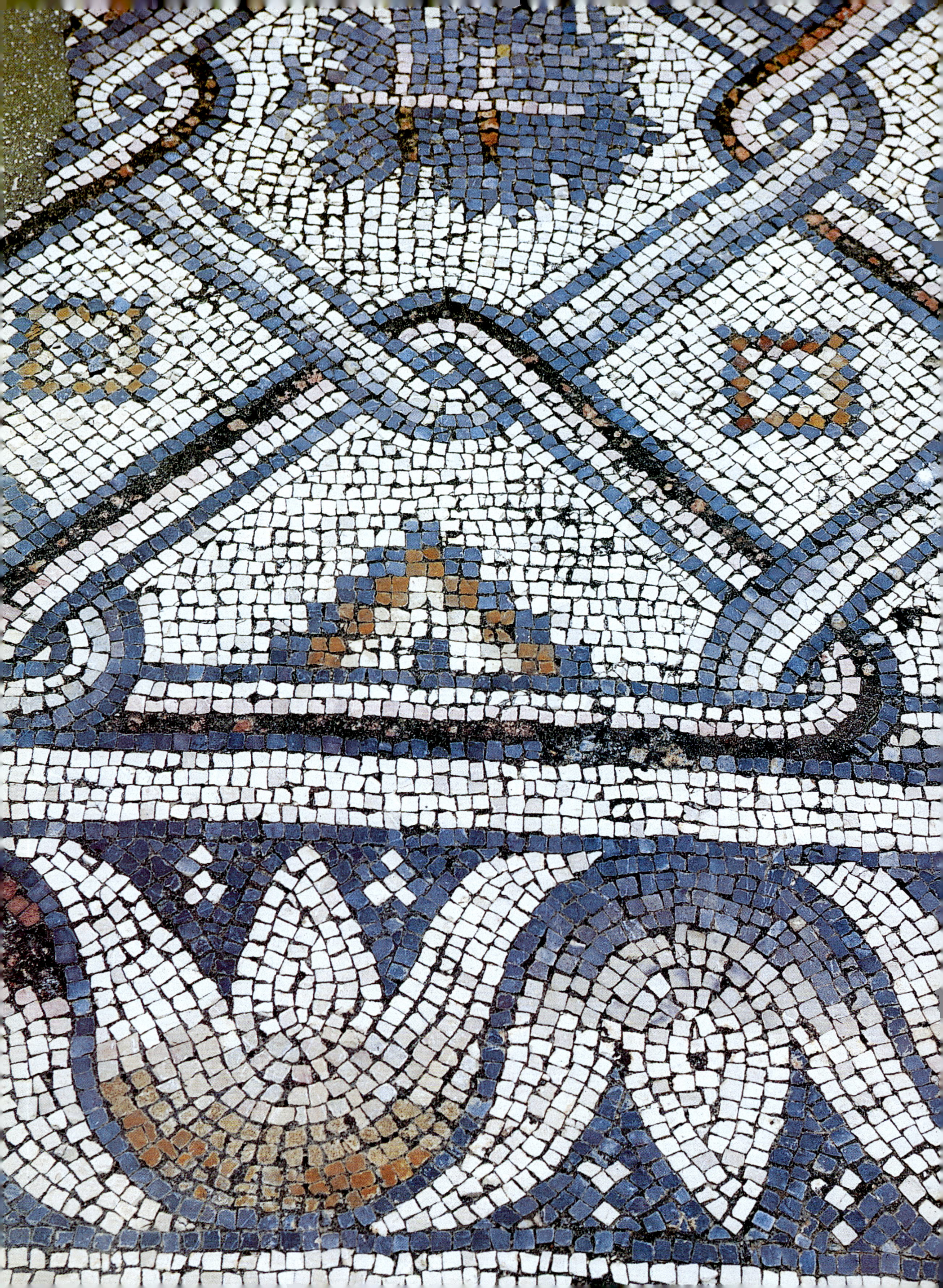

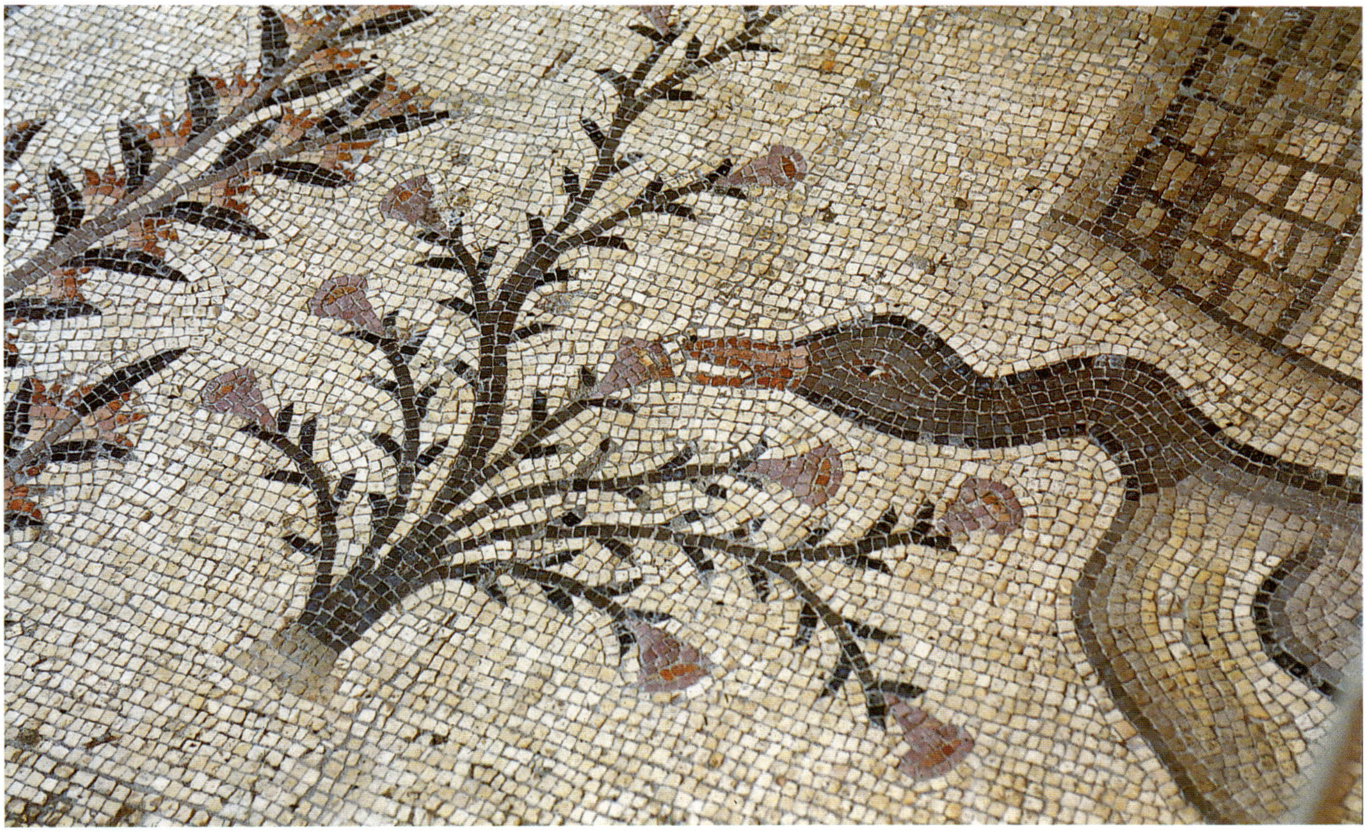

Fourth-century mosaic from Tabga.
Facing page:
Mosaic from the Byzantine convent on the site of Kursi, near Lake Tiberias.

where Jesus went to live after leaving Nazareth, must be the two most important places for Christians on the shores of the lake. Visitors can see the remains of Capernaum, which Jesus seems to have chosen for two reasons, according to historians. Firstly, unlike Nazareth, which was isolated, Capernaum was an important crossroads on the route between Damascus and Beit Shean, the big Roman city about 20 km (12 miles) from Lake Tiberias, which meant that Jesus' preaching could be heard by many people. And secondly, the town was a good way from Tiberias, where Herod Antipas had set up his capital, so that he would not have had to suffer the wrath of the political and religious leaders.

Tiberias is an important city, situated halfway along the western shore of the lake to which it has given its name – a lake which is 212 m (695 ft) below sea level. It is one of the four sacred cities of Judaism. The tombs of many of the sages of the Jewish tradition – that of the twelfth-century Moses Maimonides, for instance, who tried to show that faith and reason were not incompatible – bear witness to its sacred character.

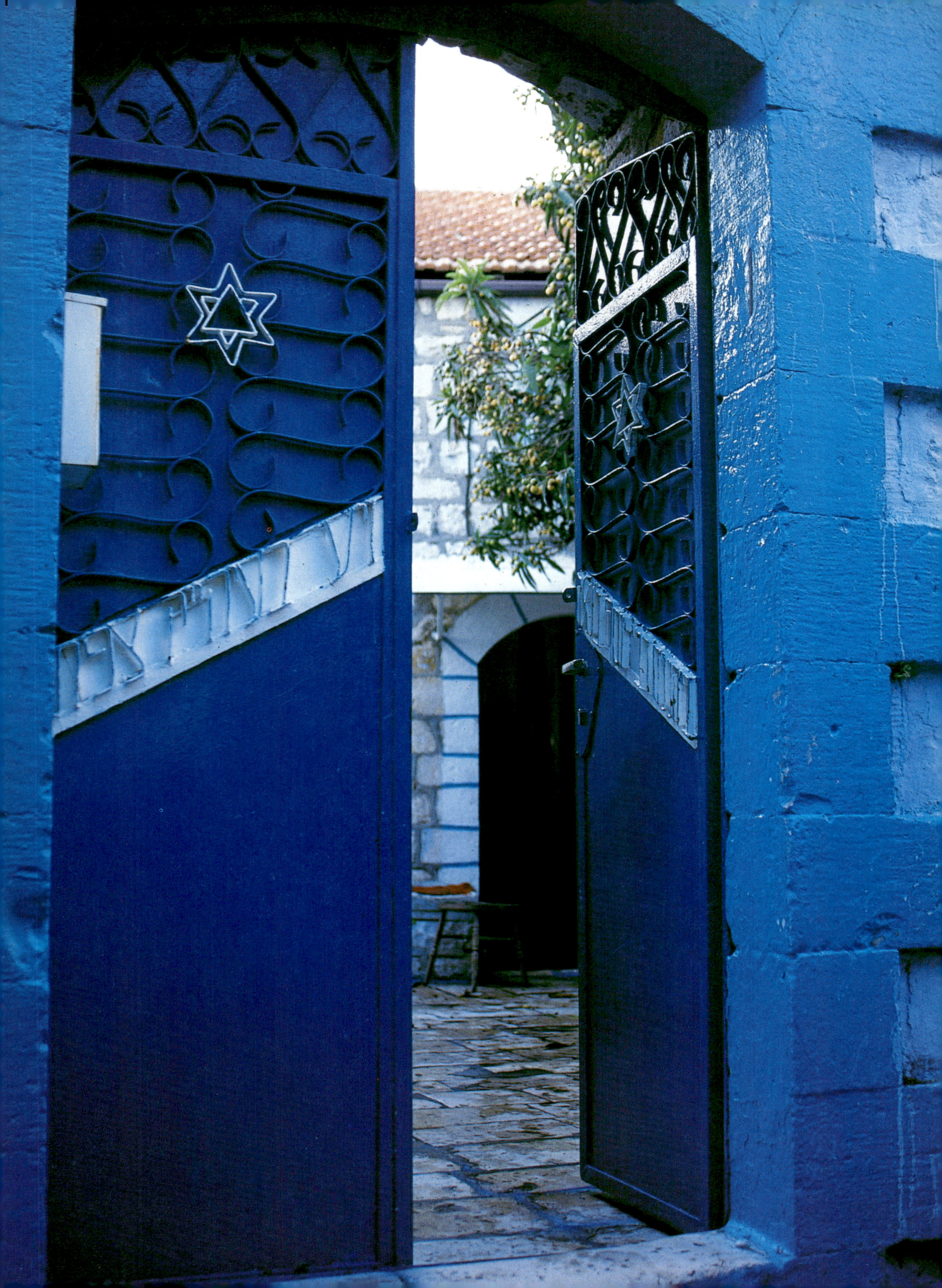

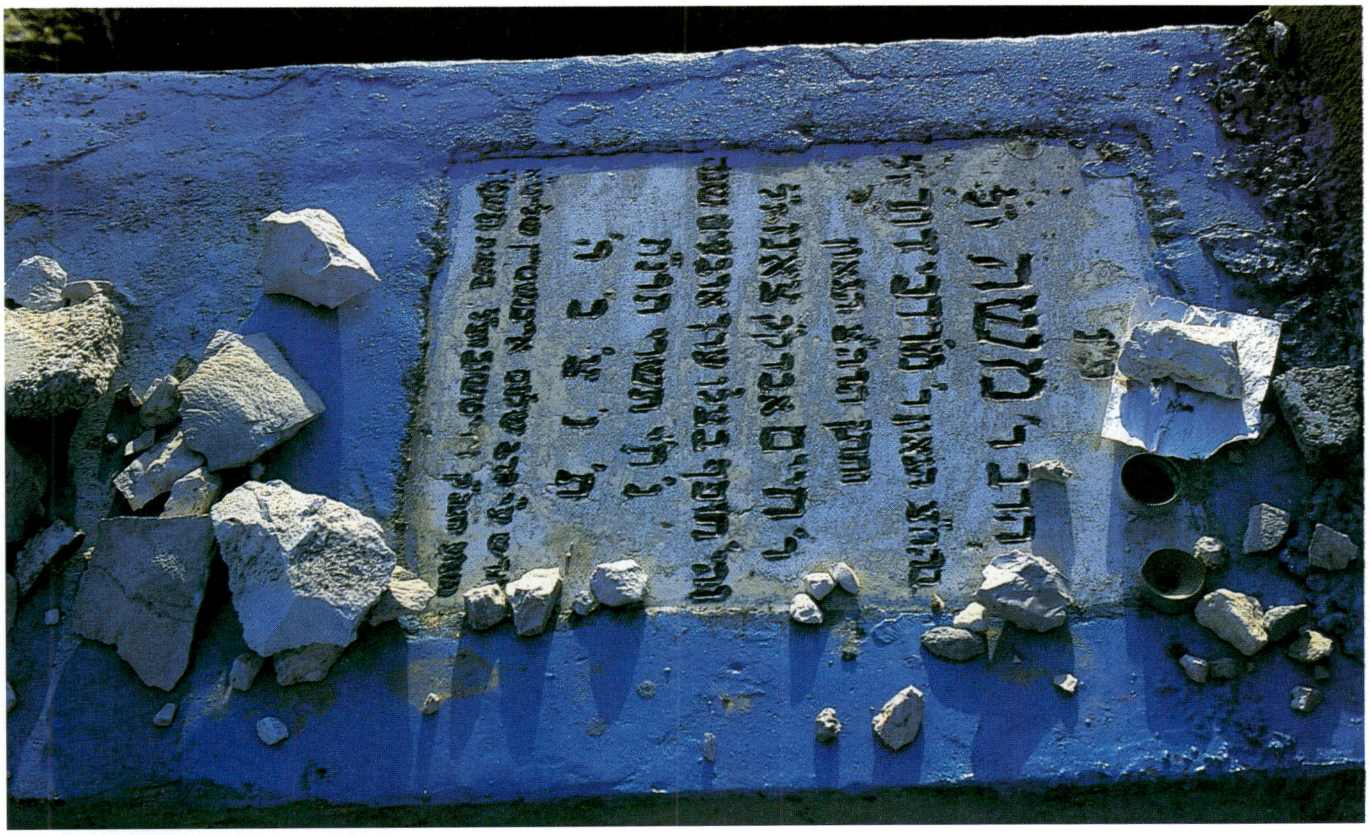

However, this aspect is no longer as vital as it was in the glorious days of the first few centuries of the Christian era, when the city was a lively centre of Jewish academic life. Nowadays, artificially created beaches on the lake shore, facilities for sailors, the spa, and the hot springs are the chief tourist attractions which give this sunny city its high reputation as a popular seaside resort. This is far from being the case for Safed (or Zefat), the other sacred city of Judaism in Galilee, which has preserved its tranquillity, tucked away on the heights of Mount Canaan. To reach it, you have to follow a twisting road, rising above of the north of the lake. The view from the road is magnificent, and puts you in the right frame of mind to approach this magical, mysterious city. In the sixteenth century it was the great Jewish cabbalistic centre, and has kept the aura of a mystical city, where each prayer seems pregnant with meaning.

The labyrinth of narrow streets winding over the hill; the doors and windows, painted blue to bring you closer to heaven and ward off evil spirits; the little synagogues, like that of Aari Akadosh, redolent of faith;

The cemetery of Safed is the most sacred in the country, next to that of Jerusalem. There are no flowers on the graves, but stones are placed there in memory of the dead.
Facing page:
The entrance to one of the sacred synagogues of Safed (Zefat). The blue brings you closer to heaven and wards off evil spirits.

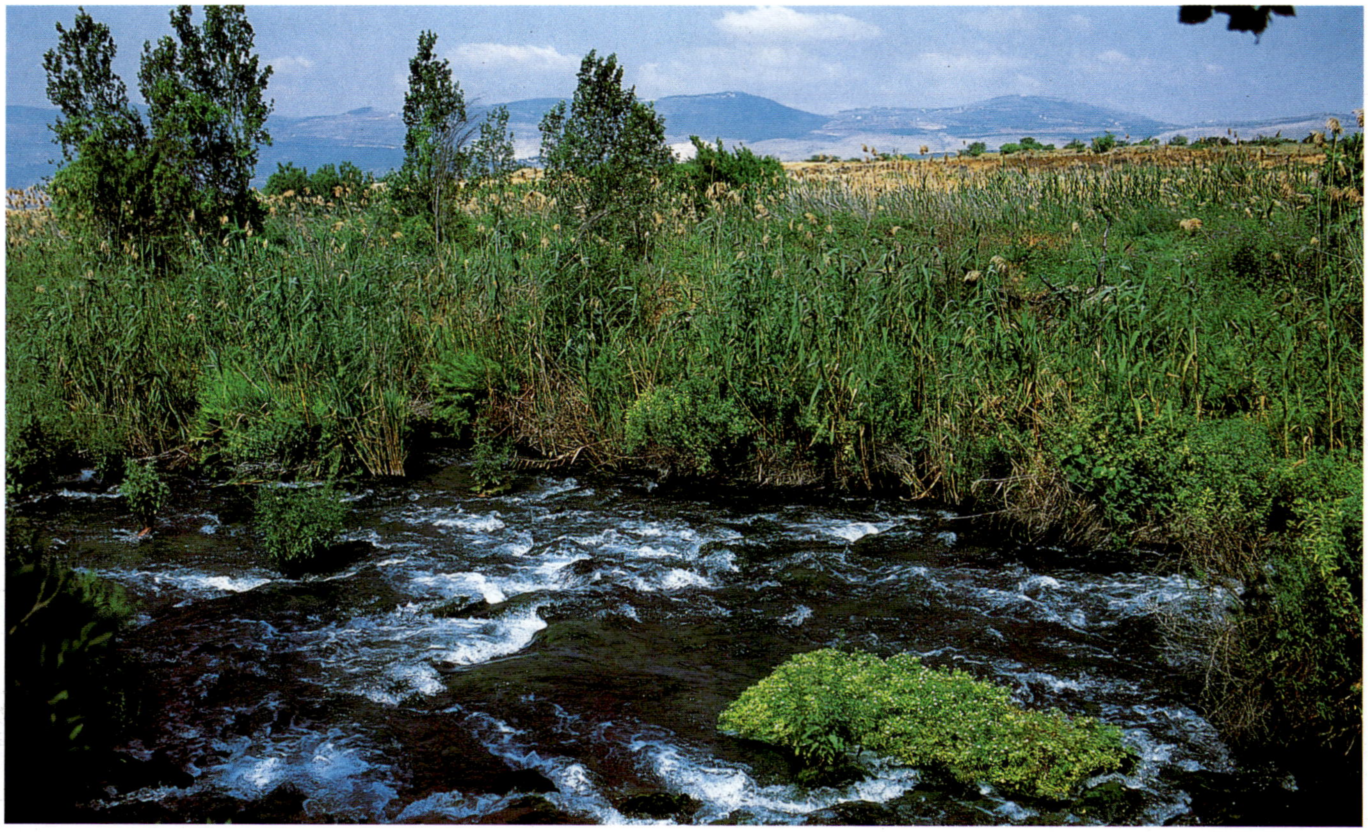

The River Dan is the longest and most important of the three Israeli sources of the Jordan.

the view over the valley formed between Mount Meron and the circle of wooded hills, rising like objects of contemplation at some distance from the city and from the cemetery – which is situated lower down the slope and considered (along with the cemetery of Jerusalem) to be the most sacred in the country – everything about this place conspires to make you fall under its spell. As you leave the city – always an emotional moment – and continue northwards towards upper Galilee, a series of remarkable landscapes is revealed. With the Golan Heights as a backdrop, there is a whole patchwork of well-kept plantations of olive, apple, peach, and apricot trees covering this part of a region mainly given over to cotton production. So the entire area is clothed in a mantle of green, but it is yellow too in summer, when the cotton is ripening, and white in autumn, at harvest-time.

Kiryat Shmona, the biggest town in the north, near the Lebanese border, is often mentioned in the media because of the rocket fire from the Shi'ite fighters of south Lebanon. It has a cosmopolitan air, especially on

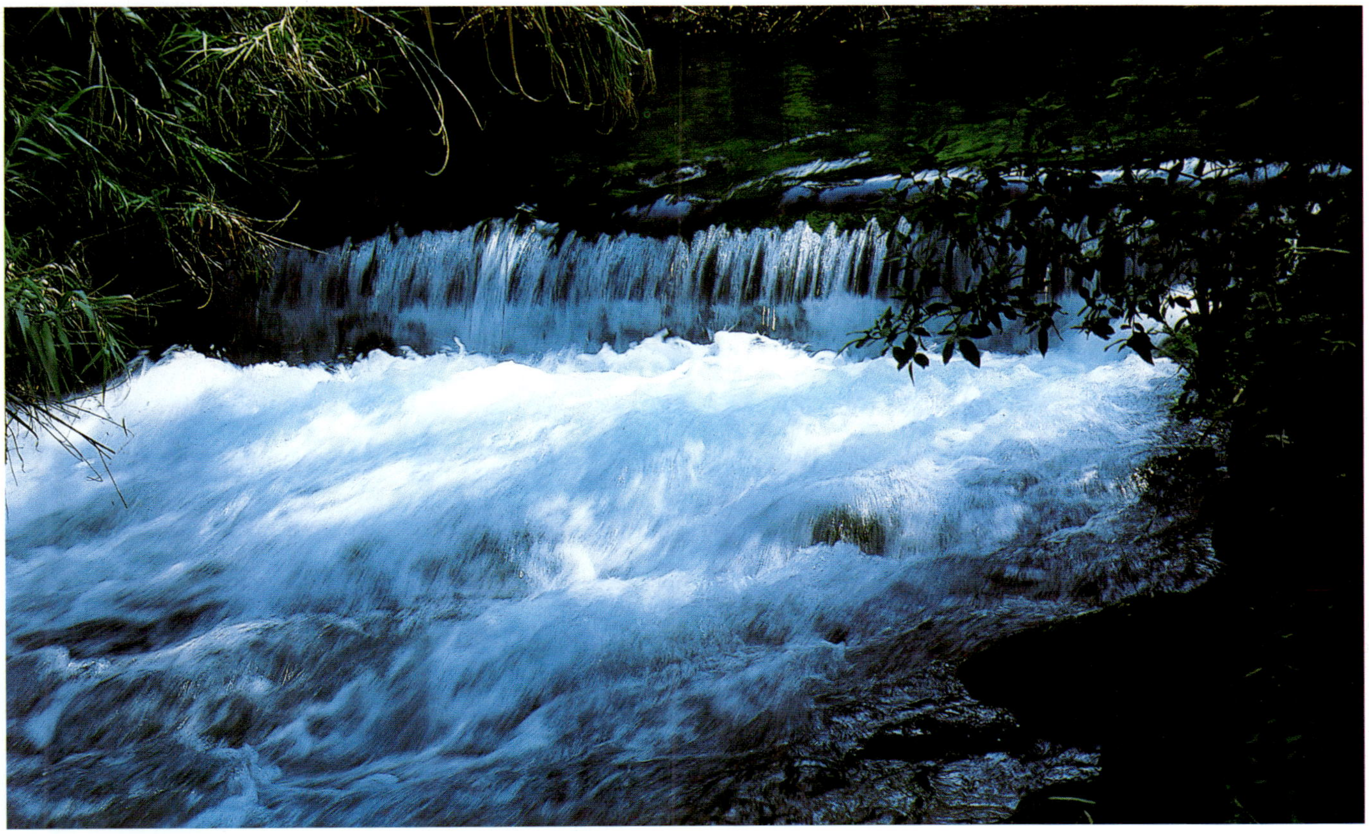

market days, when the Druzes, the Lebanese, and the Syrians all come to sell their wares. Not far from this new town lies the kibbutz hotel Hagosherim which, like most of its fellows, offers you a pleasant, restful stay, but owes its existence mainly to the River Dan. This is the longest and most important of the three Israeli sources of the Jordan (a contraction of the Hebrew Yored Dan, "descending from the Dan"), and its waters swell the river in which Christ was baptised almost 2,000 years ago at Yardenit. These are holy waters – which continue to favour the development of the region, thanks to a well-controlled irrigation scheme – and it is their duty to separate Galilee from its neighbour Jordan, by forming an obvious natural boundary in this region where borders have always been subject to question.

Washed by the Mediterranean and looking towards the setting sun, the Israeli coast is edged by a sandy coastal strip barely 200 km (125 miles) wide, but the major part of the country's vital forces is concentrated here, and the area contributes greatly to the nation's wealth.

The Coast, *a relaxed way of life, with a touch of boldness*

Tel Aviv is the main point of entry for air traffic on this Mediterranean coast, and still looks like the busy seaport it has always been. It is the chief city of this coast, with beautiful white, sandy beaches – which are as much of a delight to local inhabitants seeking for relaxation as to visitors wishing to enjoy a seaside holiday. There are currently about 357,000 people living in the centre of Tel Aviv, which means "hill of spring" in Hebrew, but the numbers far exceed this first estimate if you include the inhabitants of the adjoining towns. Among these are Jaffa, thought to be the most ancient port in the world; Ramat Aviv, an exclusive northern residential suburb, with a prestigious university harbouring 25,000 students and 1,600 teachers; Ramat Gan to the east, which is both an important financial centre and a town where the rents are much lower than in the centre of Tel Aviv; and also Bnei Brak to the east and Holon and Bat Yam to the south, which give new arrivals on low incomes the chance to settle in decent conditions. In total, Tel Aviv and its suburbs can lay claim to almost 1,500,000 inhabitants. This "hill of spring" – which attracts Jewish immigrants and many young people from other towns looking for jobs, a good place to study, a relaxed way of life, and plenty of nightlife – is becoming an independent centre, almost divorced from the rest of Israel.

The port of Jaffa is thought to be the most ancient in the world.

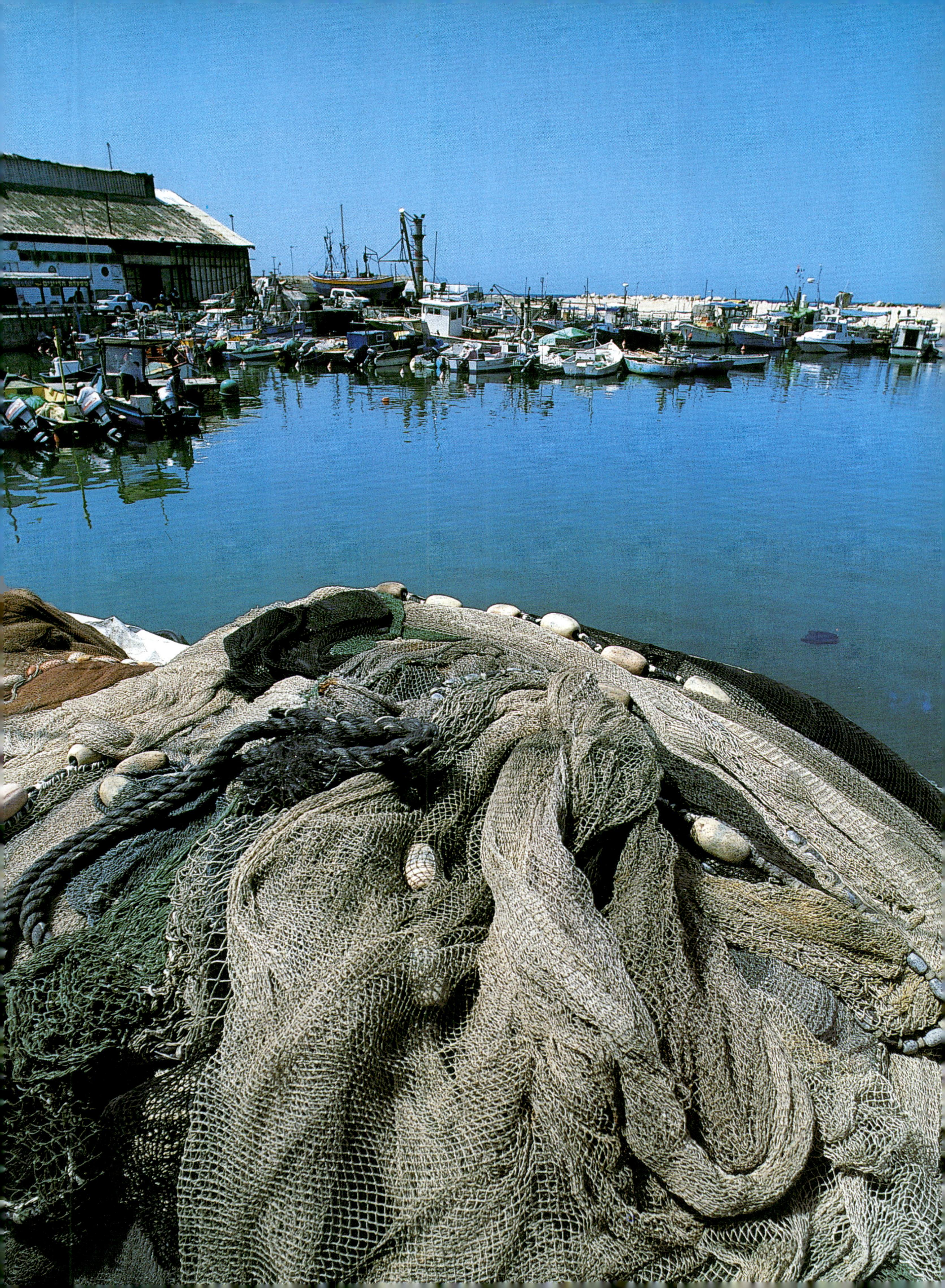

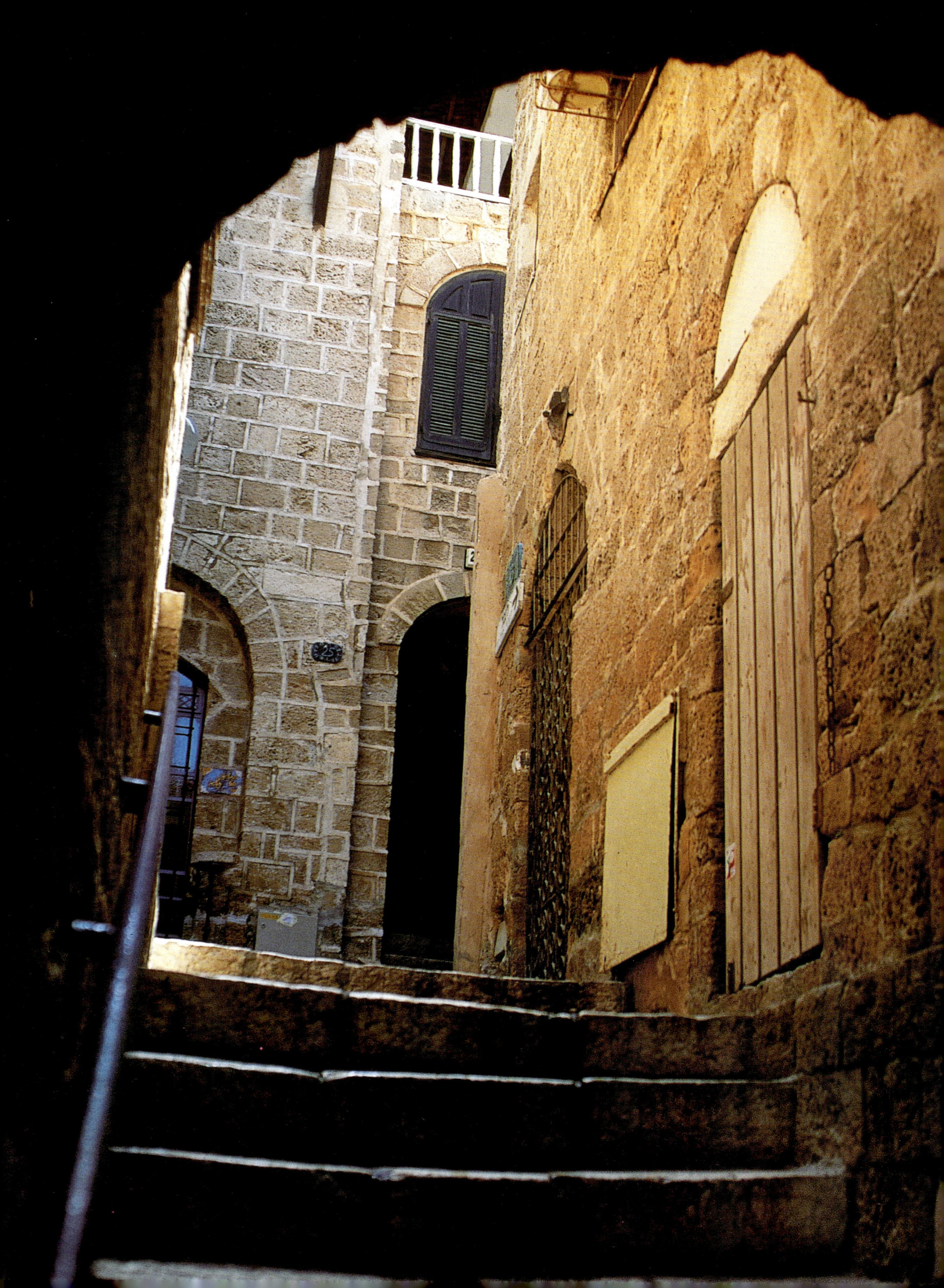

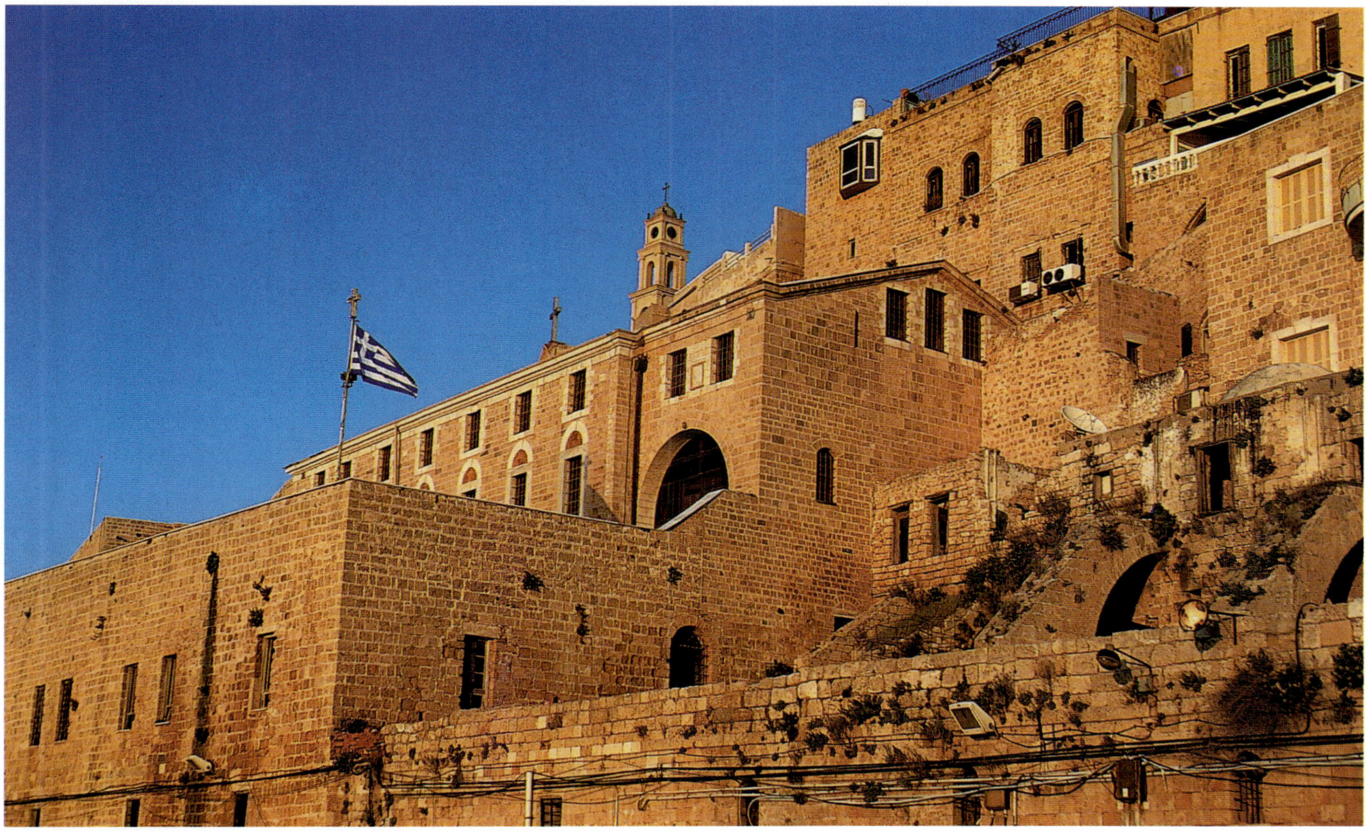

Always ready to rise to the defence of secular values, this Mediterranean city seems to be constantly at odds with the Jewish capital on such important matters as whether or not the national identity should be based on strict Judaism, whether a greater share of the budget should go to the lay or the religious communities, and even whether obedience to the rites of *kashrut* should be absolute or relative. This was reflected yet again in the recent elections. While the inhabitants of Tel Aviv voted for the socialist Ehud Barak, Jerusalem cheered Benyamin Netanyahu, the leader of the *Likhud* party. In a country whose citizens are extremely politically active and passionately involved in public life, positions do not change easily, nor are they adopted lightly or by chance. The citizens are pragmatic, most often voting in proportion to the candidates' ability to respond to specific needs. So the vigorous policies of Tel Aviv's mayor on town planning, housing, the promotion of business and commerce, and support for culture have contributed to fostering a strong attachment to the city in its inhabitants, who make up just under a quarter of the Israeli population.

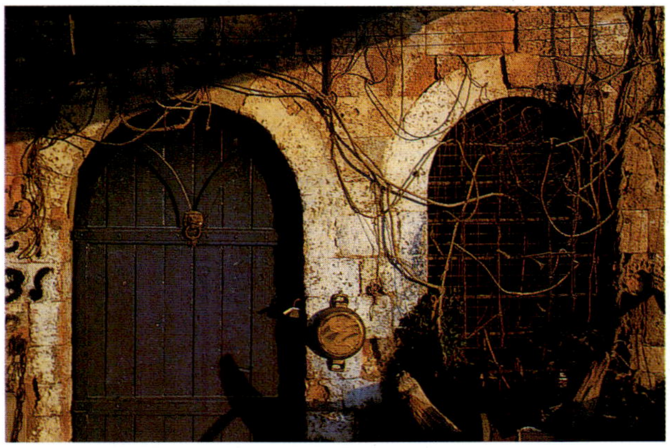

Façades of houses overlooking the harbour of Jaffa.
Facing page:
A narrow street in the old town of Jaffa.
Following pages:
The Netanya beach is the most popular one with French visitors, who flock to this city.

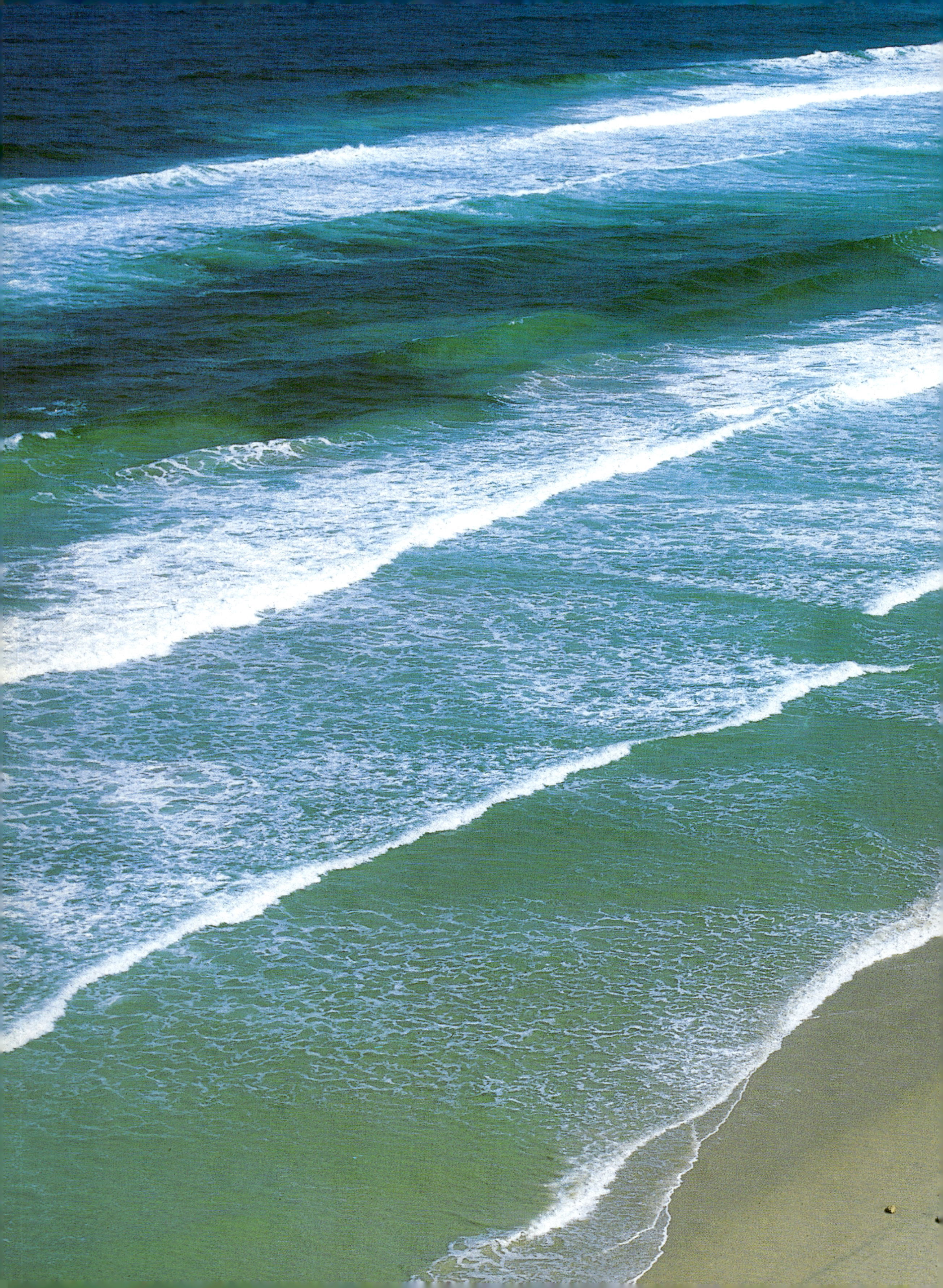

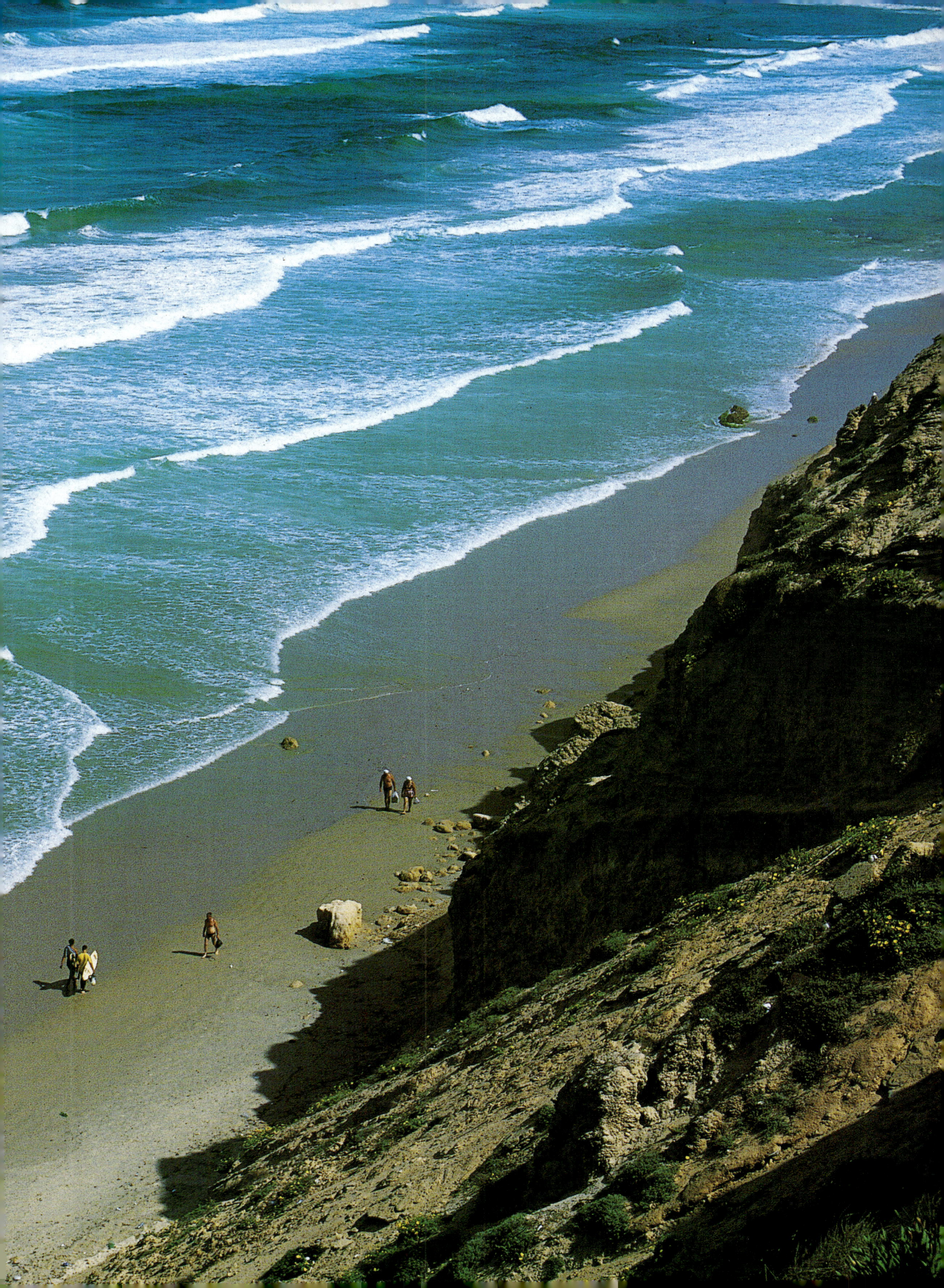

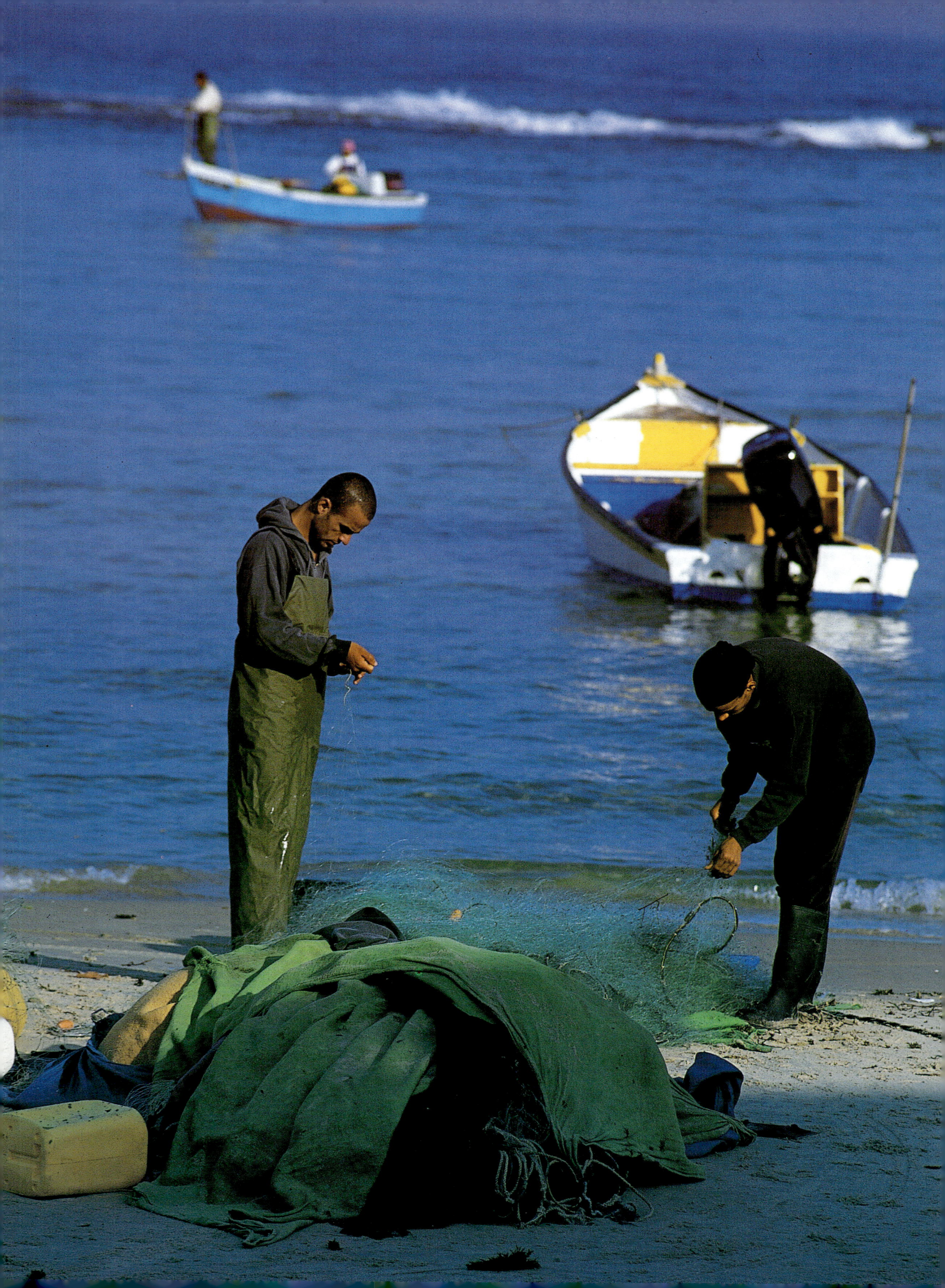

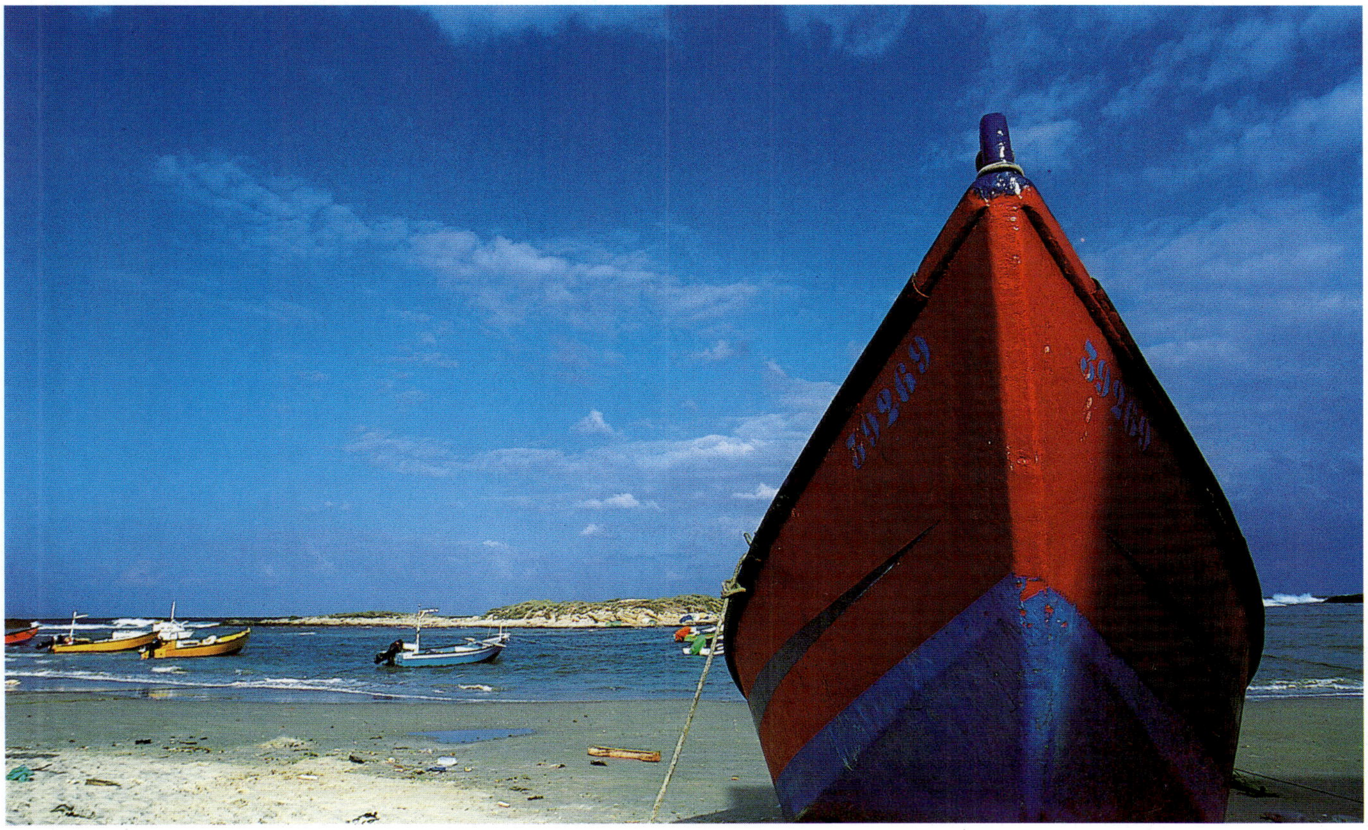

The fishing-port of Dor-Nasholim, south of Haifa.

And there is good reason for this. Even though it still gives the impression of having been built in a hurry, and has no truly magnificent buildings to show off, plunging yourself into its clever mixture of relaxation and liveliness does you good. Obviously the relaxation is represented by the magnificent sea-front, with its long ribbon of wide beaches, which are partly the reason for its existence. Lying on the sand in the baking sun; sipping freshly squeezed fruit juice in one of the bars overlooking the sea; walking lazily or athletically along the Avenue Hayarkon, dominated by high-rise blocks which seem to be stretching up to look far away to the horizon – these are just some of the ways of relaxing to which anyone can treat themselves, when they feel the need. Similarly, streets like Dizengoff Street (often compared to the Champs-Élysees for its lively atmosphere, before the wave of bombings in February-March 1996 made it less attractive), Ben Yehuda Street, and Ibn Guirol Street are major arteries with wide pavements, enabling you to discover in peace how this strange city of really rather unattractive tower blocks is put together.

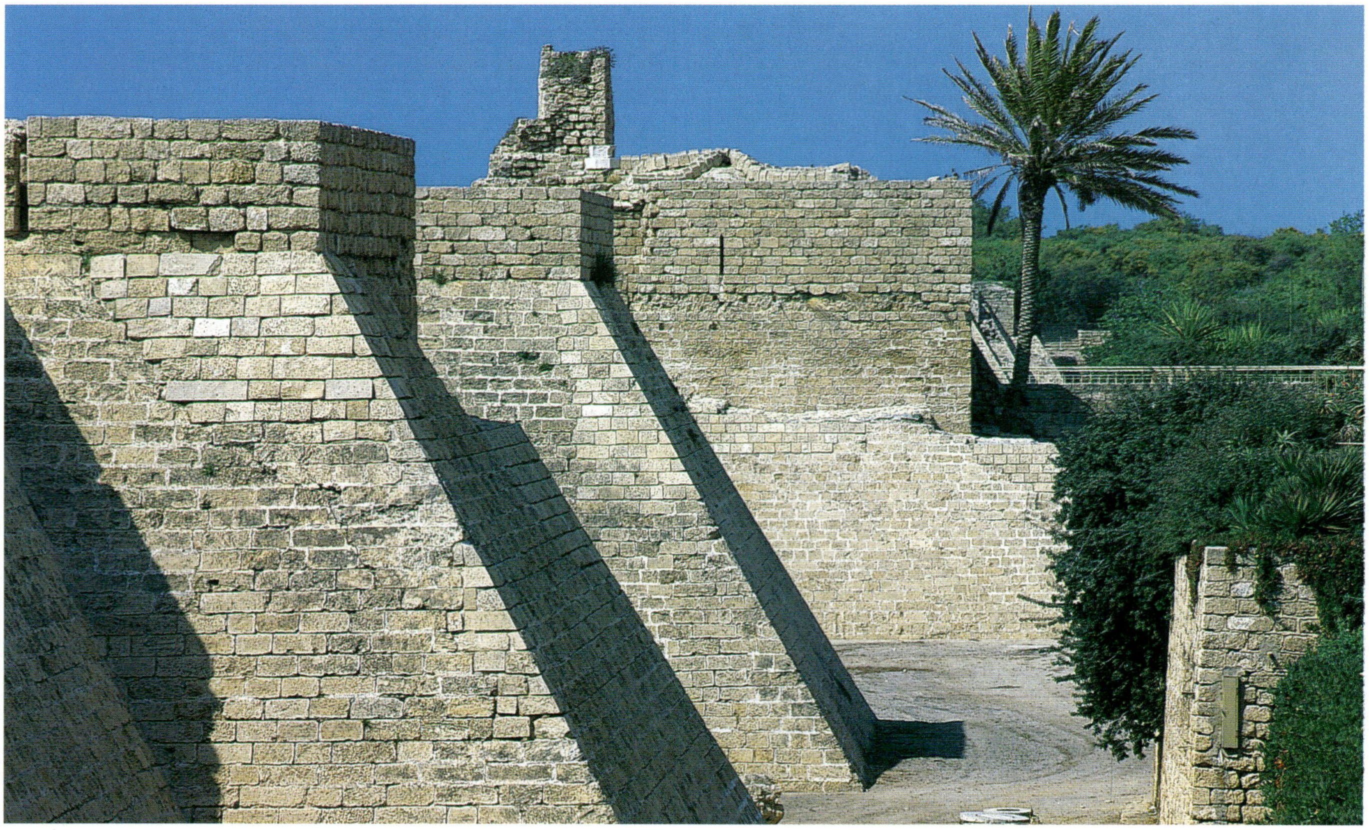

Fortifications built by the Crusaders to defend the site of Caesarea. In this famous city of Antiquity, Roman remains and arcades mingle with the minarets of mosques, encompassing two thousand years of history.

But its beauty lies elsewhere, and if you walk down these broad avenues, it is easily found, because it is the people here who are dazzlingly beautiful. Tel Aviv is a cosmopolitan city, which has welcomed Jews of the Diaspora from all over the globe. Since then a subtle interbreeding has taken place, producing a crop of radiant faces, profiles, and temperaments. The young men who got used to honing their bodies during their three years' military service, and the young women who take advantage of the sun to dress in figure-hugging sportswear, move with a sometimes casual, sometimes calculated grace, which inevitably produces a certain excitement. This sensual energy subtly pervades the city, reinforcing the impression of vitality. This vitality, which is so much a part of the essence of Tel Aviv, together with its often hectic nightlife, has gained the city the reputation of being a town which never sleeps. This famous exuberance, bordering on recklessness, takes on its full meaning at such times.

Especially on Thursdays, the last evening before the start of the Sabbath, the bars and discotheques are always full, no matter whether they are in

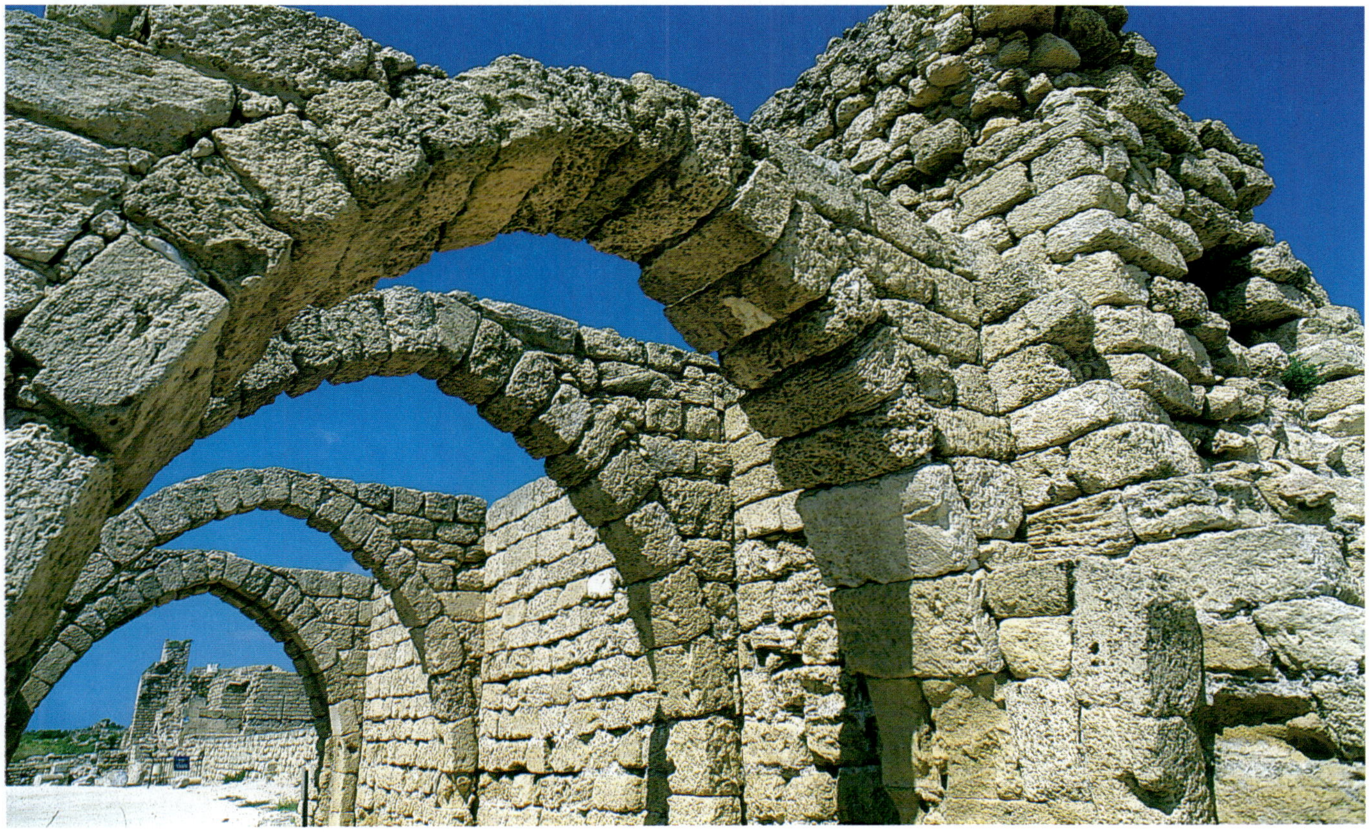

the Allenby Street area, in one of the districts of Ibn Guirol, or even where Jerusalem Street runs into Jaffa. Crowds assemble and give free rein to their high spirits. Being out in the streets, wearing tattoos and outlandish clothing, abandoning themselves body and soul to the whirl of electronic music seems – in an almost militant sense for these hedonistic young people – to be a way of demonstrating their support for that special quality of tolerance which sets Tel Aviv apart and which they feel must be preserved at all costs.

Apart from Tel Aviv and its symbolic role, the most interesting feature of the coastal region is that each of the towns strung along it has a distinct personality, a character all of its own. The Philistine towns of the southern coast, for example, are the descendants of the harbour towns founded around the thirteenth century BC by the people who arrived by sea, whom the Hebrews called "Plichtim", the invaders, the Philistines.

Though they were constantly vying with the Hebrews, they managed to preserve the integrity of their territory, which lay around Gaza, Ashkelon,

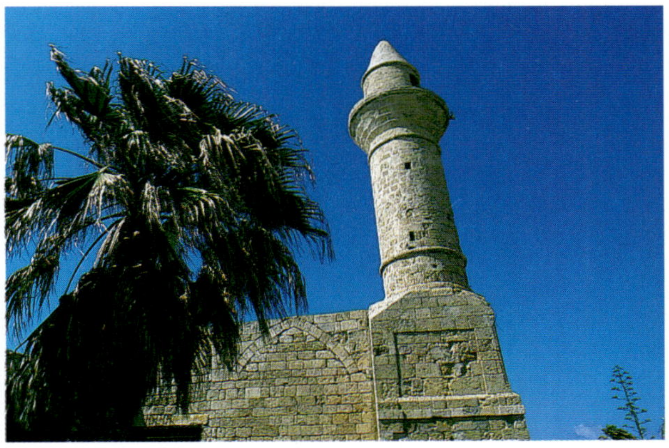

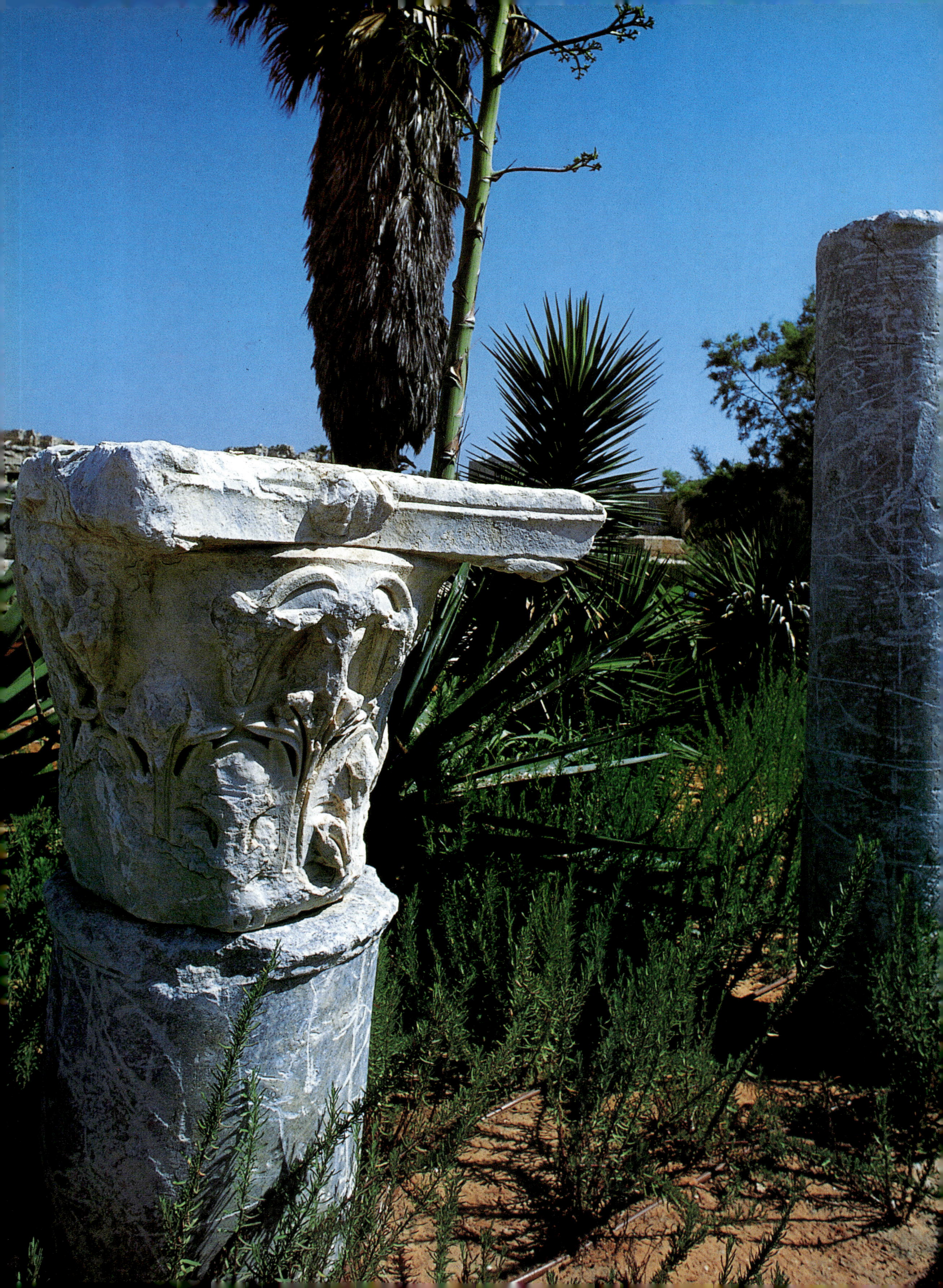

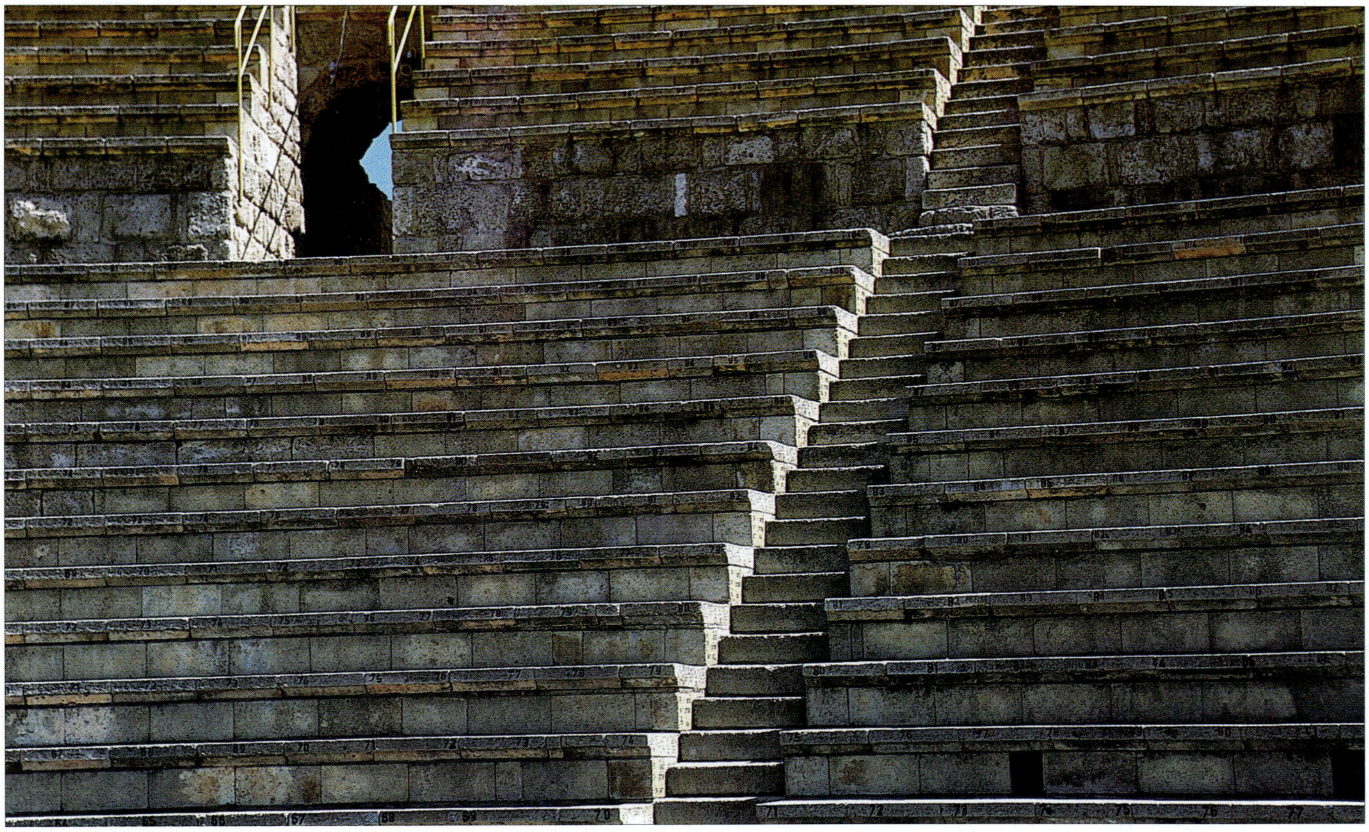

The columns and the theatre remind us that Caesarea was the capital of Palestine in the days of Roman domination.

• Caesarea •

Once the capital of the Romans in Palestine, Caesarea is one of the most popular archaeological sites in Israel today. Oriented towards the Mediterranean because of its role as a port, the ancient city, only ruins of which now remain, was considered a magnificent metropolis in the centuries immediately preceding the Christian era. In Roman times, this prosperous city was characterised by its huge harbour, large extensive amphitheatre, splendid marble palaces, columns, bas-reliefs, and statues. And there were prisons too. St Paul was imprisoned there for two years, before being transferred to Rome, and the Zealots, who shook the city in 66 BC at the time of the first great Jewish rebellion, were tortured there. The fortifications, which still surround part of the site today, and some of the ruined houses remind us that in the twelfth and thirteenth centuries, the city was an important place for the Crusaders who based themselves there.

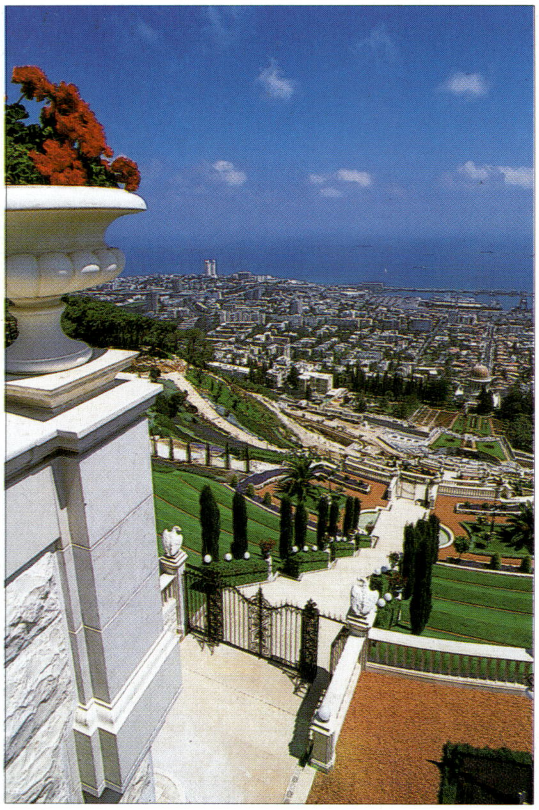

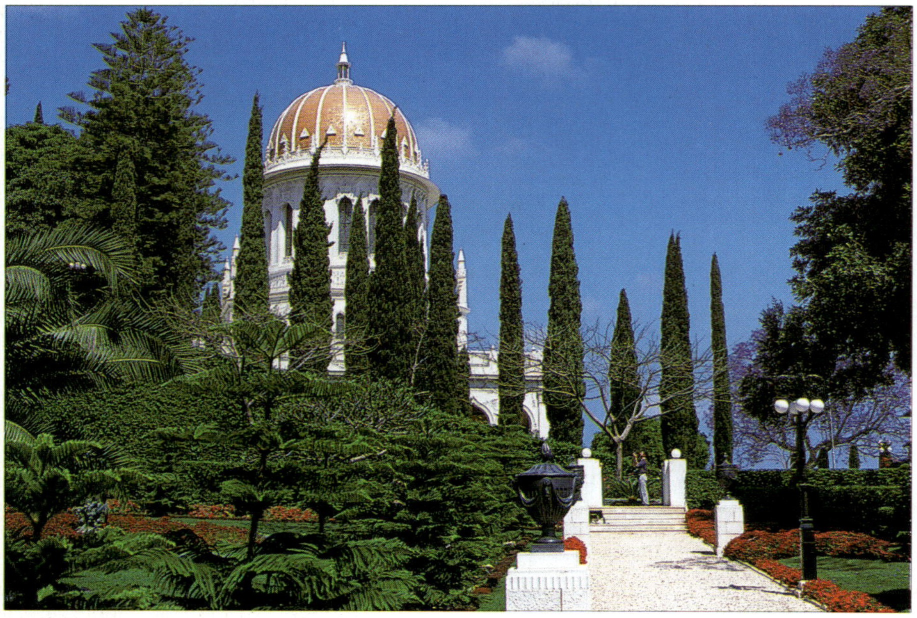

The Baha'i shrine has become the symbol of Haifa, the third largest city in the country. The gleaming red dome, emerging from a splendid garden ranged along the slopes of Mount Carmel, is one of the curiosities of this captivating harbour and industrial city.

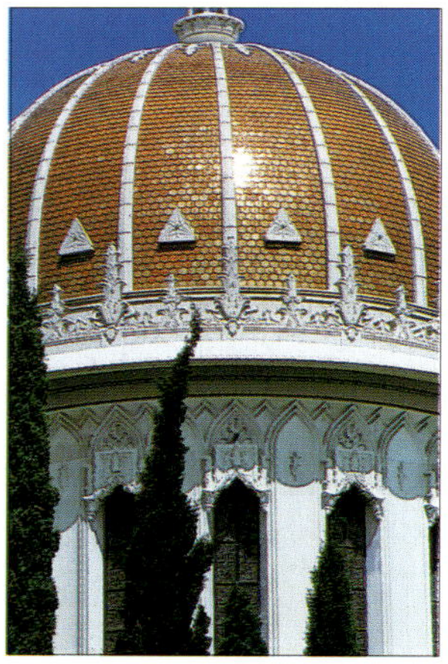

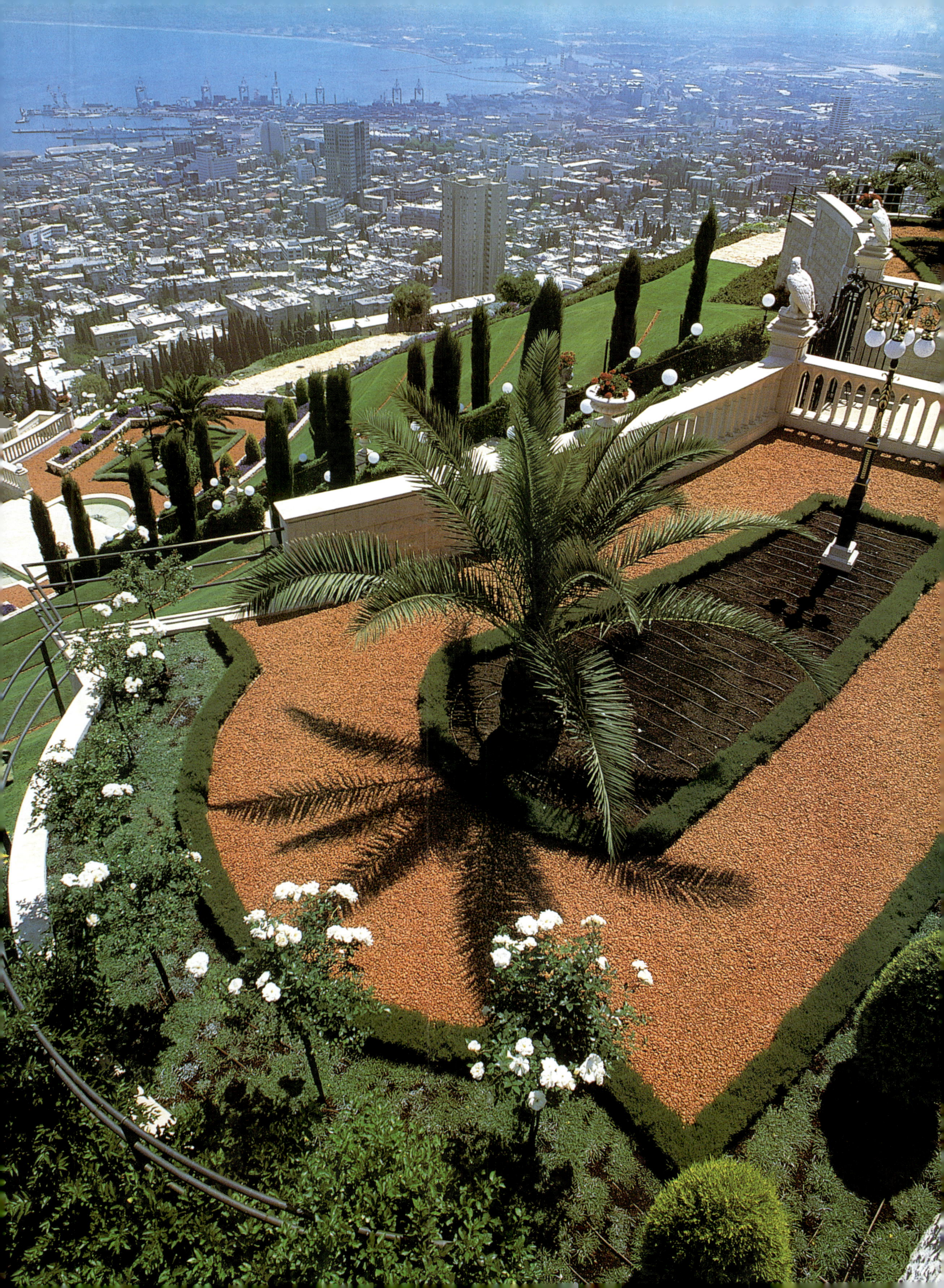

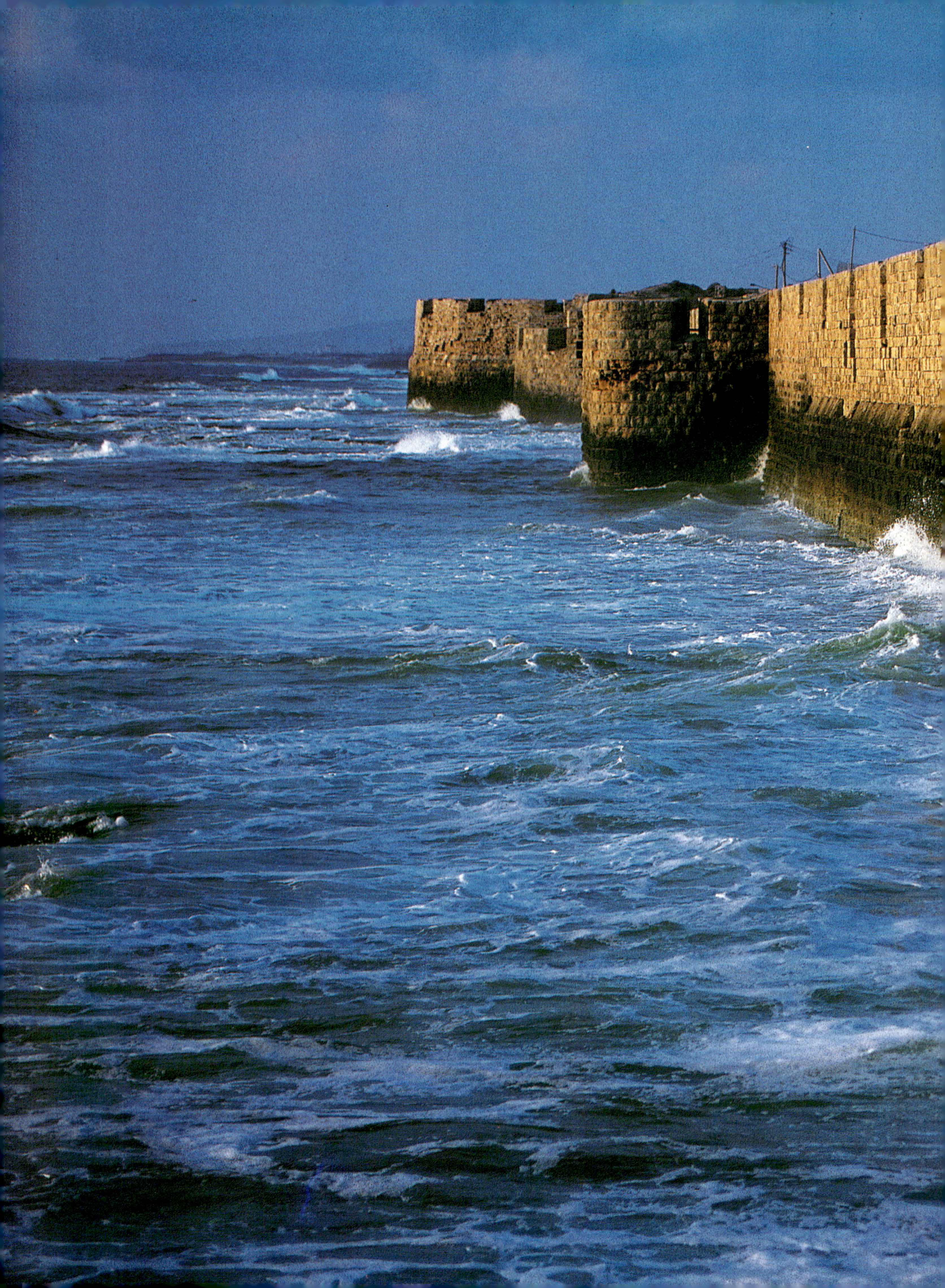

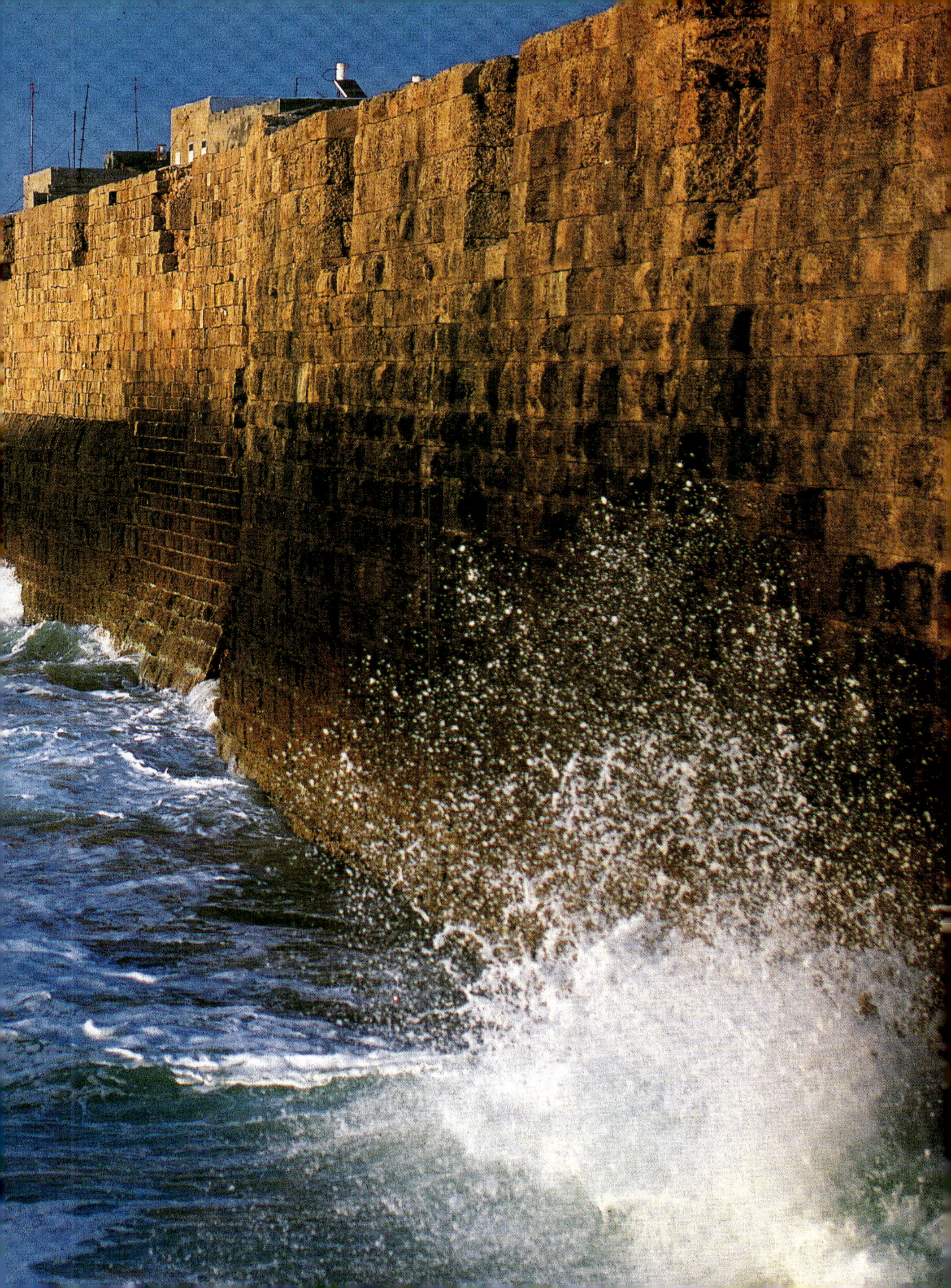

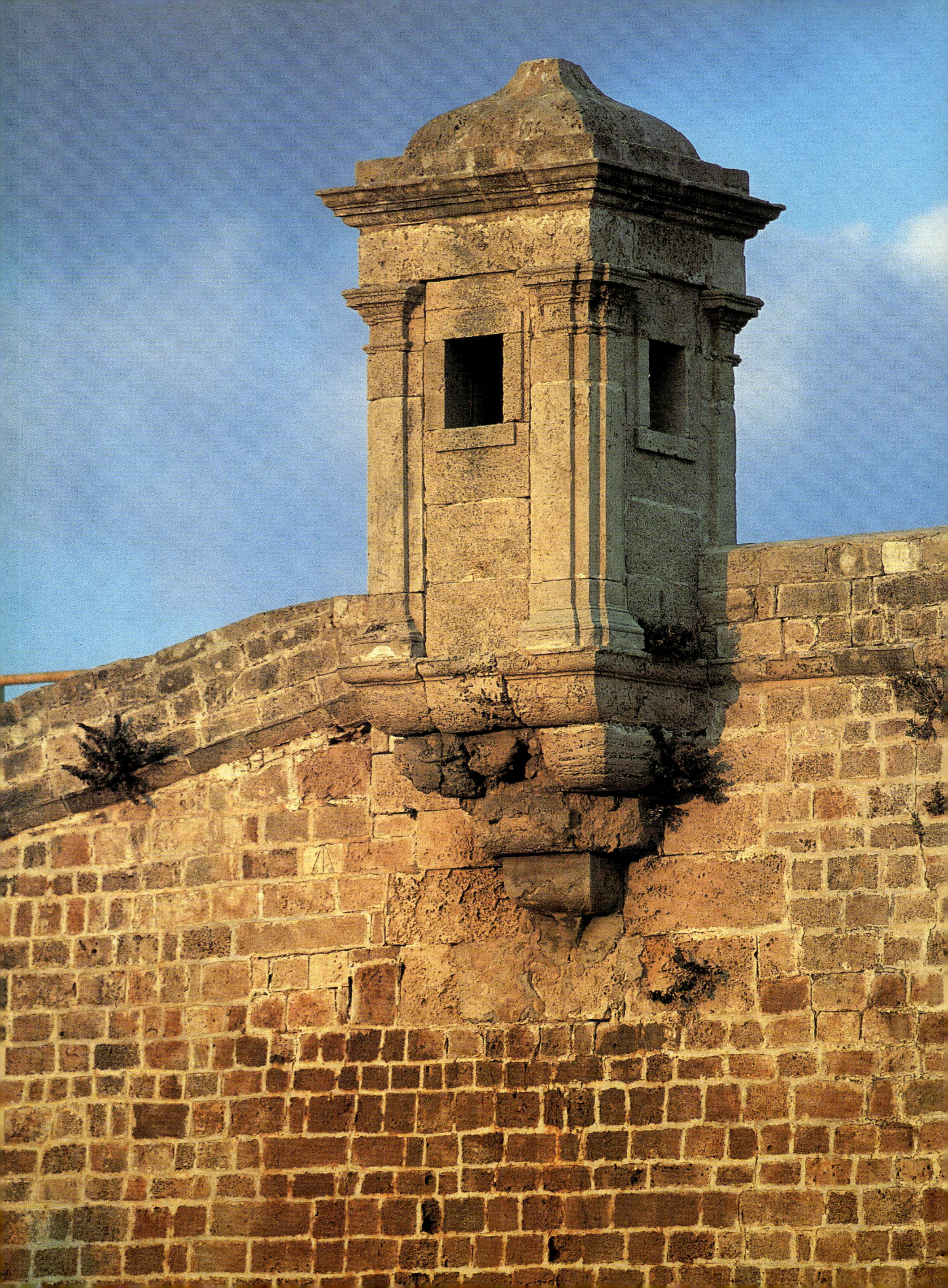

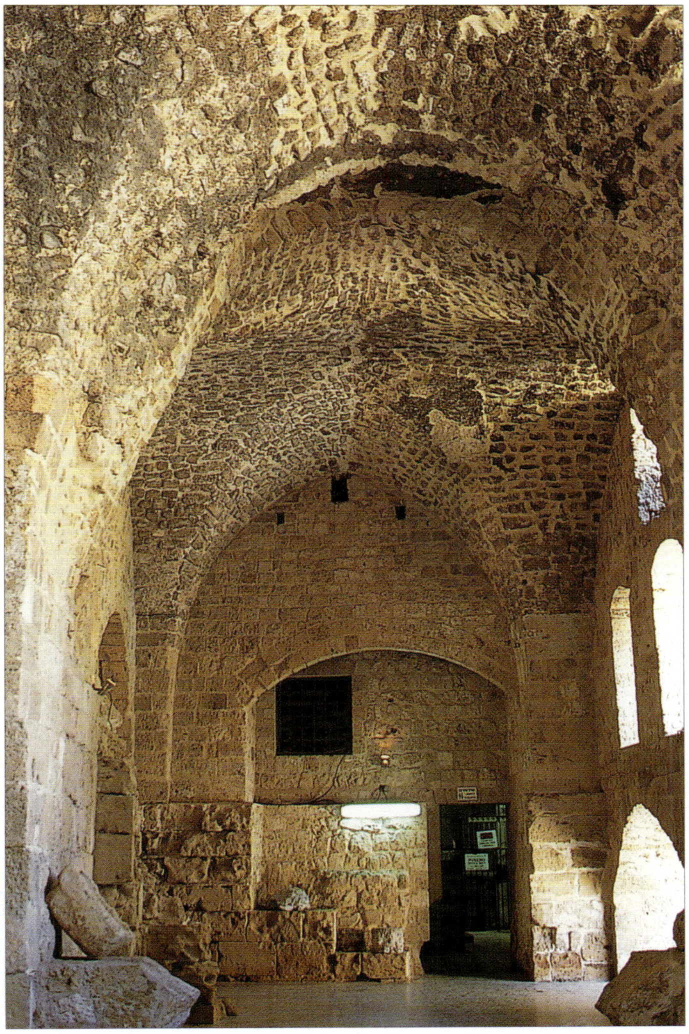

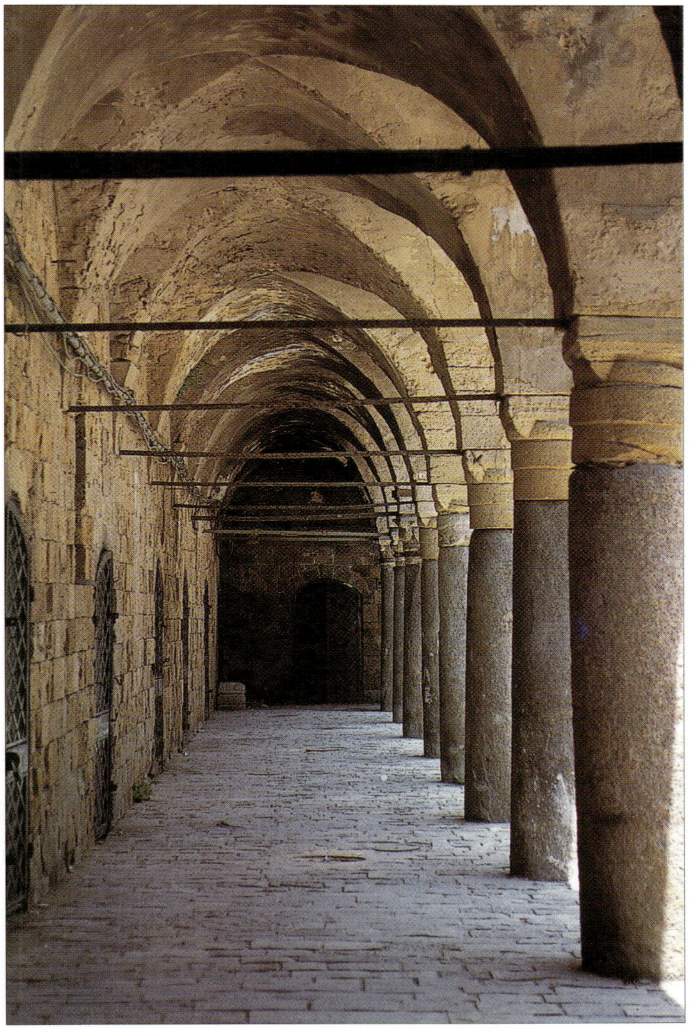

Ashdod, Gath, and Ekron (the first three are well known, but the last two have never been located with certainty). They lost Jaffa, the beautiful city which they had fortified, to David, who began to turn it into a strategic port for the Hebrews around 1,000 BC. When the Romans seized control of the region, they named it Palestine, referring to the country of the Philistines. Then the Romans made Ashkelon and particularly Caesarea into the two most important towns on the coast. Today these two cities share the distinction of having a very varied archaeological heritage and approximately defining the limits of the alluvial plain of Sharon, whose vast production of citrus fruits has become one of the country's most important resources.

Also on the coast to the north of Tel Aviv are two very famous resorts: Herzliya, which is the resort favoured by the rich and privileged; and

Interior of the Crusader fortress and entrance to the underground city.
View of the Khan el Umdan caravanserai in Acre.
Facing page:
Interior wall of Acre.
Previous pages:
The walls of St John of Acre (Akko) present an insurmountable barrier to the Mediterranean, recalling the time when Crusaders and Muslims fought over the city in the twelfth and thirteenth centuries.

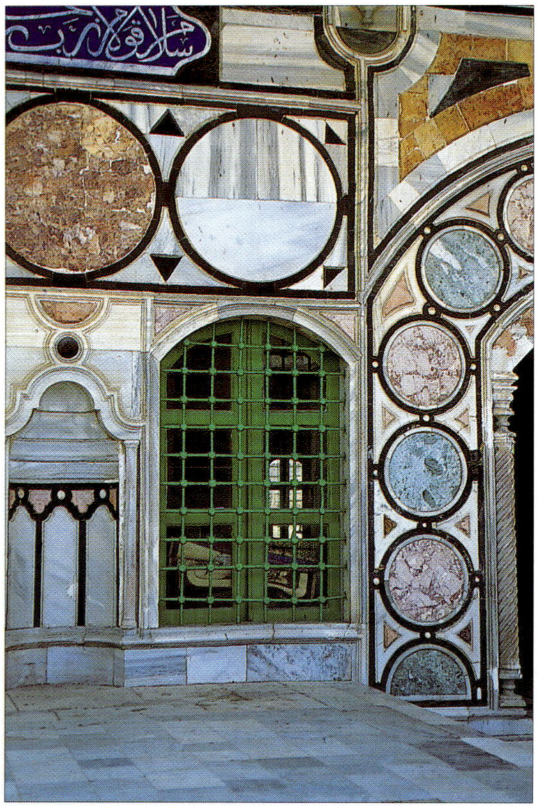

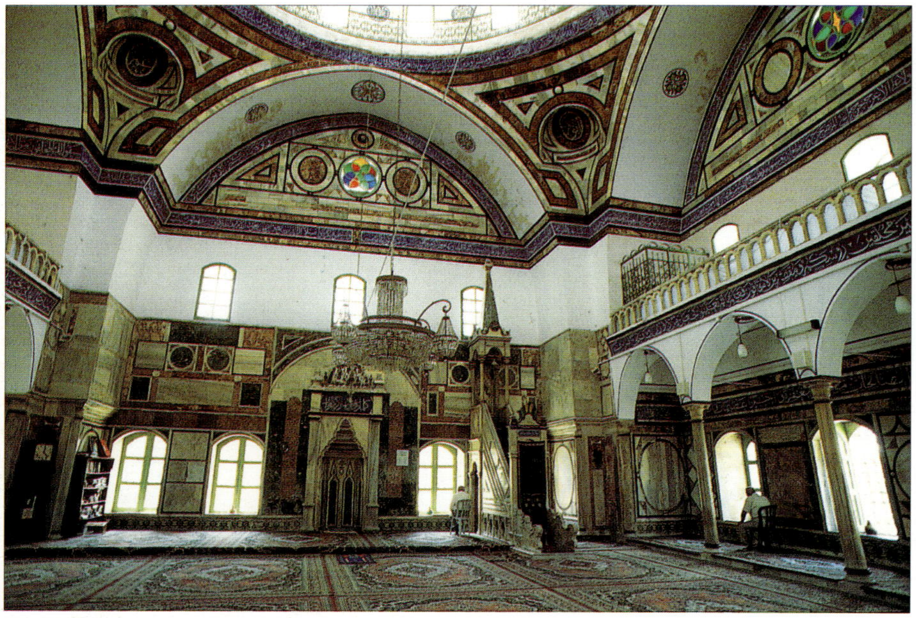

The El Jazzar mosque in Acre is the biggest in Israel. Built at the end of the eighteenth century, it has a richly decorated interior and an esplanade with a fountain, which are not to be missed.

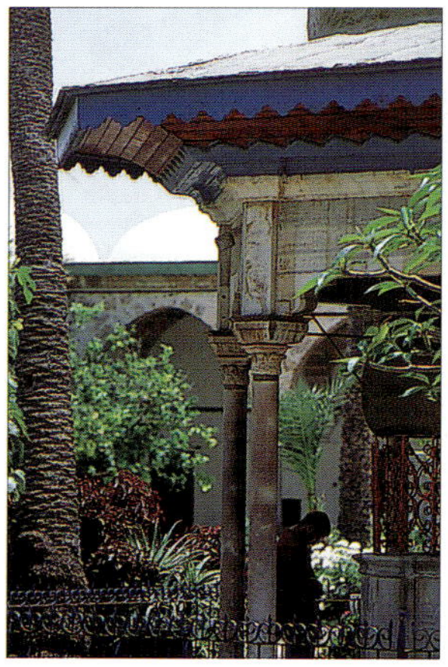

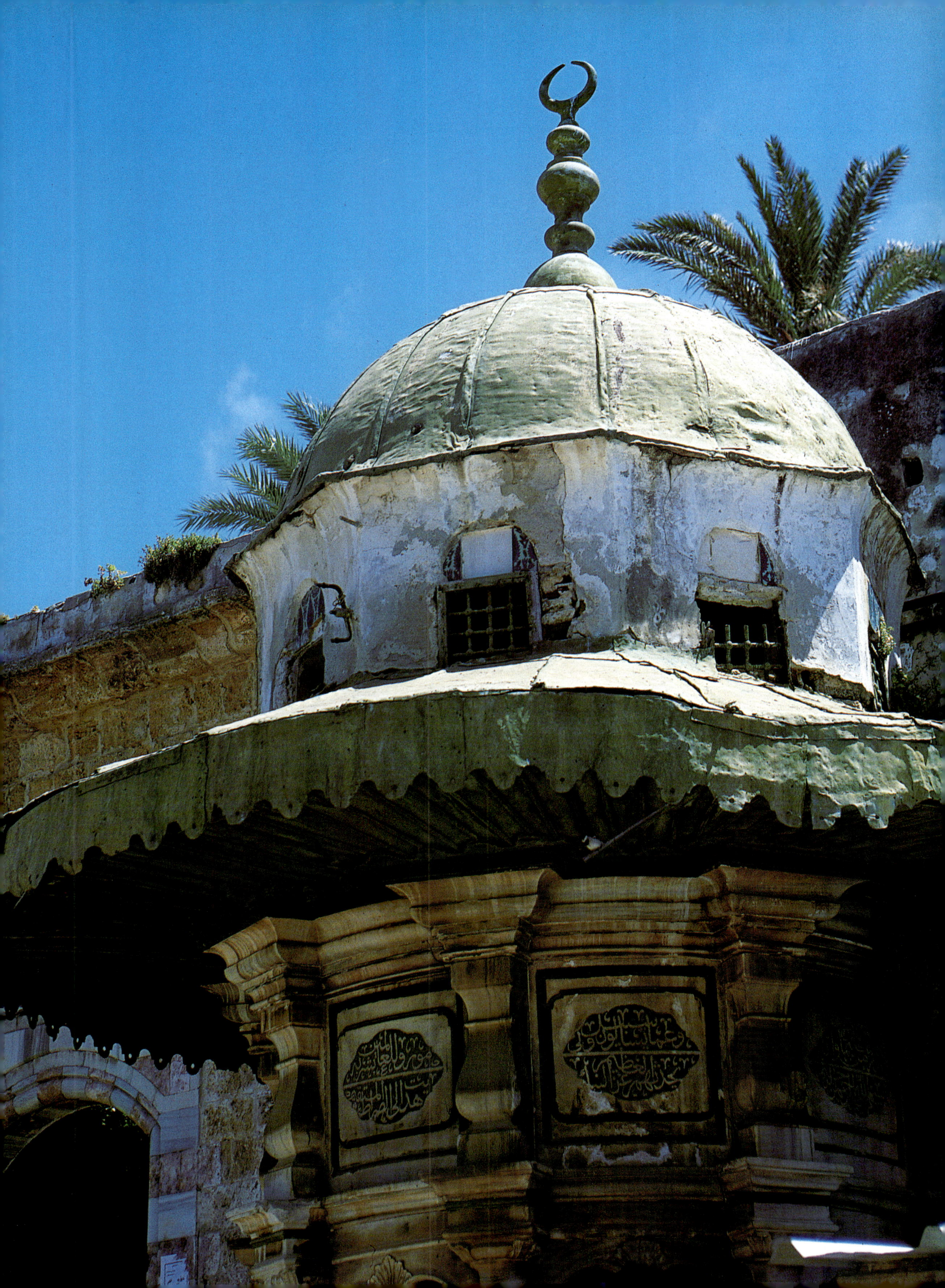

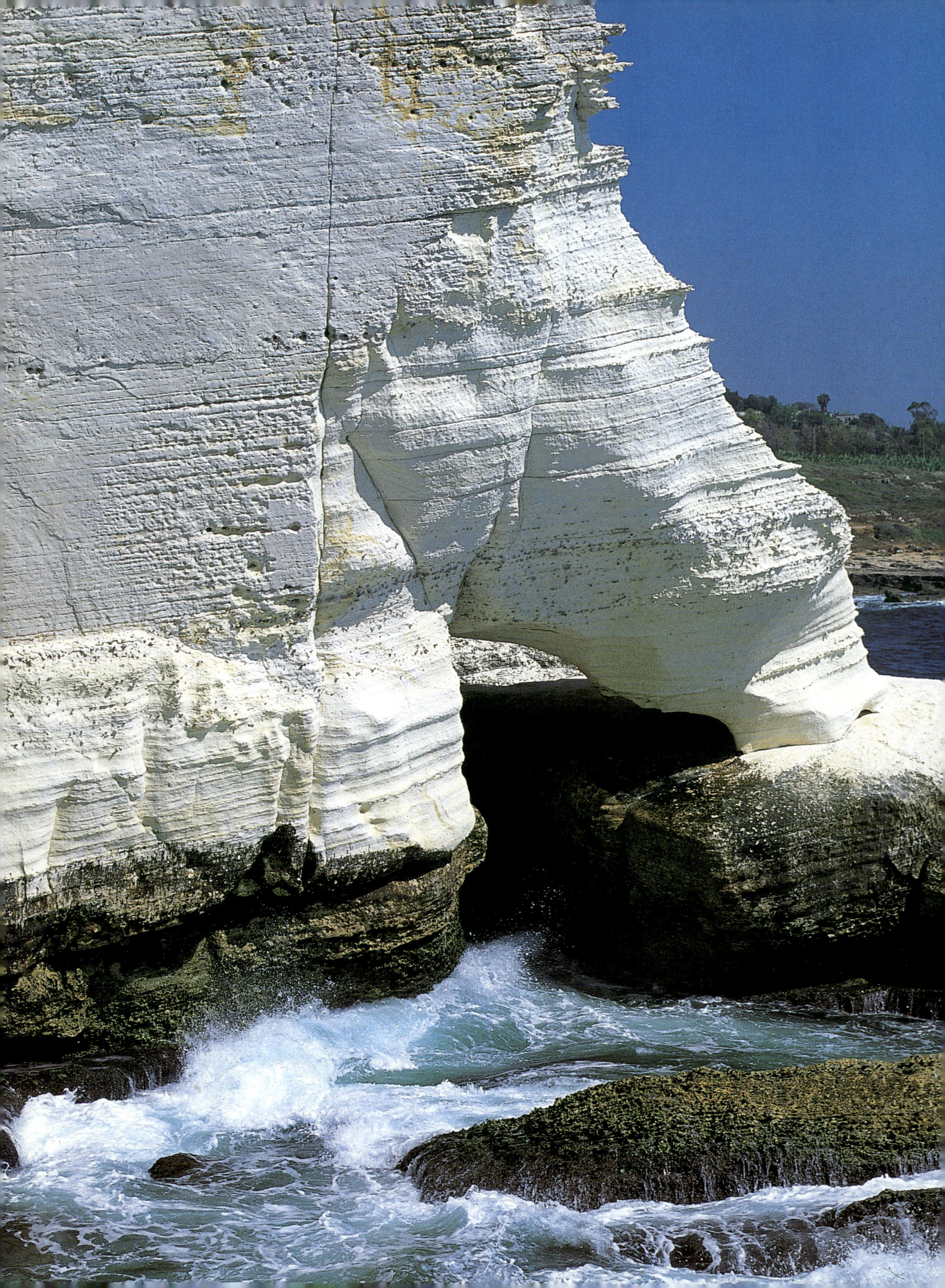

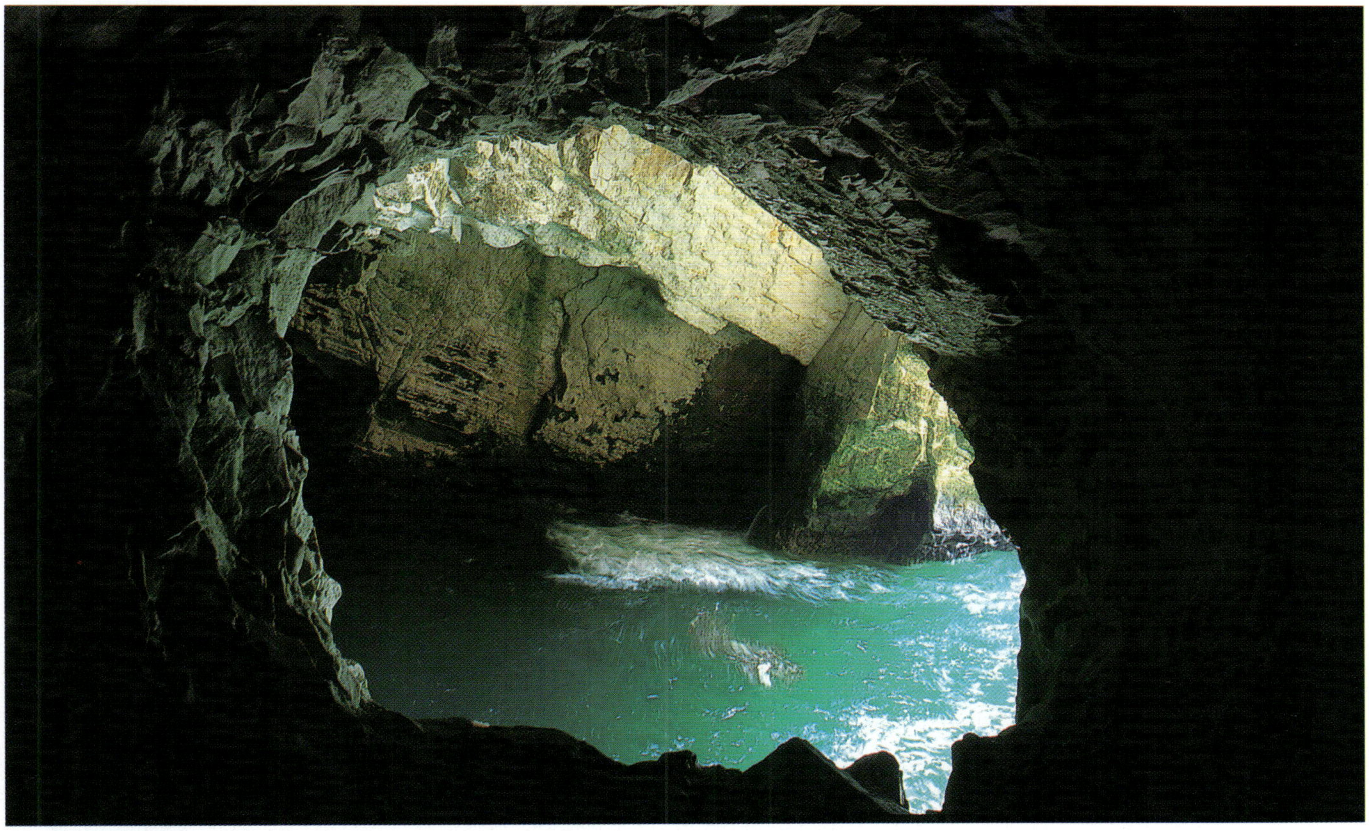

The cliffs and sea caves of Rosh Hanikra mark the coastal border with the Lebanon. You have to take a small cable-car to reach them. Jerusalem is 205 km (128 miles) away and Beirut 120 km (75 miles).

Netanya, which has become a meeting place for the French. Each one jealously guards pleasant sections of coast with very popular beaches. Further north, the coastline offers other lovely beaches, especially between Atlit and Haifa, but the chief centres of interest are those of cultural and historical importance. The north coast, stretching from Haifa and Mount Carmel to the Lebanese border, gives access to Galilee and was used as a base by the Crusaders, with Akko (Acre) as its capital. The stones of the great Crusader fortress at Akko, which became a Turkish stronghold, are a perfect illustration of the tumultuous past of this coast. Four methods of construction can be seen, one on top of the other. First came the Romans, who used big blocks, on which the Crusaders placed intermediate-sized blocks, then the Mamelukes added small, neatly cut blocks, to which the Ottomans added all kinds of loose stones. Just as it does in the old city of Jerusalem, the omnipresent stone makes the heart of the city beat, and it also has the soothing virtue of being detached from the clamour of the modern world.

A region in the form of a corridor running between Tel Aviv and Jerusalem, straddling the coastal plain and the Judaean foothills, the centre of Israel is not a defined, autonomous geographical or administrative entity, but rather an ancient crossroads. It has always linked the important cities at the four corners of the present Hebrew State.

The Centre, *at the crossroads of ancient highways*

This quite densely populated region is underrated by visitors, who often do no more than spend an hour crossing it on their way to the holy city from the big cities on the Mediterranean coast, yet developing and promoting it was one of the priorities of the founders of the Israeli State. And you do not have to go far from the main roads to find sites of interest. Rishon le Zion, 15 km (10 miles) south of Tel Aviv, is the oldest of the communities founded by the Jews of the Diaspora. This city, which today is home to more than 100,000 people, is the place where a few pioneers arrived in 1882 to develop an agricultural colony on Turkish soil, under orders from Constantinople. Fourteen ordinary people of Ukrainian origin, members of the association *Honevie Sion* (Lovers of Zion) came to attempt this difficult venture which nevertheless promised so much. In those days, at the time of this first Aliya en Eretz Israel ("climb" to the Holy Land) there were about 25,000 Jews living in Palestine. At Rishon le Zion, these Ashkenazy pioneers concentrated on growing wine and figs, and they also acquired a good reputation for their silkworms.

A short way to the east of this city, which has managed to preserve the atmosphere and way of life of a country town, the captivating town of

The White Tower, a mosque built by the Mamelukes at Ramla at the beginning of the fourteenth century, has an almost 30 m (90 ft) high minaret.

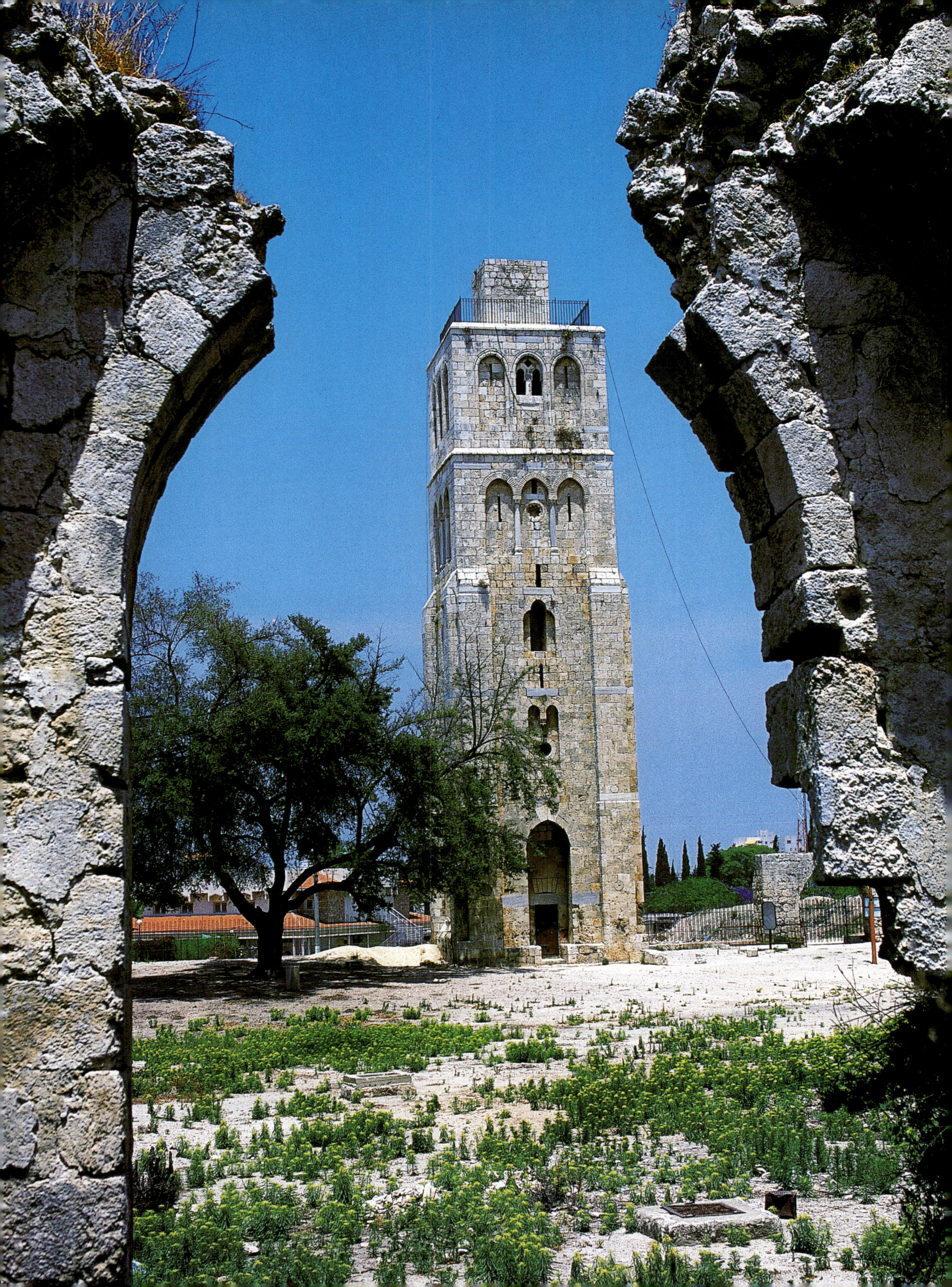

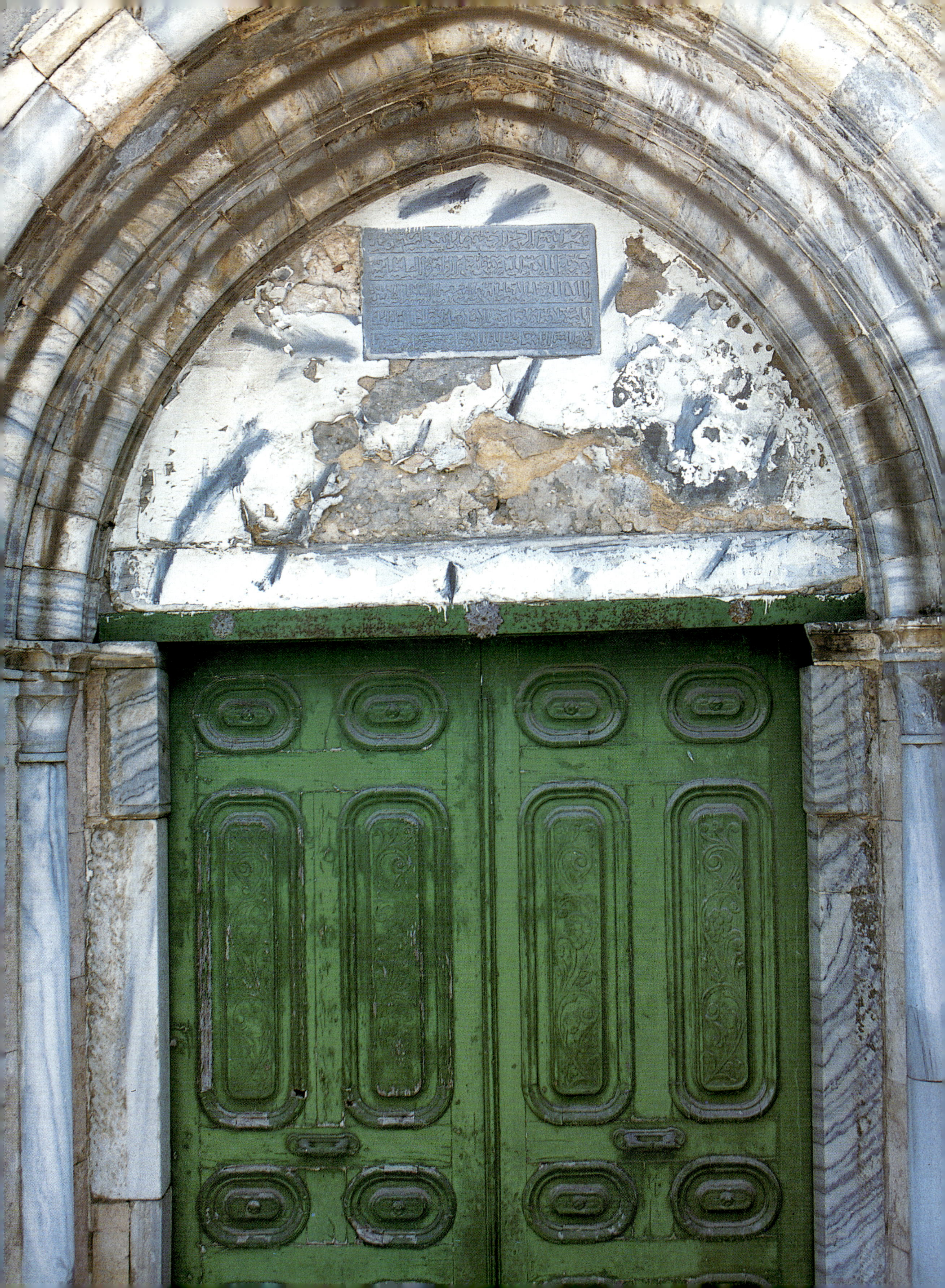

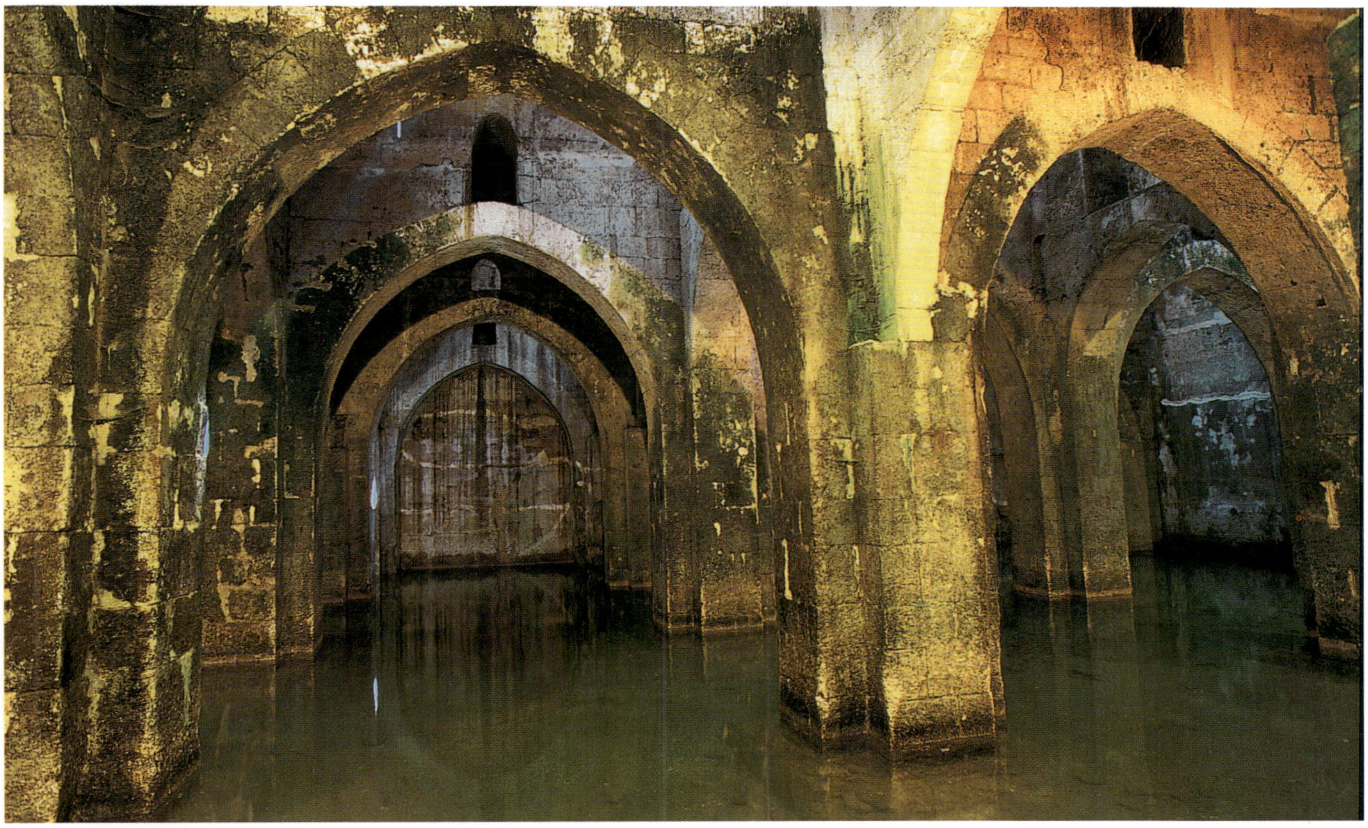

The cisterns of St Helen of Ramla date from the eighth century.

Facing page:
The door of the Great Mosque in Ramla, built in the thirteenth century on top of a cathedral.

Ramla has the privilege of being the oldest city in the region. It was the first city founded by the Muslim Arabs in the eighth century, after they invaded Palestine in 640 and seized the land that, under their influence, was shortly to become Syria-Palestine. They ruled over Jerusalem, where they built the Dome of the Rock, but they made Ramla their administrative capital and cultural centre. In this mixed-race city, where Arabs and Jews now live in harmony with one another, the two principal monuments recalling the Muslim influence are the White Tower, a mosque with an almost 30 m (90 ft) high minaret, whose construction by the Mamelukes was completed in 1318, and the Great Mosque, built in the thirteenth century on top of the cathedral of St John of the Crusades, which is still easily identifiable.

Continuing westwards, along the ancient pilgrim route to Jerusalem, visitors arrive at Latrun, famous for its fine Trappist monastery, and also for another reason recalled by Chateaubriand in his *Itinéraire de Paris à Jérusalem* (Journey from Paris to Jerusalem): "We left Rama (since the crusades, Christians had got into the habit of calling Ramla Rama) … After

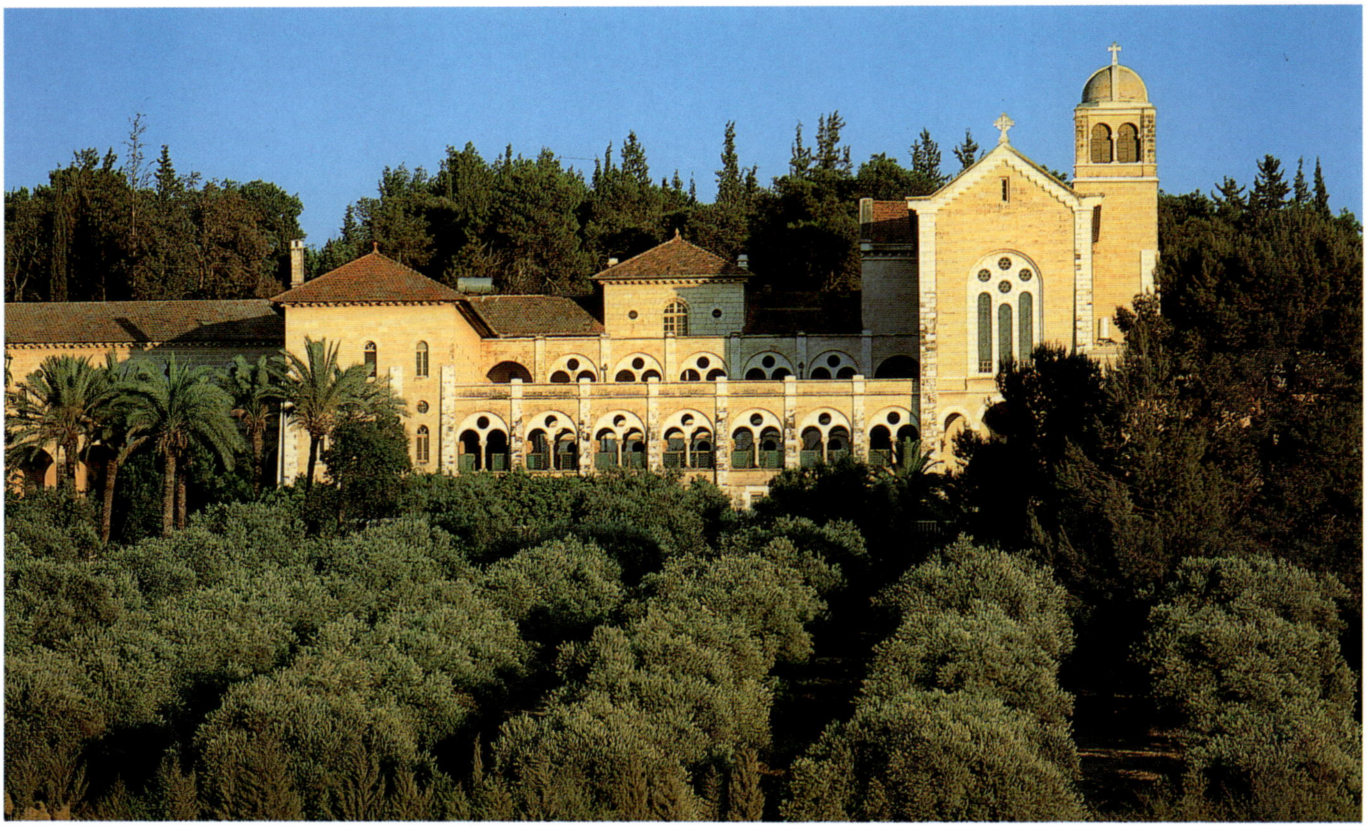

The Trappist monastery of Latrun is famous for its wines.

riding for an hour over uneven ground, we arrived at a few dilapidated hovels perched on top of a rocky crag. We crossed a rise in the plain and, after another hour's walk, we reached the first foothills of the Judaean mountains. We followed a rugged ravine around an arid, isolated hillock. At the top of this knoll we glimpsed a ruined village and the scattered stones of an abandoned graveyard. This village bears the name of Latrun, meaning robber, and was the home of the criminal who repented on the cross, and for whom Christ performed his final act of forgiveness." As described by Chateaubriand, the town of Latrun is situated in the lowest foothills of Judaea and, it so happens, on land particularly well suited to growing grapevines. The monks produced an excellent and famous wine. A little way from the abbey is the village of Amwâs, which the Byzantines acknowledged must be Emmaus, the place where Jesus appeared to two of the disciples after his resurrection.

However, the Crusaders considered the village known today as Abu Gosh – after a family who had the right to demand payment of a toll from

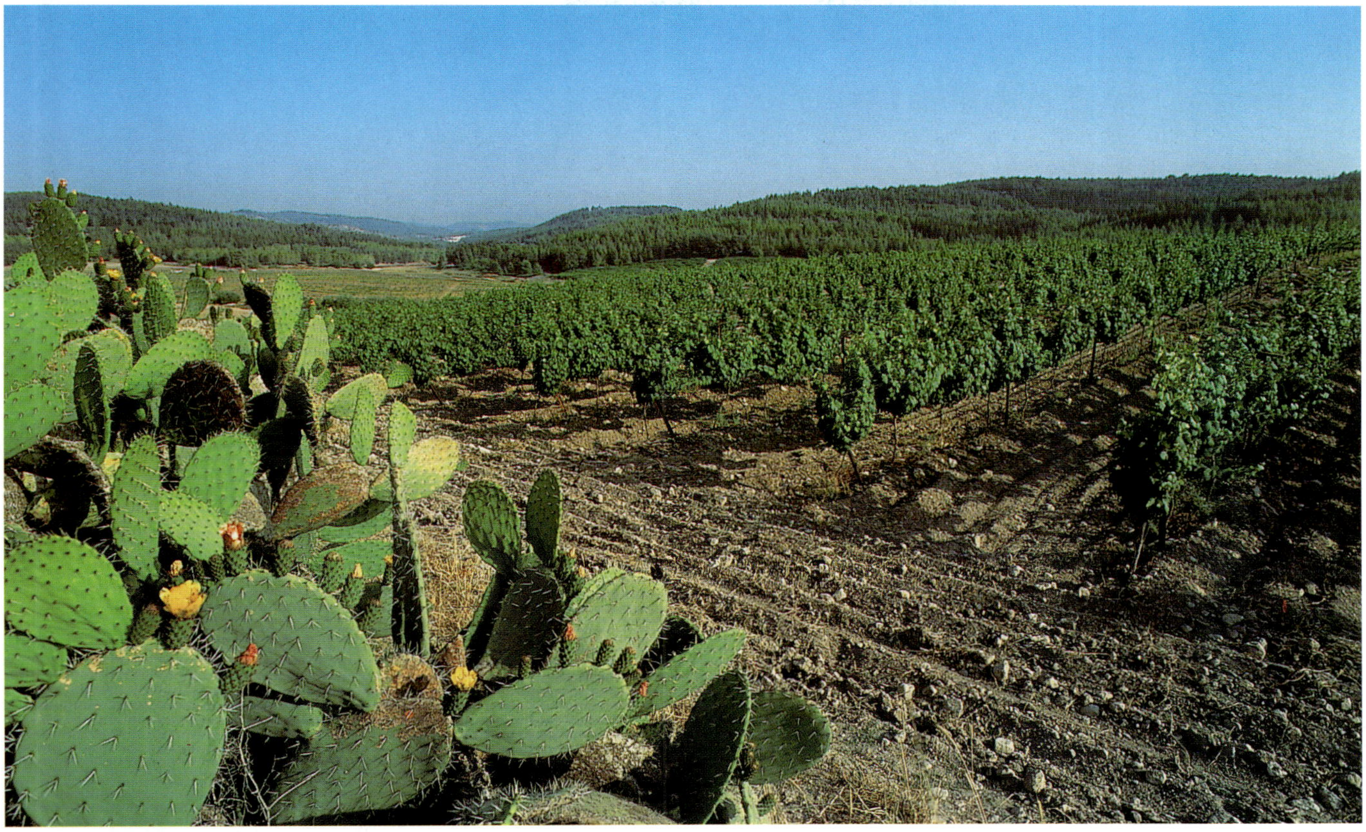

pilgrims on the road to Jerusalem – to be the place where Jesus appeared, as described by Luke (24:13 – 33): "Now that same day two of them were going to a village called Emmaus, about seven miles from Jerusalem. They were talking with each other about everything that had happened. As they talked and discussed these things with each other, Jesus himself came up and walked along with them; but they were kept from recognising him." Just as Abu Gosh, the scene of Jesus' appearance to the disciples, once guarded the route to Jerusalem and represented the main way into the city for pilgrims, so this episode from the gospels showing two disciples unable to feel with their hearts the presence of Christ, seems also to be the way to a spiritual crossroads, a route which pilgrims must follow in their search for holiness. For those who wish wholeheartedly to reach the truth, this way means giving themselves heart and soul to God.

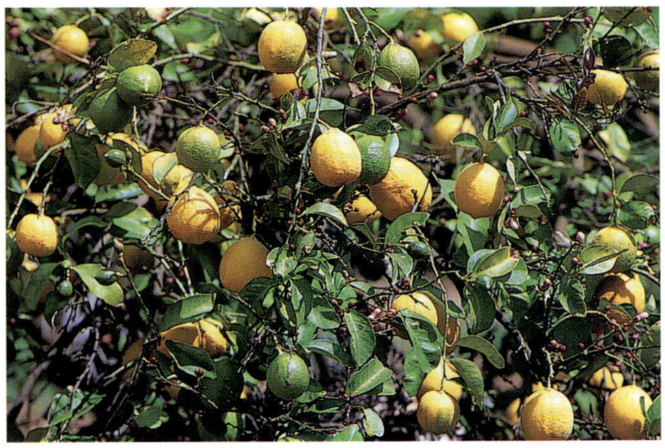

Since the time of David Ben-Gurion, the father of the Israeli nation, who had staked the Negev in a merciless struggle intended to push back its borders in order to exploit it to the limits, this desert has no longer been feared as an arid, sun-baked zone. Instead it has become a place of fabulous geological formations to be experienced, understood, and appreciated.

The South, *an ever receding border*

Though it may, as a general rule, be difficult to pinpoint and define the southern part of a country, this is not true of Israel, where the Hebrew *Negev* translates quite simply as "dry land". An awesome stony desert, baked by the sun, the Negev occupies almost half the country's surface area. It stretches from the regional capital Beersheba to the Red Sea resort of Eilat, and is bounded on the west by the Gaza Strip and the Egyptian Sinai Desert and on the east by the Dead Sea and the Arava Valley.

Since biblical times, the Negev has been seen as a land of desolation and has been feared because it is so large and so arid, yet the succession of cliffs, plains, craters, and canyons give it the special appeal of never being monotonous. In addition to these fascinating landscapes, which can be enjoyed in the course of expeditions and walking tours of varying degrees of difficulty, the south has sights to offer which can be of interest to visitors on a variety of different levels. You can journey into the history of the Hebrew nation and its Jewish heritage, especially if you travel through Qumran and Masada. You can learn more about the pioneering spirit breathed into the *kibbutzim* of the Negev – whose workers still labour tirelessly to push back the borders of the desert – by the father of the nation David Ben-Gurion. Or you can seek the simple pleasures – heightened by all the effort which has

Remains at the site of Tel Beersheba.

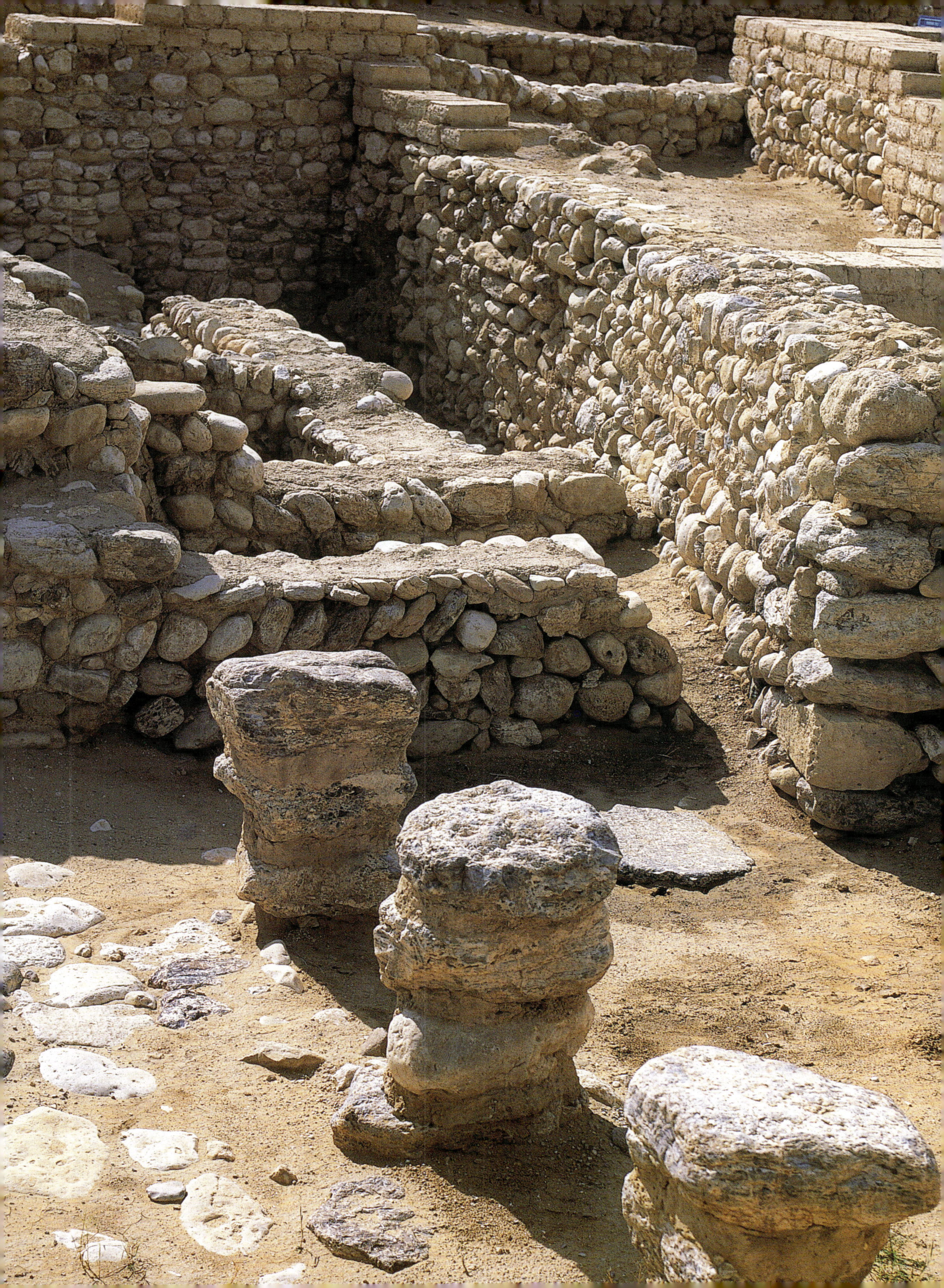

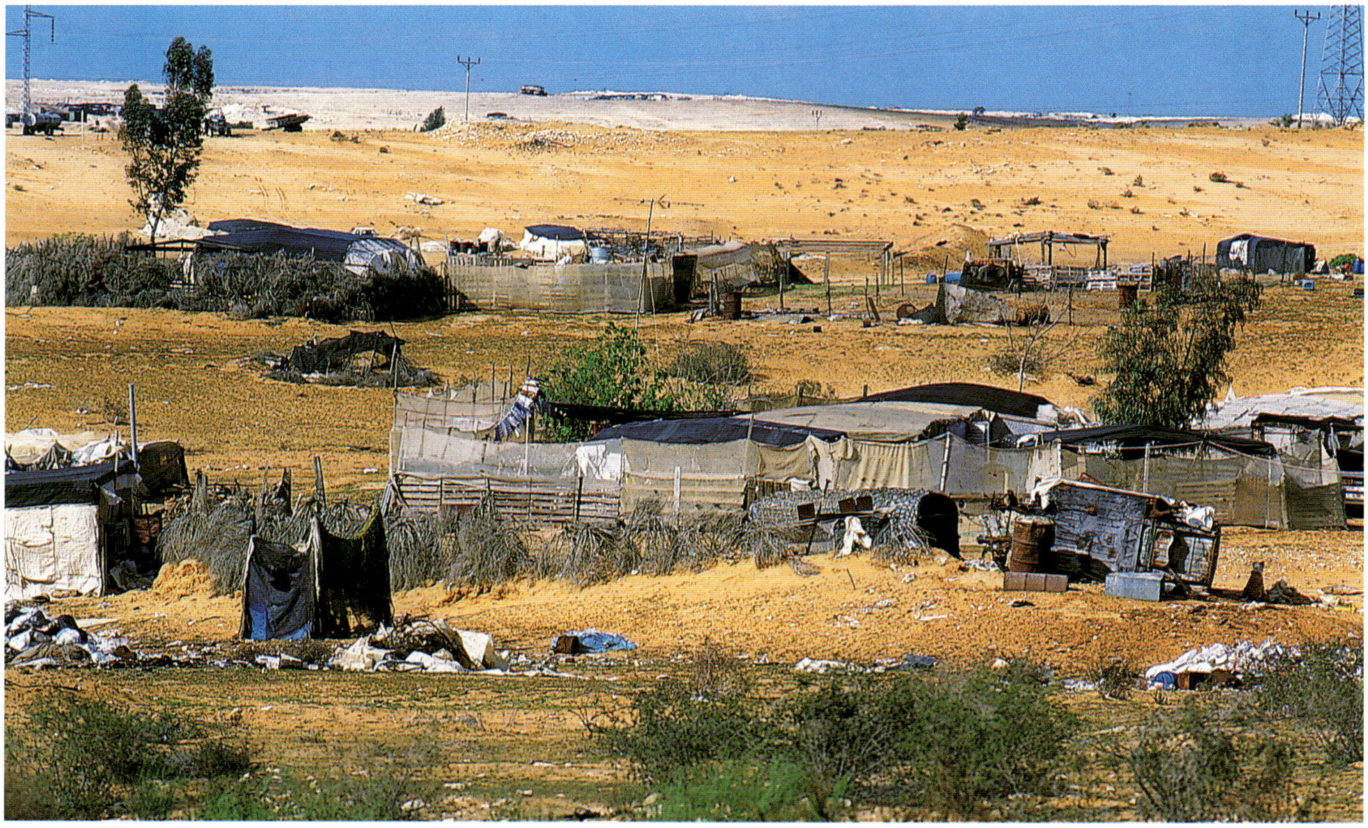

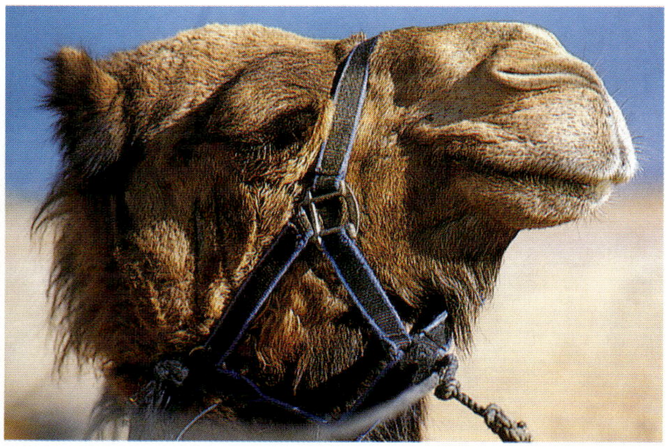

Bedouin encampments near Beersheba.

been put into providing the supporting infrastructures – of a seaside holiday on the shores of the two seas in the area.

This applies to the famous Dead Sea, for example, which is divided between Israel and Jordan. It attracts visitors as much for its unique properties as for the quality of the sites to be found there. The best way to reach it is to leave Jerusalem by the road across the Judaean Desert. After passing the Jericho oasis and reaching the northern end of the Dead Sea – at almost 400 m (1,300 ft) below the level of the Mediterranean Sea, the lowest in the world – the first of the sites of historical importance along its western shore comes into view. This is Qumran, the place where the ascetic Jewish sect of the Essenes became established during the second century BC. It was here, in 1947, that complete scrolls (among them the book of Isaiah and the Aleph Codex) and fragments of texts, known collectively as the Dead Sea Scrolls and dating from the time when the Essenes occupied the area, were discovered in caves in the cliff which the members of this sect had used as their headquarters. These manuscripts, written in Aramaic and Hebrew (800

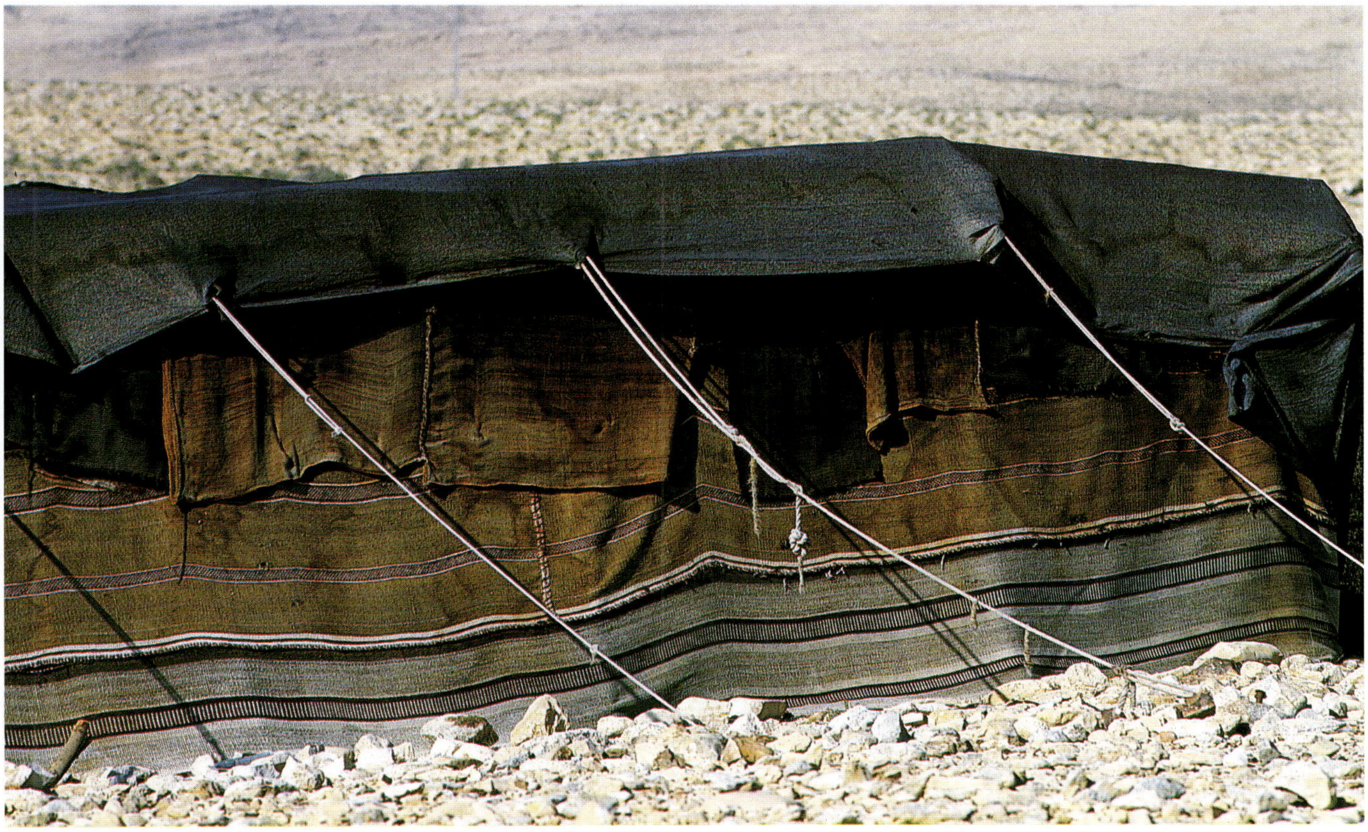

were found, 200 of which have biblical connections), are now stored all together in the Sanctuary of the Book in the Israel Museum in Jerusalem. They are the remains of the most ancient written records concerning the People of the Book.

A short distance after passing this important site – crossing here a strip of relatively green plain, squeezed between the sea and the mountains, and there an arid zone from which the date-palms and their cooling shade have disappeared – the kibbutz of Ein Gedi welcomes visitors to its spa complex, which exploits the resources and properties of the strange, mineral-rich sea. By way of comparison, whereas the Mediterranean contains 38 grams of salt per litre, the Dead Sea, with 300 grams per litre, almost reaches the limit of the amount of salt that can be dissolved in water. All the mineral elements contained in the salt – such as magnesium, calcium, potassium, and bromine – are heavily concentrated here. The Ein Gedi spa has installed facilities such as pools of sulphurous water at 39°C (102°F), which are fed directly by the natural hot springs, and baths of black mud, which are unique of their kind

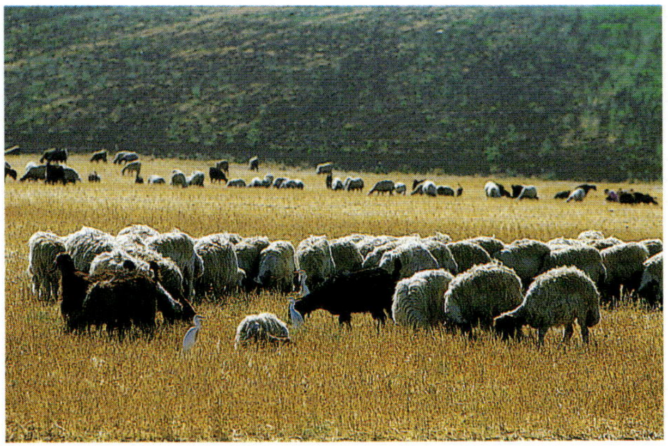

Following pages: The Negev Desert, with its succession of cliffs, plains, craters, and canyons, is never monotonous.

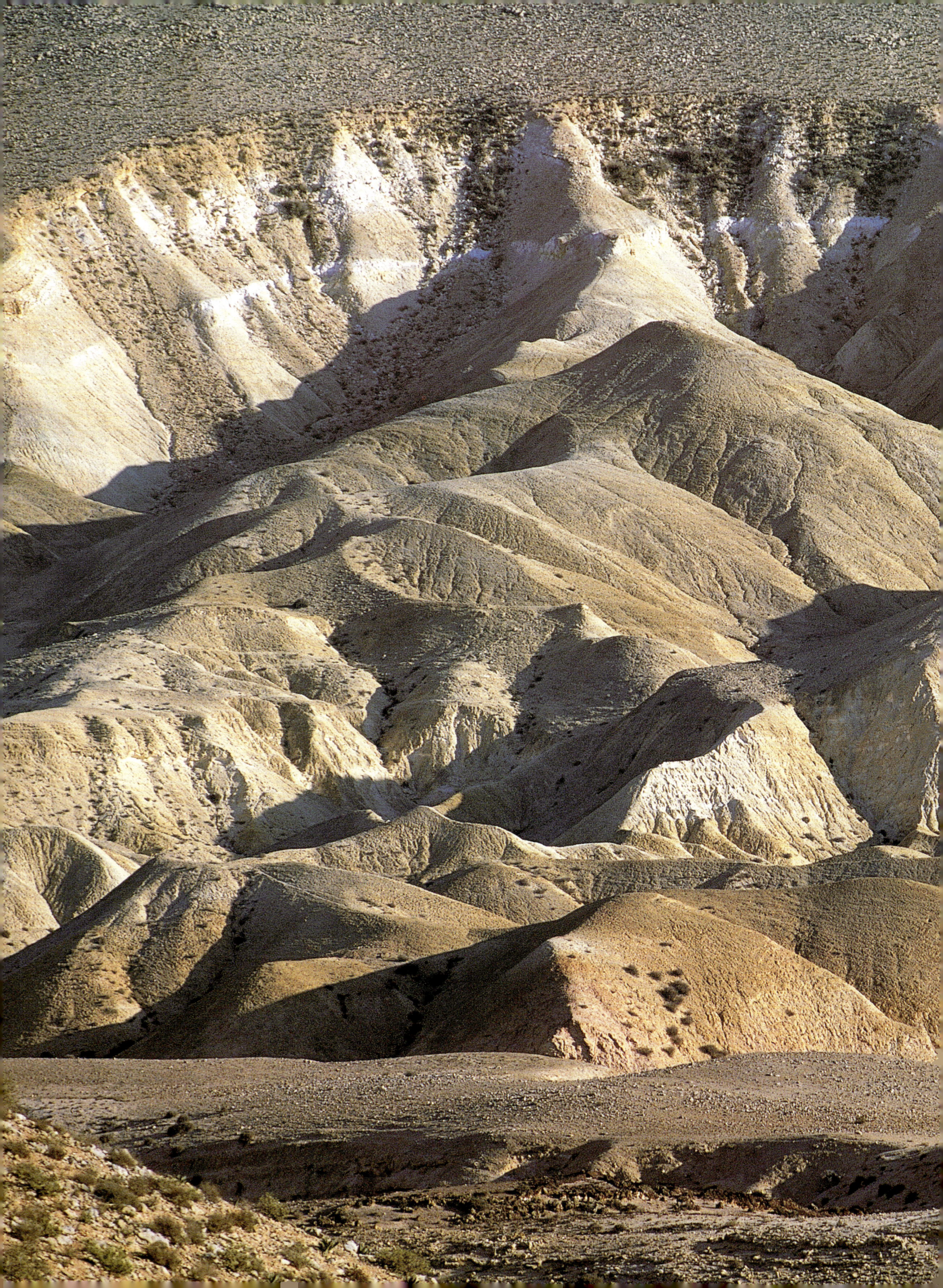

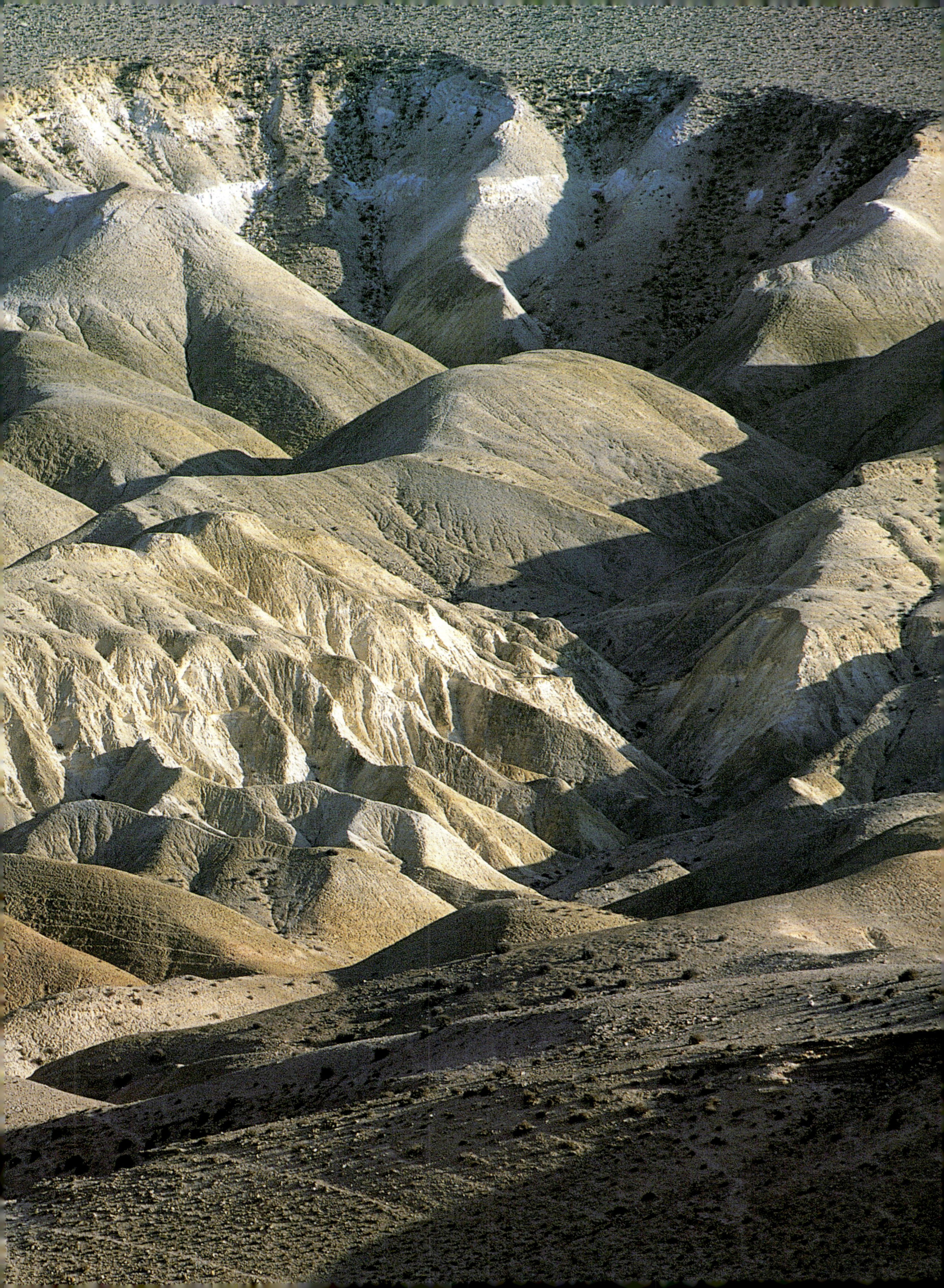

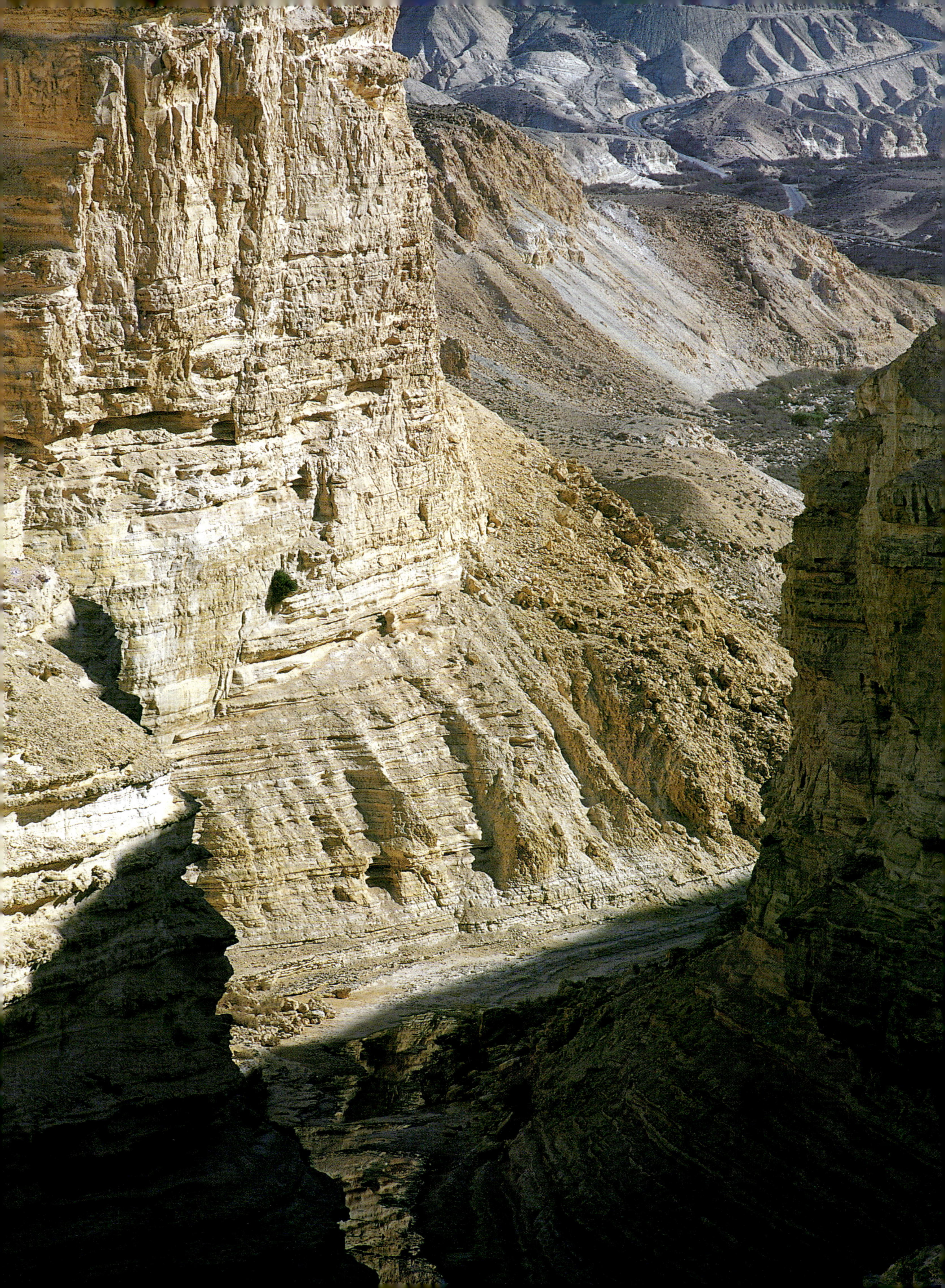

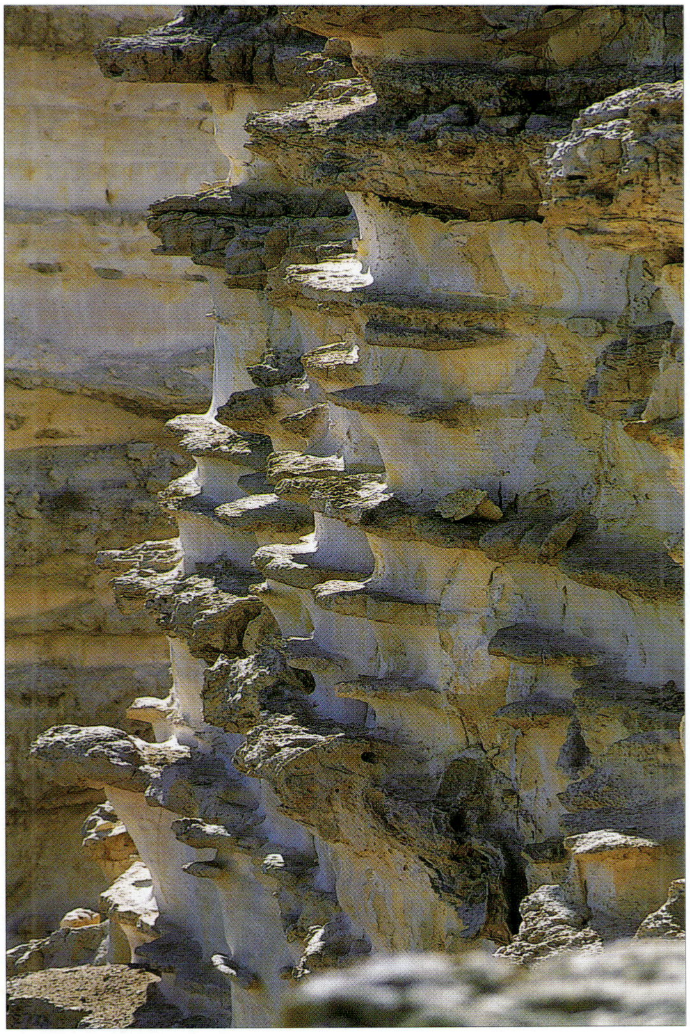

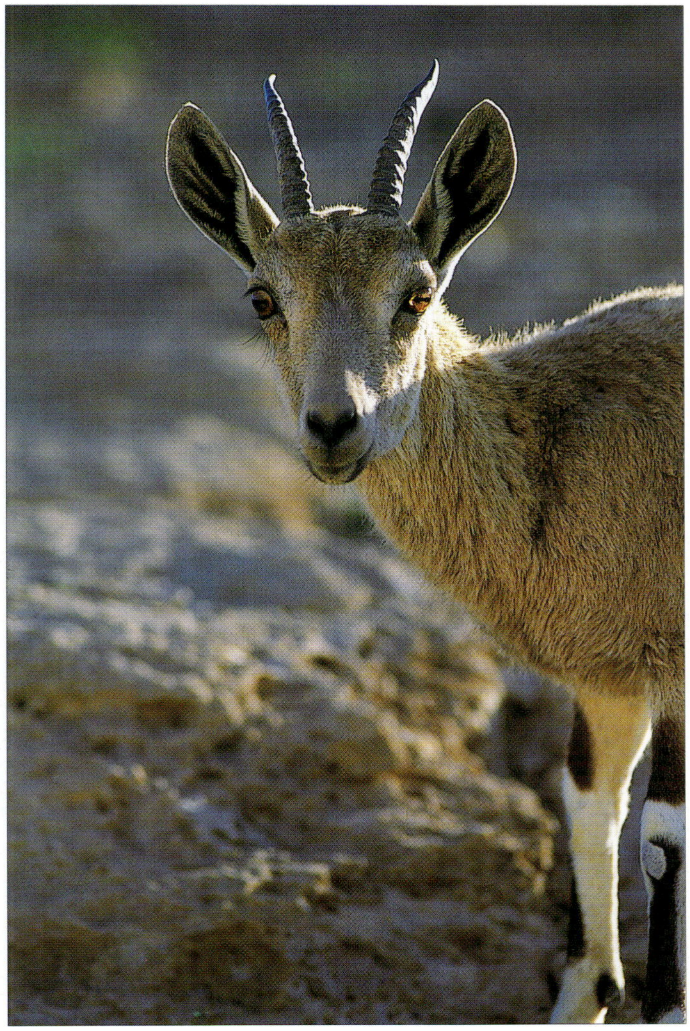

The Ein Avdad canyon is a wonderful example of the effects of erosion.
Further away, a young ibex has found a home at the site of Mitzpe Ramon.

and rich in minerals and beneficial therapeutic properties. Or there is a supervised beach on the shore of the Dead Sea, which gives you the opportunity to enjoy the strange experience of being able to float on the water like a piece of cork.

This coastal area is not only pleasant, healthy, and entertaining, but also quite simply refreshing – which is not the least of its virtues, since the heat in this basin can be stifling. It is particularly severe around Masada, which stands on top of an isolated rocky mountain in the middle of the desert, detached from a ridge of the same kind of mountains, to the south of the western shore of the Dead Sea. Masada is a natural fortress, consisting of a 440 m (1,440 ft) high cliff with vertical sides and a flat top. Today you can reach the summit – 650 m long by 300 m wide (2,130 ft by 980 ft) – by cable car. During the period of the Second Temple, this high plateau was the

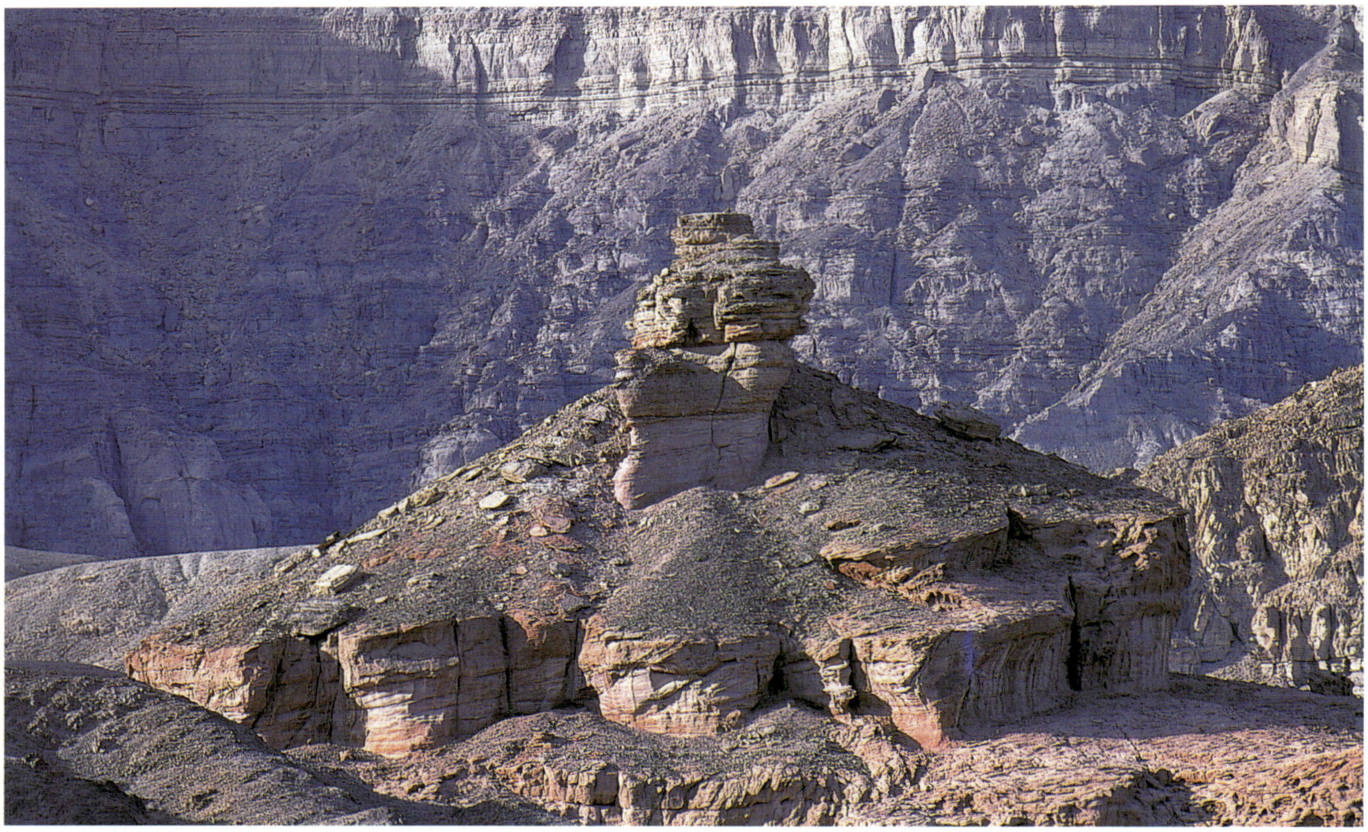

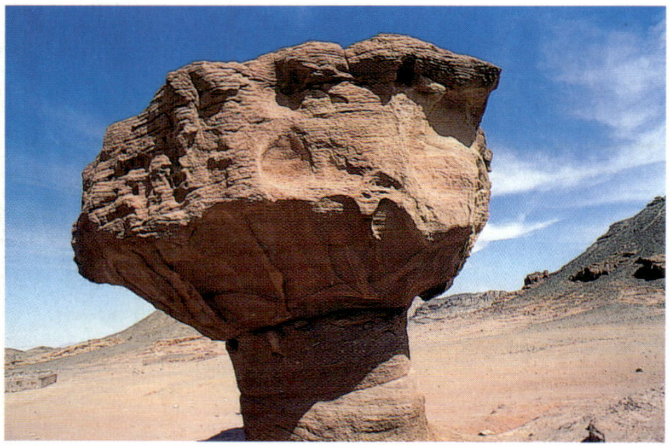

The Timna national park – with its reddish mushroom rock, spiral hill, and the Pillars of Solomon, which have become detached from the cliff by erosion – contains fabulous geological formations.

perfect example of a fortified place of safety. It was used first by King Herod, who built palaces and fortifications on it; then by a Roman garrison; before it came under the control of the Zealots, the Jews who rebelled against Roman rule between 66 and 70.

After holding out for several months against the siege of a Roman camp which housed more than 10,000 men, the Jewish defenders, seeing the building of an access ramp to their fortress nearing completion – by the very people who had recently destroyed the Temple in Jerusalem – decided on mass suicide. When they reached the summit, the Romans found the bodies of 960 men, women, and children lying on the ground. There are many archaeological relics of this event to be visited in Masada, which is still, after 2,000 years, a potent symbol of Jewish resistance. Also, the young men of the armed forces come here to take their oath of allegiance, pledging that "Masada will never fall again".

To reach the Red Sea from the Dead Sea, the most natural route is across the Arava Valley – an extension of the Jordan Valley shared by the kingdom of

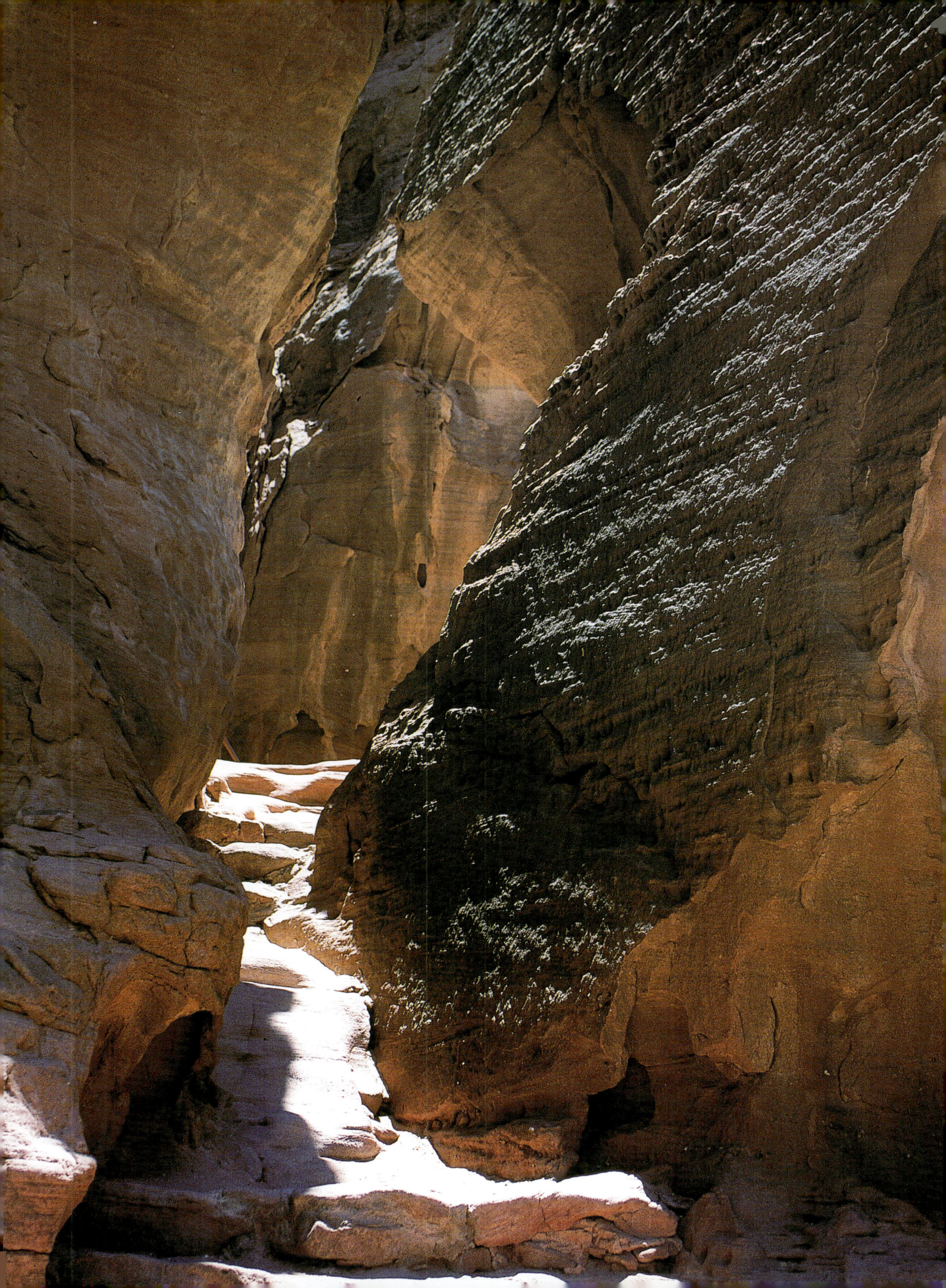

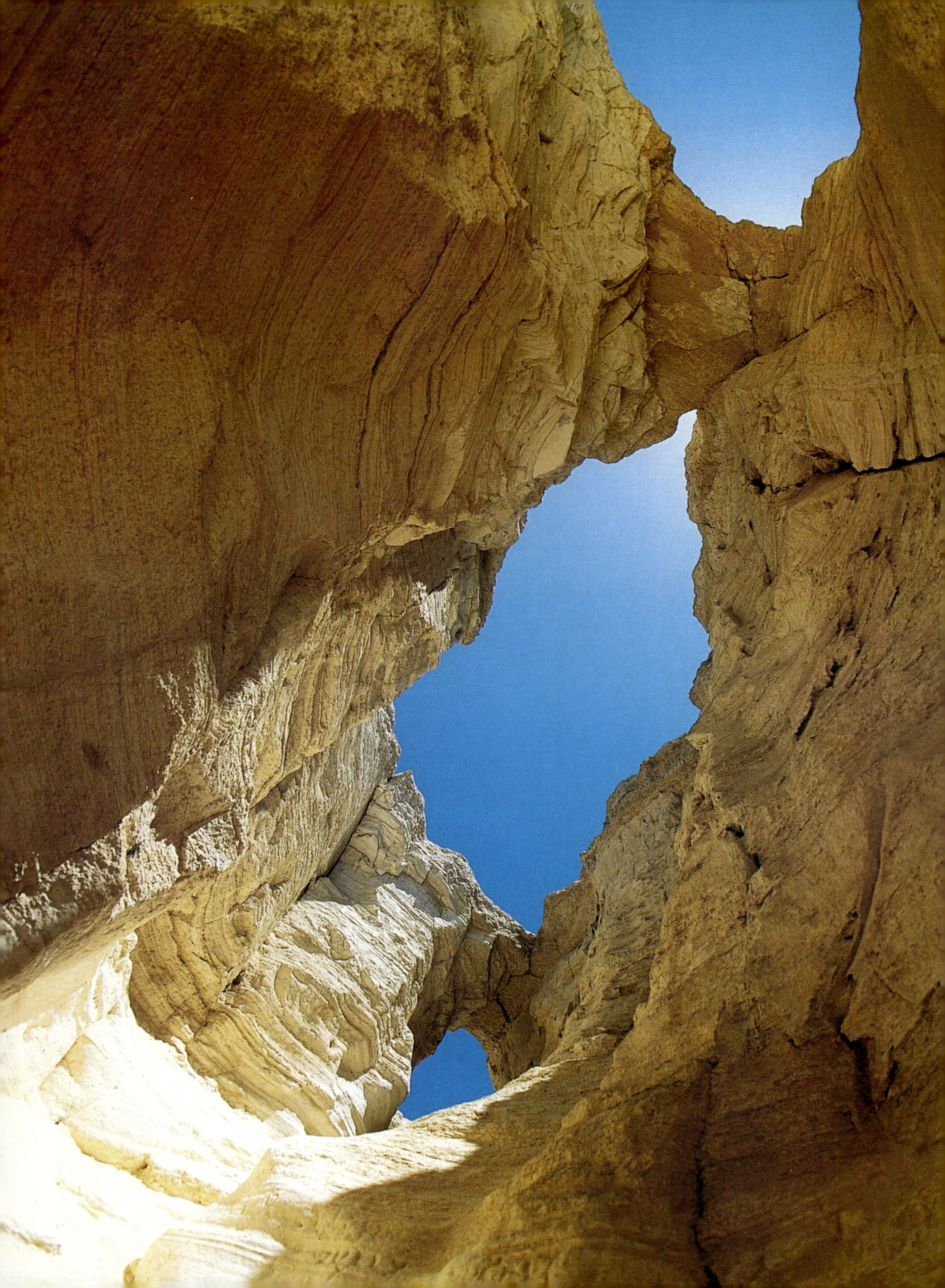

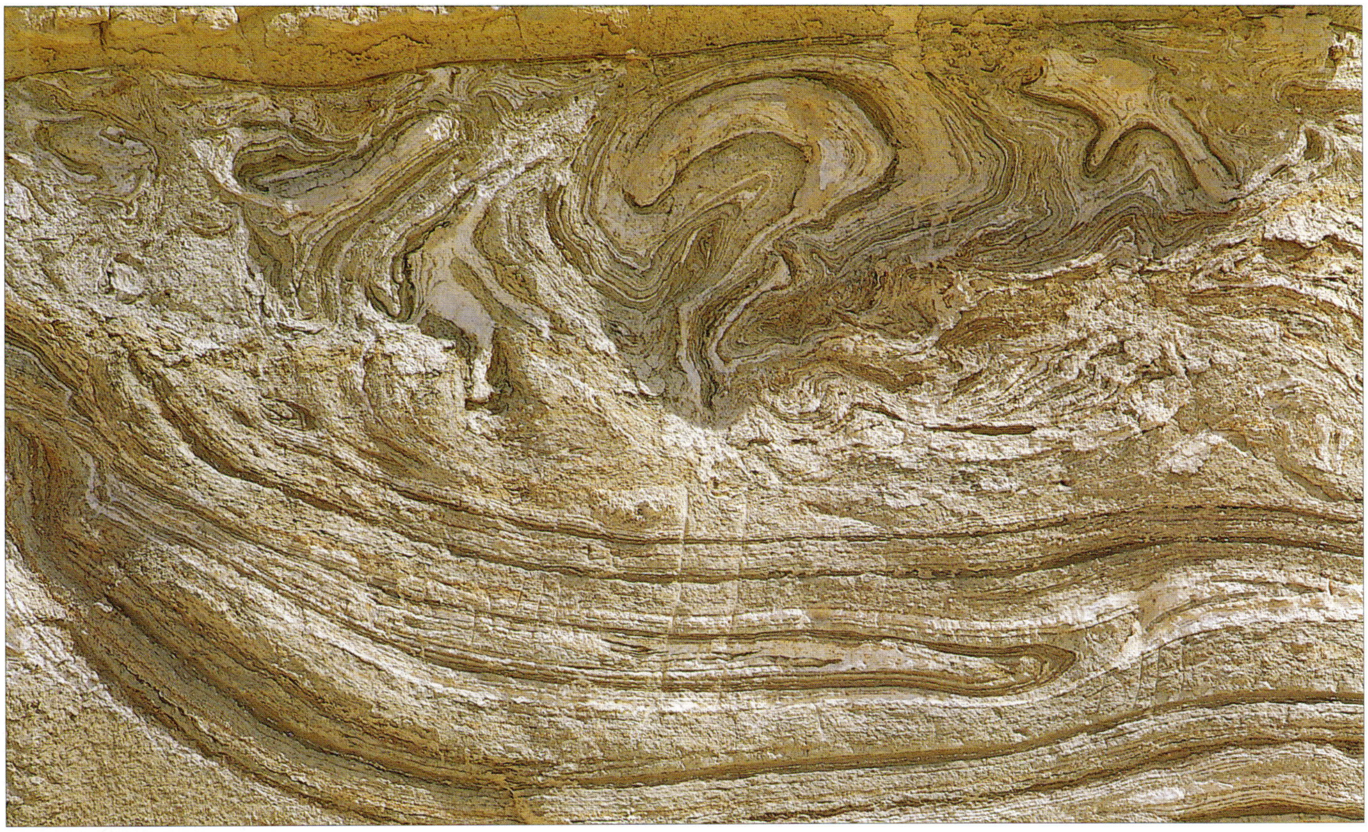

Near Sodom, erosion has created a canyon known as the "Flour Canyon".

• The Timna national park •

The ancient geological wonders of King Solomon's Mines in the heart of the Timna nature reserve attract many visitors. The Timna national park, 25 km (15 miles) north of Eilat, which covers about 60 km^2 (23 square miles) in a huge depression surrounded by mountains, has long been one of the most important employers for the inhabitants of the only Israeli city on the Red Sea. To the south of the park are the remains of the mines, where tens of thousands of people worked to extract copper in the time of King Solomon. Further away, rising out of this amazing stony landscape – created by the action of several million years on the sandstone and other marine sediments – the red rocks carved out of the cliff by erosion, known as the Pillars of Solomon, and especially the giant mushroom-shaped rock fashioned by the wind, have become the symbols of this splendid reserve. Good tracks, suitable for motor vehicles, link the many sites, and an artificial lake has been created to make a rest area.

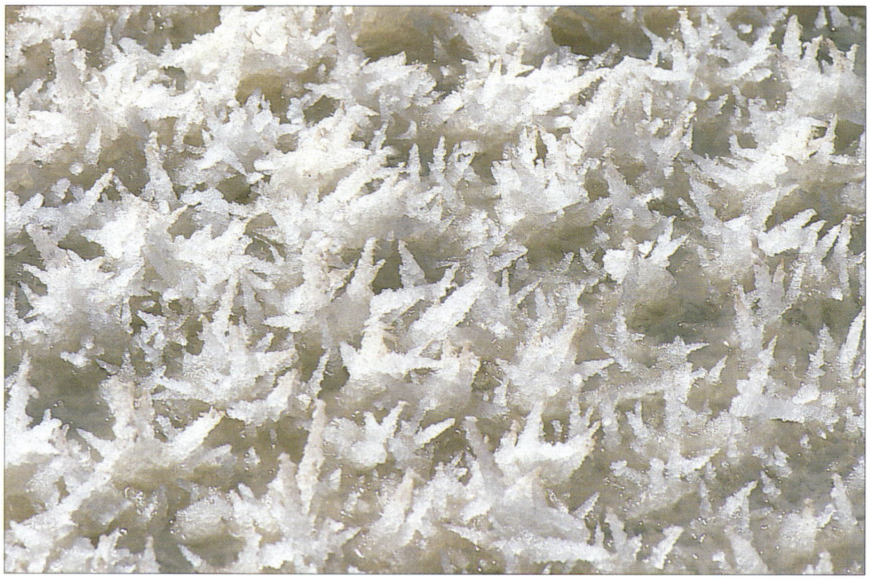

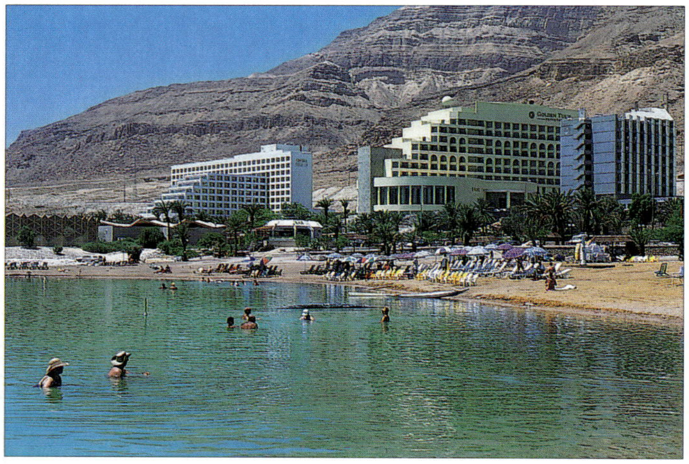

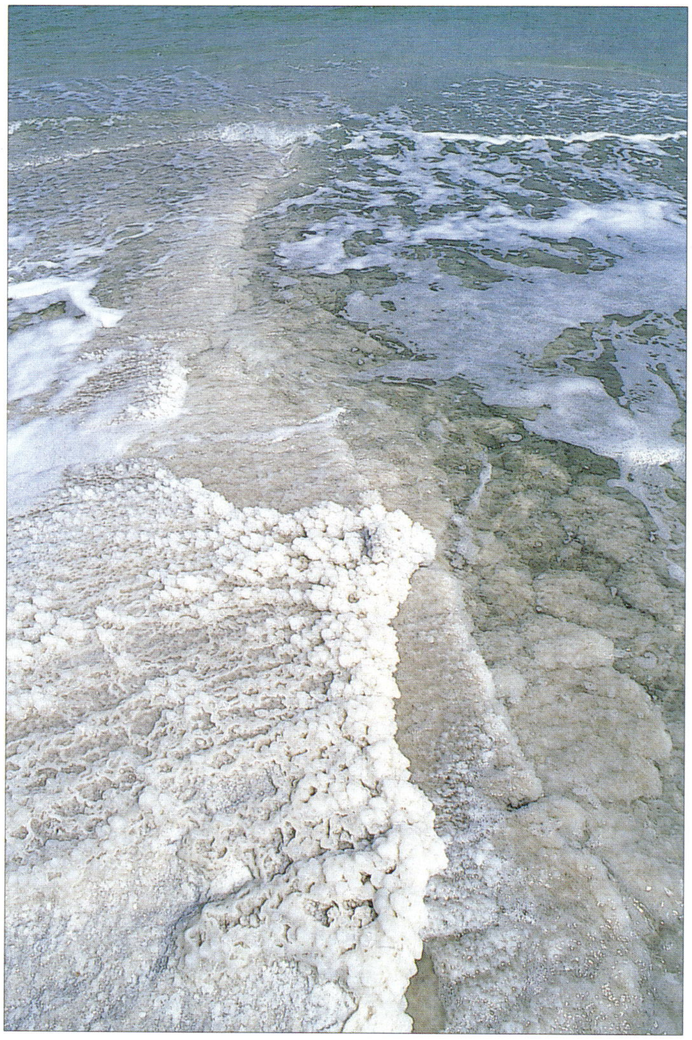

The Dead Sea is more than 400 m (1,300 ft) below the level of the Mediterranean Sea and almost reaches the limit of the amount of salt that can be dissolved in water. Resorts like Ein Gedi and Ein Bokek (pictured here) make use of the resources and properties of this sea in their spas.

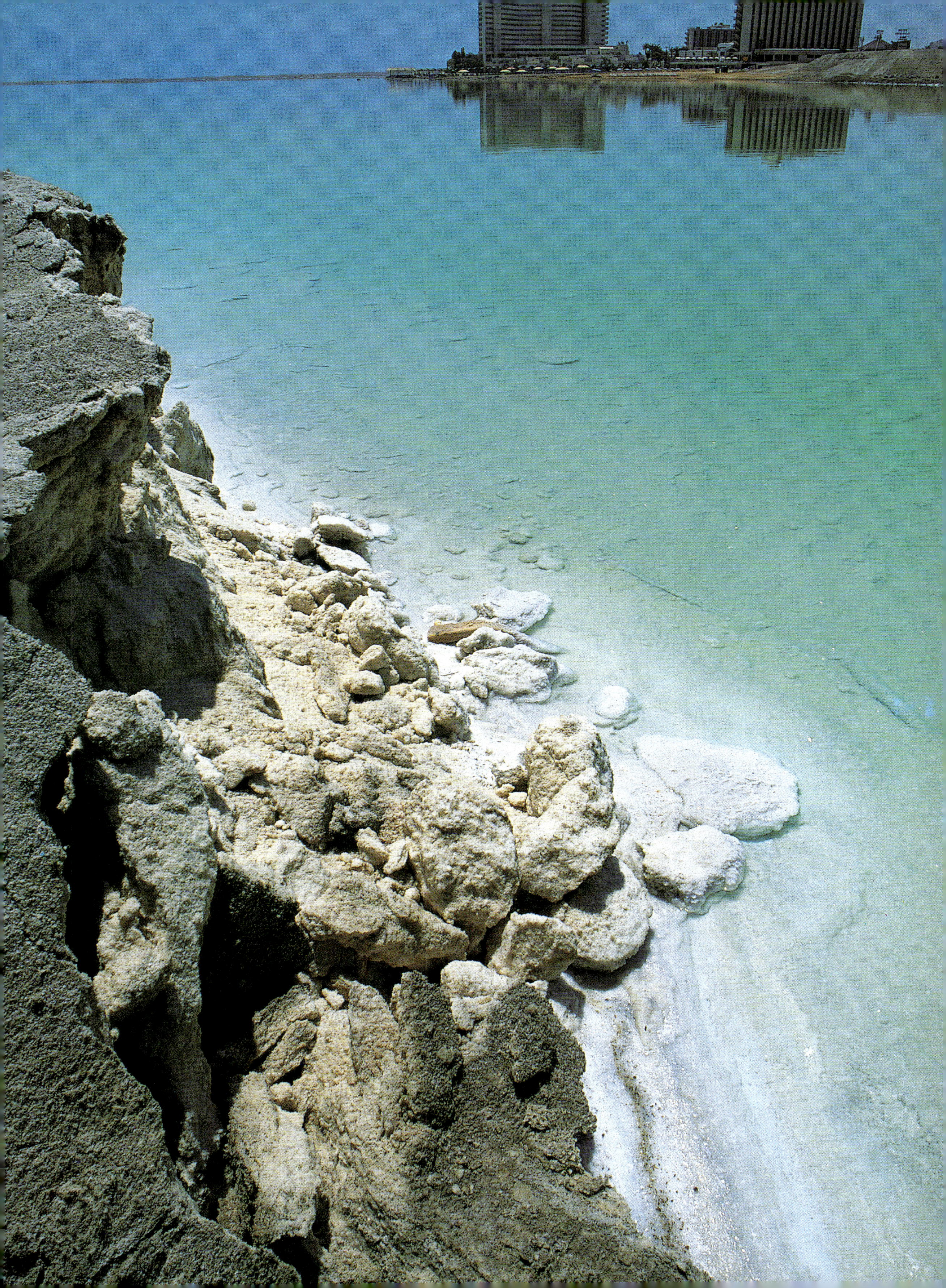

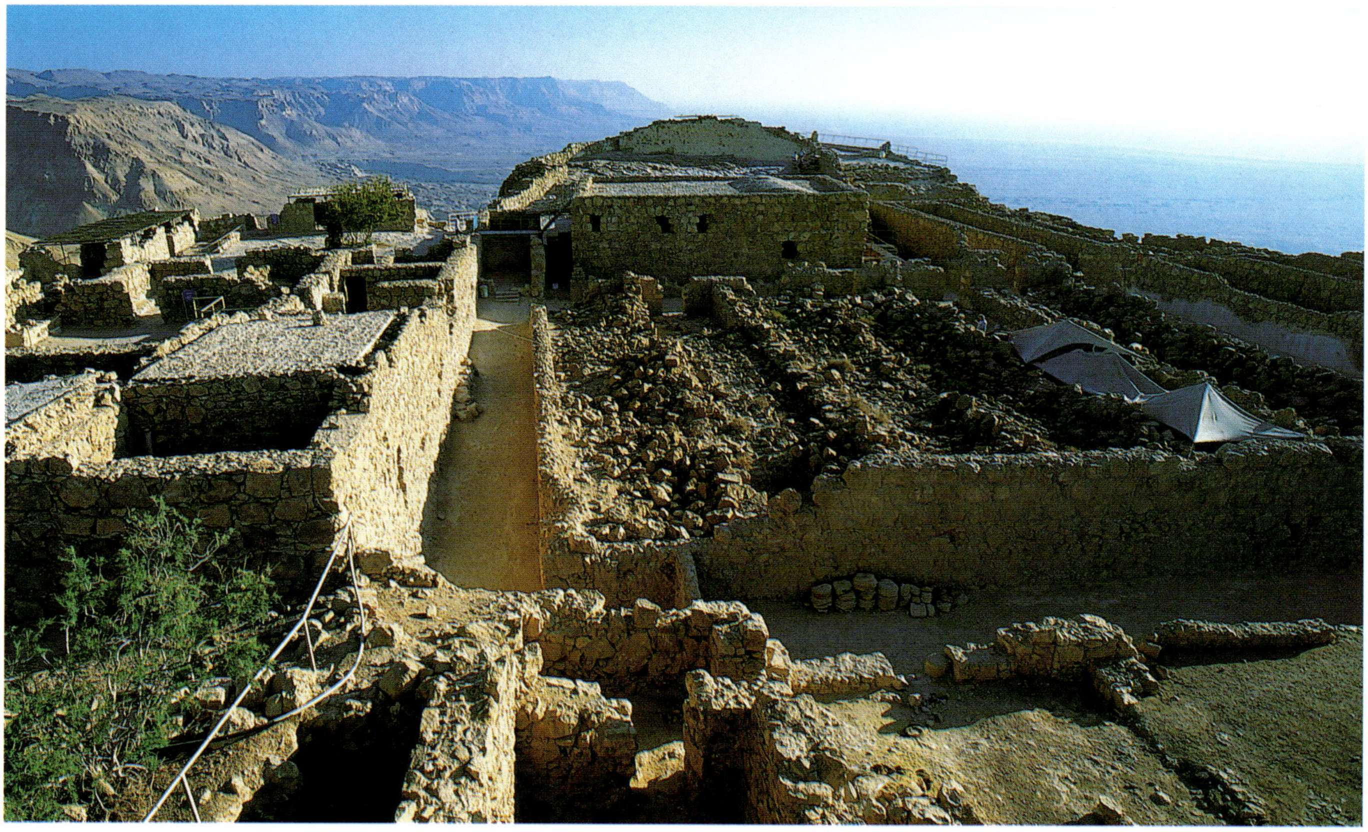

The site of Masada is on top of a natural fortress consisting of a 440m (1,440 ft) high cliff with vertical sides.
At the end of the first Jewish rebellion, some 1,000 Zealots killed themselves, rather than fall into the hands of the besieging Roman legions.

Jordan – which is part of the same geological fault as the Great Rift Valley. One incredible landscape follows another. The Arava Valley, bordering the Negev Desert, is a sight worth seeing in its own right. Sometimes it looks as if a dry plain has filled up the wide gap separating the two mountain ridges, which confront one another across the border.

This plain is sometimes dotted with little stunted trees, sometimes with a few well-kept patches of green or glasshouses belonging to the *kibbutzim.* In some places, little mounds and stony hills packed closely together give it a chaotic appearance, and in others it looks like a lunar landscape, with steep, white or ash-covered slopes showing no trace of vegetation.

The road leading from Beersheba to Eilat across the Negev is also magnificent. Route 40 gives you the opportunity to discover the *kibbutzim* which are on the way to becoming a normal part of the countryside, as in the lands around Beersheba, where the desert has been conquered by dint of the effort put into cultivation – one of many examples is that of the University of Beersheba, which has a leading-edge centre for research into

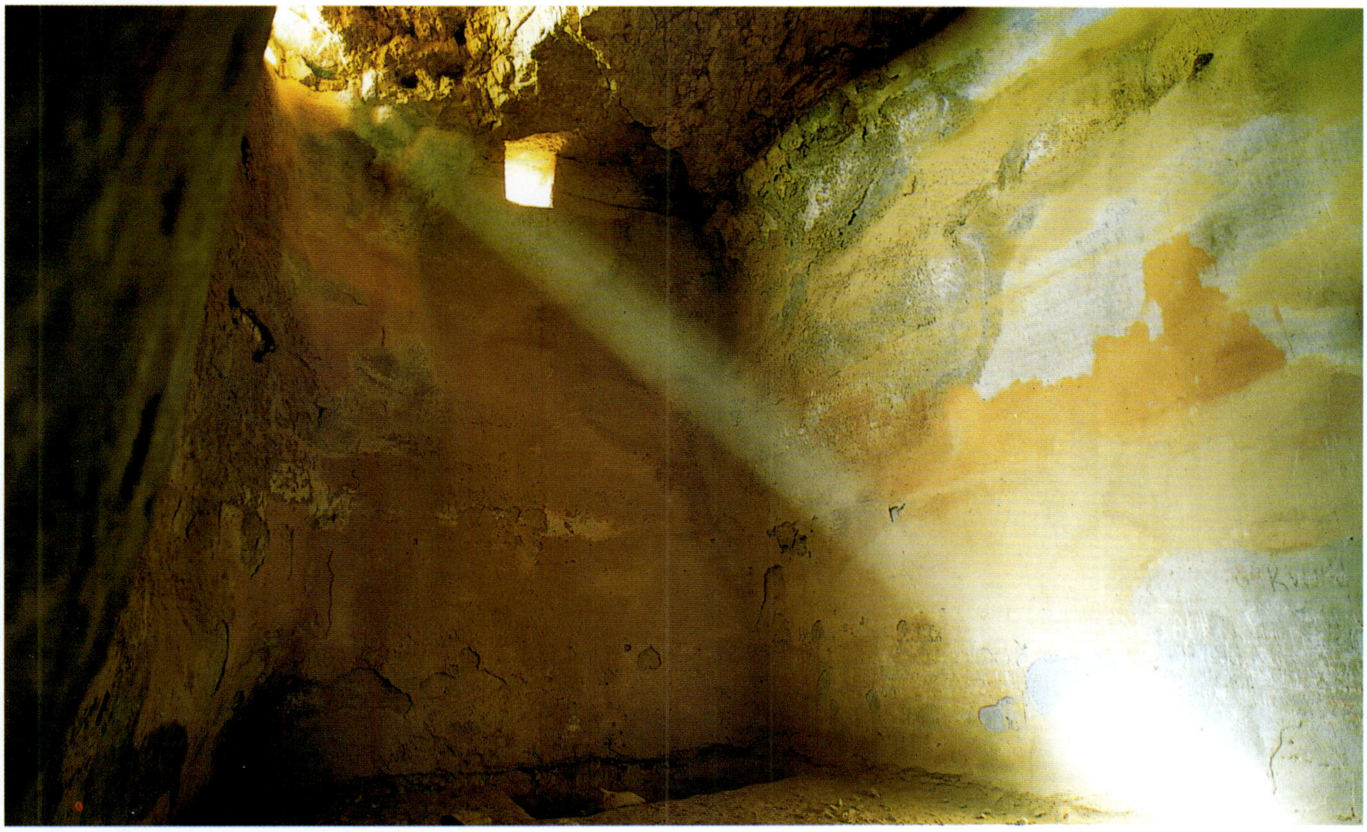

agriculture in a desert environment. It also takes you to astonishing natural wonders like Mitzpe Ramon. The Ramon crater – once used by the caravans of Nabataean traders on their way to the coast to sell their spices and other goods from the south of the Arabian peninsula – is not only impressive in size (30 × 8 km / 19 × 5 miles), but creates a subtle picture of shapes and colours with its eroded rocks.

In the extreme south of the country, the city of Eilat is a paradise for holidaymakers in search of sun, warm seas, and relaxation. Once a strategic port on the Gulf of Aqaba. Eilat has become a tourist resort determinedly given over to the pleasures of the beach. The many hotels dominate the bay, each new building more grandiose than the last.

Discovering the coral reefs, either by diving or by visiting the marine observatory, is one of the attractions of Eilat. Diving into the silent world has the extra advantage of offering a welcome cooling respite from the often torrid heat. After all, the important thing about this sun and rest cure is to be able to balance your life of leisure.

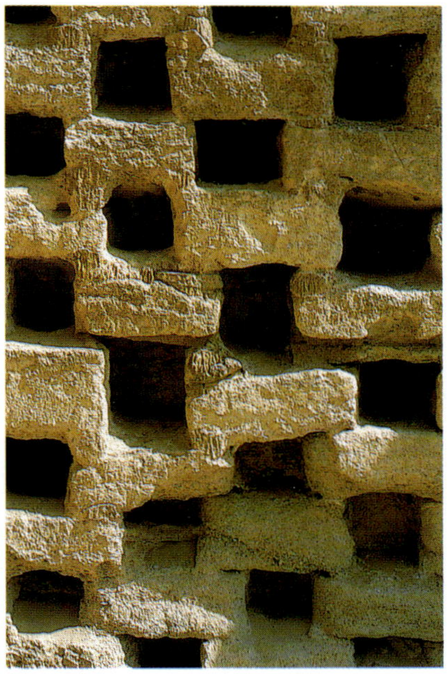

Following pages:
Canyon in the Negev Desert, near Masada.

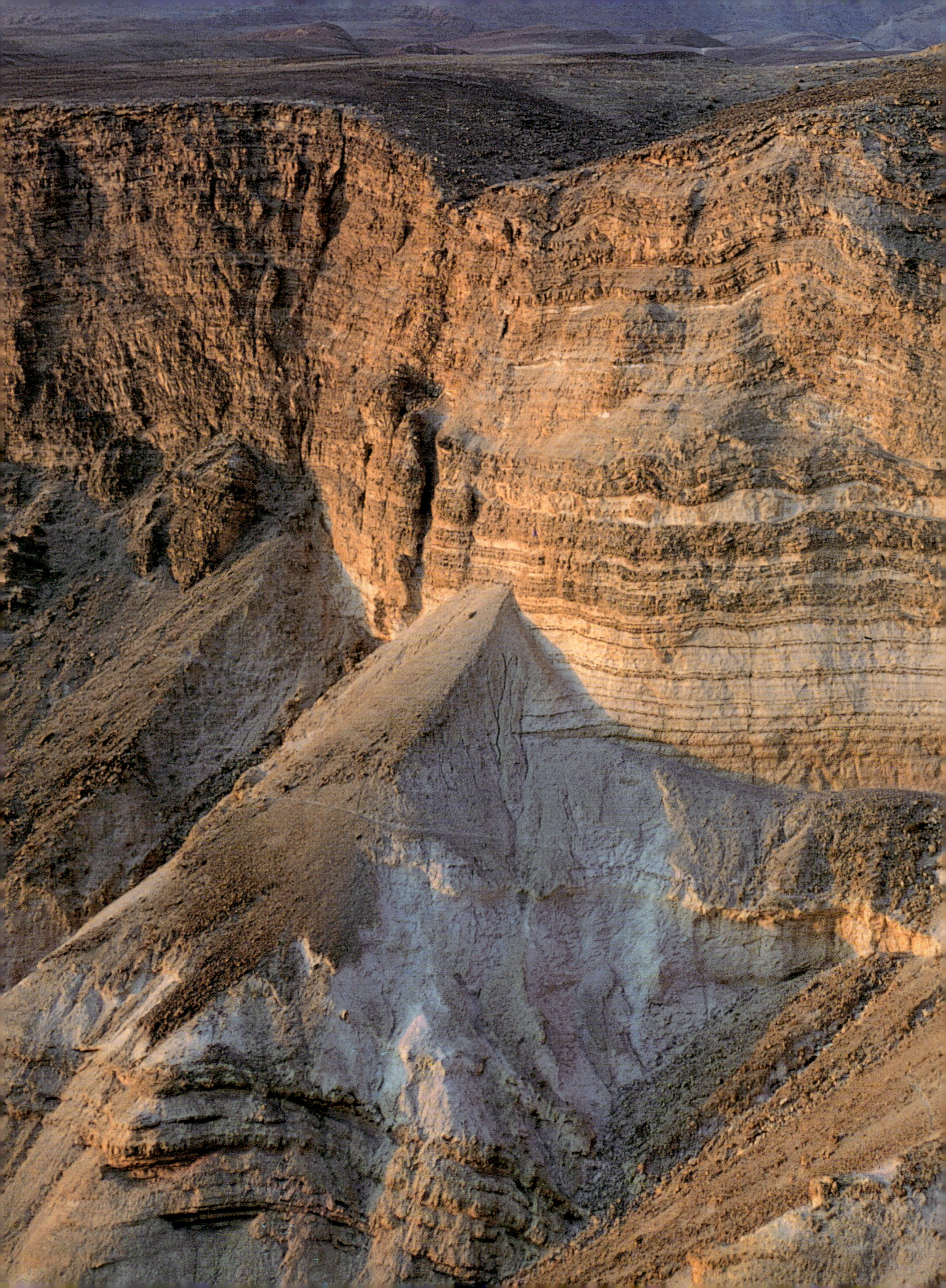

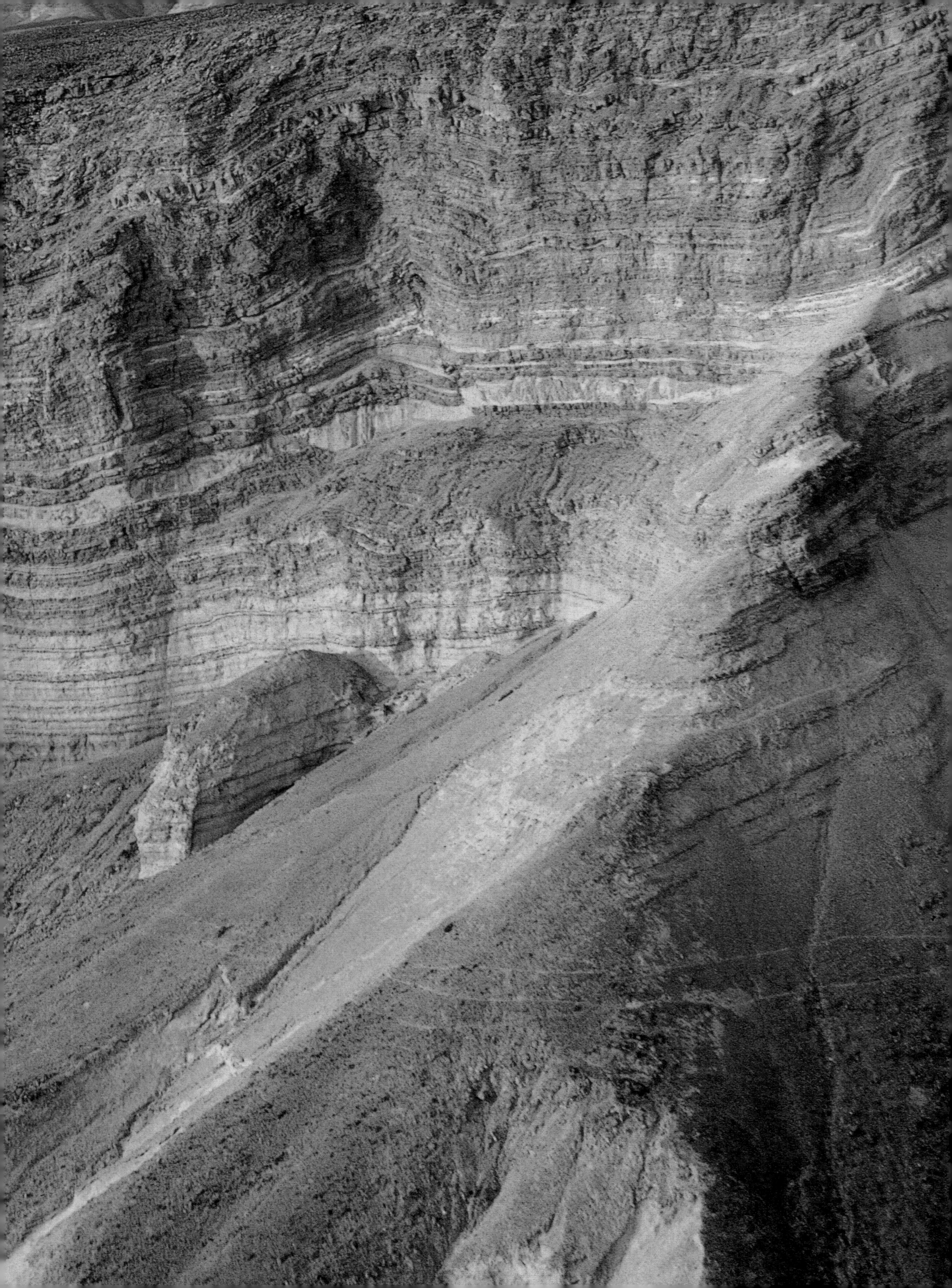

Useful Information

Tourist information in the UK: Israeli Tourist Office, UK House, 180 Oxford Street, London, W1N 0EL; tel. 020 7299 1111, fax 020 7299 1112.

Tourist Information on the Internet: www.infotour.co.il.

Tourist Information in Israel: All the major cities and places of interest for tourists have information centres, where you can find out what to see and where to stay. Tourist offices in Jerusalem: 17 Jaffa Road, tel: (00 972 2) 625 8844; Jaffa Gate (old city), tel: (00 972 2) 628 0382. In Haifa: 20 Herzl Street, tel: (00 972 4) 866 6521, fax: (00 972 4) 862 2075. In Tel Aviv: at the new bus station, tel: (00 972 3) 639 5660.

Entry requirements: British citizens require a passport valid for at least six months after the date of entry. You can obtain a free visitor's visa at the border.

Israeli Embassy in the UK: 2 Palace Green, London W8 4QB; tel. 020 7957 9500, fax 020 7957 9555; Israeli Consulate: 15a Old Court Palace, London W8; tel. 020 7957 9517, fax 020 7957 9577.

British Embassy and consulates in Israel: (general) British Embassy, 192 Hayarkon Street, Tel Aviv 63405; tel. (00 972 3) 725 1222, fax (00 972 3) 527 1572; (consular and visa) The British Consulate, Migdalor Building 6th Floor, 1 Ben Yehuda Street, Tel Aviv 63801; tel. (00 972 3) 510 0166, fax (00 972 3) 510 1167. British Consulate-General Jerusalem, 19 Nashashibi Street, Sheikh Jarrah, PO Box 19690, Jerusalem 97200; tel. (00 972 2) 541 4100, fax (00 972 2) 532 2368.

Money: The currency is the New Israeli Shekel (NIS). 1 shekel is divided into 100 agorot (singular: agora). £1.00 = about 5.5 shekels (rate in December 2000). The exchange rate in Israel is slightly better. There are notes for 10, 20, 50, 100, 200, 500, and 1,000 shekels and coins for 1 agora, 5, and 10 agorot, ½, 1, 5 and 10 shekels in circulation. Travellers' cheques (Visa and American Express) and international credit cards are accepted everywhere. Cash can be obtained from cashpoint machines using Visa or Mastercard/Eurocard. The most important currency apart from the shekel is the US dollar, which can also be used to pay for goods and services.

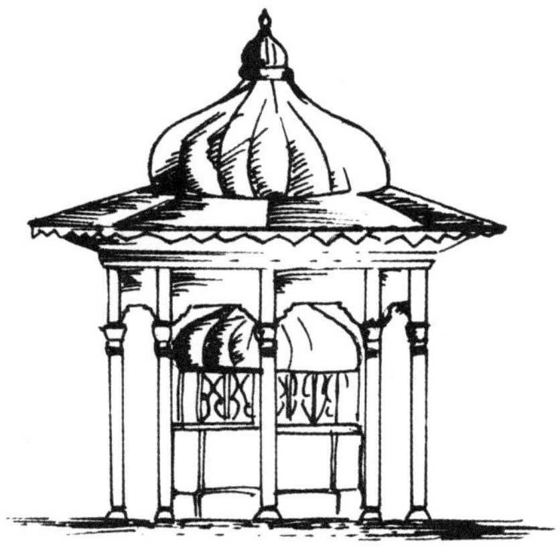

CUSTOMS REGULATIONS: Each person may take in or out 1 l spirits and 2 l wine, 0.25 l perfume, 250 g tobacco or 250 cigarettes, and personal gifts. For antiques, you must have a permit from the Antiques Authority in Jerusalem. The export of archaeological finds is forbidden and will be severely punished.

GETTING TO ISRAEL – AIRLINES: More than 20 companies fly to Israel almost every day. Flying time from London to Tel Aviv is 4 hours 30 minutes. Ben Gurion airport in Lod (18 km/11 miles from Tel Aviv and 55 km/33 miles from Jerusalem) has a shuttle bus link to Tel Aviv (20 mins). There are cheap communal taxis to take visitors to Tel Aviv or Jerusalem. It is also possible to fly to Eilat.

THE REGION AND THE PEOPLE

GEOGRAPHY: The country of Israel (Eretz Israel) lies on the eastern coast of the Mediterranean, between 29° and 33° north and between 34° and 35° east. Its length from north to south is 420 km (260 miles), but it is only between 20 km and 116 km (12 and 72 miles) wide. Israel has borders with the Lebanon to the north, Syria and Jordan to the east, and Egypt to the south and south-west. The Negev Desert takes up the whole of the southern part of the country, whereas the northern part can be divided into the coastal plain, the western mountains, and the Jordan Valley.

The highest mountain is Har Meron (1,206 m/3,957 ft); the longest river at around 260 km (162 miles) is the Jordan, which has its sources in the Dan and the Banyas, rising on Mount Hermon, and flows into the Dead Sea.

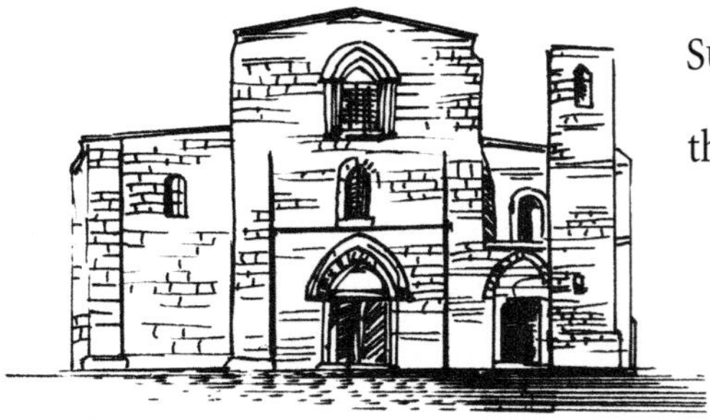

SURFACE AREA: At around 20,770 km² (8,020 square miles), Israel is slightly bigger than Wales.

CAPITAL: In 1950, West Jerusalem was declared the capital in place of Tel Aviv. In 1980, after the annexation of the eastern part of the city, the whole of Jerusalem became the capital. In protest against this violation of international law, many states refused to move their embassies from Tel Aviv.

FORM OF GOVERNMENT: Israel has been a parliamentary republic since 1948, its legislative assembly is called the Knesset. Ehud Barak has been prime minister since 1999.

ECONOMY: Two-thirds of the surface of Israel is covered by desert and mountains. However, where agriculture is possible it is very intensive, and because of the lack of water this is associated with high investment. Tinned fruit, citrus fruits, cut flowers, and poultry are important export items. There are very few mineral resources, so industry works almost exclusively on imported raw materials or semi-finished products. The high level of military expenditure and successive waves of immigration put a heavy strain on the budget. The service sector is the biggest employer with 63 per cent of the workforce, followed by commerce with 12 per cent, agriculture with 6 per cent, and the remainder working in industry.

CLIMATE: Israel lies in a transitional area between Mediterranean and desert climates. The Mediterranean climate is characterised by hot, dry summers and mild, rainy winters. Snow may fall in the mountains from November to April. The

Jordan Valley and the Negev have a desert climate, the most distinctive feature of which is a wide variation in daytime temperature. The best time to travel is in the months from September to May. In the early summer, the desert wind known as the Sharav (Arabic: Chamsin) can bring temperatures as high as 50 °C (120 °F).

Population: There are 5.6 million inhabitants, not counting the occupied Arab areas, and 1 million are not Jewish. Only 23 per cent of Jews are second or third generation inhabitants of Israel; all the rest are immigrants from more than one hundred countries. About 90 per cent of the population live in towns or cities, around 50 per cent in Jerusalem, Tel Aviv, and Haifa; 8 per cent live in rural settlements such as *kibbutzim*, *moshavim*, and *moshav-shitufi*.

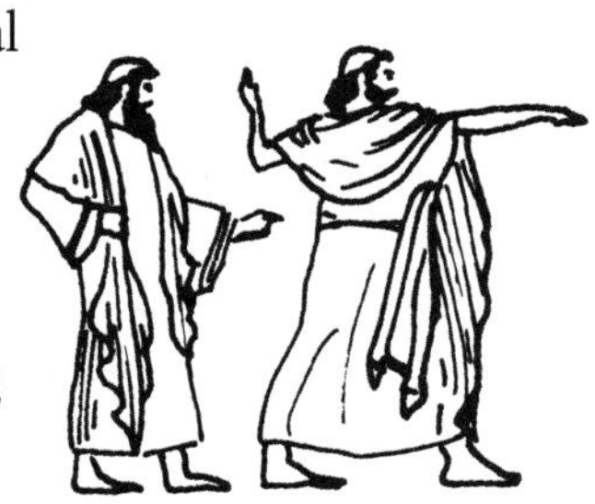

Religion: The Israeli population is 80 per cent Jewish, 14 per cent Muslim, 3.2 per cent Christian, and 1.7 per cent Druze.

Language: The official languages are Modern Hebrew (Iwrit) and Arabic. Almost all Israelis understand English.

Tourist attractions: The most attractive part of Jerusalem is the old city, which is divided into Jewish, Arab, Christian, and Armenian quarters. In the west of the old city is the Wailing Wall, the remains of the Second Temple and the Jews' most sacred place. The Dome of the Rock on Temple Mount (completed in 691) houses the holy rock of Moriah. This is a holy place for both Jews and Muslims, and its gilded dome has become the symbol of the city. The Church of the Holy Sepulchre (4th century AD), which houses the tomb of Christ, is at the centre of the Christian quarter. It stands at the end of the Via Dolorosa, the road to Calvary with the 14 stations of the cross. When tracing the events of the New Testament, the first step is almost certainly a visit to the Church of the Nativity in Bethlehem. At the heart of what was originally a Byzantine–Late Roman basilica is the Manger

Grotto. Jesus spent his childhood and youth in Nazareth, on the northern edge of the Jezreel Plain. The Church of the Annunciation, built in 1969, is the biggest church in the Middle East. Capernaum, on the northern shore of Lake Genesaret, is considered to be Jesus' real home town, and today it is the site of an archaeological excavation. Here you can see what is probably the best preserved ancient synagogue in Galilee. In Hebron, one of the four holy cities of the Jews, situated in the autonomous Palestinian area on the West Bank, you will find the Tomb of the Patriarchs, an impressive shrine dating from the time of King Herod, which contains the tombs of Abraham, Sarah, Jacob, Leah, Isaac, and Rebecca. Jericho, whose walls fell down at the sound of the trumpet, is thought to be the oldest city in the world at 10,000 years old. The most important archaeological remains are those of the Hischam Palace from the eighth century. The holy Jewish city of Tiberias on the western shore of the Sea of Galilee contains many graves of important Jewish philosophers, such as the tomb of Maimonides who, in the twelfth century, tried to resolve the conflict between faith and reason. Safed, the fourth holy city of Judaism, stands on the heights of Canaan. In the sixteenth century, it was the home of the mystical Cabbala. The synagogues here are famous for their blue colour, which is said to drive away evil spirits, and the cemetery is the most sacred in the country after that of Jerusalem. Tel Aviv on the Mediterranean coast offers cultural attractions. The Jaffa Quarter includes the oldest harbour in the world, founded by the Phoenicians in the tenth century BC. Caesarea, which lies on the Mediterranean coast between Tel Aviv and Haifa, is one of the most important archaeological sites in Israel. In Roman times, the ancient port was the capital of Palestine. Qumran on the Dead Sea is the place where the oldest written versions of the Bible were found in 1947. Jesus is said to have stayed in the caves used by the Essene sect.

Transport: Trains are slow and infrequent, so buses are the preferred means of transport. All long-distance routes start and end at the bus stations in the various cities. Local transport is provided by buses and communal taxis (*sherut*), which also do long-distance journeys. The *sherut* have fixed (low) fares. On the Sabbath and on Jewish holidays, the Jewish bus companies do not run services, but Arab buses and taxis are always available.

CUISINE: Jewish cuisine is mainly kosher, i.e. you will not find pork or camel or hare on the menu. Kosher also means that meat must never come into contact with milk or dairy products. So sauce for meat will never have cream added, and duck will never be followed by a cheese board. Among the specialities are gefilte fish (fish balls) and mock liver (made of eggs, aubergines, and onions). As well as Jewish and, of course, Arab cuisine with its kebabs (beef or mutton), falafel (little balls of chick pea paste), and shashlik (slices of grilled lamb and beef), you can find something to suit every taste in the western European or Russian world.

Although all information was carefully checked at the time of going to press (December 2000) the publisher cannot accept responsibility for its accuracy.

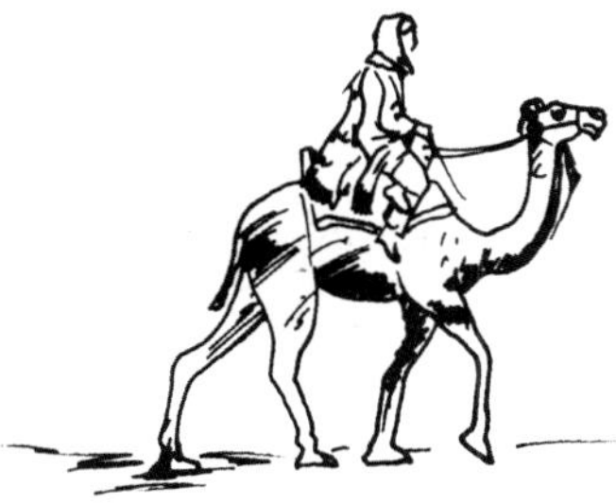